Second Edition
Practical
Fire and Arson
Investigation

CRC SERIES IN
PRACTICAL ASPECTS OF CRIMINAL
AND FORENSIC INVESTIGATIONS

VERNON J. GEBERTH, BBA, MPS, FBINA *Series Editor*

Practical Homicide Investigation: Tactics, Procedures, and Forensic Techniques, Third Edition
Vernon J. Geberth

The Counter-Terrorism Handbook: Tactics, Procedures, and Techniques
Frank Bolz, Jr., Kenneth J. Dudonis, and David P. Schulz

Forensic Pathology
Dominick J. Di Maio and Vincent J. M. Di Maio

Interpretation of Bloodstain Evidence at Crime Scenes
William G. Eckert and Stuart H. James

Tire Imprint Evidence
Peter McDonald

Practical Drug Enforcement: Procedures and Administration
Michael D. Lyman

Practical Aspects of Rape Investigation: A Multidisciplinary Approach
Robert R. Hazelwood and Ann Wolbert Burgess

The Sexual Exploitation of Children: A Practical Guide to Assessment, Investigation, and Intervention
Seth L. Goldstein

Gunshot Wounds: Practical Aspects of Firearms, Ballistics, and Forensic Techniques
Vincent J. M. Di Maio

Friction Ridge Skin: Comparison and Identification of Fingerprints
James F. Cowger

Footwear Impression Evidence
William J. Bodziak

Principals of Kinesic Interview and Interrogation
Stan Walters

Practical Fire and Arson Investigation, Second Edition
David R. Redsicker and John J. O'Connor

The Practical Methodology of Forensic Photography
David R. Redsicker

Practical Gambling Investigation Techniques
Kevin B. Kinnee

Practical Aspects of Interview and Interrogation
David E. Zulawski and Douglas E. Wicklander

Practical Investigation Techniques
Kevin B. Kinnee

Investigating Computer Crime
Franklin Clark and Ken Diliberto

Bloodstain Pattern Analysis: With an Introduction to Crime Scene Reconstruction
Virgil Thomas Bevel and Ross M. Gardner

Second Edition
Practical Fire and Arson Investigation

David R. Redsicker
Corporate Director of Investigations
Peter Vallas Associates, Inc.
John J. O'Connor
Lieutenant (Retired)
New York City Police Department

CRC Press
Boca Raton   New York   London   Tokyo

Library of Congress Cataloging-in-Publication Data

Redsicker, David R.
Practical fire and arson investigation, second edition/David R. Redsicker and John J. O'Connor
    Originally published: New York: Elsevier, 1986
    (CRC series in practical aspects of criminal and forensic investigations)
    Includes bibliographical references and index.
    ISBN 0-8493-8155-X
    1. Arson investigation—United States. 2. Fire Investigation—United States. 3. Arson—
    United States. 4. Fires—United States. I. Title. II. Series
QR749.H64G78 1997
616'.0149—dc20   97-16777
                                                          CIP

© 1986 by Elsevier Science Publishing Co., Inc.
© 1997 by CRC Press, LLC

No claim to original U.S. Government works
International Standard Book Number 0-8493-8155-X
Library of Congress Card Number   97-16777
Printed in the United States of America   2 3 4 5 6 7 8 9 0
Printed on acid-free paper

Table of Contents

4   Chemistry and Behavior of Fire   55

5   Determining Origin and Cause   91

6   Eliminating Accidental Causes   121

7   Investigating Fatal Fires   191

8   Investigating Vehicular Fires   243

9   Evidence   275

Preface

When I originally agreed to assist John O'Connor with the first edition of *Practical Fire and Arson Investigation,* it was mostly technical in nature. I provided a majority of the photographs and some personal knowledge and experience in certain areas.

Now it is ten years later and my knowledge and experience has grown. It is therefore appropriate and the time is right for updating this book with a second edition. While the knowledge and training levels of those responsible for the investigation of fire origin and cause have increased, unfortunately the rate of detection, arrest and conviction in incendiary fires has remained low. Training has reached the level of certification in many states. Several recognized organizations have supported minimum standards for fire investigators. While this book does not profess to be a certification requirement, it does support the necessity for standards or guidelines for the proper fire scene investigation. Such minimum guidelines should include the subject matter as outlined and contained in *Practical Fire and Arson Investigation.*

Keep in mind that this book, like the many others on the subject of fire investigation, has been compiled from each investigators many and varied experiences in the field. And just as their individual backgrounds and experiences are unique, so too is each fire. The guidelines outlined in this text are just that— a guide for the investigation into proper origin and cause of fires. Conclusions must be based on facts supported by scientific principles and physical evidence.

Acknowledgments

In addition to the original contributors, the following people are sincerely appreciated for their contributions.

My associates at Peter Vallas Associates, Inc.: Peter R. Vallas, President; Peter S. Vallas, Chief Executive Officer; Theodore Pantle, Northern Regional Manager; Arthur Jackson, Chief Investigator; Investigators Rich Wolfson, Aaron Redsicker, Michael Redsicker, M. Andy Hilker, Edward Valentine, Daniel Seeley, G. Bud Gordner, Douglas Gordner, Brian Johnson, and Ken Kappler; Diane Sullivan for technical support in the New Jersey office; Amy Hilker for all the manuscript preparation in her spare time; Diana Zell Robinson, Sr. Librarian at N.Y.S. Academy of Fire Science; Walter Robinson, Deputy Chief in charge of Residential Training at N.Y.S. Academy of Fire Science; William Jacobs, U.S. Fire Administration National Fire Academy; Stuart James, Consulting Forensic Scientist; Daniel V. Christman, Investigator for Snohomish Co. Medical Examiner's Office Everett, Washington; M.C. (Craig) Tomash, Sgt. Royal Canadian Mounted Police; members of the Tompkins County Sheriff's Department Marine Patrol and Divers, Ithaca, New York; Sr. Investigator Mark Dresser, Deputies Bob Lampman, Al West, and Joe Sorenberger of the Seneca County Sheriff's Department Divers; Robert Colgrove, Corning Glass Research (Retired); and Dr. P. J. Colella, Forensic Odontologist.

Special thanks to my wife Patricia for her technical support and assistance with editing.

Arson:
The American Experience

1

Arson has been described as the fastest growing crime in America. However, over the past 10 years the rate of identified arson in the U.S. has dropped by about 17%. National statistics have shown that, when measured on a cost-per-incident basis, arson is still the most expensive crime committed. The average loss per incident for arson is about ten times that for robbery.

The response to the problem of arson, when examined nationally, has improved in the identification of incendiary cause. However, few cases still lead to arrests, and only 3% of arrests end in conviction. This limited success is not difficult to accept and understand when you examine the various segments of society and the environment of the official agencies involved in the suppression and investigation of the problem.

Fire Service

About 42% of the fire protection in America is provided by volunteer fire departments. Like their paid counterparts, these people are specifically trained and equipped to suppress fire, not to investigate its causes. The dedication and personal bravery of the fire service, whether paid or volunteer, goes without question. Members of the fire services risk their lives daily to save lives and property in blazes, the causes of which may never be determined. Nationwide, 103 firefighters died in the line of duty in 1994.

Table 1.1   Estimates of 1994 U.S. Fires and Property Loss by Property Use

Type of Fire	Number of Fires		Property Loss	
	Estimate	Percent Change from 1993	Estimate ($)	Percent Change from 1993
Fires in structures	614,000	−1.2	6,867,000,000	−7.3*
Fires in highway vehicles	402,000	0	961,000,000	+9.8*
Fires in other vehicles[b]	20,000	+8.1	150,000,000	−3.2
Fires outside of structures with value, but no vehicle involved (outside storage, crops, timber, etc.)	66,500	+27.9*	120,000,000	+90.5*
Fires in brush, grass wildland (excluding crops and timber) with no value or loss involved	503,000	+13.3*	—	—
Fires in rubbish, including dumpsters, outside of structures, with no value or loss involved	292,000	+1.6	—	—
All other fires	157,000	+23.6*	53,000,000	+12.8
Total	2,054,500	5.2	$8,151,000,000	−4.6*

Note: The estimates are based on data reported to the NFPA by fire departments that responded to the 1994 National Fire Experience Survey. *Change was statistically significant at the .01 level.

[a] This includes overall direct property loss to contents, structures, vehicles, machinery, vegetation, or anything else involved in a fire. It doesn't include indirect losses such as business interruption or temporary shelter costs. No adjustment was made for inflation in the year-to-year comparison.

[b] This includes trains, boats, ships, aircraft, farm vehicles, and construction vehicles.

Police Service

The law enforcement community has not been spared from the menace of arson and fire in general. A police officer is often the first official at the scene of a fire. This is true because of the usual mode of operation, patrol. A police officer may be the first person to realize there is a problem. Many officers, after first notifying the appropriate fire department, have risked their lives while trying to save others, in fires that may receive little or no follow-up.

Most fire departments and most of the over 40,000 police agencies nationwide are too small and fiscally limited to have the people and equipment necessary to conduct detailed follow-up in fire investigation. Many state fire marshal offices are so understaffed and underfinanced that they too must be very selective in the type and number of fires they investigate.

Volunteer and paid firefighters have traditionally been investigative generalists avoiding detailed fire investigations because of a lack of appropriate training. As a result, many fires that warrant scrutiny are either entirely ignored or investigated too late for the investigation to have any legal bearing.

Table 1.2 Estimate of 1994 U.S. Losses in Incendiary and Suspicious Structure Fires

Type of Fire	Number of Fires		Number of Civilian Deaths		Direct Property Loss[a]	
	Estimate	Percent Change from 1993	Estimate	Percent Change from 1993	Estimate ($)	Percent Change from 1993
Structure fires of incendiary origin*[c]	53,000	−1.9	410	−1.2	964,000,000	−49.3*[b]
Structure fires of suspicious origin*[c]	33,000	+8.2	140	−3.4	483,000,000	+7.3
Total structure fires of incendiary or suspicious origin*[c]	86,000	+1.8	550	−1.8	1,447,000,000	−38.5*

Note: The estimates are based on data reported to the NFPA by fire departments that responded to the 1994 National Fire Experience Survey. *Change was statistically significant at the .01 level.

[a] This includes overall direct property loss to contents, structure, vehicles, machinery, vegetation, or any other property involved in a fire. It doesn't include indirect losses, such as business interruption or temporary shelter costs. No adjustment was made for inflation in the year-to-year comparison.

[b] This decrease reflects fire losses during three wildfires in Southern California in October and November 1993 and the World Trade Center explosion in New York City, resulting in estimated losses of $1,039,000,000.

[c] Should be cause, not origin.

Figure 1.1 Firefighters risk their lives daily. Unfortunately, very few of these fire scenes will receive an adequate investigative follow-up. In some cases, the cause of the fire will never be determined.

This combination of factors has resulted in the misclassification of perhaps as many as half of all the fires occurring and the inappropriate payment of millions of dollars in insurance.

Public Awareness

Americans are becoming distinctly aware of the far-reaching consequences of arson, largely because of the success of arson awareness programs. In recent years, federal, state and local governments, the insurance industry, and the mass media have disseminated substantial amounts of information regarding the crime of arson specifically and the causes of the fire in general. The best indication that these messages and warnings are being taken seriously is the tremendous growth in the manufacture and sale (in the millions) of smoke and/or flame detectors. Community groups have formed throughout the nation in an effort to curtail the seemingly unchecked spread of arson in their neighborhoods. The public is outraged and demanding swift action.

One type of official response to these demands has been the creation of arson task forces. The task-force approach represents a broad-based reaction to the fact that "arson is no longer a crime against property, but a crime against each and every citizen and a brazen attack on the entire economy of our country" (Dodson 1980, p. 20).

Fire Investigation Methodology

The investigation of fires or explosions is an art as well as a science. A combination of factual information as well as the analysis of the facts must be accomplished objectively and truthfully. The basic methodology of the fire investigation relies on a systematic approach and attention to all relevant details.

The systematic approach recommended is that of the scientific method, used in the physical sciences (such as chemistry and physics). This method provides for the organizational and analytical process so desirable and necessary in a successful fire investigation.

The scientific method forms a basis for legitimate scientific and engineering processes, including fire incident investigation. It is applied using the following six steps:

1. *Recognize the need.* One must first determine that a problem exists. In this case, a fire or explosion has occurred and its cause must be determined and listed so that similar incidents can be prevented in the future.

2. *Define the problem.* Having determined that a problem exists, an investigator or analyst must define how the problem can be solved. In this case, proper origin and cause investigation must be conducted. This is done by an examination of the scene, by a combination of other data collection methods such as the review of previously conducted investigations of the incident, interviews with the witnesses or other knowledgeable persons, and the results of scientific testing.

3. *Collect data.* Facts about the fire incident are now collected. This is done by observation, experiment, or other direct data gathering means. This information is called *empirical data* because it is based upon observations or experience and can be verified.

4. *Analyze the data (inductive reasoning).* All of the collected and observed information is analyzed by inductive reasoning. In this process, the total body of empirical data collected is carefully examined in the light of the investigator's knowledge, training, and experience. Subjective or speculative information cannot be included in the analysis, only facts that can be clearly proven by observation or experiment.

5. *Develop a hypothesis.* Based on the data analysis, the investigator must now produce a hypothesis or group of hypotheses to explain the origin and cause of the fire or explosion incident. This hypothesis must be based solely upon the empirical data that the investigator has collected.

6. *Test the hypothesis (deductive reasoning).* All other reasonable origins and causes must be eliminated. The investigator does not have a truly

provable hypothesis unless it can stand up to careful and serious challenge. This is done by the principle of deductive reasoning, in which the investigator compares his or her hypothesis to all known facts. If the hypothesis cannot withstand an examination by deductive reasoning, it must either be discarded as not provable and a new more adequate hypothesis tested, or the fire cause must be listed as "unknown."

Model Arson Task Force

A model arson task force would incorporate the intelligence gathering networks of each separate investigative agency into one cohesive, coordinated, and goal-directed entity. This would provide for a more comprehensive attack on a selected number of aspects (e.g., suspects, leads) and avoid unnecessary duplication of effort. It would also make better use of assigned personnel and available resources. The sharing of investigative specialties (fire, police, etc.) and experience in a spirit of free-flowing communication would broaden the investigative capabilities of each investigator.

Role of the Fire Investigator

The fire investigator is a specialist operating in a unique field — a person with the field experience and technical training necessary to collect and evaluate factual information and identify criminal activity in situations where others perceive only confusion and chaos.

The primary goal of a fire investigator, as of any criminal investigator, is to determine the truth. In seeking the truth, the investigator must complete a post-fire examination of the structure or vehicle that is the subject of a suspicious fire and determine the origin and cause of the fire. Interviews must be conducted, evidence collected, and comprehensive reports of all findings prepared. To complete these tasks, the fire investigator must know and understand the rules governing proper crime scene techniques, the significance of interviewing strategies, and the technical requirements of fire science.

If, during the initial stages of inquiry, actions pointing to criminal conduct or evidence of criminality are uncovered, the fire investigator must automatically shift to his secondary role: to identify and move against those responsible. A fire investigator who has reason to believe that arson was committed is morally and professionally obligated to develop the case to its fullest extent.

Figure 1.2   A fire investigator must be prepared to cope with any eventuality at the fire scene. Mobile investigative units, like the one pictured here, permit the ready availability of equipment and supplies. These highly visible units may also serve as a deterrent. A homeowner or small businessman may think twice about "selling his premises to an insurance company," if he believes that highly specialized and equipped investigative unit is likely to respond to the fire scene and may uncover his culpability.

Managing the Fire Investigation

Arson and its related offenses are universally viewed as among the most serious crimes that a person can commit; as such, they warrant the most diligent and unfaltering of investigations. To ensure that every possible avenue is adequately explored and documented, the investigator should follow an investigative checklist. A ranking officer, assigned to supervise a fire investigation unit, must continuously monitor, coordinate, and direct the cases under investigation by subordinates. The field investigator conducts the actual investigation, while the supervisor, using personal experience and expertise, monitors investigative actions and provides administrative follow-up. This type of system is used by the overwhelming majority of fire investigation units nationally.

Case Management

To optimize their limited resources (people and equipment), many agencies have developed case management systems. There is a distinction between urban and rural settings in their use of case management systems, due primarily to the difference in the volume of cases involved. Certain rural areas may refer every arson case to a case management system to ensure that every classified arson is adequately investigated. In an urban area with a high volume of cases to be investigated, the case management system is used to determine which cases should receive priority.

In some urban jurisdictions, for example, cases of fire occurring in abandoned buildings are quickly closed: the fire scene is examined and the case accurately classified, but there is no follow-up investigation unless more information is forthcoming. Even when such follow-up is conducted, no further action is taken unless the additional information provides specific data that may lead to a quick arrest in the case. The only action that may be taken would be to notify the appropriate city or state agency to order or request the demolition of the abandoned structure. Under normal circumstances, a fire intentionally set in an abandoned building and causing a death or other serious injury, or extending to and causing damage to an occupied building, is referred to the case management system.

Every case involving death or other serious injury is assigned to case management. However, for cases involving only property loss, some agencies use total dollar loss as the primary factor in designating a case for additional follow-up. For example, in Seattle, Washington, every fire causing at least $1000 in damage is thoroughly investigated.

Investigative Checklist

There are three main reasons to use an investigative checklist:

1. To ensure that every pertinent fact about the case has been identified.
2. To identify the cases to be assigned to case management.
3. To serve as a supervisory tool in evaluating an individual investigator's performance and in the assignment of additional cases based on case load.

An investigative checklist should include the following types of data:

Identity of the assigned investigator
Victim information
Suspect/defendant information
Detailed information about the incident, including time, address, identity of the fire chief, first firefighter and police officer at scene, and so on; classification of the offense (e.g., arson [occupied, abandoned], arson/homicide)

Detailed information relating to the investigative procedures and steps taken (e.g., photos, sketches, canvass)

Identification of physical evidence and follow-up procedures (e.g., assigned prosecutor)

Witness information

Crime Analysis

An integral part of the case management system is the keeping of pertinent statistical data relating to the incident or arson and related offenses occurring within the area for which the fire investigation unit is responsible.

The design of the crime analysis system depends on the length of time to be considered and the volume of cases in that period. The types of data to be extrapolated from the related reports would include: chronologic listing of incidents; date and time; classification, including whether residential or commercial, occupied or abandoned, forest or brush; point of origin (where the fire started-e.g., room, basement, attic, floor); type of accelerant used or suspected, if any; classification of damage; and death or other injury.

Basic Steps for Fire Investigation

Using the scientific method in most fire or explosion incidents should involve the following six major steps from inception through final analysis.

1. *Receiving the assignment.* The investigator should be notified of the incident, what his or her role will be, and what he or she is to accomplish.
2. *Preparing for the investigation.* The investigator should marshall his or her forces and resources and plan the conduct of the investigation.
3. *Examination of the scene.* The investigator should conduct the examination of the scene and collect basic data necessary to the analysis.
4. *Recording the scene.* The scene should be photographed and diagrammed, and notes should be made of the progress of the investigation. Valuable empirical data should be noted and preserved.
5. *Collecting and preserving evidence.* Valuable physical evidence should be recognized, properly collected, and preserved for further testing and evaluation or court room presentation.
6. *Analyzing the incident.* An incident scenario or failure analysis should be described, explaining the origin, cause, and responsibility for the incident. This analysis should be reported in the proper form to help prevent recurrence.

References

Basic Methodology, in *Fire and Explosion Investigations*, NFPA 921, National Fire Protection Association, Boston, 1992.

Braun, K. J. and Ford, R. E., Organizing an arson task force, *FBI Law Enforcement Bull.*, 50(3), March 1981.

DeLuca, T. (Battalion Chief, Los Angeles City Fire Department), Los Angeles Arson Suppression Task Force, *Arson: Resource Exchange Bull.*, Federal Emergency Management Agency, U.S. Fire Administration, Washington, D.C., July 1980.

Dodson, H.C. (Fire Marshals' Association of North America), "Is Arson Legislation Adequate/Inadequate?" *Arson: Resource Exchange Bull.*, Federal Emergency Management Agency, U.S. Fire Administration, Washington, D.C., July 1980.

National Fire Protection Association (NFPA), Fire loss in the United States during 1993, *Fire Journal*, 1994.

Sanders, Robert E., National response teams: ATF's coordinated effort in arson investigations, *FBI Law Enforcement Bull.*, 50(12), December 1981.

U.S. Department of Justice, *Uniform Crime Reports: Crime in the United States*, 1982 (also, 1983), U.S. Government Printing Office, Washington, D.C., 1983 (also, 1984).

Weisman, H. M. (Ed), *Arson Resource Directory*, Arson Resource Center Office of Planning and Education, U.S. Fire Administration, Washington, D.C., March 1980.

Wood, W. (SAC Explosives Branch, ATF), "The Bureau of Alcohol, Tobacco, and Firearms Arson Program," *Arson: Resource Exchange Bull.*, Federal Emergency Management Agency, U.S. Fire Administration, October 1980.

Arson Motives and Pathology

Some people mistakenly believe that the poor, the elderly, and the mentally ill have "cornered the market in fire." These same people believe that these groups suffer from some strange compulsion to burn themselves out of house and home. It would serve the arsonists in our society well to have us believe this nonsense.

The fact is that many supposedly respectable people are making large sums of money as arson brokers and "torches." If we examine the backgrounds of the people who have been arrested and convicted of arson, we see that they represent a complete cross section of American society. In fact, our sample would cut across the spectrum of social respectability. In the past decade, people from every walk of life have been sentenced to prison after being convicted for this, the fastest-growing crime in America. Those convicted for arson include public officials, law enforcement and fire service personnel, lawyers, doctors, accountants, teachers, and insurance and real estate brokers, as well as organized crime operatives, drug addicts, and the poor, the elderly and the mentally ill.

It has been said that there is a cause for everything people do, or fail to do. Although the person may be otherwise normal, the act of destructive fire setting is not normal (Bromley et al., undated, S4.1, p. 1).

By those who are *not* "otherwise normal", we mean those suffering from some form of mental illness. Such *pathological* motives are discussed in the section Psychological Compulsion. Most arsonists, however, are nonpathological; nevertheless, each does have a *motive*.

Motive is an inner drive or impulse that causes a person to do something or to act in a certain way. Basically, it is the cause, reason, or incentive that induces or prompts specific behavior. In a legal context, motive explains "why" the offender committed his unlawful act, e.g., murder, rape, or arson.

Figure 2.1   The motives for arson are as diverse as the walks of life from which the fire setters derive. These motives include profit (fraud), revenge, vandalism, crime concealment, and psychological compulsion.

Though motive, unlike intent (willfulness), is not an essential element in criminal prosecution, it often lends support to it. Motive, for instance, often plays a crucial role in determining the cause of a fire, as well as the identity of the person or persons responsible for setting it (Rider, 1980). The motives for arson are as diverse as the walks of life from which arsonists come. These motives include but are not limited to profit (fraud), revenge, vandalism, excitement, crime concealment, and the aforementioned psychological compulsion. The rest of this chapter describes and discusses each of these major motives for arson.

Arson for Profit

Arson for profit is responsible for about a half of all the fire-related property damage in America. It is probably the primary motive for the nearly 25% yearly increase in the rate of arson. The business of arson for profit has traditionally been one of high gain and low risk. Nationally, only 9% of all arson cases are cleared by arrest, and only 2% result in convictions. Insurance companies have paid billions of dollars in fire claims, even though many of these cases were still under active investigation by one or several agencies. As for risk, an arsonist in America has less than one chance in ten of being arrested and an even smaller chance of being convicted.

The economic gain to be derived from an arson-for-profit scheme can be either direct or indirect. A homeowner who destroys his or her home for the insurance proceeds gains directly when the insurance company settles

Figure 2.2 The expression "sell it to the insurance company" has become the call to arms for someone who views fire as a shortcut to disposing of a defective or unreliable automobile.

the claim. A security guard who starts and then puts out a fire in a warehouse where he works gains indirectly, when rewarded for quick action in saving the warehouse.

Insurance Fraud

Insurance fraud is probably the most common target in arson for profit. The expression "sell it to the insurance company" has become the call to arms for anyone who wishes to dispose of an unwanted automobile, a neglected house, or an unprofitable business. Insurance fraud has also been referred to as "the modern way to refinance."

One such scheme, most evidenced in urban areas, involves the purchase of old, economically unsound, abandoned, and dilapidated buildings in depressed areas. These purchases are made with the smallest investment possible. Over the next several months or years, the property is sold and resold back and forth among a small group of investors. In this way, at least on paper, the value of the holdings increases. The building is then insured at the inflated "paper" value.

Another example is the person who buys a new or used car and either cannot meet loan payments and fears the loss of the initial investment, or finds that the automobile is unreliable and cannot get satisfaction from the dealer. The buyer in such a position may seriously consider "selling the car to the insurance company"; in 1994 alone, there were almost 43,500 cases of automobile arson in the U.S. causing $156 million in property damage (*NFPA Journal*, Sept/Oct, 1995).

A third and all-too-common example of insurance fraud is referred to as the *redecoration fire*. A homeowner who wants to renovate his or her kitchen but cannot afford the $10,000 cost quoted by a contractor conveniently arranges a kitchen fire. The insurance settlement then pays for the renovation.

Welfare Fraud

The following rules are displayed in every social service (welfare) office in the City of New York:

> *Moving expenses:* Welfare clients may move whenever they wish. However, moving expenses will be provided only if the move is necessary and if it is determined that the fees (i.e., moving expenses, security deposit, broker's fee, rent in advance) cannot be avoided. Moving expenses will not be provided more than once in two years unless the following conditions exist:
> A. The move is the result of a fire or a disaster....

Although a disaster is impossible to arrange, a fire is not, and a large proportion of America's inner-city arson has been the direct result of welfare fraud fires.

In a typical welfare fire, the welfare recipient is either dissatisfied with his current living conditions, or needs cash. He finds a new apartment in a more desirable area. Then, usually under cover of darkness, he moves all his belongings (furniture, clothing, pets, etc.) to the new apartment. The next step is to replace some of the removed items with run-down furniture and clothing from a second-hand store or junk yard. Soon after this is done, he sets a fire. After applying to the local department of social services, he will receive funds to replace all the belongings that were supposedly lost. Besides, his moving expenses will be covered and he will get a finder's fee for having found a new apartment without departmental assistance.

It should be noted that some supposed welfare fires are actually insurance fraud fires disguised by the building owner to draw attention away from the nonresident owner to the resident welfare recipients. In other cases, the building owner encourages arson by having the services in the building (e.g., heat, hot water) rendered inoperable (usually citing economic hardship). A tenant of the building, after exhausting whatever administrative recourse is available, may then set fire as the only way to escape these conditions. Such a fire is correctly labeled a welfare fraud fire, but the conditions that precipitated it are rarely examined.

Business-Related Fraud

Eliminating Competition

One example of arson for business-related (-motivated) fraud is the setting of a fire to limit or eliminate competition. Say that a person owns a well-established business that has been operating in a particular neighborhood for many years. A new store, selling the same items, opens around the corner and, in time, cuts into the older store's business. After a series of price wars, the established store's owner determines that it is time to use other means to reduce or eliminate the competition. The simplest way is to burn them out.

In one actual case, the owner of a large piece of real estate offered to buy out one of his tenants, the owner of a five-and-ten-cent store. The owner wanted to tear down the five-and-ten to build a parking lot and restaurant, which would serve a nearby state-operated betting parlor. However, the owner of the five-and-ten refused to sell his lease. The property owner was eventually arrested and convicted for a fire that destroyed an entire block of stores.

Organized Crime

Organized crime groups in America have been and are well entrenched in the "arson-for-hire" business. The sequence of events in a typical organized crime operation, referred to as a *bankruptcy scam*, clearly highlights the magnitude of their involvement.

A person owns a successful business with an excellent credit rating; his only vice is betting on horse races or playing at the gaming tables. As the result of gambling losses, involvement with a loan shark, or extortion, he involuntarily and grudgingly accepts a new partner: an organized crime member or associate who may have bought the store owner's contract from a local loan shark. At the direction of his new partner, the store owner buys, to the extent of the store's credit, a large stock of items that can easily be fenced. When these items are delivered, they are simply reloaded onto another truck and resold (at a fraction of their original cost) to the general public by a network of reliable fences. Since the business is now in debt to the extent of its credit, the bills that come due in 90 or 120 days cannot be paid, and the organized crime partner arranges for the business to file for bankruptcy. While the bankruptcy proceedings are pending, the store burns to the ground. The fire, which was part of a package deal, was intended to: destroy the business's books and records, destroy the merchandise that was supposedly available for sale, and provide the basis for an insurance claim.

The partners then split the insurance settlement and the revenue from the fenced goods, according to a preconceived plan. Following the bankruptcy settlement, the creditors receive, at best, 10 cents on the dollar.

Figure 2.3   The investigation of conflagrations is arduous and costly. Insurance companies will often cooperate and assist by supplying or funding the heavy equipment necessary to properly excavate a fire scene.

Organized crime factions also use arson (and murder) to intimidate witnesses, to eliminate other criminal factions, and as a form of discipline to maintain order within their own ranks.

Demolition and Rehabilitation Scams

Another real estate scam in which the participants gain indirectly is one in which a speculator buys a large parcel of land that is dotted with old, abandoned buildings. The buildings are in such disrepair that the land is worth more without them than with them. The reason for the difference in value is that anyone who might consider buying and building on the property must add on the cost of demolishing the old structures. The landowner has a similar problem. The costs involved in having the building(s) torn down and carted away may be prohibitive, and fire may be seen as the only alternative. If the fire does its work, the speculator will save on the cost of demolition and the property will be more appealing to a prospective buyer.

A second and related scheme involves demolition companies themselves. Take, for example, a case in which bids are being accepted for the demolition of a 10-story building. Each demolition company (depending on the city) must add to its costs an allowance for *dumping fees*: charges for each truckload of debris dumped at a city-owned landfill. If, after winning the contract, a company realizes that its original bid was too low, it conveniently has one or more fires in the building to be demolished and blames the fire on local juveniles or vandals. The more the building burns, the less there is to be trucked away; therefore, the fewer dumping fees have to be paid. In this way, the demolition company either breaks even or makes a profit.

A third scheme, referred to as the *rehabilitation scam*, involves the rehabilitation of real property under the guise of a redevelopment project. The insurance industry and federal lending agencies, such as the Small Business Administration (SBA), are the usual targets of this type of scheme. A person buys, at nominal cost, an abandoned or nearly abandoned building in an area that has been designated for redevelopment. The purchaser then announces his or her intention to rehabilitate the old building and to make it habitable again. The old building, the builder's "good intentions," and the political climate are all used as collateral and as an inducement to secure the largest SBA loan possible. So, for example, for an investment of only $2000 or $3000 and a show of good faith, this speculator may have as much as a several hundred thousand dollars of working capital. The next step is to collect receipts for materials that were never purchased and for work that was never done. The builder may rehabilitate one apartment out of 20 in a five-story walk-up apartment building. A telephone must be installed and the utilities may be operational in that one apartment. A friend or family member is identified to authorities as a tenant, and the apartment is furnished. The building is now occupied (telephone and utility bills, rent receipts) and qualifies for insurance. Some time after the building is insured, there is a fire. An insurance claim is filed, and there are ample bills and receipts to account for the SBA loan.

Many reasons for arson have been given by practitioners of arson for profit in business-related frauds (after conviction). Among these are the following: relocation when unable to break a lease or sell the old location, dissolution of the business, ridding the business of obsolete or unsalable merchandise, completion of a seasonal business, imminent business failure (business going bad), upgrading of equipment, labor or union problems, and employees who are afraid to come to work (crime in the area).

Building Strippers

Others who profit indirectly from arson include a group of people referred to as *building strippers*. A building stripper or junk dealer is a person who strips abandoned buildings of bathroom fixtures, copper tubing, and anything else of value to be sold as junk. Most building strippers realize that there is a much easier way to expose the items they are interested in taking. Now instead of spending hours butting through sheetrock and plaster walls, they simply start several carefully planned fires, and the responding fire units do the work for them. In putting out the fires, the firefighters punch or cut holes in the floors and walls, saving the building strippers hours of work. This is in addition to the damage caused by the fire itself. As soon as the fire department has left the scene, the strippers remove all remaining items of any value. In New York City, building stripping is a summonsable offense for which a small fine can be imposed. Building strippers are rarely brought to court for the crime of arson or for the unnecessary risk their fires pose to the fire personnel who ultimately respond.

Commercial Fire Checklist

Good information is vital to the successful conclusion of an arson case. Many times a person will answer questions early in an investigation to avoid the aura of suspicion.

The investigation of an arson-for-profit scheme is very similar to many other white-collar-crime investigations. If a motive is to be discovered and documented for court presentation, the investigator must have the help of an investigative accountant. A comprehensive physical examination is usually enough to confirm that the crime of arson was committed. The "paper chase" which develops from an analysis of the business's books and records usually identifies the motive and connects the defendant to the crime.

The following is a typical line of inquiry that an investigator would follow when investigating a suspicious supermarket fire. A similar program would be used when investigating suspicious fires in most commercial establishments (Lindsey, unpublished):

- Start gathering information as soon as possible after the fire. What are the relationships among the owners of the store?
- Names and addresses of suppliers (meat, groceries, beer, etc.)
- Did the owners of the store reduce their inventory before the fire?
- What is the dollar volume of business the store does per week on meats? (An estimate of total volume can be developed.)
- What are the owner's gross earnings per week and the percent of markup?
- Does the owner have any financial interest in other stores nearby?
- Check storerooms and shelves for merchandise, beer, and meat that is the most expensive.
- Check with suppliers whether bills are overdue or checks for merchandise are bouncing.
- How much money does the owner owe suppliers?
- What is the name of the owner's insurance company and what is the extent of coverage? Check with insurance agent.

- Has the owner applied to the Small Business Administration or any similar lending agency for a loan?
- Is the store protected by an alarm (burglar or fire)? If so, what time is it turned on daily? Was it on or off at the time of the fire? Was it circumvented?
- Was the sprinkler system working?
- Ask to see business records and tax returns.
- What flammable liquids are kept in the store (charcoal and lighter fluids, spray cleaners etc.)? Where are they kept?
- Are flammable liquids used to clean the floors or areas of the store? What types and when were they last used?

"It is certainly possible to prove the arson fraud scheme without positive evidence linking the subject to the fire scene," according to Special Agent Robert E. Walsh, of the Criminal Investigations Division, Federal Bureau of Investigation (Walsh 1979). "Investigators often are required to initiate arson investigations involving fires in buildings that were torched several months previous and have since been razed." Walsh also suggests that "investigators must review available information and reports to establish the identities of fires that have been included in this scheme." Such information sources include "police/fire department records, local newspapers, state fire marshals, insurance agents, and informants. Walsh notes that while reviewing potential inner-city arson files, the following clues will indicate positive circumstantial evidence that the fire was set for an insurance fraud:

1. Presence of incendiary material
2. Multiple origins of fire (arson must be a total loss to be profitable)
3. Location of the fire in a building (look for fires near the roof, because many insurance adjusters will declare a fire a total loss once the roof is destroyed)
4. Suspicious hours (no witnesses)
5. Holiday fires
6. Vacant building
7. Renovation of building
8. Recent departure of occupants
9. Removal of objects (woodwork, plumbing, etc.)
10. Property for sale
11. Previous fire
12. Building overinsured
13. Habitual claimants
14. Fires occurring shortly before policy expiration
15. Fires where insurance has recently been obtained
16. Recent sale of building.

Agent Walsh further suggests:

> After compiling a list of possible inner-city arson fires, the investigator may
> be able to develop positive circumstantial evidence of fraud from available
> records and demonstrate the proper investor's involvement by showing
> conflicting information, deception, and false statements.... It may be much
> easier to solve an arson fraud than it would be to prove a straight arson
> case (Walsh, 1979).

Revenge and Prejudice

Arson motivated by revenge, spite, and jealousy accounts for a high percentage of the number of intentional fires occurring in the U.S. Those who
commit such arson include "jilted lovers, feuding neighbors, disgruntled
employees, quarreling spouses, persons getting even after being cheated or
abused, and persons motivated by racial or religious hostility" (Boudreau
et al., 1977, p.19).

A fire that destroyed a Hispanic social club and killed 25 partygoers in
October 1976 in the Bronx, New York City, was motivated by revenge. The
jilted boyfriend of one of the victims apparently started the fire because his
girlfriend would not leave the party to talk to him.

From an investigative standpoint, once the revenge motive has been
identified, the number of people to be investigated can be narrowed tremen-
dously because of the connection between the subject(s) and the target of
arson.

Fires motivated by racial, religious, or similar biases are investigated in
the same manner as those motivated by revenge. Most local newspapers are
laden with articles describing in detail the burning of a group home for the
retarded, a house of worship, or the home of a black family in an all-white
neighborhood. The investigator must realize that constitutional as well as
criminal statutes may have been violated in a racially or religiously motivated
fire.

Vanity

This category of arson motive is also referred to as the *hero syndrome*. A night
watchman or security guard who feels that he is being ignored may start a
fire and then "save" the entire plant. This "heroic" act may draw attention to
the splendid job he is doing and warrant a raise in pay, a bonus, or a reward.
Vanity fires have been started by volunteer firefighters who happened to live
in quiet residential areas where there were few calls for service, to gain the

attention of their family and neighbors and the respect of fellow firefighters for being the first to respond to the firehouse or scene. According to FBI Special Agent Anthony O. Rider, vanity arsonists, although few in number, have "the propensity for serious destructiveness" (Rider 1980, p. 12).

Fire Buff Arson

A special case of the vanity-motivated fire setter worth mentioning here is that of the fire "buff" — a person who enthusiastically attends the fires, perhaps to associate with and assist fire-fighting personnel. The term *buff*, in fact, most probably derives from the buff overcoats worn by volunteer firefighters in early 19th-century New York City. Says Agent Rider:

> The fire "buff," like the police "buff," is an enthusiastic "hanger-on." He generally represents a frustrated would-be fireman or would-be policeman. Although many buffs are civic-minded and constructive in their associations with the police and fire service, others are characteristically immature, inadequate underachievers. The fire buff who sets fires is seeking attention and attempting in a pathological way to win praise and social recognition for his alertness and heroism in reporting fires and helping to fight them" (Rider 1980).

Juvenile Fire Setters and Vandalism

In 1994, over 55% of arson arrests in the U.S. were due to juveniles. In some cases, the motive is certainly profit. Juveniles may be hired as incendiaries or "torches" by people who are unable to contact a professional torch or who are afraid to start the fire themselves. A juvenile hired to set a fire will generally work for much less than an experienced or professional torch. It is because of their lack of experience and their reliance on whatever supplies are available (e.g., gasoline) that these young incendiaries are likely to be trapped and die in a fire they might set.

A motive for juvenile fire setters is not always apparent. Vandalism is a common cause ascribed to fires set by juveniles, who seem to burn property just to relive boredom or as a general protest against authority. Many school fires as well as fires in abandoned autos, vacant buildings, and trash receptacles are believed to be caused by this type of arsonist (Boudreau et al., 1977).

Fire setting has been recognized as behavior that is learned at a very early age (Redsicker, unpublished). Children as young as 2 years old have started fires, destroying property and lives. An increasing number are revenge-motivated or have what is known in the profession as the "cry-for-help" syndrome. These young people often are the victims of neglect and abuse. Attempts to

Figure 2.4 The foundation is all that remains of this recently completed high ranch. Juveniles, either for a thrill or just on a dare, burnt the new home to the ground. (Photo courtesy of T. Brown.)

reach these children are being made through juvenile fire setter programs across the country. These programs are an innovative approach, not only to recognize juvenile fire setters, but, more importantly, to identify the underlying problems that surface as fire-setting behavior.

Crime Concealment

Escaped prisoners and armed robbers will often burn their (stolen) escape vehicles at the time they are abandoned. They do this to destroy fingerprints or other evidence that might connect them to the car and, therefore, to the scene of the escape or robbery. Torched getaway cars are only one example of arson for crime concealment:

> Criminals sometimes set fires to obliterate the evidence of burglaries, larcenies, and murders. The fire may destroy evidence that a crime was committed and destroy the evidence connecting the perpetrator to the crime, or, in the case of murder, make it impossible to identify the victim. People may set fires to destroy records that contain evidence of embezzlement, forgery, or fraud. Arson has also been used to divert attention while the perpetrator burglarized another building, and as a means of covering attempted escapes from jails, prisons, and state hospitals (Boudreau et al., 1977).

Figure 2.5 An employee identified this desk as the central repository for all the business records for a company that had burned to the ground over a long holiday weekend. Although gasoline has been poured throughout the structure, the desk was not destroyed as planned. The business books and records had been moved before the fire.

Evidence that might indicate arson for crime concealment includes the recovery of burglar's tools (e.g., crowbar, lock picks) from the fire scene, or personal property strewn about a room that exhibits little or no fire damage. A detailed follow-up investigation is required if: business or personal records were left out (or file drawers left open) and exposed to fire; or valuable personal items or expensive office equipment or stock are missing after a close examination of debris (and presumed to have been stolen before the fire started).

A fire set to conceal a burglary several years ago in Westchester County caused the death of more than 20 people who were attending a dance several doors away from the scene of the burglary.

Psychological Compulsion

As we have seen, there are elements of many cases of arson that might best be described as psychological: vanity, prejudice, revenge, and perhaps even a desire to "beat the system." Developing a psychological profile of an arsonist during an investigation can be an invaluable aid to the investigator. It helps him focus his investigation, identify potential suspects, and develop appropriate techniques and strategies for interviewing the various types of fire setters (Rider, 1980, p. 2).

This kind of psychological understanding is crucial in cases for which there seems to be no motive or, at least, none that is as readily comprehensible as those we have already examined. Such "motiveless" fire setting may be attributable to *psychological compulsion.*

In order to understand the role of psychological compulsion as it relates to fire setting, it is first necessary to examine the types of affective disorders that may lead to psychopathic behavior or criminal conduct.

Mania and Depression

Mania and depression are two behavioral extremes generally viewed as psychoneurotic or psychotic disorders. *Mania* is marked by mood elevation, physical and mental hyperactivity, and disorganized behavior. *Depression* may involve lethargy, lack of concentration, and sadness or dejection. Cycles or alternating mania and depression in an individual are termed *manic-depressiveness.*

Depression is a factor in some arson/homicide cases. Abhorrent as the idea may be to a rational person, people do commit suicide by fire. Suicide by fire is rare in Western culture, but common in Japan and the most common form of suicide in Bangkok, Thailand. A person in the depths of depression has one overriding concern: "How to die?" (See also Chapter 7, "Investigating Fatal Fires.")

Pyromania

The *pyromaniac* (not a maniac using the clinical definition) is a person who has an "inordinate or ungovernable enthusiasm for starting fires, who lacks a conscious motivation for his fire setting" (Rider, 1980). Some writers have argued the point that "pyros" set fires to gain some sort of sexual gratification (Battle and Weston, 1975, p. 98). Whether or not this is true, it seems that the overwhelming majority set fires to gain some type of sensual pleasure.

Pyromaniacs set fires impulsively; they do not plan their fires. Rather than carry flammables or combustibles to use as fuels in setting fires, they simply ignite whatever combustibles are close by when they have the urge to start a fire. There is generally no connection among the targets of a pyromaniac's fires other than that they may occur along a common route or path followed daily, for example, to a bus stop, to work, or to a local store.

A single pyromaniac may cause large amounts of damage and start many fires before a pattern or common thread is identified. Once the pattern becomes clear, the investigator should recommend and coordinate an extensive surveillance operation in the area.

It is important, while interviewing any suspected fire setter, to try to establish a reason (motive) for the fire-setting behavior. If the person cannot articulate a reason why they set the fire, they then may fall into the category of pyromania. However, most people, when questioned carefully about their fire setting behavior, will give reasons such as abuse, neglect, or revenge as their "reason" for starting the fires. These reasons are not the motivation of a pyromaniac.

Schizophrenia

Schizophrenia is the most serious of the affective disorders. It is generally characterized by disintegration of personality (inappropriate affect, disorderly thought and behavior) and withdrawal into self-centered subjective mental activity (autism). Of the four general types of schizophrenic personality (paranoid, simple hebephrenic, and catatonic), the paranoid schizophrenic seems to be the most likely to be an arsonist. The paranoid schizophrenic has a tendency toward excessive and irrational suspiciousness; everything is perceived from a defensive standpoint. The paranoid schizophrenic fire setter, because of this bizarre or perverted sense of reality and defensive posture, may use fire setting as a weapon against whatever is perceived as a threat.

Profile of the Pathological Arsonist

Rider (1980) found that, although there is no such thing as a "typical" pathological fire setter, the following cluster characteristics are common among them:

1. Less than 25 years old
2. Reared in distressing and pathological environments
3. Father absent from home
4. Domineering mother
5. Academic retardation
6. Slightly below average intelligence
7. Emotional and psychological disturbance
8. Social and sexual maladjustment
9. Unmarried
10. Psychological inadequacy and insecurity
11. Cowardly

The pathological fire setter may be "motivated by a multiplicity of factors" and spurred on by a "precipitating stressful situation or experience" (Rider, 1980).

Mass Disturbance (Riot)

The massive civil disturbance that rocked Miami, Florida, in May 1980 was reminiscent of our country's turbulent past. News reporters and photographers documented the all-too-familiar clouds of smoke billowing from fire-ravaged sections of the city.

The problems that plagued the authorities in Miami (arson, looting, shootings, mass arrests) were the same as those faced by the officials of New York City and many other cities during the 1960s. The words "riot" and "arson" often seem to be inextricably linked. The indiscriminate burning of businesses, homes, and automobiles during a riot, though a *consequence* of the civil disorder, is not motivated by it. People in a mob may commit acts that they would never do as individuals (*mob mentality*). Clearly, however, a riot may incite those already motivated for arson and provide chaos within which to escape.

Terrorism

In his *Minimanual of the Urban Guerrilla*, the Brazilian theoretician of urban guerrilla warfare, Carlos Marighella, defined terrorism as "an action, usually involving the placement of a bomb or fire explosion of great destructive power, which is capable of effecting irreparable loss against the enemy" (Marighella 1970, p. 32). Fire is one of the weapons in the terrorist's arsenal. This is often overlooked; media attention has traditionally focused on terrorist bombings and kidnapping incidents.

Because the primary goal of terrorists is often publicity, their violence is directed mainly against civilian targets. For example, the FALN (Fuerzas Armadas de Liberacón Nacional Puerto Rriqueña — armed forces of the Puerto Rican National Liberation movement) claimed responsibility for the extensive use of incendiary devices against department stores in New York City. A number of these devices were secreted in the merchandise on shelves and clothing racks. Terrorists have also used arson as a diversionary tactic, and their associates have used the proceeds of insurance fraud (arson) to finance covert operations and to buy weapons and equipment. In one series of cases, insurance settlements from fires that occurred in New York City were being used to further the goals of terrorists in the Middle East. Recent acts of terrorism in the U.S. include the 1993 bombing of the World Trade Center in New York City and the bombing of the Federal building in Oklahoma City in 1995.

Today's investigator must be aware of the current trends and tactics of the terrorist and maintain a liaison with local intelligence units.

References and Selected Readings

Battle, B. P. and Weston, P. B., *Arson: A Handbook of Detection and Investigation*, Arco Publishing, New York, 1975.

Boudreau, J. F. et al., *Arson and Arson Investigation: Survey and Assessment*, U.S. Government Printing Office, Washington, D.C., 1977.

Bromley, J. et al., *Cause and Origin Determination*, Office of Fire Prevention and Control, Department of State, State of New York, undated.

Fitch, R. D. and Porter, E. A., *Accidental or Incendiary*, Charles C Thomas, Springfield, IL, 1968.

Lindsey, A. (former Assistant District Attorney, Bronx, New York), "Commercial Fire Check List," unpublished course material, Arson Investigation Course, NYC Police Academy.

Marighella, Carlos, *Minimanual of the Urban Guerrilla*, New World Liberation Front (underground U.S. publisher), 1970.

Redsicker, D. (New York State Fire Academy), unpublished research.

Rider, A. O. (FBI Special Agent), The Firesetter, a Psychological Profile, *Law Enforcement Bull.*, June-August 1980.

U.S. Department of Justice, *Uniform Crime Reports: Crime in the United States*, 1983, U.S. Government Printing Office, Washington, D.C., 1984.

Walsh, Robert E. (FBI Special Agent), "Inner-City Arson," *Law Enforcement Bull.*, October 1979.

Building Construction: Fire Problems and Precautions

3

To evaluate a structural fire effectively, an investigator must have a basic understanding of building construction. A working knowledge of commonly used materials and their effect on and reaction to fire spread is essential. Under normal conditions, (e.g., no accelerants or explosives) the rate of burning and the intensity and path of a fire are directly affected by a building's construction and types of materials. Personal safety is of the utmost importance to any investigator: before entering a fire-damaged structure, an investigator must be able to evaluate its stability. The potential for internal collapse poses the greatest danger.

Classification of Building Construction

There are five nationally recognized types of building construction, though various state and local governments have further narrowed these classifications to meet their particular conditions:

1. Fire-restrictive
2. Noncombustible or limited-combustible
3. Ordinary construction
4. Heavy timber
5. Wood frame

Table 3.1   Building Construction Classifications

National Classification	NYCFD Class	Fire Resistance (hours)
Fire-restrictive	1	4
Non/limited-combustible	2	3
Ordinary construction	3	1
Heavy timber	6	1–2
Wood frame	4–5	Metal/wood: no fire resistance Fire-retardant wood: ≤1

Building Components

Walls and Partitions

Masonry, plaster, and drywall construction offer resistance to fire attack, while wood studs, wood paneling, and plywood products can greatly increase a fire's intensity and actually add to the fire load. Paint and other common finishes may burn rapidly and facilitate the lateral spread of fire. Electrical wiring, telephone lines, plumbing lines, and other service equipment may be concealed in walls and provide unprotected openings through which fire can travel. A fire that starts in or burns into a wall area can burn unnoticed for some time. If unobstructed by fire-breaks (*cats*), the fire could very well travel vertically for some distance in the chimney-like space between studs. Under heavy fire conditions, an investigator may expect a wall to collapse in an average of 28 minutes.

Floor and Ceiling Assemblies

Regardless of type or class of construction, hung ceilings and the like provide for rapid, unobstructed lateral spread of fire in the concealed space between the ceiling and the floor. This space serves as a horizontal chimney. Many materials commonly used for ceiling assemblies are combustible, and often release very toxic vapor. The associated intense, high burning has a tendency to facilitate a burn-through to the attic, roof, or living space above. The secondary burning that can result from an internal collapse may obliterate the point of origin and hamper physical examination. Older buildings that have been rehabilitated or remodeled numerous times may have two or more separate hung ceilings in any given room.

On the other hand, collapsing ceiling materials and the associated loose ash may help the investigation by both smothering the original source of the fire and insulating the point of origin from further damage. Under heavy fire conditions, an investigator can expect a floor to collapse in about 15 minutes, on average.

Figure 3.1   The intensity of this gasoline-fed fire was evident in the annealing and twisting of an 80-foot steel "I" beam.

Attics and Cocklofts

Fully attached row- or townhouses built before World War II were, for economic reasons, constructed with a common roof. Although some of these common roofs were as long as an entire city block, no provision was made for dividing parapets. Construction materials in attics and *cocklofts* (small garrets) are generally combustible, and fires that advance to a common cockloft are often responsible for the spread of fire to adjoining buildings. Torches and "fire-for-hire" rings, aware of this vulnerability, often select the cockloft or concealed ceiling space as the point of origin. The total loss of a roof, especially on commercial properties, usually results in a very favorable insurance settlement.

Many roofing materials (shingles, tar paper, etc.) are a blend of petroleum by-products and, therefore, combustible. The associated melting can facilitate the spread of fire.

Air and Light Shafts

Many older buildings were built with vertical air and light shafts. These are most obvious in row houses where the air/light shaft was meant to provide air and sunlight in the kitchen. Fully attached row houses could, understandably, have windows only on the front and rear of the building. To provide side windows and cross ventilation, vertical shafts were needed.

Figure 3.2 Firefighters and fire investigators respond thousands of times each year to single-occupancy wood frame structures like the one pictured here. (Photo courtesy of S. Grennan.)

In a fire these shafts act like chimneys, enhancing the vertical spread. Secondary fire can occur above the original point of origin. In these cases, the fire typically extends into the common cockloft and this extension facilitates its lateral movement.

Structural Loads

"Dead," "live," "impact," and "fire load" are terms describing specific circumstances that can have a direct impact on how complete structures perform in a fire.

Dead load — the total weight of the building plus the total weight of all permanent or built-in equipment

Live load — the total weight of those items added to the building, including all furnishings, stock and storage, and occupants.

Firefighting operations can greatly increase the live load. Consider the weight of firefighters in turnout gear and the total weight of the water added to the structure to suppress the fire. (One gallon of water weighs about 8 1/3 pounds.) Water can accumulate in pools or be absorbed into stock and furnishings and, in some areas, this total live load may exceed the maximum floor tolerance.

Impact load — the load that is brought to bear in a short period of time. This can result from the added weight caused by the collapse of internal structural elements and explosions.

Fire load — the total number of British thermal units (Btu) that might evolve during a fire, and the rate at which heat will evolve.

For example, consider the total potential for Btu production that might evolve from the total involvement of a five-story, brick and wood-joisted structure (type 3, ordinary construction). One could easily think of this type of structure as a lumber yard surrounded by brick walls. The best estimates available indicate that at least 12 1/2 tons of wood are introduced into the brick enclosure during construction. One pound of wood, if completely burned, produces 8000 Btu. A quick calculation clearly shows that the total potential for Btu production is astronomical.

High-Rise Construction

High-rise construction in the U.S. had its origins in the late 19th century. At that time, any building that extended above the reach of the tallest aerial ladder available was considered to be a high rise. During the last 90 years, three generations of high-rise construction have evolved.

First Generation

First-generation high-rise buildings appeared in the 1890s. They had panel-wall exteriors usually built of masonry or brick. The interiors consisted of all-wood floors supported by cast-iron or unprotected steel columns. The furnishings and interior surfaces were made almost entirely of wood. The primary design problems for buildings built during this time were the obvious danger of floor collapse and the number of unprotected vertical openings

Figure 3.3   A view of a typical inner-city housing complex.

in vertical shafts. A typical first-generation high-rise building ranged from 10 to 15 stories. The Flatiron Building in New York City is a good example of a first-generation high rise.

Second Generation

The 1920s saw the emergence of second-generation high-rise construction. The Empire State and Chrysler Buildings in New York City are perfect examples of this type of construction. Buildings built during this period had panel-wall exteriors of brick or masonry. There was very limited use of combustible materials. The interior of the buildings consisted of poured concrete or masonry floors supported by protected steel beams. The steel superstructure was protected by enclosing it in a masonry sheath. All internal walls and partitions were built of masonry, which provided for *compartmentation;* a fire in a given area would be virtually restricted to that area. Vertical shafts were enclosed, and there was no danger of internal collapse. The primary design flaws of the first generation had been corrected.

Third Generation

Modern technology and economic considerations pushed high-rise construction into its third generation in the early 1960s. The availability of and need for lighter materials, staggering construction costs, modern architectural breakthroughs, and spiraling property values in urban centers combined to produce structures that allowed the population to work and live in the clouds.

The typical exterior of a third-generation high rise has curtain walls constructed almost exclusively of lightweight steel and glass. The New York City Fire Department describes this generation of high-rise buildings as semicombustible rather than fire-resistant, because of the large amounts of synthetic and combustible furnishings that are used. These items burn hotter and produce more toxic by-products than do ordinary combustibles.

Structural Fire Precautions

Modern fire codes and construction standards address the substantive issues regarding structural fire precautions, both for new construction and rehabilitation of old buildings. These code standard changes have evolved slowly over the years; if followed, they create reasonably safe working and living environments.

It is important for the investigator to scrutinize available information (e.g., from the Department of Buildings) to determine the year in which a building under investigation was built. The building codes in effect at the time may very well explain and account for the type of fire extension and damage observed at the scene.

Two code requirements, the dividing parapet and the fire door, have been responsible for limiting the fire damage or fire extension in many cases.

Dividing Parapet

A *dividing parapet*, parapet, firewall, or *party wall* is a wall designed to prevent the extension of fire. They are usually built of masonry or other fire-resistant material. The evolution of the dividing parapet is a perfect example of the development of fire safety standards.

From 1916 to 1930, the party wall extended vertically through the building but ended at the top of the uppermost ceiling; it did not protrude into the cockloft or attic space. This type of construction was directly responsible for the loss of entire city blocks, due to the rapid travel of fire within the secluded space. From 1930 to 1940, the party wall was extended through the roof, thus subdividing the common roof and cockloft. In the late 1970s,

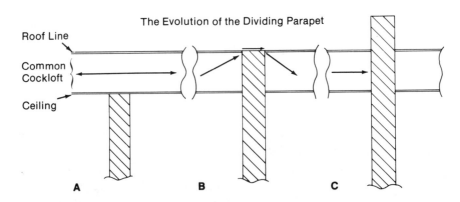

Figure 3.4 The evolution of the dividing parapet. (A) From 1916 to 1930, the party wall extended vertically through the building, but ended at the uppermost ceiling. Cockloft acted like a horizontal chimney. (B) The party wall (1930–1940) extended through the attic or cockloft, but ended at the underside of the roof. Cockloft was subdivided, but fire was still able to extend laterally over common roof. (C) In the 1940s the party wall was extended through the roof, thus subdividing the cockloft and common roof.

federal funds were selectively made available to extend party walls through the roofs of row houses that were originally built in the 1920s and 1930s with common cocklofts.

Fire Door

A *fire door* is usually made of metal and designed to prevent the spread of fire through doorways or other wall openings. Fire doors are designed to meet a variety of different standards, governed by the type of occupancy and the potential fire hazards. Glazed doors are available with and without wired glass.

A fire door may be equipped with a spring-loaded or electromagnetic closing device, or with heat sensitive fuses that, when activated, trigger the fire door to close. An arsonist will often intentionally bypass these safeguards in order to achieve the desired result.

Fire Extension and Accepted Architectural Designs

The universally recognized characteristic of a fireproof or fire-restrictive (class 1) construction is that the building will restrict a fire to one floor or other limited area (in the absence of an explosion or other unusual condition). Financial considerations, construction shortcuts, and the introduction of lightweight building materials have detracted from this recognized standard.

Civil litigation and long-term court cases have stalled the enactment of newly written building and fire codes. Some enterprising real estate holders have delayed much-needed changes by carefully using the judicial system. Meanwhile older, less expensive building codes are applied to new construction.

Design Problems

Lightweight Floor Construction

"Q" deck flooring, which is a combination of 2 to 3 inches of floated or slab concrete supported by corrugated steel sheets, offers substantially less fire resistance than the older 6- or 8-inch poured concrete floors. Much more heat is transferred by conduction through the newer floor design. It is less than half the weight of a conventional poured floor, which permits the use of lighter structural steel. This is a major factor in modern construction, since the height of the building is affected by its total dead weight.

The open-floor design reduces and, in some cases, virtually forbids compartmentation. Commercial office buildings are built with each floor exhibiting a huge expanse of undivided space; portable, quickly assembled partitions are used to separate hallways and offices. An official from the New York City Fire Department has stated,* "The life safety hazard in these buildings is increased by the omission of features which can confine fires to a single space long enough to permit evacuation. Large open floor areas in some high-rise buildings, when involved in fire, are beyond the control of manual fire-fighting operations."

Central Core Design

The central core design is characterized by having all utilities, elevator shafts, stairwells, air conditioning ducts, and electrical, plumbing, and telephone lines located and passing vertically through each floor in the central core of the building. Little fire-fighting strategy is permitted, since all fire-fighting operations must take place from the central core. Firefighters can conceivably find themselves surrounded by fire.

Curtain Wall Construction

A curtain wall is a prefabricated (non-load-bearing) exterior wall made of panels supported by the structural frame of the building. The method of

---

* During a lecture at the Victor Collingmore Institute (Advanced Training for New York City Fire Marshals), offered in conjunction with the John Jay College for Criminal Justice, City University of New York, March 9, 1981.

attachment and the details of construction between the curtain wall and the floor slab are crucial; there is usually a space between the end of the floor slab and the curtain wall. This space acts as a vent for the vertical spread of fire. The old philosophy that a building itself, by its design and construction, should aid in the control of a fire is not used today.

Atrium

In ancient times, an atrium was the main room in a Roman home, with a large open area extending to the roof. Today the term *atrium* is used to describe a large open area extending overhead from the lobby for at least several stories and possibly to the roof. A ventilation unit or skylight designed to operate automatically and vent the atrium is placed at its zenith. Living and working areas are located on corridors that front on the open area. Many fire hazards are associated with this type of construction. If a fire were to start on one of the lower floors, the heat, smoke and toxic gases produced could conceivably collect at the top of the atrium faster than the vents can dispose of them. The gas and smoke would then bank down and be forced by the accompanying increase in air pressure through the various hallways and into the living and working areas, thus trapping their occupants. If the fire were to extend into the lobby or entrance area and enough fuel were present, it could, being unobstructed, quickly rise several stories.

Construction and Materials Problems

Plenums

In an effort to save the expense and labor associated with the installation of additional ductwork, many buildings commonly use the concealed space between the ceiling and the underside of the floor as a plenum. Spent air from the living and working areas is vented into the ceiling plenum, which serves as an air shaft to carry the spent air to the building's central core. This concealed, unobstructed space is equivalent to a common cockloft located on each floor. A fire with its associated smoke, heat, and toxic gases extending into this space can easily travel great distances unnoticed. The electrical wiring and other similar materials ordinarily contained in this space would most certainly exacerbate any fire and greatly increase the types and amounts of toxic gas produced.

If the ceiling plenums vent into the central core, from which fire-fighting operations will be conducted, then a life-threatening situation awaits responding firefighters.

Central Air-Conditioning Systems

The ductwork of a central air-conditioning system acts like a chimney for any fire or smoke that finds its way into the system. Many commercial and residential high-rise buildings are equipped with several very large (multiton) air-conditioning units that serve multiple floors. Any fire problem that might contaminate that system will, therefore, affect large areas of the building.

The ducts in such a system should be equipped with smoke detectors and dampers that would warn both building security people and occupants, automatically cordon off the contaminated areas, and shutdown the affected system. The protection provided by such smoke detectors and dampers is directly related to the maintenance and testing schedules applied.

Elevators and Elevator Shafts

Elevators should never be used to evacuate a building in the event of a fire; an elevator shaft makes a very effective chimney. Moreover, in older buildings, an elevator's electronic call button may react to the heat on the fire floor, holding it there. People trying to use this elevator during the emergency may thus find themselves stopping on the fire floor and trapped as the doors open.

Most jurisdictions now require that the central elevator panel, usually located in the lobby, be equipped with an override device which, when activated, causes all the building's elevators to return to the lobby.

Elimination of the Fire Tower

A *fire tower* is a stairway enclosed in a separate structure that has its own exterior walls. It is connected to the primary building by balconies on each floor. A person using the fire tower has to leave the primary building by a fire door, cross the connecting balcony and enter the fire tower by a second fire door. Since it is a completely separate structure, people fleeing a fire in the primary building would be safe within the fire tower.

In new construction, fire towers have been replaced by interior enclosed stairways. The emergency stairwells above the fire floor may be rapidly contaminated by smoke and other hazardous by-products when occupants on the fire floor evacuate that floor. A stairwell, like an elevator shaft, acts as a chimney. Heat and smoke entering the interior, enclosed stairway at the fire floor quickly rise, trapping those above. The exit doors to the enclosed stairways are fire rated and permit access from only one side. Occupants of upper floors (above the fire floor) attempting to leave by the enclosed stairway could conceivably find themselves trapped in that stairway.

Consider the following scenario: You are working or living on the 32nd floor of a modern high-rise building. A serious fire breaks out on the fifth floor. The occupants of the fifth floor leave safely by the interior stairway but, in so doing, inadvertently jam the fire door to the stairway in the open position. Heat, smoke and gases produced by the fire enter and contaminate the stairway. You receive an urgent call from a security officer to evacuate the building immediately. You and the other occupants of your floor, who received the same call, run to the interior stairway and begin to walk down the stairs. The fire door on the 32nd floor closes and locks behind you. By the time you reach the 25th floor landing, you realize that your exit is blocked by heat and smoke below. Since all the fire doors leading to each floor are locked, your only way out of the stairway is to proceed up to the roof. You are now faced with two serious questions. First, is the roof door open or locked? You know for a fact that maintenance people often lock that door without considering the consequences. Second, can you even get to the roof before you are overcome by the smoke and carbon monoxide that are rapidly spreading up the stairway?

Plastic Furnishings

Over the past several decades, plastics and related products have invaded and changed our entire way of life. Polyvinyl chloride (PVC), polyurethane, polystyrene, and other synthetics are widely used, and virtually every phase of construction has been affected. Electrical wiring, insulation, furniture, and a wide range of other products are wholly made of or encased in plastic.

Once ignited, plastics and other synthetics tend to burn with much more intensity that other ordinary combustibles. The by-products of their combustion almost always include toxic gases.

Fire-Detection, -Alarm, and -Suppression Systems

In its earliest stages, a fire presents a minimal risk to human life and is easily controlled. The earlier in its development a fire is detected, the better the chances for escape, survival, and suppression with limited extension.

More people are killed in fires in the U.S. than in any other nation in the world. The overwhelming majority of those who are killed are asleep at the time of the fire. Deaths result from the inhalation of the gaseous products of combustion: carbon monoxide and other toxic gases. Relatively few people die of exposure to flame. Thousands of lives could be saved every year if smoke detectors were installed and properly maintained in every home and workplace.

Fire-Detection Systems

The primary purpose of fire-detection systems is to discover a fire when it is in its earliest phase and to respond by activating an alarm. There are two basic classifications of fire detectors: smoke detectors and heat detectors.

Smoke Detectors

Smoke detectors are designed to react to the products of combustion. The environment surrounding the point of origin of a fire contains particles of unburned fuel (carbon), toxic and nontoxic gases, and electrically charged atoms called *ions*. A smoke detector will respond either to the visible products of combustion (smoke) or to the invisible (chemical) changes in the atmosphere. There are two common types of smoke detectors: the ionization type and photoelectric type.

Figure 3.5 Smoke detectors are designed to react to the products of combustion.

An *ionization detector* uses a radioactive source (usually americium-241) to transform the air inside it into a conductor of electrical current (Chapman 1977). The radioactive source emits alpha particles, which ionize the air within the detector. A minute electrical current flows through the ionized air, which serves as a sampling chamber. Any visible or invisible products of combustion entering this chamber interrupt the current flow, which, in turn, activates the alarm.

A *photoelectric smoke detector* may consist of a projected light beam to cover large areas, or a reflected light beam or spot-type detector to cover small areas. In the *projected beam* detector, a beam of light is projected from a light source to a receiving unit equipped with a photoelectric cell, which

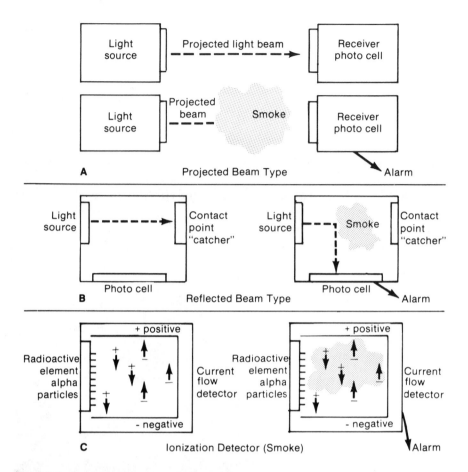

Figure 3.6 Different types of photoelectric smoke detectors: (A) projected beam type; (B) reflected beam type; (C) ionization detector (smoke).

monitors the intensity of the light beam. Smoke from a fire blocks or diminishes the intensity of the light beam and the amount of light striking the photoelectric cell, thereby interrupting the current flow. The *reflected (spot-type) beam* detector is a single unit containing a light source (projected across a narrow chamber), a light "catcher" or contact point, and a photoelectric cell positioned at a right angle to the light source. Smoke entering the chamber obstructs the directed light beam, reflecting light from the light source onto the photoelectric cell, thereby completing the circuit.

An example of a specialized smoke detector is the *air duct detector.* This is designed to mount on or within an air duct system and continuously sample the air moving within the duct pipe to detect both visible smoke particles and invisible by-products of combustion. A duct detector is usually equipped with a specially designed ionization, photoelectric, or other smoke sensor.

Heat Detectors

There are two types of basic heat (thermal) detectors: the rate-of-rise detector and the fixed-temperature detector.

The *rate-of-rise detector* is calibrated so that a rapid increase in room temperature will cause the detector to react and activate an alarm. This type of detector allows for a gradual or natural increase in room temperature due to the sun's rays, the normal operation of machinery, or the activation of the building's heat plant. It cannot differentiate between these natural increases in temperature and a slow-developing fire. It is normally calibrated to allow temperatures within a certain range, but automatically activates when the permitted maximum temperature is surpassed.

The *fixed-temperature detector* is preset to activate at a given temperature. The detection unit may come from the manufacturer with a fixed temperature rating but be equipped with a calibration screw, allowing an installer or contractor to reset the unit to avoid unnecessary or unwanted false alarms.

These are several different types of internal components in standard heat detectors. The two most common heat-sensitive components are:

1. The *thermocouple*, which converts heat energy into a small electrical current; and
2. Fusible plastic or bimetallic strips, which react to heat and either open or close a circuit.

A somewhat more unusual form of fixed-temperature heat detector is the *thermal plastic wire*. Such a wire consists of two or four metallic conductors (*actuators*) individually insulated in a special heat-sensitive plastic sheath. The insulated conductors are twisted around each other (braided) and encased in an outer plastic shell. When subjected to high temperatures, the heat-sensitive plastic layer of insulation yields and permits the conductors (which carry a minute monitoring current) to come into contact with each other. The resultant short circuit activates the alarm.

Heat and light energy radiate away from their source (the flame) in the form of electromagnetic waves, and *heat and flame detectors* have been designed to monitor the radiation of these waves. Because it would be impractical for such a system to respond to the *visible light* range of radiation without responding to any illumination source, these sophisticated detectors are equipped with electric cells sensitive to either ultraviolet (UV) or infrared (IR) or heat rays. Their activation causes the alarm to sound.

Water-Flow Detectors

One final type of detector worth mentioning is the *water-flow detector*, which reacts to the flow of water within a sprinkler system. Although designed to allow for sudden changes in water pressure in the system, this detector cannot differentiate between water flow due to a system malfunction such as a crack or rupture in the piping, breakage due to age, poor maintenance, or improper installation) and that prompted by a fire.

Selecting a Fire Detector

The following criteria are usually considered in the selection of a fire detector:

Type of structure and type of occupancy
Estimated fire load
Cost, considering budget allocations
Unique considerations (e.g., high heat sources, alarm delay factors, high hazard storage)
Local fire code requirements

Fire Alarm Systems and Components

The size, complexity, and cost of fire alarm installation in any particular building varies with the types of occupancy and the number of zones or subunits to be protected.

All parts of a fire detection/alarm system are connected to a central *control panel*. The control panel is hard-wired to an AC source with a DC (battery) backup. A modern control panel is almost exclusively divided into a series of computerized modules designed to monitor an incredible number of separate unrelated functions, including the following: operation of a wide variety of different smoke, heat, and light detectors and manual stations (*pull boxes*); activation of alarms, both audible (horn, bell, gong, sirens) and visible (flashing, strobe, and emergency lights); release of fire suppressants (water, halon, carbon dioxide, dry chemical or high expansion foam); and notification, through a *central station alarm company*, of the local fire and police departments.

The *initiating circuit* connects the individual fire (security) detectors to the central control and annunciator panels. A *receiving element* converts the activation of a fire detector into an electric, pneumatic, or otherwise-generated audible or visible alarm.

Fire-Suppression Systems

Many structures, because of either insurance requirements or local fire codes, are equipped with sprinkler systems. Sprinklers and other such systems are designed to extinguish a fire during the incipient phase by: direct wetting or cooling, cooling the atmosphere, cooling any exposed elements, or reducing the available oxygen.

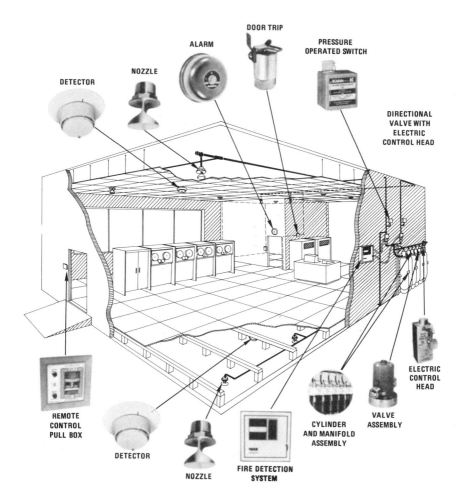

Figure 3.7   Electronic data processing and tape storage rooms — Kidde remote local and automatic operated Halon 1301 fire extinguishing system. (Photo courtesy of Walter Kidde, Division of Kidde, Inc., Wake Forest, NC.)

An investigator must be able to examine and evaluate whatever fire-suppression system might be in place in a fire-damaged structure. The investigator should interview the officers and firefighters from the "first-in" fire department company or unit to determine the suppression system's operation and effectiveness during the fire.

Sprinkler Systems

There are four common types of sprinkler systems. Many variations of these systems exist:

Figure 3.8 World's largest electrically driven Hi-Ex Foam system protects Lockheed Aircraft Company's L-1011 test hangar at Palmdale, CA. (Photo courtesy of Walter Kidde, Division of Kidde, Inc., Wake Forest, NC.)

1. *Wet pipe* — In a wet-pipe system, the supply pipes to the sprinkler head contain water at all times; thus the system is always charged. Approximately 75% of all the sprinkler systems in the U.S. are wet-pipe systems.

2. *Dry pipe* — The dry-pipe system is generally used in areas where excessive cold and the resultant danger of freezing are a problem. In this type of system, the supply pipe contains compressed air and not water. When activated, the sprinkler heads open, the compressed air escapes, and a dry-pipe valve opens to allow water to flow through the system.

3. *Preaction* — This type of system may be used in areas that are subject to extensive water damage. Water is supplied to the system by a valve that operates independently from the sprinkler heads, activated either by human action or, more commonly, by a predesigned automatic fire alarm or detection device.

4. *Deluge* — This type of system is commonly used in areas where immediate cooling is required because of extremely hazardous conditions. The sprinkler heads in the area to be protected (e.g., liquid propane storage) are open at all times. The release of water to those heads is activated by a fire-detection system.

Many variations of these sprinkler systems may be encountered; however, the combination of dry pipe and preaction is not widely used.

Specialized Suppression Systems

Certain types of occupancy require, and local jurisdictions may mandate, specialized suppression systems. In these cases, ordinary sprinkler systems could be inappropriate in terms of both cost and effectiveness. Some flammable and hazardous materials require the use of specific extinguishing agents. The owner of a multimillion dollar computer operation would certainly cringe at the mere thought of water spraying over so much valuable electronic equipment. Specialized extinguishing systems include: halogenated extinguishing agents (including Halon 1202, Halon 1211, Halon 1301, and Halon 2402); high expansion foam systems; dry chemical systems (including sodium bicarbonate, potassium bicarbonate, and potassium chloride); and carbon dioxide systems.

Neutralizing Fire-Protection Systems

Any security or fire-protection (detection, alarm, or suppression) system can be circumvented or defeated. A person or group with the proper technical expertise, given the needed time, can neutralize even state-of-the-art equipment. It is possible for an arsonist (with the technical expertise) to circumvent the electrical security and fire-protection devices in a modern computer center, empty ("blow") both the primary and backup Halon 1301 cylinders, and start a fire, the investigation of which would defy all but the most experienced experts. Arson rings with this type of expertise do exist and are active in the field.

Glossary of Building Terms

Acoustical tile   Special tile for walls and ceilings, made of mineral, wood, vegetable fibers, cord, or metal, whose purpose is to control sound volume while providing cover.

Air duct   A pipe that carries warm/cold air to rooms and back to furnace/air conditioning system.

Ampere   Unit for measuring the rate of flow of electricity (current).

Apron   Paved area such as the junction of a driveway with the street or with a garage entrance.

Backfill   Gravel or earth replaced in the space around a building wall after foundations are in place.

Baluster   Upright support of a balustrade rail

Balustrade   Row of balusters, topped by a rail, edging a balcony or a staircase.

Baseboard   Board along the floor against walls and partitions to hide gaps.

Batting   insulation in the form of a blanket (as fiberglass) rather than loose fill.

Batten   Small thin strip covering joints between wider boards on exterior building surfaces.

Beam   One of the principal horizontal wood or steel members of a building.

Bearing wall   Wall that supports a floor or roof of a building.

Bibcock   Water faucet to which a hose may be attached; also called a *bib*, *hose bib*, or *sill cock*.

Bleeding   Piece of wood or other material used to form a triangle and stiffen some part of the structure.

Braced framing   Construction method using posts and cross bracing for greater rigidity.

Brick veneer   Brick used as the outer surface of a framed wall.

Bridging   Small wood or metal pieces placed diagonally between floor joists.

Building paper   Heavy paper used in walls or roofs to dampproof.

Built-up roof   Roofing material applied in sealed, waterproof layers where there is only a slight slope to the roof, to increase the pitch.

Butt joint   End-to-end joining of two pieces of wood or molding.

BX cable   Electrical cable wrapped in rubber with a flexible steel outer covering.

Cantilever   Projecting beam or joist, not supported at one end, used to support an extension of a structure.

Carriage   Member that supports the steps or treads of a stair.

Casement   Window sash that opens on hinges at the vertical edge.

Casing   door and window framing.

Cavity wall   Hollow wall formed by firmly linked masonry walls, providing an insulating air space between them.

Chair rail   Wooden molding on a wall around a room at the level of a chair back.

Chamfer   Pared-off or angled edge, as on molding; also called a *bevel*.

Chase   groove in a masonry wall or through a floor to accommodate pipes or ducts.

Chimney breast   Horizontal projection (usually inside a building) of a chimney from the wall into which it is built.

Chimney cap   Concrete capping around the top of chimney bricks and around the chimney at each floor to protect the masonry from the elements.

Circuit breaker   Safety device that opens (breaks) an electrical circuit automatically when it becomes overloaded.

Cistern   Tank to catch and store rain water.

Clapboard   Long thin board, usually thicker on one edge, overlapped and nailed on for exterior siding.

Collar beam   Horizontal beam fastened above the lower ends of rafters to add rigidity.

Coping   Tile or brick used to cap or cover the top of a masonry wall, usually with a slope.

Corbel   Architectural member projecting from within a wall and supporting a weight, as under the overhanging part of a roof.

Cove lighting   Concealed light sources behind a cornice or horizontal recess that direct the light onto a reflecting ceiling.

Crawl space   Shallow, unfinished space beneath the first floor of a house that has no basement (or in the attic, immediately under the roof), used for visual inspection and access to pipes and ducts.

Cripples   Cut-off framing members above and below windows.

Door buck   Rough frame of a door.

Dormer   Projecting frame of a recess in a sloping roof.

Double glazing   Use of an insulating window pane formed of two thicknesses of glass with a sealed air space between them.

Double-hung windows   Windows with an upper and lower sash, each supported by cords and weights.

Downspout   Spout or pipe to carry rainwater down from a roof or gutters.

Downspout leader   Pipe for conducting rainwater from the roof to a cistern or to the ground by way of a downspout.

Downspout strap   Piece of metal that secures the downspout to the eaves or wall of a building.

Drip   Projecting part of a cornice that sheds rainwater.

Dry wall   Wall surface of plasterboard or material other than plaster.

Eaves   Extension of a roof beyond house walls.

Efflorescence   White powder that forms on the surface of brick.

Effluent   Treated sewage, as from a septic tank.

Fascia   Flat horizontal member that covers the joint between the top of a wall and the eaves.

Fill-type insulation   Loose insulation material that is applied by hand or blown into wall spaces.

Flashing   Noncorrosive metal used around angles or junctions in roofs and exterior walls to prevent leaks.

Floor joists   Framing pieces that rest on outer foundation walls and interior beams or girders.

Flue   Passageway in a chimney for conveying smoke, gases, or fumes to the outside air.

Footing   Concrete base on which a foundation sits.

Foundation   Substructure of a building, usually of masonry or concrete and below ground level.

Framing   Rough lumber of a house — joists, studs, rafters, and beams.

Furring   Thin wood or metal applied to a wall to level the surfaces for lathing, boarding, or plastering, to create an insulating air space, and to dampproof the wall.

Fuse   Short plug in an electric panel box that opens (breaks) an electrical circuit when it becomes overloaded.

Gable   Triangular part of a wall under the inverted V of the roofline.

Gambrel roof   Roof with two pitches — steeper on its lower slope and flatter toward the ridge — designed to provide more space on upper floors.

Girder   Main member in a framed floor supporting the joists that carry the flooring boards; it carries the weight of a floor or partition.

Glazing   Fitting glass into windows or doors.

Grade line   Line on which the ground rests against the foundation wall.

Green lumber   Lumber that has been inadequately dried and tends to warp or "bleed" resin.

Grounds   Pieces of wood embedded in plaster of walls to which skirtings are attached; also wood pieces used to stop the plaster work around doors and windows.

Gusset   Brace or bracket used to strengthen an angle in framework.

Gutter   Channel at the eaves for conveying away rainwater.

Hardwood   Close-grained wood from broad-leaved trees such as oak or maple.

Headers   Double wood pieces supporting joists in a floor, or double wood members placed on edge over windows and doors to transfer the roof and floor weight to the studs.

Heel   End of a rafter that rests on the wall plate.

Hip   External angle formed by the juncture of two slopes on a roof.

Hip roof   Roof that slants upward on three or four sides.

Jalousie   Window with movable, horizontal slates (louvers) angled to admit ventilation and keep out rain; also used for outside shutters of wood built in this way.

Jamb   Upright surface that lines an opening for a door or window.

Joist   Small rectangular sectional member arranged parallel from wall to wall in a building, or resting on beams or girders, to support a floor on the laths or furring strips of a ceiling.

Kiln-dried lumber   Lumber that is artificially dried; superior to most lumber that is air-dried.

King post Central post of triangular truss.

Lag screws Large, heavy screws, used where great strength is needed, as in heavy framing or when attaching ironwork to wood; also called *coach screws*.

Lally column Trademark for cylindrical steel tube filled with concrete and used to support girders or other floor beams.

Lath One of a number of thin narrow strips of wood nailed to rafters, ceiling joists, wall studs, and so on to make a groundwork or key for slates, tiles, or plastering.

Leaching bed Tiles in the trenches carrying treated wastes from septic tanks.

Ledger Piece of wood attached to a beam to support joists.

Lintel Horizontal piece over a door or window that supports walls above the opening.

Load-bearing wall Strong wall capable of supporting weight.

Louver opening with horizontal slats to permit passage or air but exclude rain or sun or provide privacy.

Masonry Walls built by a mason, using brick, stone, tile, or similar materials.

Molding Strip of decorative material having a plane or curved narrow surface prepared for ornamental application; often used to hide gaps at wall junctions.

Moisture barrier Treated paper or metal that retards or bars water vapor, used to keep moisture from passing into walls or floors.

Mullion Slender vertical framing that divides the panes of windows (or units or screens).

Newel Upright posts (or the upright formed by the inner or smaller ends of steps) about which steps of a circular staircase wind; the principal post at the foot or at a landing of a straight staircase.

Nosing Rounded edge of a stair tread.

Parget Rough coat or mortar applied over a masonry wall as protection or finish; may also serve as a base for an asphaltic waterproofing compound below grade.

Pilaster Projection of the foundation wall used to support a floor girder or stiffen the wall.

Pitch Angle or a slope of a roof.

Plasterboard Gypsum board, used instead or plaster; see *Dry wall*.

Plates Pieces of wood placed on wall surfaces as fastening devices; the bottom member of the wall is the *sole plate* and the top member is the *rafter plate*.

Plenum Dead space that is used for running phone lines, as an electrical conduit, and as a distribution area for heating or cooling systems; generally between a false ceiling and the actual ceiling.

Pointing   Treatment of joints in masonry by filling with mortar to improve appearance or protect against weather.

Post-and-beam construction   Wall construction in which beams are supported by heavy posts rather than many smaller studs.

Prefabrication   Construction of components such as walls, trusses or doors before delivery to the building site.

Rabbet   Groove cut in a board to receive another board.

Reinforced concrete   Concrete strengthened with wire or metal bars.

Ridge pole   Thick longitudinal plank to which the ridge rafters of a roof are attached.

Riser   Upright piece of a stair step, from tread to tread.

Roof sheathing   Sheets, usually of plywood, that are nailed to the top edges of trusses or rafters to tie the roof together and support the roofing material.

Sandwich panel   Panel with plastic, paper, or other material enclosed between two layers of a different material.

Sash   Movable part of a window, the frame in which panes of glass are set in a window or door.

Scotia   Concave molding.

Scuttle hole   Small opening either to the attic, to the crawl space, or to the plumbing pipes.

Seepage pit   Sewage disposal system composed of a septic tank and a connected cesspool.

Septic tank   Sewage settling tank in which part of the sewage is converted into gas and sludge before the remaining waste is discharged by gravity into an underground leaching bed.

Shake   Log-split shingle.

Sheathing   First covering of boards or material on the outside wall or roof under the finished siding or roof covering; see *Wall sheathing.*

Shim   Thin tapered piece of wood used for leveling or tightening a stair or other building element.

Shingle   Piece of wood, asbestos, or other material used in an overlapping outer covering on walls or roofs.

Shiplap   Boards with rabbeted, overlapping edges.

Siding   Boards of special design nailed horizontally to vertical studs with or without intervening sheathing to form the exposed surface of outside walls of framed buildings.

Sill plate   Lowest member of the house framing resting on top of the foundation wall; also called the *mud sill.*

Skirting   Narrow board around the margin of a floor; baseboards.

Slab   Concrete floor placed directly on earth or a gravel base and usually about 4 inches thick.

Sleeper   Wood laid over concrete floor to which the finished wood floor is nailed or glued.

Soffit   Visible underside of structural members such as staircases, cornices, beams, and eaves.

Softwood   Easily worked wood; wood from a cone-bearing tree.

Soil stack   Vertical plumbing pipe for wastewater.

Stringer   Long, horizontal member that connects uprights in a frame or supports a floor or the like; one of the enclosed sides of a stair supporting the treads and risers.

Stud   In wall framing, a vertical member to which horizontal pieces are nailed; studs are spaced either 16 or 24 inches apart.

Subfloor   Usually, plywood sheets that are nailed directly to the floor joists and that receive the finished flooring.

Sump   A pit in the basement in which water collects to be pumped out with a sump pump.

Swale   Wide shallow depression in the ground to form a channel for storm water drainage.

Tie   Wood member that binds a pair of principal rafters at the bottom.

Tile field   Open-joint drain tiles laid to distribute septic tank effluent over an absorption area or to provide subsoil drainage in wet areas.

Toenail   To drive nails at an angle into corners or other joints.

Tongue-and-groove   A carpentry joint in which the jutting edge of one board fits into the grooved end of a similar board.

Trap   Bend in a water pipe to hold water so gases will not escape from the plumbing system into the house.

Tread   Horizontal part of a stair step.

Truss   Combination of structural members usually arranged in triangular units to form a rigid framework for spanning load-bearing walls.

Valley   Depression at the meeting point of two roof slopes.

Vapor barrier   Materials such as paper, metal, or paint used to prevent vapor from passing from rooms into the outside walls.

Venetian window   Window with one large fixed central panel and smaller panes at each side.

Vent pipe   Pipe that allows gas to escape from plumbing systems.

Verge   Edge of tiles, slates, or shingles projecting over the gable of a roof.

Wainscoting   The lower three or four feet of an interior wall when lined with paneling, tile, or other material different from the rest of the wall.

Wall sheathing   Sheets of plywood, gypsum board, or other material nailed to the outside face of studs as a base for exterior siding.

Weather stripping   Metal, wood, plastic, or other material installed around door and window openings to prevent air infiltration.

Weep hole   Small hole in a wall that permits water to drain off.

References and Selected Readings

Brannigan, F. L., *Building Construction for the Fire Service*, Nation Fire Protection Association, Boston, MA, 1971.

Brannigan, F. L. et al., *Fire Investigation Handbook*, National Book Store Handbook No. 134, U.S. Government Printing Office, Washington, D.C., 1980.

Carroll, John R., *Physical and Technical Aspects of Fire/Arson Investigations*, Charles C Thomas, Springfield, IL, 1979.

Chapman, E., "Smoke Detectors for the Home: *WNYF (With New York Firefighters)*, Issue 3, New York City Fire Department, 1977.

French, H. M., *The Anatomy of Arson*, Arco, New York, 1979.

Huron, B. S., *Elements of Arson Investigation*, Reuben H. Donnelley, New York 1963.

Kirk, P. L., *Fire Investigation*, John Wiley & Sons, New York, 1969.

McKinnon, G. P., *Fire Protection Handbook*, 14th ed., National Fire Protection Association, Boston, MA, 1979.

Underdown, G. W., *Practical Fire Precaution*, 2nd ed., Bower Press, Westmeal, Farmborough, England, 1979.

Chemistry and Behavior of Fire

4

Fire has fascinated humanity since the beginning of time. Our ancestors worshipped it; we still respect it. Its value as a weapon of war and as a tool of devastation has long been recognized.

Fire is a series of chemical reactions. It is often defined as the visible, active phase of combustion. *Combustion* is a chemical process accompanied by the evolution of heat and light. More accurately, it is the rapid oxidation of fuel so as to produce flame (burning gases), heat, and light. The most common form of combustion, and that to which we address our attention, is *oxidation*. This occurs when an atom, the fundamental particle of matter, combines (i.e., forms a chemical bond) with a molecule of oxygen. Though there are other types of combustion supported by other gases, such as nitrous oxide (laughing gas), the overwhelming majority of fires are oxygen related.

Components of Fire

Traditionally, fire has been described as having three components: heat, oxygen, and fuel. This triad was illustrated by the *fire triangle*, which symbolized, in the most basic terms, a chemical relationship that would have required hours to explain. We now realize, however, that the fire triangle falls short of integrating all the components involved in producing flaming combustion. Today, the fire triangle is used to technically explain *glowing combustion*, which occurs when a fuel mass glows without flaming. This is called a *solid-to-gas* reaction (fuel being a solid, and the oxidizing agent a gas).

The additional component needed to explain flaming combustion is a *chemical chain reaction*. Such a reaction yields energy or products that cause further reactions of the same kind, and this process is self-sustaining. To

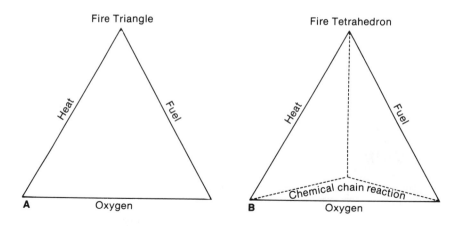

Figure 4.1 The fire triangle (A) and the fire tetrahedron (B).

show the interrelation of all four components, a more sophisticated geometric figure than the triangle is needed; the three-dimensional, four-faceted tetrahedron is the most appropriate and is commonly used.

In *flaming combustion*, fuel and the oxidizing agent are both in the gaseous state; hence this is referred to as *gas-to gas-reaction*.

Heat

A fire/arson investigator must understand and recognize how heat is produced and transferred, and how it applies to the fire's ignition and development. *Heat* is the energy possessed by a material or substance due to molecular activity. Heat should not be confused with *temperature*, which is the measurement of the relative amount of heat energy contained within a given substance. Temperature is an *intensity* measurement, with units in *degrees* on the Celsius (centigrade), Fahrenheit, or Kelvin scales. *Heat* is a measurement of *quantity* and is given in British thermal units (Btu). One Btu is the amount of heat required to raise one pound of water one degree Fahrenheit (1°F):

    1 Btu heats 1 lb of water 1°F
    1 gallon of water weighs 8.33 lb
    8.33 Btu heat 1 gallon of water 1°F
    833 Btu heat 1 gallon of water 100°F

Heat Production

There are five ways to produce heat:

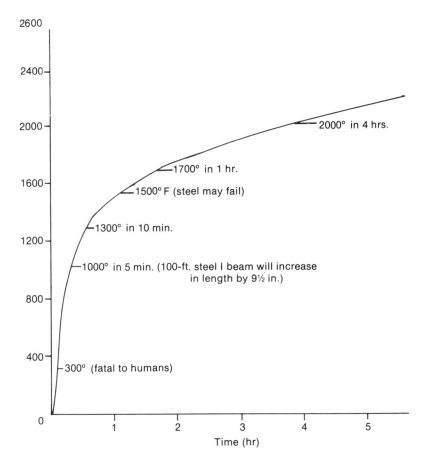

Figure 4.2   Standard time–temperature curve.

1. *Chemical.* As we have already seen, chemically produced heat is the result of rapid oxidation. The speed of the oxidative reaction is an important factor; rust is also the product of oxidation, but a very slow one.
2. *Mechanical.* Mechanical heat is the product of friction. Our ancestors rubbed sticks together to generate enough heat to start a fire. Internal metal components of machinery can overheat, due to lubricant break-down or ball-bearing failure, and cause ignition of available combustibles.
3. *Electrical.* Electrical heat is the product of arcing, shorting or other electrical malfunction. Poor wire connections, too much resistance, a loose ground, and too much current flowing through an improperly sized wire are other sources of electrical heat.

4. *Compressed gas.* When a gas is compressed, its molecular activity is greatly increased. Consider the operation of a diesel engine. The gaseous fuel is compressed within the cylinder, increasing its molecular activity. The heat generated by this activity eventually reaches the ignition temperature of the fuel itself. The resulting contained explosion forces the piston back to the bottom of the cylinder, and the process repeats over and over again. The drive train converts the energy into mechanical action that causes the vehicle to move.

5. *Nuclear.* Nuclear energy is the product of the splitting or fusing of atomic particles (fission or fusion, respectively). The tremendous heat energy in a nuclear power plant produces steam to turn steam turbines.

When more heat is produced than is lost (transferred), there is a *positive heat balance.* When more heat is lost than is produced, there is a *negative heat balance.*

Heat Transfer

There are only three ways to transfer heat: conduction, convection and radiation.

Conduction.   This refers to the transfer of heat by molecular activity within a material or medium, usually a solid. If you touch a hot stove, the pain you feel is a first result of conducted heat passing from the stove directly to your hand. Direct contact is the underlying factor in heat transferred through conduction.

The amount of heat that any item may conduct is a function of that particular item's *thermal conductivity,* represented as *K*. The *K* value for copper is 0.92, for wood 0.0005, and for aluminum 0.50. The thermal conductivity of any substance relates directly to its ability to conduct electricity as well as heat. The formula for determining the amount of heat that is passing through an object or material is:

$$H = K \frac{A(t2 - t1)7}{L} T$$

where H is the amount of heat flowing through the object (in Btu)
   L is the length of the object (in feet)
   T is the time interval of the flow (in hours)
   K is the thermal conductivity
   t^2 is the measured temperature (in °F) at the hot end of the object
   t^1 is the measured temperature (in °F) at the cold end of the object
   A is the cross-sectional area of the object tested (in square feet)

In a structural fire, superheated pipes, steel girders, and other structural members such as walls and floors may conduct enough heat to initiate fires in other areas of the structure.

Convection.   Heat transfer by convection is chiefly responsible for the spread of fire in structures. Convection entails the transfer of heat by a circulating medium, usually air or a liquid. The superheated gases evolved from a fire are lighter than air, and consequently rise. As they travel and collect in the upper reaches of the structure, they can and do initiate additional damage. In large fires or *BLEVES* (boiling liquid evaporation explosions), the high fireball that accompanies the incident is referred to as a *fire storm* and is an example of convected heat.

Radiation.   Radiated heat moves in waves and rays much like sunlight or X-rays. Radiated heat (energy) travels the same speed as does visible light: 186,000 miles per second. It is primarily responsible for the exposure hazards that develop and exist during a fire. Heat waves travel in a direct or straight line from their source until they strike an object. The heat that collects on the surface of the object or building in the path of the heat waves is subsequently absorbed into its mass through conduction.

Figure 4.3   The owner of this building made the mistake of storing mattresses too close to a gas hot-water heater in the basement. Radiated heat from the unprotected burner entrance was absorbed by the mattresses, which eventually ignited.

Oxygen and Oxidation

For combustion (specifically oxidation) to take place, a combustible fuel and an oxidizing agent (oxygen) must come together. The air we breathe is 21% oxygen. If the oxygen level drops below 15%, a fire may be extinguished in time or literally smothered, due to a lack of oxygen. This is an example of an *oxygen-regulated* fire.

Certain unusual fuels, due to their chemical composition, do not follow this basic rule. For example, pyroxylin plastics (e.g., cellulose nitrate, used in lacquer coatings and adhesives) contain enough oxygen to maintain decomposition (smoldering) or even partial combustion in the absence of additional oxygen in the air. Other exceptions include sodium nitrate, potassium chlorate, potassium nitrate, and ammonium nitrate fertilizer.

Let us examine a very basic oxidation reaction. Hydrogen (H) and oxygen (O) are two basic elements. In their natural state, they are diatomic; that is, they exist in molecules composed of two atoms, H_2 and O_2, respectively. When we oxidize hydrogen by combining it with oxygen, we form two molecules of water (H_2O) and heat. The following chemical equation describes the reaction:

$$2H_2 + O_2 = 2H_2O + heat$$

This equation illustrates a very basic *exothermic* (heat-producing) reaction. An *endothermic reaction,* conversely, is one which requires or absorbs heat.

If we oxidize an atom of carbon (C), another common element, but one that is *monatomic* (occurs in one-atom molecules), we find that carbon dioxide (CO_2) and heat are produced. This reaction is shown in the following chemical equation:

$$C + O_2 = CO_2 + heat$$

However, if we restrict the supply of oxygen or double the available carbon, we find that carbon monoxide rather than carbon dioxide is produced:

$$2C + O_2 = 2CO + heat$$

This third equation is important. The production of carbon monoxide is very common at most fire scenes; carbon monoxide asphyxiation is the primary cause of death in fatal fires. Carbon monoxide is also a fuel with an ignition temperature of 1128°F, and is the likely cause of most *backdrafts* or smoke explosions.

Fuel and Its Physical States

Fuel is matter, and matter exists in three physical states: gas, liquid, and solid. Solids melt to become liquids, and these may vaporize and become gases. The state of a substance is, therefore, an accepted characteristic of that substance under the conditions of temperature of 65 to 70°F and a pressure of 14.7 pounds per square inch.

The basic rule, unusual conditions and circumstances notwithstanding, is that at high enough temperatures all fuels can be converted to gases. Gasoline as a liquid does not burn; it is the vapors rising from the liquid that burn. Likewise, wood, the most common solid fuel, is not flammable, but gives off flammable resin vapors. Although these burn, the structure of the wood itself decomposes, yielding other flammable vapors.

Each of the physical states exhibits different physical and chemical properties that directly affect a fuel's combustibility.

Gas

Gaseous fuels are those in which molecules are in rapid movement and random motion. They have no definite shape or volume, and assume the shape and volume of their container. Other properties include compressibility, expandability, permeability, and diffusion.

Compressibility and expandability refer to the potential for changes in volume. A gas will spread and eventually equalize its distribution (pressure) throughout a fixed room or container. Its volume is directly related to two other factors, pressure and temperature. The nature of this interrelation is as follows:

$$PV = KT$$

where P is pressure
V is volume
T is temperature
K is proportionality constant

An increase (decrease) in *temperature* will cause a proportional increase (decrease) in the volume if the pressure is constant, or in the pressure if the volume is constant.

An increase (decrease) in the *pressure* will cause a proportional decrease (increase) in the volume if the temperature is constant, or increase (decrease) in the temperature if the volume is constant.

An increase (decrease) in *temperature* will proportionally increase (decrease) the pressure if the volume is fixed, or the volume if the pressure is constant.

Diffusion is the uniform distribution, seemingly in contradiction to the laws of gravity, of molecules of one substance through those of another. The rate at which gas diffuses is inversely proportional to the square root of its density (Graham's Law). *Permeability* means that other substances may pass through or permeate a gas.

How well a gas diffuses in air depends on its *vapor density* or density relative to air. The nearer this is to the vapor density of air (which has a value of 1.0), the greater the ability of the gas to mix with air. The vapor densities of several gas fuels are as follows: methane = 0.6 (lighter than air), ethane = 1.0 (same as air), and propane = 2.5 (heavier than air).

When a gas fuel (or vapor from a liquid fuel) diffuses sufficiently into air, the mixture may ignite or explode. The percentage of gas-to-air at which this occurs is the lower limit of that gas's *flammable (explosive) range.* The upper limit is the percentage at which the mixture is too concentrated to ignite (that is, there is too little oxygen; for natural gas, this range is 5 to 15%).

Liquid

Liquids, like gases, assume the shape of their containers and may diffuse. Unlike gases, they have a definite volume (though they may be compressed slightly.)

Liquids exhibit a free surface and, if left to stand uncovered, will evaporate. *Evaporation* occurs when individual molecules of the liquid escape as gas into the surrounding atmosphere. An increase in temperature will cause an increase in the rate of evaporation and, consequently, an increase in the vapor pressure. The temperature at which a liquid turns into gas by producing continuous vapor bubbles is called its *boiling point.* At this temperature, the vapor pressure is equal to normal atmospheric pressure (14.7 lbs/in^2).

Because a liquid's boiling point shows its readiness to vaporize, it is one measure of the volatility of a liquid fuel; a low boiling point means high volatility and an increased risk of fire. Other indicators include flash point and fire point.

Flash point.   Temperature at which a liquid gives off enough vapor (gas) to form an ignitable mixture (that is, a mixture within the explosive range) (see section on Gas). For gasoline, this is $-50°F$; for kerosene $100°F$.

Fire point.   Temperature at which a liquid produces vapors that will *sustain* combustion. This is several degrees higher than the flash point. For example, the fire point of gasoline is $495°F$; for kerosene, $110°F$.

The National Fire Protection Association (NFPA) defines a *flammable liquid* as one whose flash point is below $140°F$. A liquid with a flash point of

140°F or higher is a *combustible liquid*. (The temperature used to distinguish flammable from combustible liquids is defined as 100°F by the National Fire Academy and as 80°F by the U.S. Department of Transportation.)

Solid

Solids have a definite shape and volume. A solid fuel's combustibility is directly affected by the size and configuration of its mass. Finely divided, powdered fuels differ in combustibility from bulky or large-dimension solid fuels because of the obvious difference in their masses; the larger the mass of the solid fuel, the greater the potential loss due to conduction. Imagine a lit match placed against the side of a section of telephone pole. The match burns out long before there is any sign of ignition on the pole because:

1. Some of the heat generated by the match is being lost to its surroundings through convection and radiation.
2. The surface temperature at the point of contact is dissipated due to the transfer of heat by conduction evenly throughout the mass of the pole.

The temperature at which a solid turns into liquid is called its *melting point*. A solid (other than an explosive) that is likely to ignite due to friction is called a *flammable solid*.

Pyrolyzable and nonpyrolyzable solids. *Pyrolysis* is the chemical decomposition of matter through the action of heat. This decomposition may take place in the absence of oxygen, and the vapors released may include both combustible and noncombustible gases.

Pyrolyzable solid fuels include many of the ordinarily accepted solid combustibles: wood, paper, and so on. The vapors released by their chemical decomposition support flaming combustion. This exemplifies a gas-to-gas reaction: the vapors released mix with oxygen in the air to produce a flame.

Nonpyrolyzable solid fuels are difficult to ignite. A common example is charcoal. The liquid charcoal lighter that people commonly use to start their barbecue is necessary to raise the temperature so that the surface fuel will interact directly with the oxygen in the air. Chemical decomposition does not occur because there are no pyrolyzable elements present. No vapors are released. The glowing combustion that results is an example of a gas-to-solid reaction.

Pyrolysis of wood. Wood, the most common solid fuel, is composed of many tubular fiber units, or *cells*, cemented together. The walls of these cells are made of *cellulose*. The chemical decomposition of cellulose in the presence of open flame is represented by the following formula:

$$C_6H_{10}O_5 + 6O_2 = 5H_2O + 6CO_2 + heat$$

This equation represents an ideal oxidation reaction. In reality, however, the burning of a wood frame structure would most likely be fuel-regulated; that is, the rate of burning and the amount of readily available wood fuel would exceed the available air supply. This condition would lead to the evolution of huge amounts of carbon monoxide.

The first portion of the equation represents an endothermic (heat absorbing) reaction. This changes to exothermic (heat-producing) as the chemical reaction (fire) becomes self-sustaining.

Number 2 common lumber, the most common building material, has an ignition temperature of approximately 660°F. It will ordinarily burn at the rate of 1 inch in 45 minutes at 4500°F. However, when exposed to a temperature of 250°F for an extended period of time (e.g., due to the improper installation of a wood or coal stove), a condition known as pyrophoric carbon (carbonized wood) occurs. The continuous baking of the wood causes pyrolysis, resulting in the carbonization of the lumber. At first, the surface of the wood darkens and then begins to char; eventually the carbonized portion becomes deeper and deeper. Carbonized wood is ordinarily rich in oxygen and ignites at the same temperature at which it forms.

Chemistry of Fire

Hydrocarbons

Hydrocarbons are chemical compounds that contain only carbon and hydrogen. They include gases (e.g., methane), liquids (e.g., benzene), and solids (e.g., naphthalene). As fuels, they tend to burn much hotter than other compounds. Organic compounds containing carbons, hydrogen, and oxygen are called *carbohydrates*. Hydrocarbons are either saturated or unsaturated.

In a *saturated hydrocarbon*, all the available carbon atoms contain the maximum number of hydrogen atoms. Saturated hydrocarbons do not have a tendency for spontaneous combustion.

In an *unsaturated hydrocarbon*, not all the available carbon atoms contain the maximum number of hydrogen atoms; some are bonded to other carbon atoms. Such a compound can accommodate additional hydrogen atoms by breaking those carbon–carbon bonds. Therefore, unsaturated hydrocarbons have a tendency towards spontaneous combustion.

Hydrocarbons having an open-chain structure, such as methane, butane, and acetylene, are called *aliphatic*. Those containing at least one benzene-like ring, such as benzene itself or naphthalene, are called *aromatic*.

Petroleum fractions are the usable by-products of the refining of crude oil. These include gasoline, kerosene, and naphthalene. All the products of fractional distillation are hydrocarbons. As a group, they probably represent the most commonly used accelerants. They will not ignite spontaneously.

Chemical Chain Reaction

As mentioned earlier, until recently it seemed clear that: combustion = oxidizing agent (O_2) + combustible material (fuel) + ignition source (heat). In the past decade, however, it became evident that some unknown factor played a direct role in the combustion process. For years, experts in the field were at a loss trying to explain the reason that dry chemical (powder) extinguishers were so effective in the suppression of fire. We have come to realize that such extinguishers, as well as those that use chlorinated hydrocarbon gases (Halon) or several other extinguishing agents, suppress fire either by interfering with the transfer of energy or by combining with radicals generated by the combustion process. In so doing, they prevent the *chemical chain reaction* necessary to produce self-sustaining combustion. This chain reaction is a complex series of events that must be continuously and precisely reproduced in order to maintain flaming combustion. Among the events required are these two:

1. The oxidation reaction produces sufficient heat to maintain continued oxidation.
2. The fuel mass must be broken down into simpler compounds and liberated (vaporized) from the mass itself; in turn, these unburned vapors must combine with available oxygen and be continuously drawn up into the flame.

Other Terms Relating to the Chemistry of Fire

Heat of combustion. This is the amount of heat that a fuel will release during a complete oxidation reaction. It is measured in Btu per pound of fuel. The heat output may vary depending on the specific composition of the fuel. Examples are shown below:

Type of Fuel	Btu Released
Paper, wood	6,000–7,000
Coal	12,000–13,000
Common liquid accelerants	16,000–21,000
Flammable gases	20,000–22,000

Ignition. In order to be ignited, most materials must be in a gaseous or vapor state. A few materials may burn directly in a solid state or glowing form of combustion, including some forms of carbon and magnesium. These gases or vapors must then be present in the atmosphere in sufficient quantity to form a flammable mixture. Liquids with flash points below ambient temperatures do not need additional heat to produce a flammable mixture. The fuel vapors produced must then be raised to their ignition temperature. If the fuel is to reach its ignition temperature, the rate of heat transferred to the fuel must be greater than the conduction of heat into or through the fuel and the loss is due to radiation or convection. Table 3-3 shows the temperature of selected ignition sources. (see NFPA 921, Chapter 3).

Ignition temperature. Temperature at which a flammable material will ignite, whether it be gas, liquid, or solid; for example:

State	Material	Temperature (°F)
Gas	Acetylene	571
Liquid	Turpentine	488
Solid	Magnesium	1200

Note that due to the variation in the grades and octane of gasoline, its ignition temperatures may vary from 495°F to 850°F.

Autoignition temperature. Temperature to which a material must be heated in order for it to burst into flame, free of an ignition source such as a spark or match.

Autogenous ignition temperature. The lowest temperature at which an oxidation reaction can self-sustain itself to either flaming or glowing ignition; that is, the point at which the reaction changes from endothermic to exothermic.

Q^{10} value. Value assigned to the rate of chemical reaction (e.g., fire), which doubles with every 10°C or 18°F increase in temperature.

Specific gravity. The weight of a substance compared with an equal volume of water (thus, water = 1.0). Most flammable liquids have a specific gravity less than that of water. Gasoline's specific gravity is 0.70, so it will float on water. That of carbon disulfide is 1.3, so it will sink in water. (Compare vapor density for gases.)

Spontaneous ignition. This occurs if the inherent characteristics of the materials involved cause an exothermic (heat producing) chemical reaction to proceed without any exposure to external sources of spark or abnormal heat. For example, a rug soaked in linseed oil, if tightly packed and insulated, may ignite spontaneously. A substance that ignites spontaneously in air at normal temperatures (65 to 70°F) is called *pyrophoric*. (See "Materials Subject to Spontaneous Heating", Appendix 4.1.)

Behavior of Fire

The way that a fire develops is affected by many factors. At first, it is most affected by the initial fuel supply; obviously, sufficient oxygen is readily available in the surrounding air. Fire evolves and spreads to other combustibles following a natural path of least resistance. It extends up and away from its point of origin, leaving behind distinctive patterns common to all fires. The color of the smoke and flame produced by a fire is also distinctive and depends on the type of fuel and the temperature at which it is burning.

As a fire continues to grow, environmental factors become increasingly important in influencing its extent. Of particular importance is the amount of oxygen present in the immediate fire area. Other factors include fuel supply and composition, structural design, construction (see Chapter 3), and fire suppression.

Eventually, unable to sustain any one of the four components necessary for its continued existence, a fire is extinguished.

Classification of Fire

Fires may be classified according to the type of material (fuel) that is burning. There are four classifications of fire by fuel:

Class A.   Ordinary combustibles or materials that produce an ash or glowing embers or coals (e.g., wood, paper, cloth, rubber)
Class B.   Flammable or combustible liquids (e.g., gasoline, kerosene, alcohol, fuel oil)
Class C.   Energized electrical equipment (*Note:* Class C fires revert to Class A or B when the equipment is no longer energized)
Class D.   Combustible metals, (e.g., magnesium, titanium)

Structural fires are generally classified by extent of damage:

* Those that are extinguished quickly and cause little damage
* Those that, although extinguished, cause extensive damage to a limited area of the building
* Those that cause almost complete or total structural destruction.

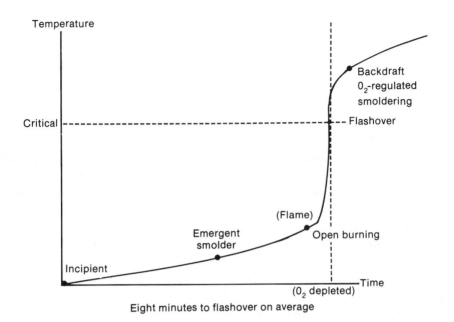

Figure 4.4   The phases of fire.

Phases of Fire

As a fire progresses, it normally passes through four phases: incipient, emergent smoldering, free burning, and oxygen-regulated smoldering. Many factors can alter the rate and intensity of a fire's evolution. No two fires are exactly the same. They vary in many ways from incident to incident.

Incipient

This earliest phase of fire may or may not occur unnoticed. The degree to which it is observable depends almost entirely upon the magnitude and source of ignition and the type of fuel. This phase may last anywhere from a fraction of a second to several hours or days, again depending on fuel and ignition source. The incipient phase for a liquid accelerant in the presence of an open flame is obviously much shorter than that of a prolonged exothermic reaction, such as in spontaneous combustion.

The products of combustion in this phase may be so minuscule as to be detected only by an ionization detector. The minute changes in atmospheric chemistry in the room or area of the fire's origin may arise without human detection. Some heat energy will be generated, but the temperature of the room or its surroundings will not be affected.

Emergent Smoldering

During this phase, the products of combustion become increasingly more pronounced. There is no meaningful change in the oxygen content of the air. Water vapor, carbon dioxide, and other gases, including minute traces of unburned fuel, may rapidly reach the level of olfactory detection. The open flames that may occur in the later stages of this phase may approach a temperature of 1000°F. The room and surrounding temperature may be only slightly increased.

It should be noted that some fires, such as a smoldering mattress fire, may pass directly from this second phase to oxygen-related smoldering (phase 4). The smoldering mattress may reduce the oxygen level in the room of origin enough to cause self-extinguishment, leaving everything in the room covered with a thick blanket of soot, with no open flame (free-burning phase 3) ever being produced (Fire/Arson Training Committee, 1981).

Free Burning

During this phase of the fire, the rate and intensity of open burning increases geometrically. The intensity of the fire doubles with each 18°F (10°C) rise in temperature (Q^{10}). Heat, rapidly evolving from the original point of the fire, is convected and collects in the uppermost areas of the structure or room. Additional heat is transferred through conduction and radiation. The convected (super-heated) gases themselves become a source of radiated heat, radiating heat energy downward onto all the surface areas directly below them. This heat is absorbed by conduction into the mass of those items whose surfaces are struck, causing surface pyrolysis (*baked effect*).

When the temperature reaches the ignition temperature of these items, a *flashover* occurs: flames instantly "flashover" the entire area. Flashover is defined as "a stage in the development of a contained fire in which all exposed surfaces reach ignition temperature, more or less simultaneously, and fire spreads rapidly. Although research has shown that the average time to flashover from open flame can be as short as 1 1/2 minutes in residential fire tests, the actual average time to flashover is 8 minutes, or it may never occur.

One condition that signals the imminent threat of a flashover is referred to as "fairies flying." This occurs when small pockets of flammable gases ignite, and may be spotted by firefighters within the building.

The lack of normal fire spread due to a flashover can exacerbate the search for the point of origin. In fact, the scene may appear as if an accelerant were used, so a careful analysis is necessary.

Figure 4.5 The photograph illustrates a condition called "baked effect." There is a demarcation line visible between affected and unaffected areas. Wood and painted surfaces appear baked and covered with heavy soot deposits, and there is a graduation in the depth of charring.

Oxygen-Regulated Smoldering

If the room or area of the fire's origin is adequately airtight, thereby limiting the amount of oxygen-rich air being drawn into that area, then the open burning that occurs in free-burning phase 3 will deplete the available oxygen. The gradual cessation of oxygen supply causes flaming combustion to end, replacing it to a large extent by flowing combustion. The room becomes completely filled with dense smoke and gases, which are forced from all cracks under pressure. The fire continues to smolder and the room to fill with smoke and gases at a temperature well over 1000°F. Such intense heat evaporizes the lighter fuel fractions, such as hydrogen and methane, from the combustible material in the room. The resulting superheated mixture of gases needs only a fresh supply of oxygen to resume free burning at an explosive rate (Fire/Arson Training Committee, 1981). This type of explosive is referred to as a *backdraft* or *smoke explosion*. "Backdraft is an explosion resulting from the sudden introduction of air (oxygen) into a confined space containing oxygen-deficient superheating products of incomplete combustion." A backdraft may result if someone opens a "hot door." This why firefighters are trained to touch a door with their bare hands and feel its temperature before opening it. Venting, the controlled removal of smoke, heat, and gases from a building, may also produce a backdraft by displacing venting combustion products with oxygen-rich air.

Figure 4.6 The area of origin of a slow-burning, smoldering fire generally shows a uniform ceiling and floor damage.

One of the superheated gases produced by fire is carbon monoxide. As mentioned in the section "Oxygen and Oxidation," carbon monoxide results from the oxidation of carbon in an oxygen-depleted atmosphere. This odorless, colorless gas collects and mixes with air (oxygen) to within its explosive or flammable limits: 12.5 to 74% of the atmosphere by volume. Carbon monoxide is highly flammable and has an ignition temperature of 1128°F. When ignition occurs, the entire cloud of smoke within the area or room literally explodes or bursts into flames. The unburned particles of fuel, which color the smoke, also burn at the same time.

Rate of Burn

Oxygen plays a key role in regulating the rate at which most materials burn. With an unlimited oxygen supply, the rate of burn increases, more heat is produced, and the fuel is consumed more completely.

The area of origin of a slow-burning, smoldering fire generally will show: uniform ceiling and wall damage, down to a line 3 or more feet below the ceiling; a baked appearance on painted or wooden surfaces and a graduation in the depth of charring; and smoke stains around windows, doors, and eaves and on window glass.

The area of origin of a fast-burning, intense fire will generally show: severe overhead damage; definite burn patterns on walls; severe charring on exposed wood surfaces; a distinct line between charred and uncharred areas or boards near the point of origin and a sharp line between burned and unburned areas around windows and doors; and crazed (finely cracked) window glass, broken in irregular rectangular pieces (see "Glass" in Chapter 5).

Fuel Load

The term *fuel load* has been used in the past to indicate potential severity of a fire, and has been expressed in terms of Btus or pounds of fuel per square foot of floor area. Btus were expressed in wood equivalent based on 8000 Btus per pound. The fuel load was determined by weighing the fuel in a room and converting the weight of plastic to pounds of wood, using 16,000 Btus per pound as the value for plastic (1 pound of plastic = 2 pounds of wood).

The total fuel load in the room has no bearing on the rate of growth of a given fire in its pre-flashover state. During this development stage, the rate of fire growth is determined by the heat release rate (HRR) from the burning of the individual fuel arrays. HRR is expressed in terms of Btu/second or kilowatts. After flashover, the heat release rate is controlled by the above factors and availability of air and exposed combustible surface.

Pine shavings, for example, burn faster than a block of wood with the same weight. Plastics can have heat release rates significantly greater than the same items made of cellulose.

Low density materials burn faster than high density materials of similar chemistry. Soft pine, for example, burns faster than oak and light weight foam plastics burn faster than more dense rigid plastics. Peak heat release rate values for typical fuels are presented in Table 4.1. These values should be considered representative for typical similar fuel items. The actual peak heat release rate for a particular item is best determined by test.

Fire Spread

Structural Fire Spread

Fire spread involves the extension of fire from one point to another. Naturally, the transfer of heat plays a large role in this extension. As we have already seen, superheated girders, pipes, and even walls and floors may initiate fires in other areas of a structure by *conduction*. In addition, superheated gases spread structural fires by both upward *convection* (the predominant means of transfer) and downward *radiation* (as in the case of a flashover; see section on Free Burning). However, heat transfer is not the only force at work in the spread of fire. *Air movement* (wind, drafts, venting) can encourage convection

Table 4.1   Representative Peak Heat Release Rates (Unconfined Burning)

Fuel (lb)	Peak HRR (kW)
Wastebasket — small (1.5-3)	4–18
Trash bags — 11 gal with mixed plastic and paper trash (2.5–7.5)	140–350
Cotton mattress (26-29)	40–970
TV sets (69-72)	120-290
Plastic trash bags/paper trash (2.6–31)	120–350
PVC waiting room chair — metal frame (34)	270
Cotton easy chair (39–70)	290–370
Gasoline/kerosene in 2 sq foot pool	400
Christmas trees — dry (14–16)	500–650
Polyurethane mattress (7–31)	810–2630
Polyurethane easy chair (27–61)	1350–1990
Polyurethane sofa (113)	3120

From NFPA 921.

to new fuel areas and can deliver additional oxygen to sustain old fires and promote new ones. Internal structural collapse may also contribute to spread, as when burning material falls through to lower floors, starting fires there.

Direction and Rate of Spread

Flames and superheated gases are lighter than air and, therefore, rise. Heat from a fire in the open rises as a column of hot gas called a *plume.* In doing so, it preheats any fuel or combustible material located above the point of origin. Once heated sufficiently, this ignites, greatly increasing the volume and upper progression of flame and heated gases. The resulting air flow draws cool air into the base of the fire from all directions. This in-flow of cool air into the plume is called *entrainment.* Thus, upward burning occurs at a very rapid rate, estimated at some 96 ft/sec (approximately 65.5 mph) (A. Dresner, personal communication). The location of the fire in the room of origin will also affect the speed of the flame growth as well as the length of time to flashover. Obviously, the higher the ceilings and larger the area of volume, the more delay in the build-up of temperature as well as time to flashover.

When a fire is burning freely in a room away from a wall or other vertical obstruction, the air is free to flow into the plume from all directions mixing with the fuel gases. This flow of cooler air into the flaming combustion zone cools the upper part of the plume — thus, the slower buildup of the rate of heat to the point of flashover.

If the fire plume is against a flat wall surface, the ability of air to enter the plume is reduced by about half of the theoretical circle around the base. This results in a longer flame and a more rapid rise in the temperature of the gases at the ceiling. Therefore, the time to flashover is quicker than in the previous example where the fire was in the center of the room.

A

B

Figure 4.7 (A) The heavy rolling char (alligatoring on the staircase) and the clean soot-free (white) spot on the walls adjacent to the stairs identified this area as one of five separate points of origin in this major commercial fire. Gasoline had been poured on the concrete floor and ignited. The rolling blisters were caused by the rapid intense movement (extension) of heat and flame. The wall surface was so hot that soot was unable to adhere. (B) An investigator holds one of the surviving heavily (deeply) charred stairs from the staircase.

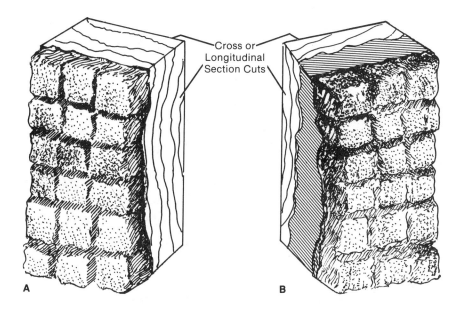

Figure 4.8 (A) Indication of a rapidly burning fire: a sharp line of demarcation separates the charred and unburned areas of the wood. (B) indication of a slow-burning fire: a gradual change from charred area of wood to unburned wood.

Finally, if the same fire is propagating in a corner of a room, about 75% of the air flow into the plume is restricted. This results in an even longer flame front, higher heat plume, and ceiling temperatures reach flashover quicker.

Downward or lateral (sideways) burning, on the other hand, moves slowly and occurs when:

- The fuel source above the point of origin is depleted
- An unusual draft condition forces the fire to progress in this unnatural direction
- A highly flammable fuel, perhaps an accelerant, is present and runs below the point of ignition and, when ignited, carries the fire downward

Chimney Effect

Since there is a natural tendency for flame and heated gases to rise, any structural element that enhances this upward movement serves as a natural chimney. Such enhancement is called the "chimney effect" (see "Building Components" in Chapter 3). Because they intensify the fire's upward movement, these areas are often deeply charred and exhibit flame and burn damage many times in excess of that at the point of origin.

Figure 4.9　The spiral staircase enhanced the upward movement of flame and heated gases. The opening for the staircase served as a natural chimney. This condition is called the "chimney effect."

In one case, for example, a young man poured gasoline on the front door to his apartment as the result of a domestic quarrel (his wife had locked him out). Although the original point of ignition was small, the fire quickly extended to a nearby staircase. The staircase acted as a natural chimney and the fire took off. The staircase and the top two floors of the five-story walkup were almost completely destroyed. The damage at the point of origin was minor in comparison.

Types of configurations that act as chimneys during a fire include staircases and stairwells, elevator shafts, laundry chutes, dumbwaiters, concealed spaces within walls, and any other unprotected vertical openings (including those created by internal collapse).

The rapid movement and vigorous burning that occur when a fire extends into a cockloft or other concealed ceiling space is akin to the chimney effect. Cocklofts and similar structures should be seen as horizontal chimneys (see "Building Components" in Chapter 3).

Burn Patterns

As the flame and superheated gases pass upward through a structure, they leave behind distinctive patterns. The most common pattern associated with this upward movement is the "V" pattern, the apex (pointed end) of the V representing the point of ignition. The formation of the V pattern is a natural phenomenon. As the flame and heated gases rise in a plume, they typically spread laterally as the atmosphere in the room or confined space attempts to equalize the temperature and pressure. This pattern is most evidenced when the point of ignition is located against a wall or other partition. When the point of ignition is located at the center of a room, away from a wall, a circular burn pattern results directly above, on the ceiling. However, when the plume is intersected by a vertical surface such as a wall, a V- or U-shaped pattern of char can occur on the surface.

The breadth or width of the V (also called the *funnel pattern*) is affected by (and, hence, indicative of) the buildup, progression, speed, and intensity of the fire. An intense rapidly moving fire produces a narrow V pattern, whereas a slow, less intense fire produces a wide V pattern. The angles of the V boundaries average between 10 and 15°F.

Rapid Movement–Slow Movement

The upward movement of flame and gases can be affected and altered by many factors. Among the most common are the following:

• A draft or crosswind from an open window, door, or skylight
• An available, secondary fuel source in close proximity to the original point of ignition
• A highly combustible fuel at the point of origin (e.g., a large pool of liquid accelerant, when ignited, causes the apex of V to be at least as wide as the pool)
• Environmental considerations, such as class and type of construction, and other conditions that might impede or block the upward progression of the products of combustion

Smoke and Flame Color

Smoke is the visible evidence of incomplete combustion; it is a suspension of the unburned by-products of solid, liquid, and gaseous products. The color of smoke and flame associated with a particular fire can show the type of material or fuel that is burning (Table 4.1). The color of the flames can also indicate the approximate temperature of the fire (Table 4.2). The colors observed in the early stages of a fire could be indicative of burning accelerants. However, in the later stages of a fire, little significance can be assigned to a

Figure 4.10 (A) Heat forms a "V" pattern on exterior wall which coincides with (B), hot spot on interior wall surface at point of origin.

color of smoke and flame because many petroleum-based building materials and contents become involved.

Fire suppression efforts will also affect the color of smoke. The application of water can produce large volumes of condensing vapor that appear white or gray when mixed with black smoke from the fire.

Table 4.1   Smoke and Flame Colors for Certain Fuels

Smoke Color	Flame Color	Fuel
Gray to brown	Red to yellow	Wood/paper/cloth
Black	Red to white	Gasoline
White to gray	Yellow to white	Benzine
Black to brown	Yellow to white	Turpentine
Black	Dark red to orange-yellow	Kerosene
Black	Blue white to white	Naphtha

Note: Overall the lighter the color of the flame, the higher the temperature. The significance of the color of smoke and flames in a fire should be considered with the time at which they were observed.

Table 4.2   Flame Colors and Temperature (°F) Ranges

Flame Color	Temperature	Flame Color	Temperature
Light red	900–1000	Salmon	1600–1700
Dark red	1000–1100	Orange	1700–1800
Dark cherry	1100–1200	Lemon	1800–1900
Medium cherry	1200–1300	Light yellow	1900–2100
Light cherry	1300–1400	White	2150–2250
Bright red	1400–1500	Bright white	2500 and over

Note: Overall the lighter the color of the flame, the higher the temperature. The significance of the color of smoke and flames in a fire should be considered with the time at which they were observed.

Smoke production is generally slower in the early stages of a fire and increases significantly with flashover.

Fire Suppression

Combustion ends when one of the four faces of the fire tetrahedron (fuel, oxygen, heat, chemical chain reaction) is removed.

Fuel — Combustion ends either when the fuel is consumed (as in the case of ordinary combustibles) or when the source of fuel is removed (as in the case of methane or natural gas).

Oxygen — Combustion ends when the oxygen level drops below that needed to maintain it (normally 15%). The foams used in certain suppression operations extinguish (smother) the fire by cutting off the oxygen supply. Remember that oxygen is not a fuel, and neither burns nor explodes. It merely supports oxidative combustion.

Heat — Water is the most commonly used extinguishing agent. It is used because of its great heat-absorbing ability. This cools the surface temperature of the burning fuel to a point below its ignition temperature.
Chemical chain reaction — When the oxidation reaction is chemically inhibited, the fire is extinguished. Certain extinguishing agents (Halon, carbon tetrachloride, potassium bicarbonate, etc.) combine with the radicals freed during the process of combustion to form new molecules. This chemical action prevents transfer of heat energy, and the fire is extinguished.

References and Selected Readings

Bates, E. B., *Elements of Fire and Arson Investigation*, David, Philadelphia, 1975 (rev. 1977).

Battle, B. P. and Weston, P. B., *Arson: A Handbook of Detection and Investigation*, 5th ed., Arco, New York, 1960.

Bradley, J. H., *Flame and Combustion Phenomena*, Barnes and Noble, New York, 1969.

Browning, B.L., Ed., *The Chemistry of Wood*, Wiley-Interscience, New York, 1963.

Bush, L. S. and McLaughlin, J., *Introduction to Fire Science*, Glencoe Press, Beverly Hills, CA, 1970.

Carroll, J. R., *Physical and Technical Aspects of Fire/Arson Investigations*, Charles C Thomas, Springfield, IL, 1979.

Carter, R. E., *Arson Investigation*, Glencoe Press, Beverly Hills, CA, 1978. Fire/Arson Training Committee, New York State Division of Criminal Justice Services, Bureau of Municipal Police, Fire/Arson Course Material, Module 1, Lesson 2, 1981.

Fitch, R.D. and Porter, E.A., *Accidental or Incendiary?* Charles C Thomas, Springfield, IL, 1968.

French, H. M., *The Anatomy of Arson*, Arco, New York, 1979.

Heidl, J. H., *Hazardous Materials Handbook*, Glencoe Press, Beverly Hills, CA, 1972.

Huron B. S., *Elements of Arson Investigation*, Reuben H. Donnelly, New York, 1963.

Ingle, H., *The Chemistry of Fire and Fire Prevention*, Spon and Chamberlain, New York, 1900.

Kennedy, J., *Fire and Arson Investigation*, Investigations Institute, Chicago, IL, 1962.

Kirk, P. L., *Fire Investigation*, Wiley, New York, 1969.

Lewis, B. and Von Elve, G., *Combustion, Flames and Explosions of Gases*, 2nd ed., Academic Press, New York 1961.

McKinnon, G. P., *Fire Protection Handbook*, 14th ed., National Fire Protection Association, Boston, MA, 1976.

National Fire Protection Association 921 (NFPA 921) *Basic Fire Science*, Chapter 3, Boston, MA, 1992.

O'Hanlon, J., *Scientific Fire Fighting*, Hubert A. Howson, New York, 1968.

Phillipps and McFadden, *Investigating the Fireground*, Prentice-Hall, Englewood Cliffs, NJ, 1982.

Roblee, C. L. and McKechnie, A. J., *The Investigation of Fires*, Prentice-Hall, Englewood Cliffs, NJ, 1981.

APPENDIX 4.1   Materials Subject to Spontaneous Heating

Name	Tendency to Spontaneous Heating	Usual Shipping Container or Storage Method	Precautions Against Spontaneous Heating	Remarks
Alfalfa meal	High	Bags, bulk	Avoid moisture extremes. Tight cars for transportation are essential.	Many fires attributed to spontaneous heating probably caused by sparks, burning embers, or particles of hot metal picked up by the meal during processing. Test fires caused in this manner have smoldered for 72 hours before becoming noticeable.
Burlap bags "used"	Possible	Bales	Keep cool and dry.	Tendency to heat dependent on previous use of bags. If oily would be dangerous.
Castor oil	Very slight	Metal barrels, metal cans in wooden boxes	Avoid contact of leakage from containers with rags, cotton, or other fibrous combustible materials.	Possible heating of saturated fabrics in badly ventilated piles.
Charcoal	High	Bulk, bags	Keep dry. Supply ventilation.	Hardwood charcoal must be carefully prepared and aged. Avoid wetting and subsequent drying.
Coal, bituminous	Moderate	Bulk	Store in small piles. Avoid high temperatures.	Tendency to heat depends upon origin and nature of coals. High volatile coals are particularly liable to heat.
Cocoa bean shell tankage	Moderate	Burlap bags, bulk	Extreme caution must be observed to maintain safe moisture limits.	This material is very hygroscopic and is liable to heating if moisture content is excessive. Precaution should be observed to maintain dry storage, etc.
Cocoanut oil	Very slight	Drums, cans, glass	Avoid contact of leakage from containers with rags, cotton, or other fibrous combustible materials.	Only dangerous if fabrics, etc., are impregnated.
Cod liver oil	High	Drums, cans, glass	Avoid contact of leakage from containers with rags, cotton, or other fibrous combustible materials.	Impregnated organic materials are extremely dangerous.

Material	Hazard	Container	Precautions	Remarks
Colors in oil	High	Drums, cans, glass	Avoid contact of leakage from containers with rags, cotton, or other fibrous combustible materials.	May be very dangerous if fabrics, etc. are impregnated.
Copra	Slight	Bulk	Keep cool and dry.	Heating possible if wet and hot.
Corn-meal feeds	High	Burlap bags, paper bags, bulk	Material should be processed carefully to maintain safe moisture content and to cure before storage.	Usually contains an appreciable quantity of oil which has rather severe tendency to heat.
Corn oil	Moderate	Barrels, tank cars	Avoid contact of leakage from containers with rags, cotton, or other fibrous combustible materials.	Dangerous heating of meals, etc., unlikely unless stored in large piles while hot.
Cottonseed	Low	Bags, bulk	Keep cool and dry.	Heating possible if piled wet and hot.
Cottonseed oil	Moderate	Barrels, tank cars	Avoid contact of leakage from containers with rags, cotton, or other fibrous combustible materials.	May cause heating of saturated material in badly ventilated piles.
Distillers' dried grains with oil content (brewers' grains)	Moderate	Bulk	Maintain moisture 7 percent to 10 percent. Cool below 100°F (38°C) before storage.	Very dangerous if moisture content is 5 percent or lower.
No oil content	Moderate	Bulk	Maintain moisture 7 percent to 10 percent. Cool below 100°F (38°C) before storage.	Very dangerous if moisture content is 5 percent or lower.
Feeds, various	Moderate	Bulk, bags	Avoid extremely low or high moisture content.	Ground feeds must be carefully processed. Avoid loading or storing unless cooled.
Fertilizers Organic, inorganic, combination of both	Moderate	Bulk, bags	Avoid extremely low or high moisture content.	Organic fertilizers containing nitrates must be carefully prepared to avoid combinations that might initiate heating.
Mixed, synthetic, containing nitrates and organic matter	Moderate	Bulk, bags	Avoid free acid in preparation.	Insure ventilation in curing process by small piles or artificial drafts. If stored or loaded in bags, provide ventilation space between bags.
Fish meal	High	Bags, bulk	Keep moisture 6 percent to 12 percent. Avoid exposure to heat.	Dangerous if overdried or packaged over 100°F (38°C).

APPENDIX 4.1   Materials Subject to Spontaneous Heating (continued)

Name	Tendency to Spontaneous Heating	Usual Shipping Container or Storage Method	Precautions Against Spontaneous Heating	Remarks
Fish oil	High	Barrels, drums, tank cars	Avoid contact of leakage from containers with rags, cotton, or other fibrous combustible materials.	Impregnated porous or fibrous materials are extremely dangerous. Tendency of various fish oils to heat varies with origin.
Fish scrap	High	Bulk, bags	Avoid moisture extremes.	Scrap loaded or stored before cooling is extremely liable to heat.
Foam rubber in consumer products	Moderate		Where possible remove foam rubber pads, etc., from garments to be dried in dryers or over heaters. If garments containing foam rubber parts have been artificially dried, they should be thoroughly cooled before being piled, bundled, or put away. Keep heating pads, hair dryers, other heat sources from contact with foam rubber pillows, etc.	Foam rubber may continue to heat spontaneously after being subjected to forced drying as in home or commercial dryers, and after contact with heating pads and other heat sources. Natural drying does not cause spontaneous heating.
Grain (various kinds)	Very slight	Bulk, bags	Avoid moisture extremes.	Ground grains may heat if wet and warm.
Hay	Moderate	Bulk, bales	Keep dry and cool.	Wet or improperly cured hay is almost certain to heat in hot water. Baled hay seldom heats dangerously.
Hides	Very slight	Bales	Keep dry and cool.	Bacteria in untreated hides may initiate heating.
Iron pyrites	Moderate	Bulk	Avoid large piles. Keep dry and cool.	Moisture accelerates oxidation of finely divided pyrites.
Istle	Very slight	Bulk, bales	Keep cool and dry.	Heating possible in wet material. Unlikely under ordinary conditions. Partially burned or charred fiber is dangerous.

Material				
Jute	Very slight	Bulk	Keep cool and dry.	Avoid storing or loading in hot wet piles. Partially burned or charred material is dangerous.
Lamp black	Very slight	Wooden cases	Keep cool and dry.	Fires most likely to result from sparks or included embers, etc., rather than spontaneous heating.
Lanolin	Negligible	Glass, cans, metal drums, barrels	Avoid contact of leakage from containers with rags, cotton, or other fibrous combustible materials.	Heating possible on contaminated fibrous matter.
Lard oil	Slight	Wooden barrels	Avoid contact of leakage from containers with rags, cotton, or other fibrous combustible materials.	Dangerous on fibrous combustible substances.
Lime, unslaked (calcium oxide, pebble lime, quicklime)	Moderate	Paper bags, wooden barrels, bulk	Keep dry. Avoid hot loading.	Wetted lime may heat sufficiently to ignite wood containers, etc.
Linseed	Very slight	Bulk	Keep cool and dry.	Tendency to heat dependent on moisture and oil content.
Linseed oil	High	Tank cars, drums, cans, glass	Avoid contact of leakage from containers with rags, cotton, or other fibrous combustible materials.	Rags or fabrics impregnated with this oil are extremely dangerous. Avoid piles, etc. Store in closed containers, preferably metal.
Manure	Moderate	Bulk	Avoid extremes of low or high moisture contents. Ventilate the piles.	Avoid storing or loading uncooled manure.
Menhaden oil	Moderate to high	Barrels, drums, tank cars	Avoid contact of leakage from containers with rags, cotton, or other fibrous combustible materials.	Dangerous on fibrous product.
Metal powders*	Moderate	Drums, etc.	Keep in closed containers.	Moisture accelerates oxidation of most metal powders.
Metal turnings*	Practically none	Bulk	Not likely to heat spontaneously.	Avoid exposure to sparks.
Mineral wool	None	Pasteboard boxes, paper bags	Noncombustible. If loaded hot may ignite containers and other combustible surroundings.	This material is mentioned in this table only because of general impression that it heats spontaneously.

APPENDIX 4.1 Materials Subject to Spontaneous Heating (continued)

Name	Tendency to Spontaneous Heating	Usual Shipping Container or Storage Method	Precautions Against Spontaneous Heating	Remarks
Mustard oil, black	Low	Barrels	Avoid contact of leakage with rags, cotton or other fibrous combustible materials.	Avoid contamination of fibrous combustible materials.
Oiled clothing	High	Fiber boxes	Dry thoroughly before packaging.	Dangerous if wet material is stored in piles without ventilation.
Oiled fabrics	High	Rolls	Keep ventilated. Dry thoroughly before packing.	Improperly dried fabrics extremely dangerous. Tight rolls are comparatively safe.
Oiled rags	High	Bales	Avoid storing in bulk in open.	Dangerous if wet with drying oil.
Oiled silk	High	Fiber boxes, rolls	Supply sufficient ventilation.	Improperly dried material is dangerous in form of piece goods. Rolls relatively safe.
Oleic acid	Very slight	Glass bottles, wooden barrels	Avoid contact of leakage from containers with rags, cotton, or other fibrous combustible materials.	Impregnated fibrous materials may heat unless ventilated.
Oleo oil	Very slight	Wooden barrels	Avoid contact of leakage from containers with rags, cotton, or other fibrous combustible materials.	May heat on impregnated fibrous combustible matter.
Olive oil	Moderate to low	Tank cars, drums, cans, glass	Avoid contact of leakage from containers with rags, cotton, or other fibrous combustible materials.	Impregnated fibrous materials may heat unless ventilated. Tendency varies with origin of oil.
Paint containing drying oil	Moderate	Drums, cans, glass	Avoid contact of leakage from containers with rags, cotton, or other fibrous combustible materials.	Fabrics, rags, etc., impregnated with paints that contain drying oils and dryers are extremely dangerous. Store in closed containers, preferably metal.
Paint scrapings	Moderate	Barrels, drums	Avoid large unventilated piles.	Tendency to heat depends on state of dryness of the scrapings.

Material	Tendency	Container	Precautions	Remarks
Palm oil	Low	Wooden barrels	Avoid contact of leakage from containers with rags, cotton, or other fibrous combustible materials.	Impregnated fibrous materials may heat unless ventilated. Tendency varies with origin of oil.
Peanut oil	Low	Wooden barrels, tin cans	Avoid contact of leakage from containers with rags, cotton, or other fibrous combustible materials.	Impregnated fibrous materials may heat unless ventilated. Tendency varies with origin of oil.
Peanuts, "red skin"	High	Paper bags, cans, fiber board boxes, burlap bags	Avoid badly ventilated storage.	This is the part of peanut between outer shell and peanut itself. Provide well ventilated storage.
Peanuts, shelled	Very slight or negligible	Paper bags, cans, fiber board boxes, burlap bags	Keep cool and dry.	Avoid contamination of rags, etc., with oil.
Perilla oil	Moderate to high	Tin cans, barrels	Avoid contact of leakage from containers with rags, cotton, or other fibrous combustible materials.	Impregnated fibrous materials may heat unless ventilated. Tendency varies with origin of oil.
Pine oil	Moderate	Glass, drums	Avoid contact of leakage from containers with rags, cotton, or other fibrous combustible materials.	Impregnated fibrous materials may heat unless ventilated. Tendency varies with origin of oil.
Powdered eggs	Very slight	Wooden barrels	Avoid conditions that promote bacterial growth. Inhibit against decay. Keep cool.	Possible heating of decaying powder in storage.
Powdered milk	Very slight	Wooden and fiber boxes, metal cans	Avoid conditions that promote bacterial growth. Inhibit against decay. Keep cool.	Possible heating by decay or fermentation.
Rags	Variable	Bales	Avoid contamination with drying oils. Avoid charring. Keep cool and dry.	Tendency depends on previous use of rags. Partially burned or charred rags are dangerous.
Red oil	Moderate	Glass bottles, wooden barrels	Avoid contact of leakage from containers with rags, cotton, or other fibrous combustible materials.	Impregnated porous or fibrous materials are extremely dangerous. Tendency varies with origin of oil.

APPENDIX 4.1 Materials Subject to Spontaneous Heating (continued)

Name	Tendency to Spontaneous Heating	Usual Shipping Container or Storage Method	Precautions Against Spontaneous Heating	Remarks
Roofing felts and papers	Moderate	Rolls, bales, crates	Avoid over-drying the material. Supply ventilation.	Felts, etc., should have controlled moisture content. Packaging or rolling uncooled felts is dangerous.
Sawdust	Possible	Bulk	Avoid contact with drying oils. Avoid hot, humid storage.	Partially burned or charred sawdust may be dangerous.
Scrap film (nitrate)	Very slight	Drums and lined boxes	Film must be properly stabilized against decomposition.	Nitrocellulose film ignites at low temperature. External ignition more likely than spontaneous heating. Avoid exposure to sparks, etc.
Scrap leather	Very slight	Bales, bulk	Avoid contamination with drying oils.	Oil-treated leather scraps may heat.
Scrap rubber or buffings	Moderate	Bulk, drums	Buffings of high rubber content should be shipped and stored in tight containers.	Sheets, slabs, etc., are comparatively safe unless loaded or stored before cooling thoroughly.
Sisal	Very slight	Bulk, bales	Keep cool and dry.	Partially burned or charred material is particularly liable to ignite spontaneously.
Soybean oil	Moderate	Tin cans, barrels, tank cars	Avoid contact with rags, cotton, or fibrous materials.	Impregnated fibrous materials may heat unless well ventilated.
Sperm oil (see whale oil)				
Tankage	Variable	Bulk	Avoid extremes of moisture contents. Avoid loading or storing while hot.	Very dry or moist tankages often heat. Tendency more pronounced if loaded or stored before cooling.
Tung nut meals	High	Paper bags, bulk	Material must be very carefully processed and cooled thoroughly before storage.	These meals contain residual oil which has high tendency to heat. Material also susceptible to heating if overdried.

Material	Tendency	Container	Precautions	Remarks
Tung oil	Moderate	Tin cans, barrels, tank cars	Avoid contact of leakage from containers with rags, cotton, or other fibrous combustible materials.	Impregnated fibrous materials may heat unless ventilated. Tendency varies with origin of oil.
Turpentine	Low	Tin, glass, barrels	Avoid contact of leakage from containers with rags, cotton, or other fibrous combustible materials.	Has some tendency to heat but less so than the drying oils. Chemically active with chlorine compounds and may cause fire.
Varnished fabrics	High	Boxes	Process carefully. Keep cool and ventilated.	Thoroughly dried varnished fabrics are comparatively safe.
Wallboard	Slight	Wrapped bundles, pasteboard boxes	Maintain safe moisture content. Cool thoroughly before storage.	This material is entirely safe from spontaneous heating if properly processed.
Waste paper	Moderate	Bales	Keep dry and ventilated.	Wet paper occasionally heats in storage in warm locations.
Whale oil	Moderate	Barrels and tank cars	Avoid contact of leakage from containers with rags, cotton, or other fibrous combustible materials.	Impregnated fibrous materials may heat unless ventilated. Tendency varies with origin of oil.
Wool wastes	Moderate	Bulk, bales, etc.	Keep cool and ventilated or store in closed containers. Avoid high moisture.	Most wool wastes contain oil, etc., from the weaving and spinning and are liable to heat in storage. Wet wool wastes are very liable to spontaneous heating and possible ignition.

* Refers to iron, steel, brass, aluminum, and other common metals, for information on magnesium, sodium, zirconium, etc.

Originally prepared by the NFPA Committee on Spontaneous Heating and Ignition which has been discontinued. Omission of any material does not necessarily indicate that it is not subject to spontaneous heating.

Determining Origin and Cause

5

The main reason for conducting a post-fire examination of the fire scene is to determine the fire's origin and cause. The factual determination of origin and cause is the principal area of expertise that separates a fire/arson investigator from other investigative specialists.

The *point of origin* of a fire is the location where the fire started — the place of beginning. The term *area of origin* is sometimes used when fire originates over a large tract or space, or when the exact point of origin cannot be determined. Multiple points of origin are said to exist when there is more than one place of beginning, or when several separate fires burn in the same structure at the same time.

The *cause* of a fire usually can be determined from a detailed inspection of the charred debris, combustibles, devices, and residues located at the point of (or within the area of) origin. Theoretically, the cause of a fire can be categorized into one of four classifications:

1. *Natural:* Act of God (e.g., lightning)
2. *Accidental:* Unintentional and explainable
3. *Undetermined:* Cause unknown, unable to be identified
4. *Incendiary:* Intentionally set

With regard to criminal prosecution, only two classifications are relevant: accidental and incendiary. NFPA 921 strongly discourages the use of the term "suspicious." Suspicion is not an acceptable level of proof for making a determination of cause within the scope of 921 and should be avoided.

Physical Examination of the Fire Scene

To improve the likelihood of a successful resolution, an investigator must approach the fire investigation systematically. It is important to keep in mind the application of the scientific method as discussed in NFPA 921 (Chapter 2, Basic Methodology). It is a six-step approach to analyzing the origin and cause of a fire starting with Step 1: recognizing the problem; Step 2: defining the problem; Step 3: collecting data; Step 4: analyzing data; Step 5: developing a hypothesis; Step 6: proving the hypothesis.

Figure 5.1 An all-too-common sight to the experienced fire investigator: the charred interior of a building under investigation. (Photo courtesy of S. Grennan.)

The first step of recognizing the problem is after the fire or explosion has occurred, and it is the investigator's responsibility to determine its origin, cause, and responsibility. It is at this point that investigators in both the civil service sector and the private sector must recognize that their determinations may lead to criminal and civil litigation which can affect many lives.

To define the problem, the investigator must conduct a thorough investigation with all the information available to him. Step 3 involves the collection of data, including documentation of the scene with photographs, reports, and collection of physical evidence. It also includes witness accounts, which may require additional statement taking, notes, and diagrams.

The fourth step is the analysis of the data (inductive reasoning). Here the investigator's knowledge, training and experience is put to the test in his analysis of the fire patterns, structural damage, fuel source, ignition source, and any other factors which may affect the correct determination of origin and ultimately the cause. This is the "fact" portion of the investigation. Your analysis must be confined to those facts which were deduced from your observations of known scientific results or through experiments and testing of physical evidence collected at the scene.

The fifth step is the stage at which an investigator may express his opinion about the origin cause and responsibility of the fire/explosion incident. This opinion is based on the facts and data collected by the investigator.

In the final step, Step 6, an investigator's hypothesis (deductive reasoning) is put to the test, based on the facts and scientific data that have been developed.

If all other possible origins and causes have been eliminated through deductive reasoning, then the investigator's opinion can stand. If not, then the cause of the fire/explosion must be listed as undetermined or unknown until such time as a logical, scientifically acceptable cause can be determined.

The physical examination of a structural fire involves a series of increasingly focused analyses: first the exterior, then the interior, the room of origin, the point of origin, and finally the determination of cause. The reconstruction and examination of the fire scene can be seriously impeded by indiscriminate or haphazard handling of the routine fire-fighting operation known as the *overhaul*. This involves the inspection of and, when necessary, the movement or reshuffling of debris in an effort to discover concealed sparks, embers, or flames that might rekindle the fire. In the case of a suspicious fire, the overhaul process should be *minimized*. If circumstances permit, the room of origin should not be overhauled before an investigator is on the scene and can supervise the operation; otherwise, evidence could be destroyed or buried. An objective estimate should be completed for each area overhauled to determine whether the debris is normal for that area, and whether items consistent with a normal life style are missing. The presence of items foreign to the environment is to be viewed with suspicion.

Exterior Examination

The exterior examination begins with interviewing of the fire department officers, firefighters, and police officers who were first at the scene. As the first-in company, they may have observations relevant to the nature and origin of the fire. The initial interviews should cover the following types of information:

Figure 5.2 In "exclusive opportunity" cases, all entrances and exits (doors, windows, etc.) must be examined. Did responding firefighters force entry? Is the damage due to natural or firematic venting or is it possible that someone else (burglar, etc.) forcibly entered the building and intentionally started a fire to conceal another crime?

1. Were any people or vehicles observed in the vicinity of the fire?
2. If so, could their conduct or actions be interpreted as suspicious? That is, were they:
   - Fighting or arguing?
   - Too eager to help or give information?
   - Attempting to obstruct fire-fighting operations?
   - Observed fleeing the scene?
   - Observed at other fire scenes?
   - Dressed in a manner suggesting obvious haste (relative to time of day/night or season)?

   If suspicions were raised, record accurate descriptions, license plate numbers, etc.
3. Was the structure fully involved?
   - Was the fire consistent with the types of combustibles readily available?
   - Was it consistent with the class and type of construction?
   - Were flames visible?
   - What side of the building was involved?
   - Was there fire through the roof?
   - Had flames extended through windows? If so, which windows?

- What color were the smoke and flames?
- Were the flames quietly lapping up the side of the structure or were they roaring violently?
4. Were the doors and windows open or closed?
   - Were they locked or nailed shut?
   - Were shades open or closed, or windows painted to obscure view?
   - Were entrances blocked (e.g., by storage or rubbish)?
   - Was forced entry made and, if so, by whom?
5. What was the approximate *reflex time* (time elapsed between alarm and first water = *response time* + *setup time*)?
6. Were any unusual odors noticed?
7. Were hydrants, standpipes, and sprinkler systems operational?
   - Were hydrants blocked, hidden, or rendered inoperable?
   - Were hydrant caps missing or cross-threaded?
   - Were fire detection or other safety systems circumvented or rendered inoperable?

After completing the initial interviews, the investigator should examine and evaluate the fire damage on the exterior. If possible, walk around the structure. Note the damage around windows and doors, under the soffit, and around vents or other outside openings. Where is the greatest exterior damage? Does it appear that the fire started outside the building and extended into the structure? Is a "V" pattern visible on the exterior shell of the structure? Where is the lowest point of exterior burning? Examine any containers or items on the ground around the structure, and photograph the outside of the building. Note the construction and use of the structure. Construction refers to the type of building: wood frame, ordinary, noncombustible, heavy timber, etc. Note the building material, such as type of roof and siding. Also note differences in multiple sections of the building; for example, a two-story main structure perhaps with a newer one-story addition. All these factors may play an important role in the fire spread and amount of destruction.

The use of the structure refers to the type of occupancy: for example, residential, multiple dwelling unit, commercial, or industrial. The type of occupancy may play a factor in the possible causes of the fire. Except in rare cases where the fire is positively identified as having started outside the building and extended into it (e.g., from burning rubbish), the origin and cause of a fire cannot be determined and should not be assumed only on the basis of an exterior examination. There is generally an inside area or room of the structure that, while exhibiting little fire damage relative to the rest of the interior, adjoins the external point of greatest damage. The extreme point of the fire's extension may be the best place to begin the interior examination.

Interior Examination

With the exterior examination completed, the investigation shifts to the inside of the structure. To the extent possible, the investigator should attempt to complete a detailed survey of the structure interior, wearing full turnout gear or its equivalent at all times.

Remember, a fire-damaged building is a dangerous place in which to work, and an investigator must evaluate its stability before entering. Floors, walls, staircases, and similar structures may be in danger of collapse, and temporary supports may have to be put in place. Heavy equipment may be needed to excavate a building that has already collapsed. Structural members of steel or, in older buildings, cast iron may be twisted and distorted or may have cracked. Steel I-beams that expanded during the heat of the fire may have punched holes in the face, rear, or sides of the building, and portions of the building may have sagged due to the failure of the steel structure.

Figure 5.3 "Exclusive opportunity" cases are difficult to prosecute. One element that must be documented is that the responding firefighters made a forcible entry. The investigator should photograph the forcible-entry damage and identify the firefighters who made the entry.

Try to reconstruct mentally what happened during the fire. All observations made during this preliminary survey should be written down, including answers to the following:

1. Does the fire spread appear natural?
2. Was the extension of the fire natural?
3. Was the intensity of the fire natural?
4. Were the furnishings, clothing, appliances, and so on normal for the type of occupancy?
5. Were personal items removed before the fire? Was there any substitution of contents (for instance, cheap or used in place of expensive)?
6. Was there fire in unusual locations (under staircase, in closets and attics, in desk drawers or file cabinets)?
7. Were the body of fire and the path of heat travel consistent with the type of construction and contents?

Figure 5.4   The investigator must be aware of and be able to explain any holes in the roof of the structure. Are they the result of burn-through or of venting by firefighters, or precut by an arsonist? The photograph shows an interior view of a hole cut in the roof by firefighters (venting). This procedure allows smoke and the other by-products of combustion to escape, and greatly reduces the danger of a backdraft.

8. Is your approximation of the burn time consistent with the combustibility characteristics of the types of material (fuel) involved?
9. Are there any holes in the floors or walls? If so, are they a natural consequence of the fire or a possible indication that an accelerant was used? (An arsonist will sometimes punch holes in walls to allow for better cross ventilation and to help the lateral spread of fire.)
10. Are there holes in the roof? Are they the result of natural burn-through from the fire or of venting during the fire-fighting operations? Are they residual damage from an earlier fire, or were they precut by an arsonist to accommodate the use of a liquid accelerant?
11. Are there any unusual puddle-like burn patterns to show that a liquid accelerant may have been used?

Room and Point(s) of Origin

By observing the burn patterns and tracing back the order in which they were formed, the investigator gradually migrates to the area of the most severe damage. This is usually the area where the fire burned the longest (except when flammable liquids were involved). A fire generally burns longest at or near its point of origin because enough oxygen is available there during the early stages (Bromley et al., undated, p. 2-2). Therefore, the room with the greatest damage is most apt to be the room of origin. Locating this room is very significant because it contains the point or area of the fire's origin* as well as clues to its cause.

Many factors and criteria are commonly used to isolate the point(s) of origin within the room of origin; these are discussed in the section on Fire Language, which follows. If the investigator finds several distinct (unconnected) points of origin, each must be carefully examined. The crime scene, photographs, sketches, and notes should clearly show that the multiple points of origin were not the result of normal fire travel, flashover, or burning material having been moved during suppression, overhaul, or salvage operations. *Fall down fires* (also known as *drop down fires*) (burning material falling to the floor) or explosions can also give the appearance of multiple points of origin (Bromley et al., undated, p. 2–9).

The discovery of multiple points of origin is *prima facie* evidence that the fire was of incendiary origin, since such a condition is highly improbable and virtually impossible under normal conditions.

After completing the preliminary scene evaluation, including the documentation of utilities, doors, and window security, the fire investigator should have evaluated areas of lesser damage back to the greatest area of structural damage in tracking the fire to its place of beginning or point of origin.

Fire Language

The step from the inside examination to the determination of the fire's point of origin and cause depends on the fire/arson investigator's ability to detect and characterize the visible remains of the fire. These give information about the fire, including the path of spread, temperatures reached, and fuels involved. The physical signs and substances that reveal, by implication, how a fire developed are referred to as *"fire language"* (NFPA 921, Chapter 4, Fire Patterns). To be effective, a fire/arson investigator must be able to read this technical language. Examples of fire language include lines or areas of demarcation, depth of char, spalling, oxidation, heat indicators (temperature determination), thermal indicators of metal, calcination, various features of glass, heat shadowing, and protected areas.

---

* Note that if there are highly combustible materials in a room adjacent to the point of origin, that room will show the heaviest damage when the fire reaches it, and might be mistaken for the room of origin.

Lines or Areas of Demarcation

The line or area of demarcation appears between the affected area and adjacent unaffected or less affected area of the structure and its contents.

These demarcations depend on the material, the rate of the heat release of the fire, fire suppression efforts, the temperature of the heat source, any ventilation, and the length of time the material was exposed to the heat.

Depth of Char

Char is the carbonization of a fuel by the action of heat or burning. The term is generally applied to the combustible residue remaining after the pyrolysis of wood. The depth of char refers to the depth of the charred material. Its value is obtained by measuring the distance from the surface of the original dimensional wood (lumber) to the boundary of the carbonized fraction, and comparing this with the remaining unburned matter.

From an investigative standpoint, the depth of char indicates the length of time that a wooden structural member was exposed to flame. Ordinarily, a section of exposed dimensional lumber ignites at about 660°F and chars at the rate of 1 inch in 45 minutes at 1400 °F. The char is usually deepest where the fire burned the longest (excluding the use of accelerants) and, thus, can be used to identify the point of origin.

It has been suggested that the presence of large shiny blisters (alligator char) and the surface appearance of the char such as dullness, shininess, or colors, have some relation to the presence of a liquid accelerant as the cause, but no scientific evidence substantiates this. The investigator is advised to be very cautious in using wood char appearance as an indicator as incendiarism.

Depth of char is often used to estimate the duration of a fire. The rate of charring wood varies widely depending upon such variables such as:

1. Rate and duration of heating
2. Ventilation
3. Surface area-to-mass ratio
4. Size, direction, orientation of wood grain
5. Species of wood (pine, hemlock, fir, oak, etc.)
6. Moisture content
7. Nature of surface coating

This condition may be associated with the use of an accelerant. The depth of charring is most reliable for evaluating fire spread rather than for the establishment of specific burn times or intensity of heat from adjacent burning materials. By measuring the relative depth and extent of charring, the investigator may be able to determine what portions of material or construction had

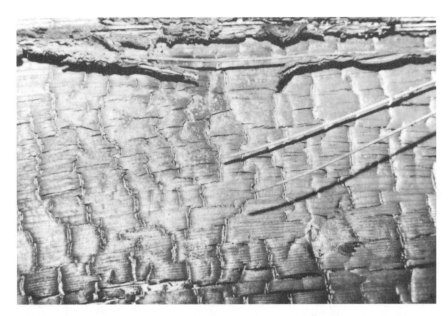

Figure 5.5 This type of char pattern (alligatoring or large rolling blisters), which ordinarily appears in floor joists or rafters above the point of origin, is consistent with uniform fire spread. Any structural members above the point of origin (accidental or incendiary) will routinely be exposed to extreme temperatures and flame for extended periods of time.

Figure 5.6 During the physical examination the investigator must recognize those patterns associated with the upward movement of flame and heat. Notice the broad "V" pattern extending from the pile of clothing and debris.

Figure 5.7 Here the burnt clothing and debris have been cleared, revealing the apex of the "V" pattern. The apex of the pattern proved to be the lowest point of burning and the point of origin. A liquid accelerant had been used.

been exposed the longest to a heat source. When measuring the depth of char, it is important to be consistent in the method of measurement. Thin blunt-ended probes, such as certain types of calipers, tire tread depth gauges, or specifically modified metal rulers are best. Char depth measurement should be made at the center of the char blister rather than in or near the crevices between the blisters. In determining the depth of charring, the investigator should take into consideration any burned wood that may already have been completely destroyed by the fire.

Spalling

Spalling is a condition ordinarily associated with masonry and cement (concrete) building materials. It may appear as a distinctive discoloration of brick or concrete and, in some cases, the surface of the material may be pitted and rough. Spalling is the result of mechanical forces in the material, particularly between the surface of the concrete and the underlying substrate aggregate. The mechanical forces react to the high temperatures and rate of heating in one or more of the following situations:

1. Moisture in uncured concrete
2. Differential expansion between reinforcing material and the surrounding concrete

Figure 5.8 It took hours of digging for investigators to uncover the accelerant pattern (spalling) on the cement floor of this nearly completed home. Several teenagers, apparently for a thrill, poured gasoline on the floor beneath a staircase. (Photo courtesy of T. Brown.)

3. Differential expansion between the concrete mix and the aggregate
4. Differential expansion between the finished surface layer and the coarser substrate layers
5. Differential expansion between the fire/heat exposed surface and the substrate material

Spalling of masonry may be caused by heat, freezing chemicals, or abrasion. Spalling is characterized by distinct lines of striation and the loss of surface material resulting in cracking, breaking, chipping, or the formation of craters on the surface.

Rapid cooling of a heated mass of concrete or other masonry material can also cause spalling. One of the most common sources of rapid cooling to a heated surface is the water from the fire fighting activities.

Although this condition may be associated with the use of an accelerant, the discovery of spalling does not in itself indicate that the fire was incendiary. Other common combustibles that burn with great intensity can also cause this condition; it may even be the result of a ruptured gas line.

Oxidation

Oxidation is the basic chemical process of combustion. Oxidation of some materials that do not burn can produce lines of demarcation and fire patterns useful to the fire investigator.

Some of the effects of oxidation include change of color and texture. The higher the temperature and the longer the exposure to heat, the more pronounced the effects of oxidation. Galvanized steel subjected to mild heating will have a dull whitish surface from oxidation of the zinc coating. The elimination of the protective zinc on the steel surface will result in a rust condition on the unprotected steel. There can be a pattern of rusted compared to nonrusted galvanized steel in the same area.

When unprotected iron or steel is oxidized in a fire, the surface turns a dull blue-gray. Continued exposure can result in thick layers of oxide (rust) that can flake. After the fire, if the metal has been wet, the usual rust-colored oxide may appear.

Stainless steel surfaces may discolor under mild oxidation; however, more severe oxidation will result in a dull gray color. Copper forms a dark red or black oxide when exposed to heat. Rocks and soil, when heated to very high temperatures, will often change to colors that may range from yellow to red. Soot and char are also subject to oxidation. The dark char of the paper surface of gypsum wallboard, soot deposits, and paint can be oxidized by continued exposure to the heat of the fire. The carbon (soot) will be oxidized to gases and disappear from whatever surface upon which it is present. This will result in what is known as a clean burn, hot spot, or white spot.

Heat Indicators

Heat indicators are those pieces of fused or molten metal (and/or glass) that suggest both the path of fire spread and the location of highest temperatures. The most severe heat damage is usually found (use of accelerants excluded) at or near the point of origin.

On finding a piece or section of fused material, the investigator must do two things:

1. Try to identify the material's composition
2. Determine its fusing temperature

This done, the investigator must endeavor to determine the source of the temperature range so indicated. The fusing temperatures of some materials are shown in Table 5.1.

Table 5.1   Fusing Temperatures of Some Materials

Material	Temperature (°F)	Material	Temperature (°F)
Solder	361	Iron	2802
Tin	449	Nickel	2651
Lead	618	Stainless steel	2462–2822
Aluminum	1220	Steel	2552–2882
Copper	1980	Platinum	3224
Cast iron	2000–2800	Chromium	3407

If the investigator knows the approximate melting temperature of the material, an estimate can be made of the temperature to which the melted material was subjected.

However, when using such variable materials as glass, plastics, and certain pot metals, the investigator should be aware of the wide variation in melting temperatures for these materials. It is best to get a sample of the material and have its melting temperature verified by a forensic laboratory with metallurgy and material science capabilities.

The melting of certain metals may not always be caused by the temperatures produced by the fire; it may be the result of alloying. During a fire, metals with relatively low melting points may drip onto other metals with higher melting temperatures or that do not normally melt in fires. If the lower melting temperature metal can mix with a higher melting temperature metal, that mixture (alloy) will melt at a lower temperature than the melting temperature of the higher-melting-temperature metal. Examples of lower-melting-temperature metals include aluminum, zinc, and lead. Metals that can be affected by alloying include copper and iron (steel). Copper alloying is often found, but iron alloying might be found in only a few cases of prolonged fire involvement.

Alloying can be confirmed by metallurgical analysis. When metals with high melting temperatures are found to have melted due to alloying, it is not an indication that accelerants or unusually high temperatures were present.

Heat discoloration of chromium materials is found in many household appliances and fixtures (toasters, ashtrays, light fixtures, etc.) which are chromium plated to prevent corrosion. Chromium has a tendency to discolor when exposed to high temperatures. This discoloration can serve as a heat indicator (Table 5.2). Many of the high-temperature colors may not remain after the chromed object cools. However, a distinctive rainbow of color may persist, suggesting high temperatures.

Table 5.2 Chromium Discoloration

Color	Temperature (°F)	Color	Temperature (°F)
Yellow	450–500	Bright red	1400–1500
Purple–brown	550–575	Salmon	1600–1700
Blue	600–875	Lemon	1800–1900
Light red	900–1000	White	2000–2400
Dark red	1100–1300	Sparkling white	2400+

Calcination

Calcination refers to the changes that occur during a fire in either plaster or gypsum wall surfaces. This may include the elimination of water from the gypsum to charring the paper surface off the wall board. The gypsum on the side exposed to the fire becomes gray in color from the charring of the organic binder. Continued heating will result in the gray color extending all the way through the gypsum board to the paper surface on the back side, which will subsequently char. The side exposed to the fire the longest will become whiter as the carbon deposits are consumed. The color itself has no significance to the fire investigator. However, the difference between colors may show lines of demarcation.

Glass as an Indicator

Glass items such as mirrors, window panes, and so on, are also affected by heat buildup, smoke, and flame. Heat damage (fusing) and smoke staining on glass items tends to occur in direct relation to: the heat buildup, the intensity of the fire, the speed of fire spread, and nearness to the fire.

A detailed inspection of glass items can give a reasonably precise determination of the items' location with regard to the fire's point of origin. The following is a classification by structure of common kinds of glass.

1. *Single-phase glass* is made up of the vitreous silica family. Among these are *fused quartz*, with a melting temperature of 3133°F (1723°C). This material softens at 2876°F (1580°C). Another member of this family is *fused silica*, used in some wood stove windows. This material softens at 2732°F (1500°C).

2. *Soda lime glass* contains a mixture of alkali and alkaline earth to make them more durable and easier to produce. This family of glass accounts for nearly 90% of all glass produced. Such glass is used for container window glass, pressed- and blown-ware, and lighting products where exceptional chemical durability and heat resistance are not required. Its melting temperature is 1005°F (695°C).

3. *Borosilicate glass* is made by replacing the alkali with boric acid, producing a lower expansion glass. These glasses are harder, more durable, and capable of withstanding higher temperatures. They can be found in oven-ware, laboratory equipment, glass piping, and sealed-beam headlights. Their melting temperature is 1190°F (780°C).

4. *Aluminosilicate glass* is made with alumina. These glasses are harder than soda lime and borosilicate glasses and are found in airplane windows, frangible containers, and stove top uses. Their melting temperature is 1670°F (910°C).

5. *Lead glass* contains lead oxide and, sometimes, lead silicate. They melt easily. These glasses are used for commercial radiation windows, fluorescent lamp envelopes, and television picture tubes. Low-melting solder glasses and frit for decorating enamels (used to decorate tableware, etc.) are based on these low melting lead glasses. Their melting temperature is 785°F (380°C).

Figure 5.9 These salt and pepper shakers are examples of soda-lime glass, which accounts for nearly 90% of all glass produced. Melting temperature is 1190°F (780°C).

The porcelain on a kitchen sink is not actually porcelain, but a vitreous glaze with a melting temperature in the range 1652–3092°F (900–1700°C). Vitreous glazes are bonded to metals at temperatures above 797°F (425°C), with aluminum bonding at a lower temperature than iron and steel.

Smoke-Stained and Checkered Glass

An increase in the temperature (heat energy) of a glass item causes a proportional increase in that item's molecular activity. The hotter the item, the greater the molecular activity on its surface. Increased molecular activity on a surface inhibits the amount of soot (*smoke staining*) that will form. An item heavily stained by smoke and soot was, therefore, cooler than one with a light buildup of soot. A heavy soot buildup on a glass surface suggests that the item was far from the fire's point of origin. However, a light soot buildup suggests that the item may be at or near the point of origin. The presence of a thick, oily soot on glass may be from hydrocarbon residues present not only in liquid accelerants, but also as the by-product of incomplete combustion of wood, other cellulosic materials, as well as many petroleum based products commonly found in today's structures. Therefore, this type of residue is not a conclusive indicator of incendiarism with the presence of an accelerant.

Checkering of glass refers to the half-moon shapes that are sometimes seen on the surface of glass items. These half-moon shapes result after droplets of water (usually from fire fighting) land on a heated surface. They usually indicate that the glass was in place or intact (e.g., in the window, door, or picture frame) when the water was applied. The presence or absence of a pane of glass in a window or door may be significant if the fire is declared incendiary and the issue of exclusive opportunity becomes manifest.

Crazed and Fractured Glass

Crazing refers to the cracking of glass into smaller segments or subdivisions in an irregular pattern. The extent to which a glass item (e.g., window pane) will crack or craze is related to the type of glass involved, its thickness, the temperature range to which it was exposed, and its distance from the point of origin.

Crazing into small segments or pieces suggests that the item was subject to a rapid and intense heat buildup. It also suggests that the items may be at or near the point of origin. On the other hand, a glass item that shows a larger crazing pattern may have been located some distance away from the point of origin.

An investigator can determine whether a particular pane of glass was *fractured* as the result of pressure applied from the inside or outside of the structure. When pressure is applied to glass, radial and concentric fractures result. *Radial fractures* start from the point of impact and carry to the perimeter

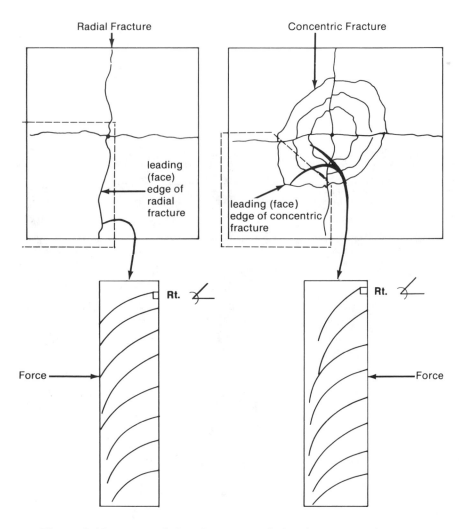

Figure 5.10 Types of glass fractures: radial and concentric fractures.

of the pane. *Concentric fractures* form around the point of impact and create a spider web-like appearance. The labeling and removal of glass fragments are simple procedures. A criminologist or laboratory expert may be needed to testify at trial regarding the analysis of the glass fragments. The steps in these procedures are as follows:

1. Carefully label (either inside or outside) a fragment of glass still attached to the window/door frame.
2. Remove the glass fragment and identify the type of fracture (radial/concentric). Carefully examine the edge of the fracture (leading edge).

3. Look at the trails of the stress fractures that result from the crackling along the lattice structure of the glass.
4. In a *radial* fracture, there is a right angle between the *striations* (fracture lines) and the *face away from* that side of the pane on which the original pressure was applied. In a *concentric* fracture there will be a right angle between the striations and the *same face* of the pane that received the pressure.

Light Bulbs

When found intact, a deformed or distended incandescent light bulb can be a valuable aid to the investigator. The glass envelope of an incandescent bulb will soften at about 900°F and distend in the direction of the heat source, which may also be the point of origin. Unfortunately, few light bulbs survive either the fire itself or the fire fighting efforts. Those that do survive are almost exclusively in ceiling fixtures. Fluorescent bulbs do not react the same way and are even less likely to survive than incandescent bulbs.

The investigation of a fire includes the identification of both the source of ignition (heat source) and the initial ignited material (fuel). The floor at the point of origin must be carefully cleaned, checking through the debris layer by layer. In some cases, the investigator has to dig through several inches of loose ash, which serves as a thermal insulator and may protect the point of origin.

Through the entire process, the investigator must be vigilant for signs of criminality. If a crime has been committed, he or she must act accordingly to build a viable case. For example, during the examination at the point of origin, the investigator may uncover certain devices, burn patterns, or other conditions that show the fire was intentionally set. Nevertheless, the investigator must still endeavor to eliminate every possible accidental cause. All fires are assumed to be accidental until absolute proof to the contrary is uncovered. (Elimination of accidental causes is discussed at length in Chapter 6.)

Heat Shadowing

Heat shadowing is the result of an object blocking the heat transfer through radiation and convection or direct flame contact from its source to the surface on which the pattern is produced. The conducted heat does not produce the heat shadowing. The object or items blocking the heat transfer energy may be solid, liquid, combustible, or noncombustible. Any object that absorbs or reflects the heat transfer may cause the production of a pattern on the material surface it is protecting.

Figure 5.11 The incandescent light bulb will soften at approximately 900°F and distend in the direction of the heat source. (A) The light bulb at the fire scene pointing to the origin at left. (B) A close-up laboratory photograph of a distended light bulb.

Protected Areas

Similar in appearance to heat shadowing is what is commonly referred to as a protected area. A protected area results when an object prohibits the deposit of the products of incomplete combustion on the material surface that the object is protecting.

Figure 5.12 The identification of the lowest point of burning is very significant. One phenomenon that serves to protect the lowest point of burning is the fact that as fire extends upward, items such as wall and ceiling materials, paintings, and wall ornaments that are damaged tend to fall or collapse and may cover the low point of burning.

Figure 5.13 It is incumbent on the investigator to sift carefully through the debris, layer by layer. This technique is called content sifting.

Figure 5.14 The hotplate pictured above was used in conjunction with a 24-hour timer and a gallon jug of gasoline by an arsonist determined to destroy his business. Portions of the molten plastic jug can be seen fused to the hot plate.

Figure 5.15 A cigarette was placed in a book of matches to serve as a crude time-delay device.

Figure 5.16 (A–C) This series of photos shows an accelerant pour pattern (trailer) on carpet and vinyl flooring.

Figure 5.17

Figure 5.18 Puddling patterns viewed from the floor below the point of origin. A liquid accelerant will seep down between floor sections and be absorbed by the supporting joists. Notice the "finger-like" patterns (accelerant splatter) on the sides of the joists, while the leading edge of the joists is untouched.

Both heat shadowing and protected areas can help the fire investigator perform the fire scene reconstruction for the purpose of determining the origin and cause of a fire.

Evidence of Incendiarism

Throughout this chapter, we have mentioned many kinds of evidence that may indicate the incendiary nature of a fire. The following list recapitulates them:

1. Suspicious behavior of people observed at the fire scene
2. Signs of forced entry unrelated to fire-fighting operations
3. Precut holes in floors, walls, or roof
4. Sabotaged fire detection or water delivery systems (e.g., hydrants, sprinklers)
5. Multiple points of origin

Figure 5.17 (A-C) Typical burn patterns resulting from the use of liquid accelerants is called "puddling." This type of pattern is distinctive enough so that it should not be confused with other irregular patterns, which might result when drapes or other cloth items burn on the floor.

Figure 5.19

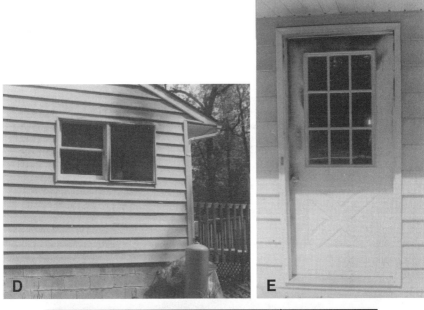

Figure 5.19 (A–F) Proper origin-and-cause investigation technique requires exterior/interior photographic documentation of security of doors and windows. Note the only open windows still had the exterior screens in place.

6. Abnormalities (inconsistencies with construction materials and contents) with regard to:
   - Rate of spread
   - Direction of spread (e.g., unusual locations of fire, burn patterns)
   - Extent of spread
   - Intensity of fire (i.e., temperature, as indicated by smoke and flame color, depth of char, burn time, spalling, etc.)

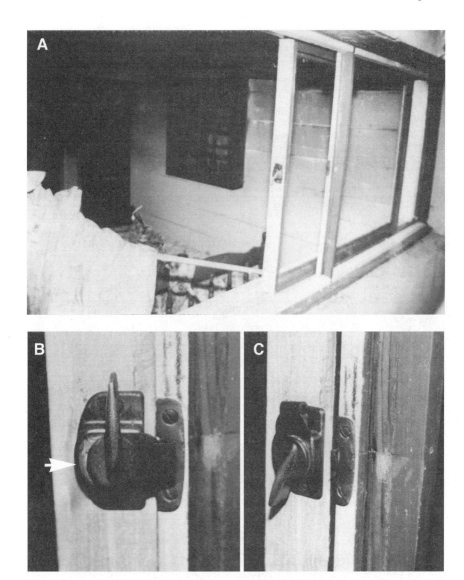

Figure 5.20 (A–C) Perimeter documentation includes status of window security. Close examination of lock reveals it was unlocked at time of fire. Note protected area indicated by arrow in B.

Figure 5.21 (A–B) A protected area results from an object prohibiting the deposit of the products of incomplete combustion on the surface the object is protecting. Note Figure B is a close-up of area indicated by arrow in A. It confirms that the screen was not in the window opening when the plastic curtain melted.

References and Selected Readings

Bates, E. B., *Elements of Fire & Arson Investigation*, Davis, Philadelphia, 1975 (revised 1977).

Battle, B. P. and Weston, P. B., *Arson*, 5th ed., Arco, New York, 1960.

Bromley, J. et al., Cause and Origin Determination, Office of Fire Prevention, Department of State, State of New York, Albany, undated.

Carroll, J. R., *Physical and Technical Aspects of Fire/Arson Investigations*, Charles C Thomas, Springfield, IL, 1979.

Carter, R. E., *Arson Investigation*, Glencoe, Beverly Hills, CA, 1978.

Fitch, R. D. and Porter, E. A., *Accidental or Incendiary?*, Charles C Thomas, Springfield, IL, 1968.

French, H. M., *The Anatomy of Arson*, Arco, New York, 1979.

Heidl, J. H., *Hazardous Materials Handbook*, Glencoe, Beverly Hills, CA, 1972.

Huron, B. S., *Elements of Arson Investigation*, Dunn-Donnelley, New York, 1963.

Kennedy, J., *Fire and Arson Investigation*, Investigations Institute, Chicago, 1962 (revised 1977).

Kirk, P. L., *Fire Investigation*, John Wiley & Sons, New York 1969.

Lewis, B. and Von Elbe, G., *Combustion, Flames and Explosions of Gases*, 2nd ed., Academic Press, New York, 1961.

McKinnon, G. P., *Fire Protection Handbook*, 14th ed., National Fire Protection Association, Boston, 1976.

NFPA 921, National Fire Protection Assoc., Batterymarch, MA, 1995.

Phillipps, C. and McFadden, D., *Investigating the Fireground*, Prentice-Hall, Englewood Cliffs, NJ, 1982.

Roblee, C. L. and McKechnie, A. J., *The Investigation of Fires*, Prentice-Hall, Englewood Cliffs, NJ, 1981.

Eliminating
Accidental Causes

6

The elimination of all possible accidental causes of fire is one of the fire investigator's most difficult duties. Unless all relevant accidental causes can be eliminated, the fire must be declared accidental, the presence of direct evidence to the contrary notwithstanding.

Consider, for example, a case where the investigator, during the examination of a warehouse fire, believed that a liquid accelerant had been splashed on and around several pieces of heavy machinery. He positively identified this section of the warehouse as the area of origin and submitted sections of flooring to a laboratory for analysis. The laboratory identified the accelerant as gasoline. The investigator believed he had an open-and-shut case and declared the fire incendiary. A motive was identified and enough information developed during the follow-up investigation to connect the warehouse owner to the fire. He was arrested and charged with arson and insurance fraud.

At the first opportunity after the arrest, the investigator discussed circumstances of the case with an assistant district attorney who would be prosecuting the case. After reviewing the reports and photographs, the assistant District Attorney asked the investigator what measures he had taken to eliminate the various electric motors, switches, junction boxes, and outlets in the reported area of origin as possible causes of the fire. The investigator, in amazement, answered, "I didn't do anything with them. I just told you, I found gasoline splashed all over the place. Why should I waste my time looking at all the rest of that stuff? Look at this laboratory report! It came back positive!"

During the first hearing, after arraignment, the assistant district attorney advised the judge that the case would not be prosecuted, and recommended that all charges be dropped.

What our fictitious district attorney had recognized was the investigator's failure to positively eliminate accidental causes of the fire. This factor alone could have had dire consequences had a prosecution been attempted. In many states, procedural codes and case law preclude an arson investigator from testifying that a fire was incendiary. In fact, this type of testimony during a trial would amount to reversible error, and a mistrial would be granted. In states where these rules apply, a court-qualified fire expert must first offer testimony suggesting that the fire was not an accident by describing the steps that were taken to eliminate all accidental causes. He could then go on to describe the conditions of the fire and any items that were found, including accelerants, delayed timing devices, plants, trailers, and so on. He could also offer testimony, based upon his expertise and experience, describing the illegal purposes for which such items are commonly used. However, the ultimate decision as to whether a fire was or was not incendiary rests with the jury.

Some typical accidental causes of a fire that may have to be eliminated are listed below:

- Electrical malfunction
- Gas or oil service malfunction
- Building heating equipment
- Improper installation or maintenance in the operation of secondary heating equipment including fireplaces, wood stoves, kerosene heaters, and electric space heaters
- Cooking-related accidents
- Misuse or failure of appliances (e.g., clothes dryers, irons, hair dryers, etc.)
- Open flame (e.g., candles, burning leaves) or sparks (e.g., static electricity)
- Children and pets
- Improper storage of combustibles/flammables
- Smoking
- Clandestine laboratories
- Construction, renovation, or demolition (e.g., welding, cement-drying heaters)
- Lightning
- Direct sunlight

Electrical Fires

An investigator must be able to determine conclusively whether or not a fire was caused by electricity. To do this he he needs a basic understanding of

Figure 6.1   An investigator must be well acquainted with the electrical code in force in the state or county in which he is conducting an investigation. Note and photograph all code violations.

electricity and a working knowledge of the basic electrical system. He must also be able to differentiate between electrical damage caused internally (within the system) and externally (by flame).

The investigator should know whether each appliance was on or off at the time of the fire. (In a commercial fire, the investigator should examine the types of equipment and appliances common to that occupancy.) At the same time, he should evaluate the particular appliance (or piece of equipment) in terms of its involvement in iniating the fire. Doing this may eliminate potential accidental causes of the fire, and the investigator can develop an overall opinion as to possible negligence on the part of the occupant.

The elimination of electrical wiring, appliances, and apparatus as a fire cause has been an area of considerable controversy over the past decade. Recent research shows that fires of electrical origin occur far less often than previously believed or reported.

Before a fire is declared to be of electrical origin, the investigator should have hard evidence to that effect. The traditional reliance solely on a visual inspection of electrical components at or near the apparent point of origin of a fire often leads to an erroneous conclusion and mislabeling of the fire cause. If, after careful examination, some reasonable doubt exists as to the involvement (or lack thereof) of the electrical components, the fire investigator should seek a second opinion from a qualified electrical expert.

Terminology

To express clearly what he found during his field examination, the investigator must know the basic terminology of electricity:

Electron — the basic unit involved in electricity. An electron is a negatively charged particle of the atomic structure of matter.

Circuit — an unbroken path through which electricity can pass. When a circuit is interrupted (for example, by opening a switch), it is said to be *open*; when uninterrupted, *closed*. A circuit charged with electricity is said to be *alive*; one free from electricity, *dead*.

Current — the rate at which free electrons pass through a conductor or circuit. Current, which is measured in *amperes* (A), determines the size, diameter, or gauge of the conductor to be used in a given circuit. Too much current flowing through an inadequate conductor will cause it to overheat, possibly starting a fire. *Direct current* (DC) travels only in one direction: out one side (negative) of the circuit and back into the other (positive). All batteries are DC. *Alternating current* (AC) reverses its direction many times per second. Standard U.S. house current reverses 60 times per second and is known as *60 cycle current*. Because of the constant alternation, the terms "positive" and "negative" are inapplicable to the sides of the circuit. When part of the circuit is bypassed, thus making a new circuit of much lower resistance, it is called a *short circuit*.

Potential — the ability of a source of electrons to overcome resistance. Potential is measured in *volts* (V), which are also used to measure differences in electric potential between any two points within an electrical system. The voltage difference between two points determines the insulation required for the conductor(s) connecting them. The greater the difference, the thicker the insulation needed to prevent arcing (luminous electrical discharge) and insulation breakdown.

Resistance — the amount of opposition offered by the conductor or circuit to the flow of electricity (passage of electrons). Resistance, which is measured in Ohms (Ω), is a form of friction and, as such, dissipates some of the electrical energy as heat.

Ohm's law — the electric current i flowing through a given resistance r equals the applied voltage v divided by the resistance. That is:

$$i = \frac{v}{r}, \quad r = \frac{v}{i}, \quad v = ir.$$

The various equations of Ohm's law explain, in readable terms, principles that, though invisible to the naked eye, are measurable with an electric meter for AC circuits; the law becomes:

$$i = \frac{v}{z}$$

where z is the *impedance* (resistance plus *reactance*, another kind of opposition to current flow).

Watt — a measurement of *power* — electrical energy (in *joules*) consumed per unit time (in seconds).

$$1 \text{ watt} = 1 \text{ joule/sec} = 1 \text{ V} \times 1 \text{ A}$$
$$746 \text{ watts} = 1 \text{ horsepower}$$
$$1 \text{ kilowatt} = 1000 \text{ watts}$$

One kilowatt-hour (kw-h) is a unit of energy equivalent to 1000 watts of power being used for 1 hour.

Ground — an area or point used as an arbitrary zero of electrical potential and a common return for an electric circuit; especially, an object that makes an electrical connection with the earth.

Transformer — a device that changes an alternating current or voltage from one circuit to another via *mutual electromagnetic induction*. Changing the current in a given circuit will *induce* a difference in potential in a nearby but unconnected circuit. Transformers can be set up to transfer potentials that are lower (*stepped down*), higher (*stepped up*), or the same as that of the original circuit.

Typical House Service

Normal house service, also referred to as *Edison/single-phase power*, is probably the most common electrical system examined by investigators in the field. A typical house service can be outlined as follows:

1. A utility company generates power (in a generating plant) at 10,000 to 20,000 V.
2. The power is distributed through transmission lines at a suitably high voltage.
3. The high voltage carried by the transmission line is stepped down (by a transformer) to a lower voltage for distribution to individual customers (residential, commercial, etc.)

4. An overhead service connection (*drop line*) permits current to flow from the step-down transformer through the company's meter and into the *service main* (service panel or fuse box).
5. Within the service panel or fuse box, the power is divided into the smaller load-carrying paths called *circuits* or *branch circuits.*
6. Each circuit is protected by an over-current protection device (*circuit breaker* or *fuse*). The circuit consists of a system of insulated wires or conductors. Power flow through selected sections of the circuit is controlled by switches or devices to open and close the passage of current. Finally, there is an electric *load* or demand for power (e.g., lamp, electric appliance).

Figure 6.2 (A) Typical residential electrical meter. (B) Residential distribution panel with circuit breaker type of over-current protection.

One side of a typical house service should be grounded. Usually the service (entrance) cable is grounded at the service panel to a water pipe. The voltage (potential) is the same as that of the earth, about zero. Unless a system is grounded, the fuses or circuit breakers will not blow or trip. A poorly made ground can overheat when it is carrying too much current and can cause an electrical fire.

Overcurrent Protection Devices

As previously stated, each circuit should be provided with an *over-current protection device*, that is, a *circuit breaker* or *fuse*. The service panel itself is protected by a main circuit breaker. The ampere rating of this breaker usually indicates the total ampere rating for that particular electric service (e.g., 100 A). A fuse box would have the same form of protection, but, instead of a circuit breaker, would contain a main fuse (usually of the cartridge or blade type) that also indicates the total rating of the service.

The type of fuse used in any particular circuit should give some indication as to the purpose of that circuit (see Table 6.1). The investigator should count the number of individual circuits branching out from the service panel and note the ratings of the circuit breakers or fuses. In a typical household fuse box, ratings of 30 A or higher should be questioned. The total value of all circuits may exceed the overall service rating, the assumption being that not all circuits are fully used at the same time.

Table 6.1 Type and Rating of Overcurrent Protection Devices

Type	Rating (amperes)
Hexagonal window	15 or less
Round window	20–30
Edison	Up to 30
Cartridge (ferrule)	30–60
Blade	60 and up

The *S-type fuse* is unique in that each rating comes with its own distinct socket to prevent misfusing. Another type is the *time-delay fuse*, normally used with high-horsepower motors. It permits a brief overload of the circuit (by timed-delayed response) to allow for the high power demand when the motor starts. *Cartridge* or *blade fuses* are used to protect the main service panel or for high-demand circuits.

Circuit breakers (CBs) open and close the circuit either by means of internal electromagnets that react to the amount of current, or by bimetallic strips (similar to those in a fuse) that, when heated, separate to open the circuit. Switching device circuit breakers (SWDs) should not be used as on/off switches; such improper use wears them out.

Circumvention and Tampering

Someone who wishes to disguise an intentionally set fire as an accidental electrical fire may tamper with a circuit breaker. This person has to know how to reset the calibration screw set by the CB's manufacturer. If the investigator suspects that such a condition started the fire, he should examine the CB to see if the plastic seal covering the calibration screw has been removed and replaced.

Figure 6.3 Residential distribution panel with fuse-type over-current protection.

Fuses are often circumvented, but the intent is not always criminal. Some people, because of constantly blowing fuses, will overfuse a circuit. This radically increases the danger of fire in that circuit, since the wire insulation may burn before the oversized fuse blows.

Similarly, some people will substitute a spark plug for the S-type fuse. Typical means used to circumvent the protection provided by a properly sized fuse are as follows:

Water in the fuse — People may intentionally place several fuses in a washing machine with the clothes they intend to wash. In time, the water seeps into the fuse. Once the fuse is full, the water is almost impossible to see except for air bubbles.

Penny behind the fuse — In order for the circuit to open, the penny would have to burn through completely.

Packing with aluminum foil — This requires that the glass on a fuse be broken. The interior of the fuse is then packed with aluminum foil.

Driving a nail through the cartridge — The current passes through the nail, completely bypassing the fuse.

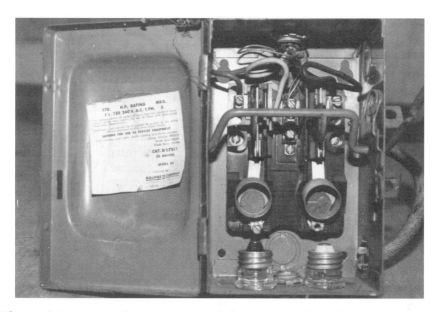

Figure 6.4   A typical fuse type switch box that has had the fuse protection circumvented with pennies.

Service Panel/Fuse Box

A fire that starts within a service panel (or fuse box) is usually accompanied by an explosion. This will usually cause the door or cover of the service panel to blow open. When primary supply lines of opposite potential contact each other due to the action of the internal fire, a rather substantial and violent explosion can occur.

Before handling any electrical components of the service panel, the investigator should verify that the utility's meter or clock *has been disconnected* or unplugged. During the inspection of the service panel, the following should be carefully noted:

- Rating of each fuse or circuit breaker
- Gauge of the wire used as compared with the purpose of each circuit
- Total rating of the service panel vs. total potential load
- The age of the service
- Whether the installation is UL approved
- Whether the service was converted from fuses to circuit breakers
- Whether the service size was recently increased (say, from 60 to 150 A)

A fire within a service panel is usually accompanied by deep charring and extensive heat damage in the area immediately surrounding (and especially above) the panel. In most cases, a clear V pattern is visible on the wall to which the panel is mounted. The base of the V will be approximately as wide as the service panel. Substantial arcing within the box may well be evidenced by the presence of *pop-outs*, holes formed by melting in the metal walls and cover of the service panel.

Disguised Use of Accelerants

Several years ago, numerous accelerated fires were mislabeled as having started in the service panel. These fires were classified as accidental, their cause listed as being of electrical origin.

Various radical publications had printed an outline and diagram recommending the suspension of gasoline-filled balloons as close to the service panel as possible. Delayed-ignition devices were also suggested. The fires that followed this plan were traced back to the area of the service panel, where the deep charring, restricted scope of damage, and the virtual destruction of the service panel itself closely resembled the circumstances that would follow an accidental fire of electrical origin. Time constraints due to burdensome caseloads were probably the chief reason for the ineffective cause and origin determinations in these cases. In any event, countless numbers of such fires were misread before an investigator discovered their true cause and published his findings.

Electrical Wiring

Current is carried away from the service panel by insulated conductors (wiring). Local electric codes mandate the type of wire to be used in any particular region, city, or town. Any electrical code violations observed during the investigation should be photographed, and written notes prepared describing the circumstances. The written analysis of the total electrical system should include all violations or hazards encountered, regardless of their involvement (or lack of involvement) in the fire.

A length of standard electrical wiring consists of a conductor (copper or aluminum), an insulated covering surrounding the conductor (designed to prevent conductors of opposite polarity from coming into contact with one another), and an outer covering.

The diameter (gauge) of the conductor is determined by the amount of current that it is intended to carry. The amount of current is, in turn, determined by the purpose of the circuit. The thickness of insulation is directly related to the line potential: the higher the voltage, the thicker the insulation required to prevent arc-over and insulation breakdown.

Electrical wiring may be sheathed in a variety of different coverings. Armored cable, commonly referred to as BX, is wrapped in rubber and encased in a flexible steel covering. There is also a nonmetallic sheathed cable, commonly called "Romex." Depending on the purpose of a particular line, electrical codes may require that the wire (whether hard- or soft-covered) be encased in a rigid metallic conduit. Ordinarily, electrical wiring is color-coded, with the same color denoting the same potential.

Electrical wire diameter is measured in the American Wire Gauge (AWG) system. Each gauge is represented by a numerical value (e.g., 10 or 14 gauge): the higher the gauge number, the smaller the wire. The carrying capacity, measured in amperes, is directly related to a conductor's gauge. The recommended maximum current rating for a given gauge is the maximum amperage circuit breaker or fuse that should be protecting that line. (See Table 6.2.)

As current flows through a wire, the individual conductors become heated and may anneal. In time, the conductor thins and its total length increases; this accounts for the sagging wires found in the walls of older buildings.

Table 6.2   Wire Gauge and Maximum Current

Gauge (AWG)	Max Current (amperes)	Uses
8	45	House/commercial service
10	30	House/commercial service
12	20	House service
14	14	House service
16	7	Extension cord
18	5	Lamp cord

Aluminum Wire Controversy

In 1979, the National Consumer Product Safety Commission released the results of a comprehensive study that brought a long-debated point to a head. The Commission stated that "for an aluminum-wired home, the risk of having at least one (electrical) receptacle reach fire hazard condition was 55 times as great as for a copper-wired home." The problem with aluminum wire is not that it is a poorer conductor than copper; it is not. Problems seem to result, however, from the method and type of installation and the lack of proper maintenance.

Public awareness was raised by several highly publicized fires whose cause was attributed to aluminum-related electrical fires. Many home owners who lived in aluminum-wired housing developments brought in electricians to correct any electrical problems. Since the cost of rewiring a home with copper wire was prohibitive, *"pigtailing"* — connecting copper conductors within a receptacle to the aluminum wire buried within the walls — was seen as the only viable alternative. Thus, all the connections (duplex outlets, light switches, etc.) would be copper.

The copper-to-aluminum splice, like any wire connection, should be made with great care. The following factors must be considered:

Aluminum has a coefficient of expansion 38% greater than that of copper; therefore, specially designed connectors must be used. The installation of an improper (all copper) connector counterpart may create more problems than it prevents. Experts have suggested that the aluminum wire used be one gauge size larger that its copper counterpart.

Aluminum is electrically positive with respect to copper; an aluminum-to-copper connection, in the presence of moisture, acts like an electrolytic cell, and the resultant electrolysis can create copper salts which interact with and corrode the aluminum. The aluminum wire should be elevated in relation to its copper counterpart and coated with an oxide inhibitor.

Copper fuses at approximately 2000°F, and aluminum fuses at about 1200°F. As a general rule, and depending on the temperatures reached during a fire, an investigator is likely to find that copper has survived at or near the point of origin more often than aluminum wire.

Electrical Wiring Checklist

Probably 99% of all electrically initiated fires are accidental when viewed from a purely criminal-law standpoint. No mental culpability attaches. Yet although negligence, code violations, and the like may not have criminal significance, these same elements could serve as the basis for a civil trial. A criminal investigator could find himself subpoenaed to testify in civil court about a case which has long been closed. In addition, investigators in the private sector must carefully document all electrical aspects of a fire, whether a cause or consequence, when pursuing potential subrogation against either a product or service associated with the electric wiring.

Wiring problems commonly encountered are listed below.

1. Incorrect and inappropriate use of (flexible) extension cords:
    a. Extension cords are designed to radiate heat to the surrounding air; they should be uncoiled when used
    b. If damaged or broken, they should be discarded and replaced
    c. They should not be used in place of permanent or fixed wiring (e.g., snaked through walls)
    d. They should not be spliced
    e. They should not be exposed to physical hazards by being:
        • Run under rugs and other high-traffic areas where walking, rolling, or pushing objects are likely to damage the wire
        • Suspended without support
        • Made accessible to pets
        • Used in areas where there is tension on or a high risk of impact with wires
        • Subjected to sharp bends, knots, twists, pinches, etc.

2. Poor handling of splices:
    a. Mismatched splices
    b. Wires spliced and buried in walls or under floors
    c. Spliced wires not protected within a junction box
3. Other problems, such as:
    a. The familiar "octopus" where more outlets are needed
    b. Nails or staples piercing insulation and contacting conductors
    c. Junction boxes buried in walls
    d. Power strips, either misused or defective

Figure 6.5   In the course of a physical examination, an investigator may observe serious building or other violations. All such violations should be noted and photographed, even if they have no direct bearing on the cause of the fire. This type of photographic evidence may be used later to depict graphically either negligent or reckless conduct. (Photo courtesy of S. Grennan.)

Internal or External Damage?

The most difficult problem when evaluating electrical wiring located at or near the point of origin of a fire is to determine whether the damage to the wire resulted from some (internal) electrical malfunction or was caused by the (external) natural spread of fire. Several factors may be examined in this regard.

Cherry discoloration.   Heat applied to a copper conductor will normally discolor it to a cherry-red hue. The depth of this cherry discoloration will, to some extent, identify the source of the heat. A common pocket knife is sufficient when field-testing a section of involved wiring. Using the blade of a knife, the investigator scrapes the surface of the conductor (carefully — the conductor is likely to be brittle). If, after scraping the surface of the wire, the original color is visible, the source of the damage was most likely *external*, since the discoloration occurred only on the wire's surface. If, on the other hand, the investigator finds that the cherry discoloration runs throughout the diameter of the conductor, then the source of the damage is most likely *internal*, and may involve an electrical short, arcing, or other internal electrical problem.

Sleeving. Rubberized or PVC insulation covering a conductor will react to and move away from a heat source. Therefore, if the insulation on the conductor is loose, the conductor was probably the heat source and the problem was internal. If the insulation is melted to the conductor, however, then the heat source was external.*

Figure 6.6 Before any fire is declared to be of electrical origin, the investigator should have hard evidence to that effect. The traditional reliance on a visual inspection of electrical components at or near the apparent point of origin alone will often lead to an erroneous conclusion and the possible mislabeling of the fire's cause.

Pop-outs. When a short and arcing occurs with BX cable or sheathed wire, the investigator may find *pop-outs* (holes caused by melting) in the external

---

* This particular field test has been recently challenged by experts who question its validity.

covering of the wire. If the wire in question is at or near the fire's point of origin, the investigator must determine if the shorting was due to internal forces or resulted from the normal spread of fire. To make this determination, the ends of the conductors at the pop-outs must be examined. A wire that has been cut by an electrician will have a sharp, pointed end; one that has broken due to an internal electrical short will be rounded (*beaded*) and blunt; and a wire that burned through and collapsed under its own weight will be pointed and annealed.

Overheated wires and connections.   If the electric service at or near the area or point of origin is suspect, the following indicators may suggest a fire caused by an electrical malfunction.

Indicators of overheated electrical connections:

1. The electrical components of the connection (switch, outlet, etc.) show signs of localized heating
2. Discoloration, arcing, pitting, and erosion of the surfaces of the connectors, terminals, and wires
3. Heavier charring to the combustible wood studs/support for the boxes as compared to other nearby stud surfaces
4. Partial or complete deterioration of connections as compared to intact connections in the same enclosure. (e.g., a heavily damaged terminal connector screw on one side of an electrical outlet as compared to the opposite side)
5. Isolated arcing, pitting, or deterioration at the point of origin in a normally nonenergized portion of the electrical system

Indicators of fire cause by overheated wires:

1. Damage to the insulation from internal heating through the length of the circuit from the point of the arc failure to the point where the circuit receives current. This condition must be present on the suspected circuit, even outside the area of fire damage. Signs of internal heating are loose, sagging, or swelling insulation, and insulation charred inside and not outside
2. The overcurrent protection (fuses or CBs) serving the suspect circuit have been bypassed, tampered with, or are of improper size
3. Numerous points of fire damage along the same circuit
4. Charring inside the holes where the circuit passes through wooden structural members

Figure 6.7 Examine all duplex outlet receptacles in the area of origin. This outlet and wiring were a consequence of the fire, not a cause.

The following conditions are necessary for electrical fires:

1. A completed energized electrical circuit
2. Electrically powered equipment or lighting fixtures that depend on the suspected connection must be drawing current at the time of the fire
3. An overload or fault condition allowing excessive current to flow
4. Improper overcurrent protection
5. Suitable combustibles present at the point of origin*

Electrical Outlets and Switches

Electrical receptacles are usually rated at 15 A; snap switches may be rated at 5 A. With constant use, either of these may become worn, resulting in pitting and arcing on the contact surface — the term *hot switch* is sometimes applied. As the contact surface loses tension, additional resistance may be created, which may cause overheating when used. Foam-type insulation, which was recently banned due to health hazards, had been widely used in place of fiberglass home insulation. When the foam was introduced into the space between the inside and outside walls of a house, it completely filled the void. However, in so doing, it formed a tight and complete blanket around

* From NFPA 907M, "Determination of Electrical Fire Causes."

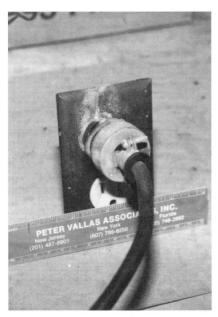

Figure 6.8 Electrical fires generally start slowly and are usually preceded by odor or other indicators of an electrical problem.

all junction, switch, and outlet boxes in the wall, preventing these boxes from dissipating heat from their surfaces. The heat trapped in the junction boxes may cause premature breakdown of the insulation of those wires housed within them.

Electrical Lighting

Fluorescent Lights

Fluorescent light fixtures should be individually protected with a 3-ampere fuse. The basic components of a fluorescent lighting fixture are a fluorescent bulb, the base, the *ballast* starter, and a fuse. Older ballasts still in use are considerably more hazardous than the newer, thermally protected ones now required by electrical codes. This protection takes the form of a system of internal bimetallic strips that open and close to alter the flow of current as the ballast heats and cools.

Poor maintenance schedules are one factor in fires started by fluorescent lights. When old fluorescent bulbs are left in fixtures for too long, the ends of the bulbs become dark and eventually black. These older blackened bulbs draw increased voltage, which may cause the ballast to overheat dangerously and possibly ignite. To avoid this condition, fluorescent bulbs should be replaced regularly.

Incandescent Lights

Incandescent bulbs have caused many accidental fires. They have also served as the source of ignition for a number of incendiary fires. Many times, tracing the cause of the fire to a light bulb is much easier than determining whether the fire was set or accidental.

New light fixtures, whether they are traditional (e.g., a desk lamp) or distinctive (e.g., a recessed unit), are generally rated by the manufacturer as to their maximum allowable bulb wattage. When this is exceeded, a condition called *overlamping* exists. The danger in overlamping is that the envelope temperature of the oversized bulb may ignite a lamp shade or other nearby combustible. The high temperatures trapped in an installed recessed fixture can cause pyrolysis of the adjacent ceiling joists or actual ignition of certain commonly used ceiling materials or insulation.

In several instances, people have intentionally buried or insulated a bare light bulb in combustible material to create a delayed ignition device. In one case, a person wrapped a 60-watt bulb several times with toilet tissue, then buried it in a pile of dry rags and clothing on an upper shelf in a closet. He then turned on the light switch and energized the bulb. The tissue paper ignited in about 25 minutes. Ignition occurred because the bulb's envelope temperature was absorbed by the toilet tissue, rather than dispersed into the surrounding air. Table 6.3 illustrates the temperatures associated with various bulb wattages.

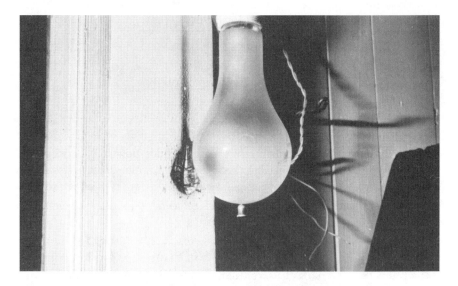

Figure 6.9 An excellent example of pyrolysis from a low heat source. The oversized (150-watt) bulb was installed in a do-it-yourself fixture, too close to combustibles. Notice the charring on the closet door frame.

Table 6.3 Filament and Envelope Temperatures

Wattage (W)	Filament Temp. (°F)	Envelope Temp. (°F)
100	4000–5000	200–350
200	4000–5000	295–500
300	4000–5000	380–650

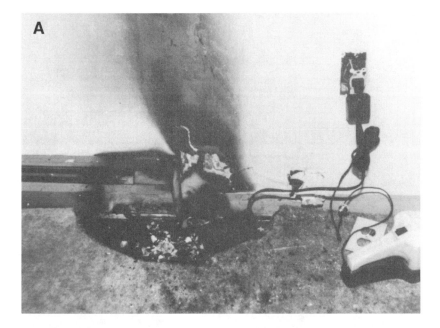

Figure 6.10 Improperly installed electric baseboard heater (A) failed at connection between distribution wire and manufacturer's connector wires (B).

Figure 6.11 Confirm that electrical equipment alleged to have caused fire was, in fact, plugged in. (A) Arrow shows extension cord alleged to be plugged in; (B) note the weather-tight outlet covers are closed. Plug end of extension cord is indicated by arrow.

Although incandescent bulbs rarely survive fires (or routine fire suppression and overhauling operations), an investigator can readily determine whether or not a particular bulb was energized at the time of the fire by examining its filament. If the bulb was energized (live) when the envelope ruptured, the filament is blackened by sudden exposure to the surrounding cooler air. On the other hand, if the filament has maintained a shiny metal appearance, then it was cool (not energized) at the time the envelope ruptured.

Sunlamps and Heat Lamps

Because of their purpose, sun or heat lamps are worthy of special mention. Sunlamps are designed to generate heat rays and are have specially designed bulbs. When energized, a 250-watt sunlamp can have an envelope temperature anywhere between 400° and 700°F. The fixture itself must be equipped with a porcelain or other heat-resistant receptacle, because the socket can easily exceed 300°F.

Electric Motors

The operation of an electric motor is based on the principle of electromagnetism. Reversing magnetic fields (like and unlike poles) cause the motor to turn. Magnetic forces are concentrated in a magnetic field that surrounds each pole. The strength of the field is directly related to the amount of current carried. Problems occur when foreign objects (dust, moisture, metal filings etc.) get into the housing, the motor is subjected to vibration, or its bearings are worn or misaligned.

To field-test an electric motor, spin the motor shaft. If it is stuck, the problem is most likely internal damage caused by a breakdown in lubrication and fusing of the ball-bearings (internal friction). Any electric motor should be operated on a separate circuit (have its own circuit breaker or fuse).

Electric Blankets

To eliminate an electric blanket as the source of ignition for a fire, the investigator should examine the contact points in its thermostat for signs of pitting or arcing. Electric blankets should not be tucked in under the mattress, left on all the time, folded up into a ball on the bed, or insulated or covered with other blankets.

Low-Voltage Circuits

Because of their low arcing potential, low-voltage circuits rarely cause electrical fires. A typical low-voltage circuit might consist of a step-down transformer connected by 20- or 22-AWG insulated wire to a doorbell or alarm system. Most electrical problems that involve a low-voltage circuit can be attributed to some transformer malfunction. Such a malfunction can cause the insulation to burn completely off the light-gauge wire.

Lightning

Lightning, although comparatively rare, has started many accidental fires. The physical signs of a lightning strike will be obvious to the trained investigator: holes blown in concrete, shattered wooden beams, and scorch marks that follow the course of wiring. A lightning strike is usually verifiable through interviews and weather records.

Figure 6.12 Lightning is one of the natural causes of fire.

An investigator should know that when lightning strikes a transformer, two to three times the normal voltage will go to ground even when lightning resistors are in place. Even so, the fuses may not blow; the lightning-induced surge of current is too brief. It has been estimated that the electricity released by one bolt of lightning (if harnessed) could power a small town for 3 months. Lightning bolts average 24,000 A, but can exceed 200,000 A and their potentials can range up to 15,000,000 V.

Lightning strikes occur in two basic ways, cloud to cloud and cloud to earth. However, in the cloud to earth case, charges of opposite polarity are generated in the cloud and the ground below. Subsequently, a discharge occurs and the lighting bolt (discharge), which appears to be from cloud to ground, actually extends from both cloud and ground, meeting in mid-air to complete the strike.

There are four basic paths by which a lightning discharge may enter a structure:

1. By striking a metal object, such as a television antenna, air conditioning unit, metal flashing, or other protrusion above the building's roof
2. By direct strike to the structure

3. By a strike to a nearby taller object or structure allowing for transient horizontal surges to the building through trees or other paths of current discharge
4. By striking nearby public utility power lines, phone lines, or television cable

The transient high voltage surge follows a path of least resistance to ground. During its travel, there may be transient surges to the distribution wiring, plumbing, or other grounded items in the electrical system.

When electrical storms are to be ruled out as a possible accidental fire cause, it is necessary to obtain a certified copy of weather records for the time span surrounding the date of fire loss. National weather service organizations as well as private companies can supply both surface weather observations and weather radar data to confirm the presence of thunderstorms in a specific area. Such information may include a lightning strike map which records the actual number of strikes in an area.

Gas Fires

Gas and Flammable Vapors

Natural gas, liquid petroleum gases (LP), and other flammable vapors have been involved in numerous fires and explosions. Experience indicates that most gas- or vapor-initiated fires are accidental. Negligence, human error, simple ignorance, and mechanical defect are the leading contributing factors. Thus, an insurance company may refuse payment on the grounds that the fire or explosion was the result of negligence or some unreasonable conduct on the part of the insured. The fact that criminal (arson) charges are not forthcoming does not preclude insurance companies from seeking relief in *civil* court.

Gaseous fuels have, however, been used to accelerate incendiary fires. In such cases, the "torch" is either one of two extremes: *highly* skilled or blatantly amateurish. The unpredictability of gaseous fuels and the inherent danger associated with their use virtually preclude their use by professional torches. After all, a torch's intent is to destroy a building, not to risk his life. Generally, when a gaseous fuel is used as an accelerant, the investigator should focus on the owner of the property or on the person who will profit the most from the fire.

Figure 6.13

Figure 6.13 (A) Arrow indicates point where lightning hit the building; (B) charred facia board. Many lightning strikes result in only minor fire damage. However, confirming the cause as lightning may require extensive investigation and documentation of physical evidence (C–D).

Natural Gas

Composition

Commercial natural gas is a mixture of methane (90 to 95%), ethane, and other flammable and inert gases. It contains no carbon monoxide (CO) and is, therefore, nontoxic. By itself, it is colorless and odorless. Commercially produced mercaptan, which contains sulfur in place of oxygen, is added as a safety measure to give natural gas its distinctive odor and serve as an olfactory warning, protecting against the inadvertent accumulation of natural gas (e.g., due to leakage or appliance malfunction).

Combustion

The combustion of natural gas is clean and smokeless. When oxidized, it produces a nonluminous flame (Bunsen type), blue in color. The inner and outer blue cones of the flame should blend, and yellow flame tips should be absent. A yellow flame indicates an insufficient primary air supply.

The burning of an overrich gas–air mixture results in a condition called *carboning*; as a result of incomplete combustion, free carbon is deposited and collects on surfaces surrounding the gas jet (e.g., the burner cap head).

The oxidation of too lean a mixture can also be seen with the naked eye. This condition is indicated by a clear distinction between the inner and outer

Figure 6.14 (A) A natural gas explosion is evidenced by structural components (walls, roofs, foundations, etc.) moved or shattered, and followed by fire. (B) It is important to document and preserve the gas supply equipment.

blue cones that make up the flame, and is usually accompanied by popping noises.

The ideal oxidation of methane is shown by the following formula:

$$7 \text{ air } (O_2 + N_2) = 4CH_4 > 7N_2\uparrow + 2CO_2\uparrow + 8H_2O6 + 2CO\uparrow$$

The complete oxidation of one cubic foot (1 foot³) of natural gas produces approximately 1055 Btu. (Btu is the technical name for the British thermal unit, which is the amount of heat needed to raise the temperature of 1 lb of H_2O 1° F.)

Residential Gas Service

The local gas utility company supplies natural gas to customers through underground transmission pipes, commonly known as mains. The mains traverse the area serviced in a grid-like configuration. The gas pressure (*service pressure*) in a main can be as low as 1 pound per square inch (PSI) and as high as 35 to 100 PSI.*

A *house service* line branches off the main and connects the main to the house meter. House service is generally a lower-pressure line than the main; where necessary, a *pressure regulator* reduces the main pressure for house service.

The *gas meter* is a mechanical device that measures, for billing purposes, the flow of gas as it is used. Gas meters are generally made of tin, with soldered joints, or of an aluminum alloy, with screwed joints (the latter is called a *hard-cased* meter). A utility's liability generally ends at the inlet cone of the gas meter.

The various gas appliances (*loads*) in the customer's home are connected to the gas meter by rigid gas pipes called *house piping*. The gas requirement for a load (in cubic feet) is determined by dividing its Btu output by 1055 (the maximum Btu output derived from oxidizing 1 ft³ of methane). The Btu output of a gas appliance, along with the make and model number and other pertinent information, appears on a plate (usually metal) attached to it.

Venting

All automatic gas appliances should be vented. No unvented gas appliance should be operated continuously. Where venting is required, the diameter of the flue pipe must be properly sized, and its length must not exceed the maximum specified on the appliances or by local code. A flue pipe should also be properly *pitched* (sloped): ¼ in./ft is common. Certain appliances, such as a gas clothes dryer, must be vented independently and not to an existing furnace chimney. The oxidation of methane creates large amounts of water vapor as a by-product. This moisture can create problems and should be vented. A gas clothes dryer will evaporate approximately 1 gallon of water per load in addition to the water vapor created during the oxidation of the fuel.

---

* Gas pressure is measured with a manometer, which is a water filled, U-shaped glass tube. The manometer is read in inches of water (1 inch H_2O = 0.036 PSI). Service pressure is either *low* (below 1 PSI), *medium* (1–15 PSI), or *high* (15–100 PSI).

Liquid Petroleum Gases

In many parts of the country, bottled liquid petroleum gas (LP) is used for heating and cooking. For example, so-called suburban propane is 90% propane, 5% ethane, and 5% butane. These gases, which include propane, butane, and acetylene, are also commonly found at the scenes of industrial fires. Their presence at the scene of any fire requires that the investigator clearly document and explain whether and how they were involved.

Gas Investigation

To correctly evaluate the role, if any, that gas may have played in a fire, the investigator must identify the suspected gas or vapor, determine its source, and locate the point of ignition.

Identifying the Gas or Vapor

A suspected gas can be identified by laboratory analysis. Characteristics include: ignition temperature, flammable (explosive) limits, vapor density, and boiling point (see Table 6.4 "Fuel and Its Physical States" in Chapter 4, p. 61). Once quantified, the values associated with each of these properties serve as a "fingerprint" (set of parameters) that differentiates one gas from another.

Table 6.4   Characteristics of Several Common Gases

Gas	Ignition Temp. (°F)	Flammable Limits (%)	Vapor Density	Boiling Point (°F)
Methane	999	5.3–14.0	0.6	−259
Propane	871	2.2–9.5	1.6	−44
Butane	761	1.9–8.5	2.0	31
Hydrogen	1085	4.0–75.0	0.1	−422
Acetylene	571	2.5–81.0	0.9	−118
Ethane	959	3.0–12.5	1.0	−128
CO	1128	12.5–74.0	1.0	−314

The investigator should carefully select and package samples of porous materials, such as cinder blocks, plasterboard, and carpeting. In any fire investigation where evidence or samples are collected, great care should always be taken in the selection process. It should not be done in a haphazard fashion. Consider the following:

- Where was the concentration of the suspected gas the greatest? Many small samples, packaged correctly, are better than a limited number of large (bulk) samples.
- Where might I find samples that were least affected by the fire itself or by fire suppression operations?

Determining Source

In any gas-related explosion (pressure release) or fire, the investigator must identify the source of the suspected gas. The type of gases that are most often encountered are natural, propane, methane (sewer, sump) and, on rare occasions, hydrogen.

The accidental sources of *natural gas* and *propane* are similar enough to be discussed together. In general, the pressure of the gas is due to some form of leakage due either to mechanical failure or to defective piping; for example:

- Cracked pipes, especially around threaded fittings, due to sudden impact against or excessive weight placed on the damaged pipe
- Improper use of flexible gas tubing (e.g., between floors or through walls)
- Malfunctioning or improperly installed gas appliance (e.g., furnace, water heater, dryer, or space heater)

Note that the piping in a gas supply system will *never* unscrew as the result of a fire or explosion. If a threaded pipe *is* unscrewed from a fitting, examine the pipe for fresh tool marks.

Sewer or *sump gas* may be found as the result of a faulty or improperly built water (sewer) line — for example, if there is no trap in the plumbing to prevent sewer gases from escaping back into the structure, or if there are cracks in the sewer line. In the case of methane gas, an investigator may also have to examine the history of the land on which the structure was built: it might have been the site of a landfill (dump), which would account for the presence of methane (sewer gas).

To the best of my knowledge, little is known about the source of hydrogen gas which has occasionally been found in the basements of private homes. In one case, an expert called to the scene of a gas explosion in a private home positively identified the cause of the explosion as the ignition of hydrogen gas. However, he was at a loss to determine the source of the gas, other than to state that it may have worked its way up to the surface from some point in the earth.

Locating Point of Ignition

The point of ignition in a gas-related fire or explosion is obvious in some cases, and determined by the investigator's educated assumption in others. When a flash fire results, causing only scorch damage, the burn patterns may indicate the fire's extension away from the point of ignition; backtracking locates the point of ignition. However, when a structure has suffered severe damage, the investigator may develop a list of several probable points of ignition. Typical ones include: heated machine parts, due to friction; spark

or arc from a nearby piece of electrical equipment or other electrical installation; and gas-fired furnace or water heater suddenly "kicking on."

In one actual case, the point of ignition was determined to be a short
circuit in an energized doorbell. A neighbor testified that when he rang his
neighbor's doorbell, the house literally blew up.

Gas-Related Hazards

During the post-fire evaluation, an investigator must determine if any hazards
related to the provision or use of natural gas service contributed to, caused,
or existed before the fire. In completing this evaluation, look for the following:

- Signs of tampering at the meter
- Evidence of tampering (e.g., tool marks) at any connection of the
  house piping
- Improper installation of appliances
- Misapplication of equipment
- Incorrect burner adjustments
- Code violations (e.g., improper use of flexible pipe)
- Improper or inadequate venting
- Missing or loosened house piping components (*note*: Under no cir-
  cumstances will a threaded fitting unscrew by itself. This includes caps
  or plugs on pipe endings)
- Appliances used in inappropriate locations (e.g., in the presence of
  flammable or explosive vapors or dusty atmosphere)
- Auxiliary (e.g., portable) heaters used as the primary heat source

The investigator must also document and evaluate the building's history:

- Have there been complaints alleging gas odor?
- What do the utility's records show for service calls at that address?
- How do meter readings compare over time? Are there unusual volumes
  or recent changes in use?

Role of the Gas Company

Most utility companies have well-trained investigative units, which will
respond to any fire where gas is suspected, since any such fire potentially
represents a substantial financial liability to the company. In my experience,
these investigators are very professional and eminently qualified in the analysis of gas-related incidents.

Such "in-house" investigative staffs are not restricted by personnel and
budgetary constraints, as are their state and municipal counterparts. They

examine and document every scene where gas is suspected with an eye toward eventual court presentation. Their laboratory results, photographs, and investigative reports are usually available to other interested parties. (Any investigative results obtained from the company should, of course, be double checked for accuracy.)

A typical utility-run investigation includes the following procedures:

1. Inspect every gas-fueled appliance
2. Note dial settings (whether on or off)
3. Examine piping and connections
4. Check local fire department records for number of false alarms
5. Check for thermostat failure
6. See if copper or plastic inserts are needed in the feedline*
7. Photograph burn patterns and/or damage due to explosion
8. Identify gas-related scorch pattern
9. Determine whether the explosion was soft (gas) or high order (explosives, etc.)
10. Identify point of ignition and source of ignition
11. Trace source of gas

Fuel Oil Fires

Building Heating Equipment

As a general rule the investigator should examine the building's heating equipment. This should be done even where the fire does not involve the heating system. In every case, the investigator should be able to describe (at deposition or trial) the steps taken in eliminating the heating system as a cause of the fire. Local utility companies are usually very cooperative in helping in the evaluation of the heating equipment (furnace or boiler).

Combustion theory is the study of combustion under perfect conditions, which cannot be achieved in the field. The percentages referred to are approximate, i.e., air contains approximately 21% oxygen — it is 20.9% oxygen.

Fuel oil used in home heating — which includes one-, two-, or three-family dwellings, up to approximately 400,000 Btu's — comes in two grades: #1 and #2 fuel oil.

---

* Because of the effects of moisture, the cast iron feedlines from the main to the house have been known to become porous. To correct this condition, copper inserts (inner sleeves) are used. However, because of the value of copper, such inserts have sometimes been stolen, leaving the feedline in disrepair. More recently, plastic inserts have been used to discourage such thefts, but these are still subject to vandalism.

Figure 6.15   As a general rule, the investigator should locate and examine the building's heating equipment.

Number one fuel comes in varying grades which vary slightly in viscosity and purity. Among these are "K" kerosene, "K #1" kerosene, and various grades of jet aircraft fuels. The #1 fuel group produces about 135,000 Btu/gal when properly burned.

Number two fuel comes in two basic grades: home heating oil and diesel engine fuel. However, diesel fuel varies with the additives used for different applications. Because of the additives in diesel fuel, only home heating oil should be burned in a home heating system. This will produce 140,000 Btu per gallon when properly burned.

Combustion is the rapid oxidation of a mixture of combustible matter and oxygen. The process begins when heat in an adequate amount is added to the mix. The combustible matter we will be dealing with is fuel oil, containing 85% carbon and 15% hydrogen. The oxygen is in the air, which contains 21% oxygen and 71% nitrogen. The heat comes from an electric spark.

The chemical reaction which produces heat #1 begins with a spray of oil from a nozzle which breaks the oil into small droplets. This is mixed with air and ignited by an electric spark. The carbon in the oil combines with the oxygen in the air to produce heat #1. The nitrogen in the air passes through the process unchanged. Heat #2 begins with the same droplets of oil. It is mixed with air and ignited. The hydrogen in the oil combines with the oxygen in the air to produce heat #2. The nitrogen in the air passes through the process unchanged. Heat one is produced by the chemical reaction of the mixed carbon and oxygen. The by-products of this reaction are carbon dioxide, nitrogen, heat, light, and smoke. Smoke is produced only if the carbon is not completely converted to carbon dioxide. This can be illustrated with the formula

$$C + O_2 + N_2 = CO_2 + N_2 + \text{heat \#1}$$

Heat two is produced by the chemical reaction of the mixed hydrogen and oxygen. The by-products of this reaction are water vapor, nitrogen, heat, and light. This can be illustrated with the formula

$$2H_2 + O_2 + N_2 = 2H_2O + N_2 + \text{heat \#2}$$

Heat three is the combination of heat #1 and heat #2 with the presence of unused oxygen or excess air. The unused air enters the reaction chamber (the combustion chamber) at room temperature and thus cools the reaction. Heat #3 is a cooler heat. This can be illustrated with the formula

$$C + O_2 + N_2 = CO_2 + N_2 + O_2 + \text{heat \#3}$$

The combustion chamber is the area in the appliance where the chemical reaction takes place. Although it is not involved in combustion, it plays an important role in and has an effect on this reaction.

Combustion chambers are divided into four basic designs: round, irregular pentagon, rectangle, and square. The round chamber is one of the most commonly found in warm-air heating equipment. This shape is one of the best suited for combustion chambers. The irregular pentagon is the best shape for a combustion chamber, because it conforms most closely to the shape of the flame produced by the oil burner. This shape is not widely used because it is difficult to incorporate in the design of heating equipment. The rectangle is the shape found in most boilers of larger residential sizes. The earlier ones were constructed of hand-laid refractory fire brick. This produced eddy current pockets or cool spots in the chamber. To solve part of this problem, a soft fiber refractory in the shape of a bathtub was produced. The square shape has the same eddy current problems as the rectangle; these were solved in the same manner. The square and rectangle are widely used in boilers because the shape helps distribute the heat evenly over the heat exchanger.

Reflected heat from the combustion chamber helps in the more complete combustion of the oil fuel. This reflected heat vaporizes the fuel, allowing the oxygen in the air to come in close contact with oil, causing more complete combustion. The temperatures reached in an oil flame from a modern gun burner can, if allowed to come in contact with it, damage the metals of the furnace or boilers.

Combustion chamber size is measured in square inches of volume. The size (in.²) of the chamber determines the amount of fuel that can be properly burned. A chamber too small for the amount of fuel and air entering it will cause incomplete combustion (soot) and allow the flame to impinge on unprotected metal areas. If the chamber is too large for the amount of fuel being burned, the reflected heat decreases, the vaporization of fuel drops, the efficiency of the equipment drops, and the water vapors produced are not properly expelled, causing deterioration of metal parts. The height of the chamber is also an important factor. If it is too high it will interfere with the transfer of heat; if it is not high enough, metal surfaces will be exposed to excessive heat.

Types of systems to be discussed here are residential and light commercial; these systems are most common and make up the bulk of the heating related fires.

Residential systems have a firing rate (gal/hr input) of from 0.50 to 3.00. They include mobile homes, single family homes, and small apartment buildings. The input of these systems is from 70,000 Btu to 420,000 Btu. Light commercial systems are those with a firing rate of from 420,000 Btu to 1,120,000 Btu; they include apartment buildings, office buildings, schools and stores.

Operation of Systems

How an Oil Heating System Works and How It Relates to Fire

Fuel delivery is generally made by a specially equipped tank truck. Oil is pumped from the truck's tank through a flexible hose into the building's storage tank. The fuel is pumped under pressure at a high speed which, under certain conditions, can cause a build-up of static electricity. Although extremely rare, this static electricity can ignite oil vapor causing an explosion and fire.

The fuel system is made up of several different component parts:

Storage Tank

These come in different sizes and shapes. The most common residential size and shape in use is the 275-gal obround tank. In investigating fire or explosions, it is important to note the location of the tank. The measurement of distance between the level of the oil in the tank and the oil pump is critical in determining the amount of lift or pressure on the oil pump system. To determine this critical distance, an accurate measurement of the oil in the tank is necessary.

Fill-and-Vent System

Although this may look unimportant to the untrained person, it is quite important. The fill pipe must be of adequate size to allow the free flow of oil discharged from the delivery truck fill nozzle (it should be 2 inches inside diameter). In some installations, polyvinylchloride (PVC) pipe has been used. Although unacceptable under today's standards, it can still be found as both fill and vent pipe in some homes. One of its disadvantages is that it becomes brittle and breaks when cold. When heated above 165°F, it begins to melt. In a fire this can cause pressure to build in the storage tank because of the lack of venting, and a rupture can occur. It has been documented that within the vent cap, insect action (the building of nests) can restrict venting. At the time of filling, the pressure becomes so great that it causes a rupture of the storage tank.

With reference to static electricity causing an explosion and fire, a rather unusual incident in Broome County, New York can be cited. The oil storage tank was a 275-gal obround vertical tank. The tank was in the basement. The fill pipe consisted of a short length of 2" pipe mounted on the top of the tank. Delivery was being made into the tank with very little fuel remaining. This meant that the fuel being pumped into the tank under pressure, had to drop 3 feet into the existing oil, causing a build-up of fuel vapor in the upper portion of the storage tank. This vapor mixed with the air in the tank to form an explosive mixture, which was ignited by a static spark. Under normal circumstances, the oil fill pipe would have extended outdoors through the sill of the structure. This would have kept the fuel vapor and the static spark separated.

The use of plastic pipe for fill and vent piping in a fuel storage system can cause difficulties to both fire suppression and fire investigation efforts. This can be documented with a fire in Ulster County, New York: this system consisted of two 275-gal vertical obround tanks joined at top and bottom to form a 550-gal storage capacity. In this case, the fire started in the basement. As temperatures rose, the plastic pipe distorted, causing the tanks to be sealed from the environment. Pressure inside the tanks rose because of heat expansion, and one ruptured. Between 450 and 500 gal of fuel was spilled into the super-heated basement. This occurred just as firefighters were about to mount an attack through the front door of the structure, creating a few tense moments among the firemen. During the ensuing investigation, because of the large quantity of spilled fuel, sampling was not possible.

Fuel Supply Systems

There are two types of fuel supply systems. A one-pipe system which exits the tank from the bottom through a spring-loaded valve is commonly referred to by the brand name Fire-O-Matic valve. (Fire-O-Matic Corp., Shrewsbury, MA). This is a fused valve designed to snap closed when the fusing element reaches the preset temperature of 160°F. The handle and fuse have a left-hand thread so as not to allow an unfused handle to be installed.

The second type of system uses two pipes. One pipe supplies fuel to the oil burner, and the second pipe returns unneeded oil to the tank. When a two-pipe system is used, an internal bypass plug must be installed in the oil pump. The two-pipe system is commonly found on mobile home systems, homes with underground storage tanks, or where the storage tank is lower than the burner. This system allows the oil pump to bleed air from the system without the air bleed valve.

When inspecting fuel lines at or involved in a fire, an important point to consider is the return line of the two-pipe system. If restricted, it will build pressure and cause a leak. Restrictions are caused by a number of problems including underground line crushed by heavy equipment driving over it, or by improper installation of the oil return line in the tank (i.e., tight to the bottom of the tank) or ice forming when condensation freezes during cold weather, blocking the return line. This can be difficult to determine because the ice tends to melt during a fire. The place to start is a check of the oil tank for water. This can be done with a paste that changes color when it comes in contact with water. The most common color change is to red or pink. (A check of manufacturer's instructions is recommended.)

Oil Filter

The oil filter is usually made of cast iron and steel. It can withstand heat far above that which destroys the brass fittings and copper piping usually attached to it. Because of this, it is sometimes the only part of the system (fuel delivery) remaining to examine. The manufacturer, size, and location should be noted. In many models, this information is cast into the top cast-iron part of the filter. On a standard residential fuel system with an inside storage tank, the filter is located next to the Fire-O-Matic valve at the bottom of the oil tank. In two pipe systems, the oil filter is usually located near the oil pump at the burner. The Fire-O-Matic valve is a spring-loaded valve designed so the valve shaft is forced into the valve by the spring closing the valve. The shaft is threaded with a left hand thread so the only valve handle it will accept is the fused one designed for it. The valve body is cast brass and, because it is usually located just above floor level, it will be found intact. If it is not, this is an indication that oil from this area fueled the fire.

Oil Burner Assembly

The oil burner is made up of several systems that function as a unit to efficiently burn oil for heating purposes. With the energy crisis of the 1970s,

Figure 6.16 The oil burner assembly is made up of several components designed to efficiently burn oil for heating purposes.

many new and innovative oil burners came into being. As new technology was developed, burners of new design came onto the market; this new breed of burners is known as flame retention burners. In general, combustion temperatures of high speed flame retention burners will be 100 to 200°F higher than nonflame retention burners even though the same oil rate, air fuel ratio, and chamber are used. The first part of the oil burner to be dealt with is the oil pump, which is also part of the fuel system.

Oil pump. The oil pump draws oil from the tank and delivers it to the burner nozzle at a preset pressure, in most cases, 100 lbs/in.[2]. Oil pumps are manufactured by several companies. The most common are Suntec (Sunstrand, Rockford, IL) and Webster (Frankfort, KY). There are limitations as to how high a single-stage pump (standard pump) can lift oil from a storage tank. Care should be taken to document the distance of the lift from the top of the oil reservoir to the inlet of the pump. The lift capabilities of pumps are available from the manufacturers. When a two-line system is used to supply oil to the pump, a bypass plug is installed. If this is installed in a single-line system, the pump will build internal pressure and damage the pump shaft seal. This will let oil flow into the burner at an uncontrolled rate and out of the burner into the surrounding environment.

There are two types of oil pumps used on oil burners: the single-stage (standard) and the two-stage (high lift) pump, which can lift oil to a greater height than a single-stage pump. These two pumps look similar and must be examined closely to identify them. The two-stage pump is usually found on overhead (hung) furnaces.

Booster pump systems are also used in the delivery of fuel in some applications where the oil storage is a great distance from the oil burner. These systems consist of some of the components of an oil burner (i.e., oil pump, drive motor, and flex coupling), and also include a small auxiliary tank, float assembly, and switch. This system is located in a remote area away from the heating equipment. Its function is to draw oil from the oil storage to its auxiliary tank. As the oil burner uses the oil from the auxiliary tank, the float assembly senses the drop in oil level and closes the switch, starting the pump and refilling the tank.

Figure 6.17 The nozzle and electrode assembly is the component responsible for producing the correct combination of fuel, air, and heat (spark). Improper adjustment can cause carbon/soot build-up as shown here.

Nozzle assembly.   The nozzle assembly, also known as the *electrode assembly,* supplies fuel and electric spark to the combustion chamber. The fuel part of this system consists of a flexible copper tube which connects the oil pump outlet port to this assembly. Two types of fittings are commonly used on this tube. They are the standard flare nut and the aircraft flare, which includes a steel sleeve and a long shank nut. Care should be taken in examining these fittings because when exposed to extreme heat they will expand and when cooled they will not fully contract, giving the appearance of a loose fitting. It should be noted that this does not usually exceed $1/8$ turn. If more travel is found, a loose fitting is likely. The oil is carried down the blast tube through a steel pipe with a $1/8$" inside diameter. This pipe also serves to hold the head end of the assembly the proper distance from the blast tube head. This distance is critical to the proper performance of the burner. The nozzle adapter is a special fitting designed to accept the steel pipe at the rear and the nozzle at the front. At the junction of the nozzle adapter and the nozzle, the area is protected from a hostile fire by the steel blast tube. The nozzle should not be loose. When a loose nozzle is found, this indicates that oil may have entered the combustion chamber at an uncontrolled volume, causing overheating of the equipment. In some heating equipment, the internal temperature is not monitored. This will be dealt with later when controls are discussed.

The nozzle is a precision-machined mechanical metering device which atomizes the fuel, breaking it into a fine mist and forming this mist into a cone shape. The cone will be one of three basic types: hollow, semisolid, or solid. The angle of the cone can be from 45 to 90°; as determined by the internal design of the nozzle. The amount of oil that flows through the nozzle is controlled/metered by the diameter of the hole (orifice) and the passageways through which it travels.

Information as to the nozzle design is coded and stamped in the body. An example of this would be ".50 80° A" which translates to $\frac{1}{2}$ gal/hr at 100 PSI pressure. The cone is 80° and it is hollow. Nozzle manufacturers use varying codes to identify cone shape (i.e., A can mean hollow, but H can mean the same). Some special nozzles also are in use; for example, the 6601 181 is used in the Intertherm mobile home furnace.

The passages through which the oil travels are slots cut into the surface of a cone-shaped insert. These slots serve two purposes: they spin the oil, causing the shape of the cone and controlling the amount of oil leaving the nozzle. To help protect the internal passageways and discharge orifice from blockage, a filter screen covers the rear of the nozzle. One problem that can occur is that one or two of the slots can become blocked, causing an uneven cone in the oil discharge. This can cause ignition delay or puff-back. Cases have been found where the cone insert was removed, and this causes over-firing and overheating of the furnace.

Energy to drive the oil burner is supplied by an electric motor. This drives a fan (squirrel-cage type) and the oil pump. The fan is fastened to the motor shaft with a set screw, and the pump is driven by a flexible connector or belt. Motors come in two speeds: 1725 rpm and 3450 rpm. A check of the motor speed should be made and compared with the oil pump speed. If a 3450 rpm motor is installed on a 1725 rpm pump, the oil pressure to the nozzle is significantly increased, and the internal pressure in the pump also rises. This can cause the pump shaft seal to rupture, causing fuel to spray into the surroundings. The speed of the motor and pump can be determined by the windings of the motor and the internal parts of the pump if no markings remain. The outer part of the motor consists of a steel cylinder with caps at both ends, which are called end bells. The outer one supports a bearing in which the motor shaft turns. The inner end bell supports a bearing through which the shaft is extended. This extension is where the fan is fastened. In belt-driven models, the pulley is attached to this shaft extension. In flex connector models, the connector is attached to the end of the shaft. The bearings have lubricating ports into which lubricating oil is supplied during normal yearly maintenance. Excessive oil in these ports can cause lubricating oil to be expelled from the bearings onto the windings and armature, where it can ignite and cause fire in the motor.

The armature is made of laminated steel secured to the shaft. Solid in mass and cylindrical in shape, it acts as a fly wheel as well as the point at which the electromagnetic energy from the windings is applied which causes the motor to turn.

Combustion air is an adjustable air supply that is mixed with the oil exiting the nozzle to support the controlled fire in the combustion chamber. This air is drawn into the oil burner by the fan, and its volume is controlled by an air metering device. In most oil burners, air bands located on the oil pump side of the burner are used for this purpose, and an air shutter (door) is used in some models. Intake air ports can become partially blocked with dust, lint, or pet hair. This causes a rich burn and produces soot. Things to look for in the surroundings are pet beds or dishes, a clothes dryer, or dirt floor.

Look closely at the fan after an oil burner has been in service for some time. The fins can become coated with dust from the air passing through it. As this buildup occurs in the fins, it produces a flat surface instead of the scoop of the concave design.

Many oil burners in service today have an air pattern control device located in the blast tube. This device is a steel plate attached to the oil supply pipe and located part way down the tube.

When evaluating the building in which the heating equipment is located, look for air intakes. The burner needs enough air to support proper combustion. Also important is negative air (vacuum) in the building. This can be caused by vent fans or several chimneys in the structure.

Ignition system.   The ignition system supplies a high voltage electrical spark to ignite the atomized fuel–air mixture to be burned in the combustion chamber. The high voltage used (10,000 volts) is produced by a *step-up transformer*. This transformer contains two coils of wire known as *windings*. The coils are wrapped around a steel core. The winding assembly is housed in a steel outer shell. After assembly of the internal components, a tar insulating material is poured into the outer shell. House current (110V AC) is supplied to the primary winding. This current produces a current in the secondary winding of 10,000 volts. This high voltage current leaves the transformer through threaded brass bolts affixed to the winding ends. The brass bolts are protected from the steel shell by a porcelain insulator. Several types of connectors can be attached to the brass bolts. These range from clips to a flat brass surface.

The aforementioned tar filler can be an asset in fire investigation. The tar melts and flows from the transformer at approximately 400°F. This fact is a good indicator of temperature ranges at the burner location. However, as a trade-off, this can also become a liability as temperatures continue to increase in the surrounding environment. The filler produces a combustible gas which can ignite and cause an internal fire within the burner, consuming both the tar and with burners containing the flexible coupling design, the flexible coupling. In most cases where this phenomenon occurs, if the burner housing is of aluminum, it melts away. This melt-down can be misleading to an investigator who is unaware of this phenomenon.

Oil burner safety shut-down is the job of a control known as the *protector relay*. This relay can be one of two types: heat sensitive or light sensitive. *Heat sensitive relays* use a bimetallic sensing element to create mechanical energy which opens and closes electrical points in the relay. If the proper points do not open in a preset amount of time, the relay locks out. Once in lockout, the control must be reset manually by pressing a button on the cover (usually red). The heat-sensitive protector relay is located with its sensing element in the exhaust gases directly above the combustion chamber or in the smoke pipe close to the furnace or boiler.

Light sensitive relays use a flame detector to sense the existence of a flame in the combustion chamber. In residential equipment, this flame detector is a cadmium cell, which is an electric switch that reacts to light. The cadmium cell will not allow electric current to pass when it is in darkness. When light strikes the face of the cell, current can pass through the cell.

The cadmium cell is usually located in the burner housing area at the rear of the blast tube facing the combustion chamber. Upon start up, if electric current does not flow through the cad cell in a preset amount of time, the relay locks out. This relay must also be reset manually by engaging a red button on the face of the unit. In some boiler applications, this relay is incorporated into the boiler aquastat.

Controls

The control of heat in air furnaces, steam boilers, and hot water boilers is the same whatever the heat source may be: oil, natural gas, liquid petroleum gas, or electric.

When we think of burner controls, the best known one is the *thermostat*. This is also most often blamed for problems in the heating system. The thermostat is the simplest of the burner controls and the least likely to malfunction. It is an electric switch which in most cases contains a set of points which are opened and closed by the heating and cooling of a bimetallic strip or coil. The after-market does have some solid-state thermostats that use a heat sensitive transistor instead of points. When points are used, they are often in a glass tube which uses a small droplet of mercury to bridge the points.

In the discussion of the control of heat we must understand how the heat is sensed. Most of the common controls in service today convert a change in temperature into mechanical energy. The two types of conversion devices use the expansion of a gas or the expansion of two metals laminated together. The laminated metal or bimetallic system uses the principle of different metals expanding at different rates when heated. If steel and brass are joined or laminated at room temperature to form a straight strip, as the temperature of the strip rises, the brass will expand faster than the steel, causing the strip to bend toward the steel side. This movement can be used to open and close electrical points or switches, which is an effective method to start and stop motors or open and close valves. In most controls today, this principle is refined to create a more accurate response by forming the bimetallic into a coil or helix (screw shaped) design. The gas type control uses a sensing bulb at the end of a capillary tube. This tube can be of different length to allow the control to be located some distance from the point of sensing. A bellows is located at the opposite end of the capillary tube. As the sensing bulb is heated, the gas expands and forces the bellows outward. This movement is used to open or close points. A third type of system uses the bimetallic principle in the form of a concave disk called a *thermodisk*. As the bimetallic is heated, the center snaps to the opposite side. This action is used to move a micro switch. This device is commonly called a "clicks on." It is also common in clothes dryer control systems.

The most widely used bimetallic heliac-driven control is the fan and limit switch of a warm-air furnace. This control is located on the furnace with its heliac inserted into the warm air chamber or in the warm air chamber, just above the furnace. This chamber is known as the *warm air plenum*.

The function of the *fan* and *limit switch* is to monitor the temperature in the air chamber surrounding the heat exchanger of the warm air furnace. When a preset temperature is reached, the furnace blower motor starts and the produced heat is distributed through the area being heated. The second purpose of this device is that if the air temperature in the air chamber exceeds the specified limit, the unit denies electrical current to the burner until the temperature in the heat chamber is dropped sufficiently to reengage the burner. It should be noted that the most common device is the fan limit, which accomplishes both functions. However, some manufacturers incorporate two separate units, a fan switch and a limit switch, to produce the same effect. Although few gravity furnaces are still in use today, the furnace design which is referred to as "gravity flow," does not have a blower to force air through the air chamber. The principle used to move the air is that of air rising through the heat distribution system above the furnace and being replaced at the bottom with cooler air from the area being heated. In this particular type of application, only a high limit switch will be found. In some furnace manufacturer's designs, a combination of a fan limit switch using the heliac sensor and the thermal disk (clicks-on) controls is incorporated.

The use of a sensing bulb to control heat is most common in the hot-water boiler system. The sensing bulb is attached to a control device known as an *aquastat*. Depending on its particular design, the aquastat can perform a number of functions. It can maintain a minimum temperature within the boiler, energize a water circulating/hydronic pump, or deny electric current to the burner mechanism if the water reaches or exceeds the preset high temperature mark. The principles of the aquastat are also used in water heaters which use either natural or LP gas or oil as a heat source. The sensing bulb for the aquastat control is inserted into a brass well which is called an immersion well. The well is immersed in the water in the unit being controlled. Other control devices found on hot water heating systems include the *zone valve*. This is an electrically operated valve which opens and closes to allow water flow into a particular area of the heated space by the use of a thermostat which energizes the valve, allowing it to open. A set of points is usually incorporated in the valve. Upon opening of the valve, the circulating pump of the boiler is energized and water is forced through the particular portion of the heat distribution system that the zone valve controls. Zone valves can be divided into two different categories. One type of valve produces heat. The heat moves the mechanical portion of the device through a bimetallic apparatus. This mechanical energy opens the valve and closes the points. The second type is a motorized valve. These are divided into two categories. One is continuous motion, meaning as it revolves in one direction one quarter of a turn opens the valve and the second quarter turn closes it. The third type is a reverse motor which is spring-loaded. The motor energizes and opens the valve. Upon denial of electricity to the valve, when the thermostat is satisfied, the spring-loaded mechanism of the valve causes it to close.

Another type of control system used in hot water heat is the *pump and relay system*. This consists of a thermostat located in a specific area of the heated building, which energizes a relay. The relay in turn energizes a pump which pumps heated water to this specific area of the building. This system is most commonly found in multiple residential dwellings and light commercial applications. However, it can also be found in single family residential applications.

The other common type of boiler is the *steam boiler*. The control for a steam boiler is known as a *pressure troll*. This control monitors steam pressure in the system, including the vessel of the boiler and its attached distribution piping. The pressure troll is a simple electrical switching device which uses steam pressure against a bellows to open and close the points within the control. In multiple dwelling applications, a combination of more than one pressure troll can be found. Some states require a 100% shutdown secondary pressure control. This second control is set at a higher pressure than the operating pressure troll. It shuts the system down should the pressure reach the preset pressure limit. This particular pressure troll does not reset itself when the pressure drops, and the boiler must be checked by service personnel to reset the unit and determine the cause of the excessive pressure.

Although the *pressure relief valve* is a mechanical device, it can be grouped with the controls of boiler systems, both hot water and steam. Its function is to relieve excessive pressure in the system. The pressure relief valve is a simple mechanical device which uses a predetermined pressure on a valve mechanism. The pressure is produced by a spring. When the pressure on the boiler side of the valve seat exceeds the force being applied by the spring, the valve opens and allows excess pressure to be vented into the atmosphere around the boiler. The excess pressure can be in the form of steam or hot water in the hot water boiler application. A similar device is installed in water heaters; it also includes a temperature sensing portion which uses a sensing bulb. When the temperature of the water exceeds the preset temperature, the valve opens and allows discharge of hot water and its replacement with cold water through the *water fill valve*. The water fill valve on the hot water boiler application is also referred to as a *pressure reducing valve*. This can also be considered a control since it monitors the water pressure in the hydronic system and adds water as needed. In most residential and light commercial applications where the building does not exceed three stories, the usual pressure within the hydronic system is 12 to 15 PSI. This water feed apparatus is attached to the domestic water system and reduces the pressure of that system to the operating pressure of 12 to 15 PSI, thus the term, "pressure reducing valve."

The steam boiler has a device known as the *low-water cut-off*. This device incorporates a float or other water sensing device (usually electronic) to sense the water level in the boiler. If the water drops below the operating level, the low water cut-off interrupts the current to the burner and shuts the boiler down. These devices are designed with a combination of mechanical and electrical components or are strictly electrical switching devices. The type which combines electrical and mechanical components shuts the burner down electrically, and mechanically opens a water feed valve, which replaces the missing water in the steam boiler. On reaching operating level, the burner is re-energized to continue the heating cycle. The electrical type has two sets of points. As the water level drops, one set opens and denies the burner electrical power, and the second set energizes, closes, and supplies electrical current to an electric solenoid valve that replaces the missing water. When the water level reaches operating height, the burner is re-energized and the heating cycle continues. At the same time, the fill valve is de-energized and no additional water enters the system. Attention should be given to this particular device when investigating fires with origin in and around a steam boiler. Several versions of this device are designed for mounting on the exterior of the boiler and are mounted at two points, one above and one below the water level. The sensing device is *a float*. Several documented cases of failure in this device have resulted in structure fires. This can occur when the float area fills with rust and debris from the heating system and pulls the float in an operating position. As the water boils away, the structural material of the boiler continues to heat to extremely high temperatures. In many cases, the high temperatures are conducted from the boiler into the surrounding combustible materials by the steam pipes directly above the boiler and/or the jacket surrounding it. The float type devices are designed so they can be disassembled to determine if a quantity of this rust and debris is located in the float chamber. This is recommended procedure in all cases where a steam boiler is located in or near the area of origin of a structure fire.

Another device found connected to a steam boiler is referred to as a *condensate pump* or *injection pump*. This device is located on the return line system. Its function is to return the water produced when the steam condenses and flows back toward the boiler. The pump is connected to a sealed reservoir containing a float system. As the water level from the returning condensed steam reaches a certain point, the motor to the injection pump is energized and the water is returned to the boiler.

How a Gas-Fired Heating System Works and How It Relates to Fire

In addressing the use of gas as a fuel in residential and light commercial heating, we start with the fuel supply, which is, in most cases, natural gas or liquified petroleum (LP) gas. In the case of LP gas, the gas is delivered to a storage tank under pressure by a delivery truck. The gas under pressure is in a liquid state and is pumped from the truck's tank to the storage tank. The pressure of the gas within the tank varies in direct proportion to the ambient air temperature and the actual temperature of the gas contained in the storage tank. A rule of thumb for gas pressure is temperature $\times$ 2. This means that at 70°F, the internal pressure within a storage tank would be approximately 140 PSI. The 0 pressure point of LP gas is reached at $-14°$. With this in mind, it becomes obvious that if LP gas is used in a heating system, some control over the pressure introduced to the system must be maintained.

This is achieved through a device or a series of devices known as a pressure regulator. A single regulator is located at the tank in residential and light commercial applications. In larger storage tanks, a series of two pressure regulators are installed. The first regulator reduces the tank pressure to a mid-range, usually in the neighborhood of 15 PSI. The second pressure regulator is located near the appliance on the exterior of the building. It reduces to operating pressure, which is less than 1 PSI and is measured in inches of water column. This measurement is usually reduced to three capital letters, IWC. Failures in the pressure-regulating devices have been documented. When failure occurs and allows the full pressure in the storage tank to enter the heating system far above its design specifications, damage and uncontrolled fires can occur.

You will note, when examining a pressure-regulating unit, a vent is present. This vent allows outside atmospheric pressure to equalize on the external portion on the interior bellows. Weather-related failures of gas regulators have been documented when the vent area becomes restricted due to icing conditions on the vent port.

In a documented case in south central New Jersey in the late 1980s, several LP gas pressure regulators suffered similar malfunctions in a concentrated area; all were directly attributable to adverse weather conditions. These failures allowed excessive pressure to do varying degrees of damage within the residences to which they were supplying fuel.

In addressing natural gas as a fuel source, it should be noted that the gas is supplied to residential and commercial customers at varying pressures depending on the type of main. These pressures can vary from pressure low enough to allow use directly from the main — in this application, no regulator is used to systems considered midpressure — to high pressure systems in which the gas from the main passes through a regulator before entering the residence for utilization by the equipment being supplied. Although in many areas the pressure regulator is located outside the residence immediately adjacent to the foundation, in some cases the regulators are located near the roadside and/or just inside the foundation wall in the basement area. Although not as common, the aforementioned weather-related failure in a regulator can occur with natural gas as with liquified petroleum. Another possible failure of the natural gas regulator is caused by oil which travels with natural gas in the distribution piping of the natural gas utility system. This oil can accumulate in the regulator to a sufficient quantity to hinder proper operation of the device and can allow pressure to increase. Failures of this type are not as sudden with a gradual increase of temperature, and are usually noticed by residents and reported to the utility company for correction long before a dangerous situation exists.

In exploring the possibilities of oil traveling with the system, a device at the apparatus, the furnace, or in the case of a natural gas water heater, near the valve is located an arrangement of piping referred to as a *drip leg*. This simple configuration consists of a "T" with the gas coming in through one of the arms and a short nipple with a cap on the end protruding out the other arm. The "T" lying on its side has its outlet connected to the gas appliance. This allows any oil traveling with the fuel to drop past the outlet portion of the "T" and into the nipple and cap and be trapped there. If a regulator failure is suspected, remove the nipple and cap from the bottom of the drip leg, closely examine the interior; if no oil is present, a distinct line where the oil had been before it boiled away during the hostile fire will still be present. In a gas-fired heating system, the gas is introduced to the burner through a regulator and valve. These can be a combination of two separate devices or what it known as a *combination gas valve*, which incorporates a regulator and a solenoid type valve in a single entity.

In the case of a standing pilot, which is the first system we will address, a safety shut-down device is also incorporated as part of the system. This consists of a pilot sensor in residential applications, most generally a *thermocouple*, connected to either a mechanical or electrical shut-down device, and in the case of a combination gas valve, it is incorporated into the valve body. The electrical safety device consists of a thermocouple sensing the pilot flame. The thermocouple can be best described as a thermoelectric generator. It consists of two different types of metals which, when heated, generate electrical current. The thermocouple most generally used produces 750 mV (3/4 of one volt) of DC. This current passes through an electromagnet and energizes it. The energized electromagnet holds a set of points in the closed position. These points allow current to pass to the burner. When the thermocouple is denied heat, the electrical generation process contained within that entity ceases and the points open with the assistance of a spring mechanism, thus denying electric current to the burner and causing shut-down. The mechanical pilot safety device is installed in the gas supply usually beyond the gas valve and gas regulator and before the gas enters the burner. This mechanism also uses a 750-mV electromagnet to hold a gas valve in the open position. When the pilot flame is extinguished and the thermocouple stops generating electricity, the electromagnet releases the spring-loaded valve and it closes, shutting down the gas burner. It should be noted that in most applications using this system, a separate pilot tube will supply a small quantity of gas to the pilot assembly even though the larger main gas burner has been shut down. In the combination gas valve, a similar mechanical spring-loaded valve is incorporated. However, when denied electric current, the spring-loaded valve closes on both the pilot and main burner gas, completely denying the unit all gas supply.

All these systems use a 24-volt control system. This 24 volts is supplied by a step-down transformer which produces the control voltage. However, a second type of system, commonly known as a *power pile system*, is designed to operate independently of an outside electrical power source. This system is considered desirable in areas where frequent interruptions to electrical power occur, or in cases where there is no electric utility, as in some rural applications. This system has a device known as a pilot generator which operates on the same principle as a thermocouple (i.e., two metals). It can generate larger quantities of electricity at 750 mV. This electrical current directly energizes a 750 mV gas valve controlled through a thermostat specifically designed for this voltage range. In certain applications, the power pile gas valve is fitted with a bulb type sensor and switch which opens and closes the gas valve at a set temperature. This type of system is most generally found in gas-fired space heaters or room heaters.

Gas burners can be divided into three basic types: the ribbon burner, the jet burner, and the power burner. The *ribbon burner* produces a long, thin flame which burns between two heat transfer surfaces. In the case of a warm air furnace, the design is called "clam shell." This type of burner is used in boilers of cast iron configuration, and the flue passageways beneath which the burners are set are referred to as flues. The *jet burner* is also fired into a clam shell design, usually in a forced-air furnace. This burner does not extend into the clam shells, but merely fires a mixture of air and gas into the unit ignited by a pilot light. The third type, the *power burner*, consists of a gas orifice and a forced air intake fan. This type of burner is commonly used to convert oil-fired heating equipment to gas fired. It is also used in certain mobile home furnace applications. The most common problem with the jet burner and ribbon type burner is failure to spread the pilot light to all of the burners used in a multi-burner configuration. Some ribbon type burner assemblies are produced as a single unit with multiple burners and a single small ribbon across the front exterior of the clam shells. This small ribbon ignites the pilot gas and spreads the flame to all of the burners in use for ignition, although some manufacturers' designs include smaller ribbons to each burner. This allows the individual removal of a burner and also makes possible misalignment in these ribbons, which causes improper spread and can allow a large amount of gas to collect in some of the clam shells. When this ignites, a miniature explosion takes place, which can allow burner gases to escape from the combustion chamber into the surrounding environment. The situation is similar in the jet burner application. In examining the power burner, this unit uses an intake air blower of squirrel-cage design with a centrifugal switching device which operates the gas valve. The start-up sequence is as follows. When the thermostat switch closes to call for heat, the electrical blower motor is engaged. When the motor reaches full speed,

Figure 6.18 Some heating systems use a combination of fuel supplies, such as this furnace, which runs on either oil or wood.

the centrifugal switch closes and energizes the gas valve, allowing fuel to flow into the burner. This fuel is ignited with a standing pilot. The problem most commonly found in this type of burner is sticking of the centrifugal switch. When a stuck switch occurs, the make-up air blower can shut down, denying the unit proper make-up air and allowing the gas valve to continue feeding fuel to the burner. This causes an erratic uncontrolled burn which can, under proper circumstances, extend outside the burner into the surrounding area.

An important part of all heating devices is the *exhaust system,* which removes the products of combustion from the structure and transports them to the outdoors.

Incorporated as part of the exhaust system on a gas-fired heating unit is a mechanical device called a *draft diverter.* This is simply an open area which allows the exhaust gases to travel upward and outward to the environment. However, in the event of a downdraft on the exhaust system, it allows the exhaust gas to enter the surrounding environment so as not to affect or blow out the pilot light. Affixed to this downdraft diverter is a sensing unit referred to as a *spill switch.* This monitors the air surrounding the downdraft diverter. In the event that exhaust gases spill out of this diverter, the spill switch opens and shuts down the main gas burner electrically. This is accomplished either through the 24V control voltage or, in some applications, it is installed between the gas valve and the thermocouple which denies the unit the necessary 750 mV to maintain combustion. In this application, the shutdown is identical to that of a pilot light failure shutdown.

With the advent of the modern high-efficiency gas furnace and the increased demand of architectural design for the absence of a chimney, the *direct vent* or *power venting system* for removing exhaust gases has become

Figure 6.19 A fire hazard results from failure to adhere to manufacturer's recommended clearances from combustibles. Note lack of space between hot air plenum and structural wood floor joists.

increasingly popular. This system does not require a chimney, but can be vented directly through a wall. This is accomplished through a booster fan which removes the exhaust gases to the outdoors. Power vent systems can be divided into two basic types. One type contains a centrifugal switching device similar to the one described in the power gas burner, and the second depends on pneumatic pressure changes in the venting system. As with the power gas burner, the power vent which uses the centrifugal switch is susceptible to a stuck switch situation. In this case, if the switch is stuck in the on position at the end of one firing cycle, at the beginning of the next firing cycle, a failure in the power vent exhaust motor can cause an extreme heat build-up in the attached exhaust pipe and the introduction of combustion gases into the surrounding environment and the living space. The pneumatic system operates on the pressures developed in the exhaust pipe. These are monitored through tubing to a bellows and microswitch. As the power vent fan produces a positive pressure in the exhaust pipe, the bellows move and close the microswitch, allowing the gas burner valve to be energized electrically and fire the burner unit. In both cases, the thermostat actually controls the power booster and the point system in the power booster controls the gas burner to produce heat. It is recommended that, when investigating a loss involving a power vent system, careful inspection and tracing of the electrical circuits be made. Instances have been found where the thermostat was wired directly to the gas valve rather than to the power vent. Such improper wiring negates the safety devices built into in the system's design.

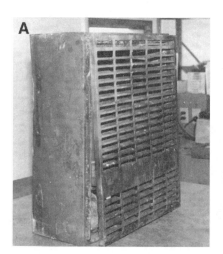 

Figure 6.20 Heating equipment in the area of origin must be evaluated to determine whether it was involved in the cause of the fire. (A) Note that heat patterns on front and side of this wall-mounted heater are external; (B) inside of heater with cover removed.

Auxiliary Home Heating Equipment

Approximately 20% of residential fires in New York State are the direct result of the improper installation, operation, or maintenance of auxiliary heating equipment. The tremendous increase in the price of home heating fuels,

Figure 6.21 The popular use of alternative heating appliances has been responsible for the increase in heating related fire causes. (A) Improper chimney construction; and (B) a cracked flue liner resulted in a fire.

brought about by the Arab oil embargo of 1973, created an almost frenzied interest in supplementary heating units. Millions of home owners turned to solid fuel heating appliances (wood, coal, corn, pellets, etc.), direct vent, propane heaters, kerosene heaters, electric space heaters, and the like in an effort to save on home heating costs. Their presence at the fire scene warrants

Figure 6.22

Figure 6.22 Supplemental heating appliances include: (A) Air-tight wood stove; (B) coal-burning stove; (C) wood pellet stove; (D) convection type kerosene heater; and (E) radiant type kerosene heater.

thorough investigation. Problems associated with use of these heaters include the following:

- Death from asphyxiation due to unvented or improperly vented operation
- Improper installation — location near combustibles, failure to follow minimum clearances, improperly sized flues, and poorly made chimney connections

Figure 6.23 Creosote will quickly accumulate in any chimney that is not adequately maintained and cleaned regularly. Creosote is a major fire hazard.

- Incorrect operation — improper storage of flammable fuels, spillage and overfilling, overheating, improper choice of fuels, use of heater to dry clothes, and use of spot/area heaters as a primary heat source
- Improper maintenance — failure to replace worn or damaged components, and failure to clean and/or inspect components on a regular basis

Cooking-Related Fires

Most kitchen fires start as cooking accidents and are preventable. Thoughtlessness and panic are the two human characteristics that are chiefly at fault. People leave pots cooking on the stove and roasts baking in the oven. When a minor fire starts, they panic in an attempt to extinguish it. For example, people try to carry a flaming pot from the stove to the sink, and one of three things inevitably occurs:

1. They drop the flaming pot on the floor after burning their hands
2. They make it to the sink and set the kitchen window curtains on fire
3. They pour water on the flaming grease or oil and find that small droplets of flaming grease "spit" about the room

Here are some typical accidental causes of cooking-related fires:

- Barbecue grill left to burn next to the house or in the garage until tank is empty
- Food left heating in toaster ovens and counter-top broilers
- Shortening, vegetable, or similar cooking oils overheated and igniting in the pan, or boiling over and igniting on the cooking surface
- Ignition of grease built up in a kitchen exhaust fan
- Dish towels and oven mitts thoughtlessly dropped on or close to hot cooking grills

- Appliances may be defective. Many kitchen appliances have caused devastating loss of lives and property due to overheating or failure of the products' heating components. For the private-sector fire investigator, it is important to preserve these items for future potential subrogation procedures. The manufacturer, distributor, and retailer all may be held responsible in civil litigation. It is important to preserve the remains in efforts to identify the manufacturer of the product and the ultimate failure.

Some of the appliances involved include toasters, toaster ovens, microwave ovens, coffee makers, stoves, ovens, refrigerators, freezers, dishwashers, etc. Also included in this group are outdoor grills, particularly LP, propane, or natural gas fired type.

There are standards and guidelines to protect against the inadvertent or deliberate destruction of evidence through invasive or destructive analysis (ASTM Standards E860-82 and E1188-87).

Exposed or Unprotected Flames and Sparks

Exposed or unprotected flames and sparks may cause many fires, most of which are accidental. However, after close scrutiny, some evince gross neglect or reckless conduct of such a nature as to call for civil if not criminal sanctions. Common sources of exposed flame and sparks include: candles (decorative or religious), chimney exhaust, welding equipment (arc or acetylene torch), static electricity (discharge can produce gas-igniting sparks), electric motors and equipment (sparks from friction or electric discharge), and open burning (leaves, rubbish, bonfires).

Figure 6.24 (A) View of a kitchen counter. The lowest point of burning is on the right end of the counter next to the refrigerator. A "V" pattern can be seen on the kitchen wall above that point. The holes in the wall and ceiling were cut by firefighters checking on possible fire extension. (B) The point of origin was cleaned, and a toaster found on the kitchen floor was put back in its proper place. (C) A view of the interior of the toaster revealed internal flame damage and the residue of a molten, tacky substance. Investigation revealed that a fruit-filled pastry had apparently jammed when being toasted. A child had forgotten about it and had gone outside the house. The pastry ignited and the fire extended to the wall.

A

B

C

Figure 6.24

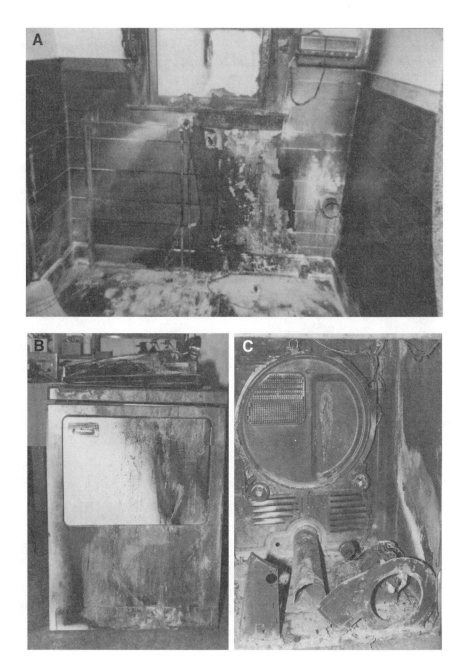

Figure 6.25 Appliance fires have caused devastating loss of property and life. (A) Classic fire patterns from dryer fire. (B–D) This series of photos documents the origin of the fire from within the dryer lint trap area.

Figure 6.25 (continued)

Figure 6.26 Exposed or unprotected flames cause many fires, most of which are accidental. This candle had a defective wick, which ran along the vertical surface. It ignited and burned through, tipping over onto the table and igniting the tablecloth.

Children and Pets

Children, household pets, and farm animals may recklessly knock over candles, kerosene heaters, or other auxiliary heating units, accidentally starting a fire. In one case, the family dog carried or dragged a large throw pillow from the living room couch and dropped it against the protective screen of a smoldering fireplace. A spark ignited the pillow. Fires caused by children playing with matches are an all-too-common occurrence. In New York State, children under the age of 7 years are considered to be infants and not criminally responsible for their conduct. However, the child's parents may be held to be civilly liable for any damage.

Improper Storage of Combustibles/Flammables

All too often, warnings printed on packages or simple common sense considerations are ignored when storing and handling combustible/flammable materials. Some examples of *improper* storage follow:

- Combustibles/flammables are stored too close to heat sources (e.g, furnace, heat vent, or auxiliary heater)
- Pool chemicals or metallic sodium and potassium are stored in damp, moist areas
- Magnesium slowly oxidizes in moist air
- Oxidizing agents or acids (e.g., sulfuric, nitric, hydrochloric acids) are stored too close to combustibles
- Phosphorus may be stored in a damaged container or otherwise exposed to possible contact with the atmosphere
- Vinyl acetate used in paint or other monomers may be stored in close proximity to peroxides or other catalysts

The U.S. Department of Transportation publishes numerous periodicals that list literally hundreds of hazardous and flammable/explosive substances. Any investigation of large numbers of unknown or suspect chemicals may require the involvement of outside experts.

Spontaneous Combustion/Ignition

All things being equal, spontaneous combustion (defined in Chapter 4) will progress more rapidly and efficiently in a warm or hot atmosphere (say, preheated by the sun's rays) than in a cold (wintery) atmosphere. For spontaneous combustion/ignition to occur, at least three factors must exist:

1. The fuel mass or materials involved must be subject to spontaneous combustion; for example, fresh-cut sawdust, grass clippings or hay, soft coal or coal dust, charcoal, or rags or paper soaked with linseed oil (boiled oil)
2. Oxidation (heat production) within the fuel mass must be slow, and sufficient heat must be generated to reach and initiate ignition
3. The self-heating core of the fuel mass must be insulated well enough to prevent the generated heat from dispersing into the surrounding atmosphere

The preheating qualities of direct sunlight (i.e., the greenhouse effect) may very well be a factor in expediting spontaneous combustion.

Smoking

The purpose of our original comments on smoking and smoking-related material as an ignition source was to bring to the fire investigator's attention its overuse as a cause of fire. Although the statistics in the early 1980s confirmed its overuse, nevertheless it is still one of the leading causes of accidental fire death and serious injury. Since our early reporting, there have been two significant studies on cigarettes, smokers, and their relationship to cigarette-related fires. The first was the Cigarette Safety Act of 1984, which was subsequently followed by the Fire Safe Cigarette Act of 1990.

National fire incident databases have shown consistently that cigarettes are the leading heat source in fatal fires in the U.S. However, the frequency of fire death is known to vary among different age groups and gender groups. At the same time, laboratory studies show that under standard test conditions, the propensity of cigarettes to ignite fires is different for cigarettes with different physical characteristics.

Improperly discarded cigarettes, cigars, and pipe ash have been responsible for many structural, vehicular, and forest/brush fires and countless deaths. However, it is also true that smoking products have long been the scapegoat in cases where no cause of the fire could be determined. Detailed and extensive experimentation conducted over the past decade has painted a much clearer picture of the role of smoking products in the creation of fire. Research conducted by the author indicates that careless disposal of smoking material is highly overrated as an accidental cause. The average burn time for cigarette tobacco is between 5 and 15 minutes — an additive to the cigarette tobacco aids in sustaining glowing combustion. Cigars, which do not have such an additive, rarely sustain burning for more than a couple of minutes. Stick matches will burn up to 35 seconds, and cardboard matches

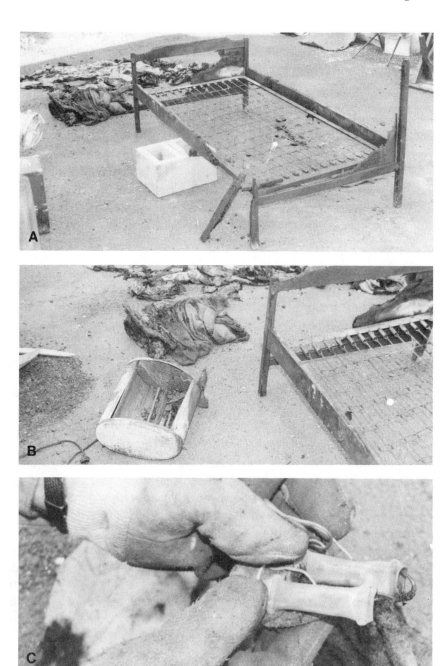

Figure 6.27 (A) View of a reconstructed bed that had been removed from the room of origin. Notice that the headboard had almost totally burned away. The fire was ruled accidental, caused by careless smoking in bed. (B) All other accidental causes had to be ruled out, including an electric heater and an electric blanket. (C) Note the close-up of the contact points.

for only 25 seconds.* Meanwhile, the average time span from the smoldering phase to open-flaming combustion is at least an hour. In addition, the increased use and effectiveness of flame-retardants has significantly reduced the frequency of such incidents.

A cigarette fire is the result of three elements, each of which is necessary if the fire is to occur and each of which may be characterized by greater or lesser degrees of susceptibility. First is the contact between the heat source (the cigarette) and the potential fuel source. Second is the susceptibility of the fuel source to ignite when so exposed. Third is the propensity of the cigarette to light fires when put in this position.

Contact between a cigarette and a potential fuel source is usually the result of carelessness, and people differ in the degree of their carelessness. Therefore, smokers will have different probabilities of discarding cigarettes in places where ignition is possible, and cigarettes may have different probabilities of being discarded.

Once discarded, the cigarette must maintain glowing combustion in order to ultimately ignite whatever combustible it comes in contact with at the time of discarding. Many factors are taken into consideration for this smoldering ignition to occur, not the least of which are the length of the cigarette (not counting filter), the diameter, the porosity of the paper and the density of the tobacco. The average smoldering time in tests has ranged from a minimum of just over 10 minutes to a maximum of 18 plus minutes. Maximum temperatures of smoldering cigarettes vary between 1100 and 1300°F. Most fires originated in mattresses or bedding, upholstered furniture, and trash receptacles.

As for the propensity for matches to ignite combustibles when discarded, the statistics and data to date have not shown any increase in the figures from previous studies. Basically, our original figures regarding stick matches and cardboard matches have remained the same.

Clandestine Laboratories

A *clandestine laboratory* can be defined as a place where controlled substances (i.e., drugs) are illegally prepared or processed. Many of the *precursors* (substances from which others are formed) used in the preparation of illegal drugs can be categorized as dangerous flammable materials. In addition, the gaseous by-products resulting from cooking, baking, or mixing phases in the drug-making process result in the creation of a critical (explosive) atmosphere

---

* Values are for matches in horizontal position, as they might be if accidentally left or carelessly tossed away. Respective burn times for vertical position are 70 and 47 seconds; held down at 30° angle, 12 seconds for both.

in the apartment, basement, or garage where the lab is hidden. A careless act can easily cause a disastrous and/or fatal explosion.

The huge demand for illicit drugs on the open market and the exorbitant profits associated with their manufacture and sale have led to the creation of many such illegal labs. Narcotic investigators speculate that thousands are operating throughout the nation, many under the cover of legitimate business.

If, as an investigator, you inadvertently discover such a lab facility, *proceed with extreme caution*. Several law enforcement officers have been killed and/or seriously injured by explosions at clandestine labs. Follow the same procedures you would at the scene of a natural gas emergency. If you discover a lab as the result of an explosion or fire, immediately contact the local narcotics investigation unit or the regional Drug Enforcement Administration office. They may supply the technical personnel and expertise necessary to complete the investigation safely.

The presence of any of the following may be due to the operation of an illicit drug laboratory:

Odors
  Burnt almond
  Ether
  Peppermint (often used to cover the ether)
  Gas (especially if passersby or nearby residents constantly complain of such an odor)
Equipment
  Gas (Bunsen) burners
  Electric mixers and grinders
  Gas, electric, or portable ovens
  Electric hot plates
  Plastic welding machines
  Pharmaceutical scales or other measuring and weighing devices
Controlled substances
  Heroin (from morphine or morphine base)
  Cocaine
  THC (cannabis extract)
  Mescaline (peyote, trimethoxyphenethylamine)
  Methadone
  Amphetamines
  Methamphetamines
  LSD (lysergic acid diethylamide)
  DMT (dimethyltryptamine)
  DET (diethyltrptamine)
  PCP (phencyclidine, "angel dust")
  STP/DOM (methyl-dimethoxy amphetamine)

Precursors

- Acetone (propane)
- Acetonitrile (methyl cyanide)
- Ammonium chloride
- Benzene
- Chloroform (liquid)
- Dimethylamine
- Dimethylformamide
- Diphenylacetonitrile
- Ethyl alcohol (ethanol)
- Ethyl ether
- Hexane
- Hydrochloric acid
- Lithium aluminum hydride
- Methanol (methyl alcohol)
- Methylformanilide
- Nitraethane
- Potassium permanganate
- Propane
- Sulfuric acid
- Tetrahydrofuran

Construction, Renovation, and Demolition

Many construction or demolition fires involve the use of electric or gas welding or cutting torches without the user having followed minimum safety standards. Molten metals may come in contact with combustibles, starting a fire. In some cases, the inexperienced or untrained welder inadvertently permits the torch flame to touch nearby combustibles or rests the still-hot torch (after use) on combustible material. Propane heaters, which are either used to heat a work place or to dry cement work quickly during winter months, may malfunction and result in a flash fire or explosion.

A common sight at construction and demolition sites during the winter is workers feeding wood scraps into flaming 55-gal drums to stay warm. Sparks and burning embers carried aloft by the heated gases and smoke may come to rest on combustibles elsewhere in the structure and start a fire.

Direct Sunlight

Under unique conditions, the sun's rays may strike a curved section of auto or window glass in such a way that the refracted (bent) or distorted rays passed through the section of glass are slightly more concentrated than they might be ordinarily. This type of condition could not occur with standard flat or sheet glass. An exceptional combination of factors is required before any type of ignition is possible:

1. The room or car interior must be preheated (a greenhouse effect would be sufficient)
2. The fuel to be ignited must be of small mass with a low ignition temperature
3. The slightly concentrated light energy must strike the fuel mass for the length of time required to cause ignition

A working knowledge of the unique combination of condition required to cause ignition through the action of direct sunlight clearly justifies its infrequent linkage to or listing as the accidental cause of fire. However, children playing outdoors with magnifying glasses have been known to start both structural and brush or forest fires.

Product Liability and Subrogation

Once a fire cause has been determined to be accidental, the local authorities have satisfied their legal investigative obligations. At this time, the private sector fire investigator is just beginning the systematic analysis, identification, documentation, and preservation of the cause of the fire. Whether the ultimate cause is the result of a product or service failure, the proper procedures for preservation of the evidence are essential.

Product liability refers to the legal liability that arises out of the design, manufacturer, and sale of products that are either dangerous or defective. Appliances, electrical equipment, vehicles, and television sets are but a few of the recent examples of products that have been involved in such litigation. The idea that a seller may be found liable for injuries caused by a product he/she sells is a relatively new concept. Until recently, the principle of "caveat emptor" was applied (meaning "let the buyer beware"). Under this principle, an individual who purchased a defective product had no one to blame but himself/herself. But, as products became more complex, some sellers began to take advantage of customers by selling them defective or substandard merchandise. Slowly, the courts began to allow the customer to bring civil actions against the seller because of deceit. The civil action bought by the buyer was in tort.

In early product liability cases, the right to sue another because of defective merchandise was limited to those in privity with the sale of the product. This meant that a person had to be an actual party to the sale before suit could be brought.

Over the years, the use of privity as a defense was eliminated by the court. Today, most courts are concerned with the tests of duty, negligence, and causation in deciding product cases.

Under the law, there are three methods of recovery for damages that result from products. They are: negligence, breach of warranty, and strict liability in tort. The recent use of strict liability in tort has greatly increased the number of cases where insurance carriers and individuals may now pursue recoveries for injuries or damages due to dangerous or defective products.

Negligence

Negligence is the failure to use that duty of care which is required to protect others from an unreasonable chance of harm. Before a charge of negligence can be established, specific conditions must be met. These include:

1. There must be a duty owed to the person harmed.
2. The duty owed must be violated.
3. The breach of that duty must be the proximate cause of the injury/damage.
4. There must be actual damages or injuries.

A duty owed to consumers of products and to bystanders is to reasonably foresee harm that might arise out of the use of the product. The negligent act may then be termed the *proximate cause*.

For example, a home suffers heavy fire damage when fumes from a flooring adhesive are ignited by a pilot light. The homeowner sues the retailer for negligence. What relationship would the consumer have to establish between the retailer's conduct and the accident to recover?

The homeowner would have to show that the retailer breached a duty in selling a product and then show that this breach was the proximate cause of the fire. If the consumers asked the sales person if there were any danger of fire in using this adhesive and the salesperson said "no", despite his/her knowledge that prior fires had occurred, the retailer might then be held liable.

The concept of negligence is vital to make product liability cases, since it was the means of breaking the "no privity, no suit" rule. Where negligence is obvious or willful in placing a dangerous product on the market, it is easier to obtain a favorable judgment against the responsible party.

Duties of the Manufacturer

The manufacturer is the entity that makes the product or assembles it and markets it under its name. A company is considered a manufacturer even when it uses components supplied by other companies.

The degree of reasonable care depends on the foreseeable danger if the product is defective. The greater the danger, the greater the degree of care. The manufacturer is required to use reasonable care in designing its product and in anticipating harm from any unsafe design. A manufacturer's duty of care extends only to the expected or intended use of the product. Injury/damage resulting from abnormal use of a product is generally not chargeable to the manufacturer. Abnormal use means that a manufacturer would not reasonably anticipate that its product would be used in an unforeseen or abnormal manner. The manufacturer must warn of any danger from the use of its product. The warning must be adequate (large enough and in a conspicuous place).

As an example, the manufacture of an adhesive is sued by a homeowner who was severely burned while smoking a pipe during the installation of a kitchen counter top using the adhesive. The product failed to contain a clear warning on the label that the adhesive is highly flammable and should be used only in well-ventilated areas away from flame or fire. If the manufacturer knew, or should have known of such danger, but failed to provide an adequate warning. Warnings must be large and in a prominent place on the label.

In cases where the manufacturer becomes aware of a danger after the product is on the market, the manufacturer must then conduct a campaign to warn consumers of the newly discovered danger and/or problems. It is this duty that often causes product recalls.

Defects

The following are a few examples of defects:

1. A physical flaw or impurity in the material/materials of the product
2. A product that uses a dangerous design
3. An unfit, unmerchantable, or unsafe product
4. A product that did not receive adequate testing
5. A product with inadequate warnings or poor directions

Identification of Products

Often during the course of an investigation, the product or components are severely damaged by the fire/explosion. Identification labeling or warnings are not present on the equipment. The following is a list of methods and considerations the investigating engineer may use to establish the manufacturer and proper identification:

1. A careful search and evaluation for any paper products, remains of labels, packaging, or individual names of manufacturers on components which are a part of the item in question.
2. A visual inspection and nondestructive/invasive analysis of the various component parts may help to establish the type of product.
3. Obtain invoices, receipts, bills, and place of purchase from the owner or user of the product. (You should also ask these individuals if they recall the manufacturer's name on the product.)
4. Conduct an exemplar analysis of the same product reviewing the manufacturer's owner's manual, instructions, and cautions.

5. Visiting an appliance or hardware store to evaluate the product and/or similar products.
6. Evaluating other manufacturers products for design, construction, and improvements compared to the product that is the subject of your investigation.
7. Recall research through the U.S. Consumer Product Safety Commission (toll free hot line: 1 (800) 638-2772).
8. Experiments and testing of burned and/or exemplar products.

Defenses

Several defenses are available to the defendant in product liability cases. By recognizing these defenses, the claim representatives can conduct a more thorough investigation. The primary defenses are:

1. Contributory negligence on the part of the plaintiff
2. Assumption of risk by the plaintiff
3. Abnormal use by the plaintiff

The most common defense used is that of *contributory negligence*. In states where comparative negligence is recognized, the plaintiff's negligence may reduce his or her ability to recover.

Assumption of risk is another defense to an action brought in negligence. This defense is used when the plaintiff willingly and knowingly exposes himself or herself to the possibility of danger. Assumption of risk overlaps contributory negligence, but there are some cases in which it can stand alone as a defense. For example, the driver of a car realizes that his brakes are starting to fail, but he continues to drive despite the fact that the red brake light is on and the fact that the brakes feel spongy. That driver may be completely barred from any recovery against either the manufacturer or repair facility.

The final major defense is that of *abnormal use*. A manufacturer/seller is entitled to expect that a buyer will put a product to normal use. Therefore, a manufacturer/seller is generally not found liable if the buyer uses the product in a way it was not intended to be used.

Property/Evidence Securing, Storage, and Destruction

Having conducted your investigation and potential product liability analysis, this equipment is now maintained in your custody. There are very important procedures and guidelines that must be followed prior to testing and evaluating certain types of damaged products or evidence.

The methods of testing and analysis must be determined and approved by all parties concerned. All parties must be advised of the potential testing and have the opportunity to inspect and evaluate the evidence prior to any testing.

Once notification has been made and the testing and/or inspections have taken place, the most critical part is the preservation and/or storage of the evidence. At no time should the investigator destroy or discard any evidence in his/her possession. Your client, the owner of the equipment, and all parties involved in the litigation must be notified and respond with written authorization before any such disposition of the evidence is undertaken.

The two generally excepted standards used for guidelines in the collection, preservation, and analysis of evidence are the following:

ASTM Standard E1188-87, "Standard practice for collection and preservation of information and physical items by a technical investigator."
ASTM E860-82, "Standard practice for examining and testing items that are or may become involved in product liability litigation."

References

NFPA 921.

NFPA 1033.

ASTM Standards E1188-87 and E860-82.

NFPA Handbook 7th Edition.

Peter Vallas Associates Incorporated Research Material.

AccuWeather Inc., State College, Pennsylvania.

Investigating Fatal Fires

7

The impact of unchecked incendiarism on society is most often delineated in economic terms. Arson is described as one of the predisposing causes of the economic blight so evident in our cities. Its costs are often measured in terms of the dollar value of shrinking tax revenues, the high cost of insurance premiums, and the increased burden of welfare benefits. Although accurate, such a price tag approach is blatantly deficient in describing the grief and suffering of the burn victim, or the loss to society, family, and friends of a fellow human being.

This year alone, arson will dramatically impact the livelihood and well-being of millions of Americans. More important, well over 1000 people will die and ten times that number will be injured or frightfully disfigured. Every arsonist, regardless of motive, is a potential mass murderer.

Six-Phase Investigative Approach

The multiplicity of problems confronting an investigator at the scene of a fatal fire is not always obvious. The underlying investigative dilemma is the separation, with absolute certainty, of those incidents that are tragic accidents from those that need detailed criminal investigation.

In the initial stages of the investigation, many questions will be raised that may be hours or even days away from credible answers: Was the fire intentional or accidental? Was the victim alive or dead before the fire? (Arson is sometimes used in an attempt to disguise a crime scene or to destroy evidence of criminality; see "Crime Concealment", Chapter 2.) Who last saw the victim alive? Who discovered the fire? Can enough solvability factors be identified to warrant an aggressive prosecution?

Table 7.1   Estimates of 1994 U.S. Civilian Fire Deaths and Injuries by Property Use

	Civilian Deaths			Civilian Injuries		
Property Use	Estimate	Percent Change from 1993	Percent of all Civilian Deaths	Estimate	Percent Change from 1993	Percent of all Civilian Injuries
Residential (total)	3,465	−9.4	81.0	20,025	−11.4**	73.5
One- and two-family dwellings[a]	2,785	−8.2	65.1	14,000	−10.8*	51.4
Apartments	640	−6.6	15.0	5,475	−13.1	20.1
Other residential[b]	40	−61.9**c	0.9	550	−8.3	2.0
Nonresidential structures[d]	125	−19.4	2.9	3,000	−21.5**a	11.4
Highway vehicles	555	+2.8	13.0	2,325	−3.1	8.5
Other vehicles[e]	75	+36.4	1.8	300	+9.1	31.1
All other[g]	55	−8.3	1.3	1,500	+20.0	5.5
Total	4,275	−7.8		27,250	−10.6**	

Note: Estimates are based on data reported to the NFPA by fire departments that responded to the 1994 National Fire Experience Survey. Note that most changes were not statistically significant; considerable year-to-year fluctuation is to be expected for many of these totals because of their small size. *Change was statistically significant at the .05 level. **Change was statistically significant at the .01 level.

[a] This includes manufactured homes.

[b] Includes hotels and motels, college dormitories, boarding houses and so on.

[c] This decrease reflects 20 deaths in Paxton Hotel fire in Chicago, Illinois, on March 16, 1993, and 47 fire deaths in Waco, Texas, at the Branch Davidian Complex on April 19, 1993.

[d] This includes public assembly, educational, institutional, store and office, industry, utility, storage, and special structure properties.

[e] This includes trains, boats, ships, aircraft, farm vehicles, and construction vehicles.

[f] This includes outside properties with value, as well as brush, rubbish, and other outside locations.

The answers to these and similar questions provide the investigative blueprint for determining the truth.

The following six-phase approach is presented as an aid to the investigator in a fatal fire case:

1. Fire incident
2. Examination of the body
3. Cause and origin/investigative canvass
4. Investigative procedure
5. Follow-up investigation
6. Arrest and trial

The strategy used in this approach is applicable in every case involving a fire fatality. However, the information to be collected during each of the phases may be tempered by unusual or unique conditions. The utility of each phase must be evaluated in light of the facts and circumstances presented in the case at hand.

Fire Incident

The first phase in the process deals with the duties and responsibilities of the first fire-fighting units to respond to a fire in which a person dies or is seriously injured and likely to die. It begins at the time the fire is discovered, and ends with the arrival of the fire/police investigator. The ultimate responsibility for this phase rests with the officer in command of the fire scene. If the fire is considered suspicious, the officer should immediately request the assistance of a fire investigator. In the case of a fatal fire, he should also request the assistance of a *police* investigator; the investigation of unusual or unnatural deaths generally falls within the jurisdiction of the local police department.

Maintenance of the Fire Scene

The credibility of the scene investigation and, to a great extent, any future prosecution is directly affected by the extent to which the fire scene has been disturbed. The person responsible for preserving the integrity of the fire scene until the first (fire/police) investigator arrives is the chief fire officer. A chronologic list of all authorized persons entering the crime scene should be kept and given to the investigator when he arrives. Those authorized to enter the fire scene would include police and fire officials assigned to the investigation, the medical examiner or medical investigator, the district attorney/prosecutor or his representative, and so on. In the case of a fatal fire, the scene in its entirety should remain *intact* until the medical examiner arrives. Therefore, line firefighters and other emergency personnel should be prevented from removing a human body found in the charred debris. There are some obvious and reasonable exceptions to this rule:

- Any doubt as to whether the person is, in fact, dead
- Danger of fire-structure collapse or falling debris creating a serious hazard
- A serious threat that the body will be further damaged by the spread of flames
- The continued presence of the body being a serious hindrance to fire-fighting operations

However, in the absence of special circumstances, the body and its immediate surroundings should be left as originally found. If the responding fire/police investigator is nearby, the overhauling process should be delayed

Figure 7.1 (A–D) A fatal fire scene (A) must be handled like any crime scene; (B) document the position of the body *in situ* (original position); (C–D) identify any artifacts which will assist in the identity of the victim.

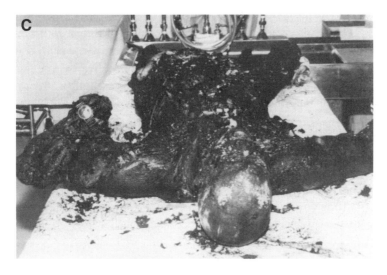

Figure 7.1 (continued)

until he is present. This is to prevent the inadvertent destruction of any evidence near where the body was found or at the point of origin.

Arrival of the Investigator

An experienced investigator should know that the timeliness of his response to the scene can, to a great extent, make or break the investigation. Survivors and people with an interest in the fire may still be present, and firefighters with first-hand knowledge of conditions within the building during the fire may be available. In addition, a rapid response — one made before the fire department releases the building to the owner — can preclude certain legal problems regarding crime scene searches (see Chapter 14).

Upon arriving at the scene, an investigator must make a conscious effort to maintain his professional objectivity and avoid getting caught up in the confusion and hysteria that will immediately confront him. Other uniformed personnel (fire and police) may be looking to him for direction. Rather than jumping headlong into the case, an investigator must pause long enough to assess the situation and develop a preliminary plan of action. One way to secure the needed time is for the investigator to maintain a low profile at first, to give the investigator a few minutes in which to record some basic information and collect his thoughts while taking a walk around the perimeter.

The type of information to jot down initially includes:

- The exact address of the fire (which may differ from that received from a dispatcher)
- The time you arrived at the scene
- General observations (weather conditions, lighting, entrances, exits presence of smoke and/or heat detectors, sprinklers, fire extinguishers, fire escapes, etc.)

The next step is to ensure that "pedigree" (detailed background) information on all injured or evacuated persons is recorded by subordinate uniformed personnel. This should be done even if the injured are to be treated at the scene and released. Also to be noted are the names of the ambulance attendants, paramedics, and Red Cross volunteers who are treating and transporting the injured; and pertinent information regarding the ambulances, and the hospital(s) or other emergency centers(s) to which the injured are being moved. Everyone displaced and all the injured will have to be interviewed when the investigator has finished at the scene. The paramedics and attendants should also be interviewed to see whether any of the people being transported made statements while in the ambulances. These statements could be material to the case or may contradict statements already noted. (The reasons for and an analysis of such contradictory statements are covered in Chapter 12.)

Once the investigator has evaluated the situation and is satisfied that the necessary background information has been recorded, he should identify himself to the chief fire officer or his aide. The chief or his aide can then fill the investigator in on what happened at the scene before his arrival, as well as confirm whatever information he may have received up to that point. Other information that should be sought at this time includes the identity of anyone missing or unaccounted for, an estimate of the fire damage, and whether the fire's cause is suspicious (and the rationale for this classification).

Remember that this scene involves a death investigation. It is crucial to determine anything that took place before the investigator's arrival that may have an impact on the investigation. The fire scene is to be treated as a *crime* scene, even though it is not yet known whether a crime has, in fact, been committed.

Chief's Report

The ranking officer will prepare a fire report describing the actions taken to extinguish the fire. A copy of this report is usually available to the fire/police investigator. This after-action report will include, among other things, a determination as to whether the fire's origin and/or cause were suspicious. A fire may be declared suspicious for a variety of reasons. The fire report should list and explain any factors that led to such a determination. Some common factors are the following:

- The rate of burning was not consistent with the type of combustibles present in the fire building
- A person died in the fire
- There were questionable or multiple points of origin
- The cause of the fire could not be readily ascertained
- Firefighters noticed an odor of gasoline or other accelerant

Although "suspicious" is not a recognized cause (see NFPA 921, Chapter 12-2), it is frequently misused by the untrained or inexperienced investigator.

Examination of the Body

The second phase of the investigation involves the visual inspection and physical examination of any human body discovered in phase 1. In most jurisdictions, the office of the *medical examiner* or *coroner* is responsible for ensuring that both an investigation at the scene and a subsequent autopsy on the body of the victim are conducted. The autopsy should be conducted by a *forensic pathologist,* but the scene investigation is usually carried out by either a medical examiner's or coroner's representative or a physician (non-pathologist) who holds the title of *medical investigator.* Although it is often preferable for the pathologist to visit the scene, the vast number of medical examiner cases, from all sources, and scarcity of forensic pathologists do not permit this except in unusual cases.

The fire/police investigator should advise the local medical examiner's office as soon as possible as to the known facts and circumstances relating to the fire and victim(s). In all fire cases where a body is found, a medical investigator should respond to observe the scene, the condition of the body, and its relationship to the origin of the fire.

There are four main tasks facing an investigator during phase 2:

1. Recording the scene
2. Identifying the victim (to whatever degree possible)

3. Determining (tentatively) whether the fire occurred ante- or postmortem (i.e., whether the victim was dead before the fire or died as a result of it)
4. Examining and collecting whatever physical evidence may be present that might corroborate a finding in tasks 2 or 3 and would help the pathologist performing the autopsy

Recording the Scene

Photographs of the body *in situ* (i.e., its original position) and of the room or area in which it is found will prove to be very valuable later in the investigation. These photographs, along with investigative notes, and any rough sketches prepared at the scene, are used to serve the following purposes:

1. To give an overview of the body and its surroundings so that its relative position can later be established
2. To provide close-up photographs of any evidence that indicates (a ruler should be used for true size comparison):
   a. The identity of the victim
   b. Circumvented alarm or fire-suppression systems
   c. Point(s) of forced entry or exit
   d. Another (underlying) crime or signs of a struggle
   e. The presence of gas cans, trailers, plants, etc.
3. To clarify the condition of the body regarding:
   a. The extent of burning or cremation
   b. The flow of fire patterns on the body and whether they are consistent with the damages to the surroundings. (Was a victim who died on the second floor found buried in an ash-filled basement because of the collapse of the interior structural members?)
   c. Whether the body was found face up or face down, and the degree to which it insulated the floor below it (or failed to do so)
4. To identify furnishings (e.g., bed, coffee table, desk) in the area where the body was found
5. To indicate the relative position of the body in relation to the point(s) of origin
6. To identify any other factors of importance to technical or forensic procedures

In some cases, especially where the victim is found quite a distance from the point of the fire, it is necessary to trace the connection between the fire and the resultant death. The connection may seem obvious when the investigator is at the scene, but on the witness stand some 12 or 15 months later, it may not be as clear. To illustrate this problem, let us examine the particulars of a fire that occurred in the Bronx, New York, late in 1978:

At 5 A.M. a fire started in the basement of an abandoned five-story walkup. The adjoining buildings were fully occupied and were evacuated by the responding fire units. One of the evacuees was a 9-year-old, retarded boy. During the ensuing confusion, the boy was separated from his parents and, apparently frightened by the crowd, sought the safety of his room. The boy's father, searching for his son, found him under his bed. The boy had died from carbon monoxide asphyxiation.

The fire damage to the abandoned building was extensive, but did not communicate to the adjoining buildings. The boy's body was found one building away and four stories above the source of the carbon monoxide that caused his death. The investigators involved in this case traced and (wisely) photographed the path that the billowing smoke and gases took between the source and the boy's room.

On occasion, the medical examiner will, after autopsy, refer a case to a police investigator for further investigation. The autopsy may have revealed insufficient and/or contradictory data or may have raised additional questions that the medical examiner wants to have clarified before signing a death certificate. These cases are referred to as CUPPIs (circumstances undetermined pending police investigation). If the crime scene was processed and recorded accurately, the investigator, in many cases, should be able to review the crime scene data and provide the medical examiner with satisfactory answers. (See Chapter 10 for more on crime scene documentation.)

Psychological Profiling

If, during the course of the investigator's analysis, it appears that the fire was set to conceal the scene of an especially gruesome or sex-related homicide, the investigator should evaluate the evidence collected and the documentation of the scene in terms of their possible value in the development of a psychological assessment.

> The purpose of the psychological assessment of the crime scene is to produce a profile; that is, to identify and interpret certain items of evidence at the crime scene which would be indicative of the personality type of the person or persons committing the crime (Ault and Reese 1980, p. 23).

The following are necessary in order for a psychological profile to be conducted properly:

1. Complete photographs of the crime scene, including photographs of the victim, if it is a homicide. Also helpful are some means of determining the angle from which the photographs were taken and a general description of the immediate area.

2. The complete autopsy protocol including, if possible, any results of lab tests which were done on the victim.
3. A complete report of the incident to include such standard details as date and time of offense, location, weapon used (if known), investigating officer's reconstruction of the sequence of events (if any), and a detailed interview of any surviving victims or witnesses. Also included in most investigative reports is the background information on the victim(s). (Ault and Reese, 1980, p. 24.)

The background information on the victim should be as detailed as possible. Information provided by such a profile may include the following:

1. The perpetrator's race
2. Sex, age range, and marital status
3. General employment
4. Reaction to questioning by police
5. Degree of sexual maturity
6. Whether the individual might strike again
7. The possibility that he/she has committed a similar offense in the past
8. Possible police record (Ault and Reese, 1980, p. 24)

If the investigating officer's agency or department does not have the trained personnel to develop a psychological profile, then the assigned investigator should contact the nearest FBI field office. The agents assigned to the field office may be able to evaluate the submitted material in terms of its applicability to the profiling process. If the field office does not offer this service, the investigation should forward his request directly to the Behavioral Science Unit, FBI Academy, Quantico, Virginia.

In light of the FBI's success in this field, some of the larger state, county, and municipal law enforcement agencies in the country may well develop their own procedures in this area. Many law enforcement agencies already have the personnel (studying the effects of stress on job performance and conducting preemployment psychological testing) who could conceivable provide this service.

The role of psychological profiling is covered in more detail in *Practical Homicide Investigation*, 2nd Ed. by Geberth (1996).

Identifying the Victim

Determining the identity of a fatality discovered at the fire scene can be difficult, involving the efforts of several specialists. The investigator must, therefore, collect any items that might directly or indirectly facilitate the proper identification of the victim (e.g., remains of the victim's clothing or objects found on or near the body). Some obvious questions should also be answered:

- Who was most likely to have been within the fire structure when the fire started?
- Who was seen entering the structure during the fire?
- Who, among these people, is missing or unaccounted for?

If these preliminary avenues of investigation seem to make the identity of the victim clear, the field investigator should make every effort to identify and record the names, addresses, and phone numbers of relatives and friends of the deceased. This information should be supplied to the office of the medical examiner. Many victims are identified by these relatives and friends during a viewing of the body conducted at the morgue. Such visual identification is referred to as *gross identification.* The feasibility of such a viewing is obviously determined by the condition of the body.

The degree of destruction of a body depends largely on the intensity of the fire and on how long the body was exposed to it. In extreme cases, the body may be so badly damaged that it is impossible to determine even sex or race, let alone identity and cause of death, without an autopsy. Position of the body relative to the fire is another significant factor: Suspension over flames (e.g., on a bed, couch, or reclining chair) will lead to more complete bodily destruction because body fat and tissue fuel the fire.

The investigator should know that in most fires, the body is almost never totally consumed and is usually recognizable as human even if the sex, race, and so on are undiscernible due to massive charring. This is because it is extremely difficult to maintain the open burning of a human body. Even when a body is cremated — burned for approximately 2 hours 2000°F — teeth and dental work are rarely destroyed.

Beyond gross identification, there are several other approaches to victim identification available. One is by means of *fingerprint comparison.* Palm and sole prints should also be made at the time fingerprints are taken. These are all forwarded to the Federal Bureau of Investigation for comparison with prints already on file. The value of finger, palm, and sole prints for identification purposes is limited, of course, by the condition of those areas to be printed. If a complete set of prints cannot be taken, the incomplete set and tentative identification should be forwarded to help in the comparison.

Another method of positive identification is through the use of dental records. As mentioned earlier, teeth and dental work are usually found intact. Furthermore, the shrinking of the victim's facial skin and the swelling of the tongue tend to protect not only the teeth, but also the inner mouth. This means that a *forensic odontologist* can identify three or four times as many points of identification as can a fingerprint technician. These include the shape of fillings, sinus cavities, nerve paths, signs of root canal work, and so on.

At autopsy, the odontologist takes dental X-rays and then removes the upper and lower jaws for charting purposes. These charts are then compared with earlier X-rays and charts based on any tentative identification. If no tentative identification is available, the odontologist can at least greatly narrow down the possibilities of identifying the *style of dentistry* (e.g., type of materials used in fillings). This may help identify the socioeconomic class of the victim.

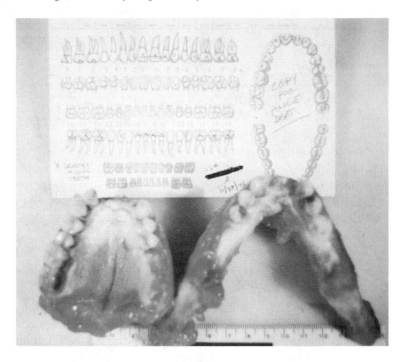

Figure 7.2   Fire victims are very often identified through an examination of antemortem and postmortem dental records. As seen here, the victim's jaws were removed during the autopsy, and a dental chart was prepared. This chart and X-rays are compared with the antemortem records of suspected victims. (Photo courtesy of Dr. A. Goldman.)

A fourth method of identification is based on information discovered during the medical/physical examination and autopsy. These factors include:

- Tattoos and scars
- Evidence of prior surgical procedures or bone fractures
- Unique or unusual deformity
- Sex, race, build, features, and approximate age
- Personal papers, jewelry, clothing, etc.

Time of Death: Before or During the Fire?

One of the most important questions in any fatal fire investigation is the time of death. Was the victim alive or dead before the fire? This piece of information, coupled with the cause of the fire, will set the tone of the entire investigative process that is to follow (as we shall see in phase 4).

The police, fire, and medical investigators, working as a team, may be able to make certain tentative determinations regarding the status of the victim during the fire, based on an analysis of ante-or postmortem burns and injuries. Any determination made at the scene is obviously tentative the precise analysis of ante- and postmortem injuries can only be determir and interpreted at autopsy.

Body Decomposition Time In Fire	
	10 Min. – Arms charred
	14 Min. – Legs charred
680°C (1256°F) *for:*	15 Min. – Face, arm bones showing
	20 Min. – Ribs, skull showing
	25 Min. – Shin bones showing
	35 Min. – All leg bones showing

Figure 7.3   Body decomposition time in fire.

In some jurisdictions, an investigator may have to wait several days to receive the final disposition of an autopsy. This is a crucial factor. It is therefore, incumbent upon the investigator to pursue whatever investigative data are available on the basis of his initial, on-site investigation.

In many cases, the medical investigator, with the help of the police and fire investigators, can develop a defensible and medically accurate conclusion as to whether death occurred before or during the fire, based on what he sees at the scene. There are several factors that, when analyzed, can provide the empirical data upon which to base such a conclusion. These factors examined separately (like the pieces of a puzzle) can be misleading; but when compared and connected chronologically, they can provide a reasonably clear picture of what happened.

The first thing that the investigator should note during the physical examination is whether the victim is face up or face down. Except for those found in bed or on a couch, most victims are found face down. A person who succumbs while staggering or crawling through a smoke-filled room can usually be expected to fall forward and thus, be found face down. However, it is reasonable to expect to find a person sleeping face up in bed or on a couch. The fact that a body is found face up elsewhere is not in and of itself necessarily suspicious, but it does warrant additional attention and inquiry. If the victim was alive during the fire, he or she may have inhaled smoke and soot. If so, the body should show signs of soot and smoke particles (*carbonaceous material*) in and around the mouth and nose, indicating that breathing continued during the fire.

Certain physical changes occur after death or when varying degrees of heat and flame are applied to a human body. In most cases, these are natural phenomena and should not be misinterpreted by an investigator as indicative of foul play.

Postmortem Lividity

The natural settling of the blood after death is called *postmortem lividity*. It is due to the gravitational pooling of the blood, and it is usually purplish to blue-black in color. Its location depends on the position of the body after death. Although it begins *at* death, lividity becomes *visible* from 30 minutes to 4 hours later. Over the next 8 hours, it becomes fixed. It is during this period (before lividity becomes permanent) that *secondary lividity* may occur. If a body is turned from the position in which it originally rested — as might occur if a body were moved several hours after death and repositioned — lividity will develop in this second position. The medical investigator arriving at the scene will note the presence of lividity corresponding to two positions (Gross, undated, p. 5). Unless the repositioning can be attributed to structural collapse or operational intervention, secondary lividity would seem to indicate foul play.

Concentrations of carbon monoxide in the blood cause postmortem lividity to be pink to cherry-red in color. Redness of the lividity might, therefore, indicate that the victim was alive and breathing at the time of the fire. Should the examination of the body take place before lividity has developed, the pink to cherry-red color may appear in the victim's lips and eyelids.

Pugilistic Attitude

A victim may be found in what appears to be a defensive boxing pose or fetal position. This is called the *pugilistic attitude*. It occurs when the stronger muscles in the limbs are exposed to high temperatures over a prolonged period of time. The intense heat causes the large muscles in the arms and legs to contract, thereby pulling the limbs toward the torso. In addition, the hands may be cupped (clawlike) as the fingers are drawn toward the palms. This movement is a gradual one, and not a spasmodic or jerking action.

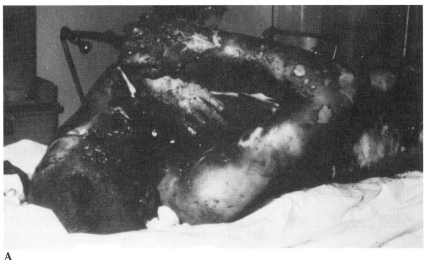

A

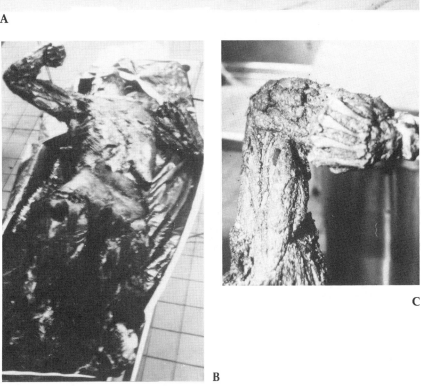

B

C

Figure 7.4 (A–B) The body pictured appears to be in a defensive boxing pose. This condition is called "pugilistic attitude." It is a natural phenomenon of fire. (C) The close-up of the victim's right arm illustrates how the limbs are drawn toward the torso and the fingers are cupped. The extent of the burning makes fingerprint identification impossible. (B and C courtesy of Dr. A. Goldman.)

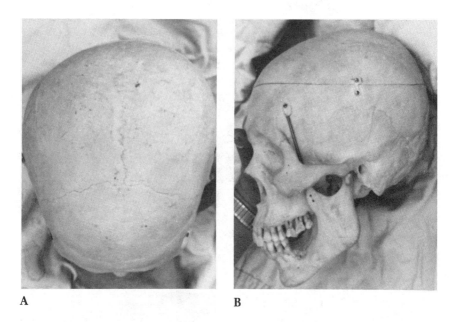

A   **B**

Figure 7.5 (A) Photograph illustrates the natural suture appearing on the skull. (B) A side view of a normal human skull. (Photos courtesy of Dr. A. Goldman.)

The absence of the pugilistic attitude in a body that has been exposed to ample stimuli may very well be questionable. One possible reason for its absence might be that the body was in rigor mortis before the fire. *Rigor mortis* is the stiffening of the body after death due to the postmortem contraction of the muscles as the result of changes in protein content. It first develops to completeness in the muscles comprising small tissue masses and is, therefore, first visible in the face, jaws, and hands. It develops in about 2 to 4 hours, becomes complete over a period of 12 to 24 hours from death, and remains for another 24 to 48 hours before it begins to disappear.*

A body in rigor mortis before the start of the fire will develop only a limited pugilistic attitude or none at all, depending on the time and extent of rigor mortis.

The pugilistic attitude might also not occur if the heat necessary to cause the muscle contraction was not long or intense enough. This might be the case in a flash fire. Regardless of the suspected cause for the lack of pugilistic attitude, the responding medical investigator should routinely examine the body for rigor mortis.

---

* The onset of rigor mortis may be hastened by heat or cold. It may even develop instantaneously in the case of a fatal head injury. Its disappearance is accelerated in a warm environment and with the development of putrefaction.

Skull Fracture

Another factor that may easily be misconstrued is the discovery that the victim's skull is fractured. Care must be taken to determine whether the fracture is implosive or explosive. An *implosive fracture* may have been caused by a fall, may be evidence of a prior felonious assault or homicide, or may result from a collapsed structural member. The exact cause will be determined at autopsy and evaluated during the follow-up investigation. An *explosive fracture*, however, is usually a natural consequence of fire. The extreme heat may cause the fluids in and around the brain to boil and expand. The resulting steam produces enough pressure to cause an explosive (pressure-release) reaction. The resulting fracture(s) usually follow the natural suture lines of the skull. In extreme cases, the cranium may burst, causing the expelled brain and skull matter to form a circular pattern around the head. This is more common in children than in adults — the *fontanel*, or membrane-covered opening between the uncompleted parietal bones, is the weakest point in a fetal or young skull. The resulting circular pattern (0 to 12 inches from the skull) is significant when compared with the type of spattering that might result from a shotgun blast or high-order explosion.

Blistering or Splitting of Skin

The new investigator may be somewhat apprehensive in attempting to evaluate the effects of heat and flame on the skin of the victim. The medical investigator is in the best position to render a judgment in this area. The formation of blisters (*vesicles*) is part of the body's natural defense system. The exact distinction between ante- and postmortem blistering can only be made at autopsy. There are however, certain signs that a medical investigator can evaluate in the development of a hypothesis. *Postmortem blisters* are generally limited in size and may contain only air or air mixed with a small amount of body fluid. *Antemortem blisters* are larger in size and contain a complex mix of body fluids. The precise determination of the fluids requires microscopic analysis. A blister surrounded by a pink or red ring can be considered as having occurred before death; the reddish ring is the result of an antemortem inflammatory reaction.

Note that, in some instances, temperatures may not have been high enough to produce blistering. Likewise, if the skin is burned off or otherwise heavily damaged, blistering will not be in evidence.

The heat and flame inherent in the fire also cause the skin to shrink or tighten and ultimately split. The splitting or lesions may be seen on the arms, legs, and torso. At first glance this condition, coupled with pugilistic attitude, could be misinterpreted as indicating defense wounds.

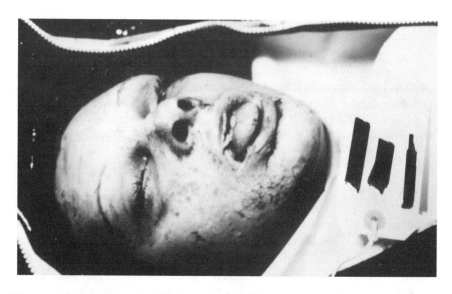

Figure 7.6 Photograph illustrates the effects of varying degrees of heat and flame on human skin. The victim's skin is sloughing or separating from the tissue below and has experienced some charring. (Photo courtesy of Dr. A. Goldman.)

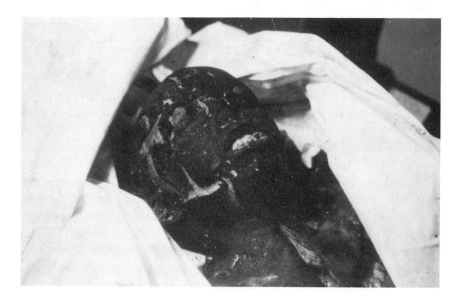

Figure 7.7 The skin on the victim is split or ripped.

Note that, in some cases, a seriously burned person survives the fire and is removed to a local burn center. In an effort to save the person, the medical staff at the center may attempt to duplicate the natural splitting of the skin with a surgical technique known as an *escharotomy*. This technique is used

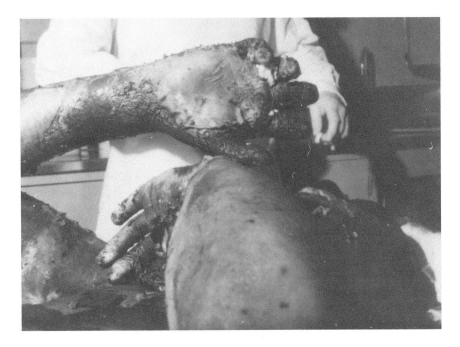

Figure 7.8 Victim's skin is sloughing or separating from tissue.

to help foster circulation and to prevent the onset of gangrene. Should the burn victim expire some time after the fire, these splits should not be misinterpreted as fire-induced.

Origin and Cause/Investigative Canvass

In this third phase of the inquiry, two separate investigative operations take place simultaneously. The *fire investigator*, who is responsible for determining the fire's origin and cause, begins the physical examination of the structure (or automobile in the case of a vehicular fire). The *police investigator*, who is responsible for the death investigation, begins an investigative canvass.

Also at this stage, the medical investigator authorizes and supervises the removal of the body and associated debris. This debris may contain evidence that would resolve the circumstances of death and the possible origin of the fire (e.g., remnants of a charred mattress). The body itself is a crucial part of the physical evidence, and a chain of custody must be maintained. Remember, too, that the body may be heavily charred and very fragile. Special care must also be taken to ensure that personal items that might aid in the identification process (e.g., dentures, jewelry, clothing) are not lost. No attempt should be made to separate these items from the body prematurely; this should be done at the morgue where the autopsy is to be conducted.

Origin and Cause

Determination of origin is covered in detail in Chapter 5, and automobile salvage is covered in Chapter 8. However, several additional points deserve mention at this time, in that fire fatalities call for the generation of many additional reports and their eventual referral to the medical examiner's office.

The medical examiner's interest in the results of the physical examination or automobile salvage will focus on several narrowly circumscribed factors.

1. He will want to know the cause of the fire (accidental or incendiary), since this may provide information regarding the circumstances of death.
2. He will want to know if the use of an accelerant (e.g., gasoline or kerosene) is suspected and the possible type(s) of material(s) that were ignited. At autopsy, the pathologist may then order additional toxicologic analyses of the victim's blood and lung residue to test for the presence of the flammable vapors of toxic gases. (If these are present, then the location of the point(s) or origin in relation to the location of the body at the scene would also be considered.)
3. A third area of interest, especially if the victim died in the fire, is *survivability*. The medical examiner will be concerned with any fact that would provide insight into the victim's failure to escape safely.

Investigative Canvass

Interview and interrogation strategies and the investigative canvass are covered in detail in Chapter 12. The investigator conducting a canvass must remember that the neighbors and friends of the victim, who may themselves have just escaped the flames, may make threatening and accusatory statements that they will rarely make or repeat at a later date. The investigator must learn to make use of the tension and stress manifested by the fire survivors as a motivating factor to elicit information.

Determining Investigative Procedure

In phase 4, all the information amassed from the investigative steps already completed (phases 1 to 3) is assembled and analyzed by the medical examiner, together with the results of the autopsy (cause of death). The product of this synthesis serves as a blueprint determining how the follow-up investigation (phase 5) is to be conducted.

Medicolegal Autopsy

After the body is removed from the fire scene (phase 3) but before the investigative procedure can be determined, an autopsy must be performed.

Although the external areas of the body may be very heavily charred, in most cases, the internal organs will be relatively undamaged. The *medicolegal autopsy* is a systematic examination of a dead body, following standardized procedures, conducted for multiple purposes. The predominant purpose of a medical examiner's autopsy is to determine the cause of death. Many other factors are considered in the course of the examination, some of which are a continuation of examinations initiated at the scene:

- Identification
- Time of death
- Circumstances of death
- Correlation of injuries
- Evidence
- Survivability (Gross, undated, p.8).

X-Rays

The forensic pathologist's first action will be to X-ray the body and the associated debris. By examining the X-rays, the pathologist will isolate and identify any foreign objects (e.g., spent bullets, cartridges, knife blades). If an explosion preceded the fire, shrapnel may have been blown into the body and may, indeed, be the cause of death.

Carboxyhemoglobin

Carbon monoxide (CO) is an odorless, colorless gas present at hazardous levels in all structural fires. Carbon monoxide asphyxiation is probably the single most common cause of death in fires. Exposure to as little as 1.3% carbon monoxide can cause unconsciousness after only two or three breaths, and death in a few minutes. As we have already seen, CO causes the cherry-red color of postmortem lividity (as well as that of internal organs and muscle tissue).

At autopsy, the pathologist will test the victim's blood for the level of *carboxyhemoglobin*–carbon monoxide present in the pigment of the red blood cells. Carbon monoxide has an affinity for red blood cells that is approximately 210 times greater than that of oxygen. The concentration of carbon monoxide in the blood is a very important element in determining if the victim was alive before and during the fire. Its concentration is given in terms of a percentage of saturation. Because carbon monoxide in the blood is generally due to the inhalation of CO during the fire, the absence of CO in the red blood cells (less than a 10% saturation) would be rather conclusive evidence that the victim was dead before the fire.*

---

* It is possible for a charred body to absorb small quantities of CO, which accounts for the low levels (10% or less) of CO found in a body proved to have been dead before a fire occurred.

Alcohol and Controlled Substances

At autopsy, the pathologist should routinely test a sample of the victim's blood for the presence of alcohol or drugs (controlled substances). The purpose of this test is threefold.

1. The first objective is to determine if the presence of alcohol and/or drugs was a relevant factor in the death, due to the *synergistic* (enhanced-effect) reaction between alcohol or drugs and carbon monoxide. When a person is "high" on alcohol or drugs, the oxygen carried to the brain is restricted. When that same person inhales carbon monoxide, the CO quickly replaces the already restricted oxygen in the blood, and unconsciousness and death quickly follow.
2. The second purpose is concerned with the question of survivability. Did the presence of alcohol or drugs in the victim have any bearing on the fact that the victim failed to escape safely?
3. It affords the investigator and district attorney an opportunity to evaluate and prepare for a possible contention by defense attorney that the victim himself accidentally started the fire while in a drunken stupor.

Toxicology

If the fire investigator or fire marshal has reason to suspect that an accelerant was used, he should advise the medical examiner of this fact. Based on the information supplied, especially the distance between the point of origin and the body, the medical examiner may choose to send blood and lung samples to the lab for gas chromatographic or mass spectrophotometric analysis. The lab would both analyze and attempt to identify any flammable vapors present in these samples. If flammable vapors are found, this would both indicate that the victim was alive and breathing these vapors during the fire and corroborate the suspicion and findings of the fire marshal.

Cause of Death and Investigative Procedure

During the course of the autopsy, the pathologist will make a determination as to the cause of death. Death may have resulted from a single factor or from several contributing factors. The cause(s) may include, but are not limited to, the following:

- Burns
- Burns plus CO asphyxiation
- Spasm of the epiglottis

- Acute alcoholism plus CO asphyxiation
- Edema
- Shock
- Gunshot wound or stabbing

After fixing the cause or contributing causes of death and evaluating the circumstances of death, the medical examiner will generally classify the case and refer it to the local police department. As shown in Table 7.2, the medical examiner's classification is usually the determining factor in how a case will be investigated.

Table 7.2 Determining Investigative Procedure

Cause of Fire	Cause of Death	Investigative Procedure
Accidental	CO asphyxiation No additional factors (Accidental)	Close case during follow-up investigation
Incendiary	CO asphyxiation No additional factors (Homicidal)	Investigate as an arson/homicide Motive for the fire important

Accidental	Gunshot, stabbing, manual or
	  ligature asphyxiation, blunt force
	  trauma, etc., prior to the fire
	(Homicidal)
		Investigate as a homicide
		
		Reevaluate physical examination of
		  fire scene

Incendiary	Prior to fire (Homicidal)	Investigate as a homicide Fire used to conceal Motive for homicide is important

Accidental	CO asphyxiation plus other natural
	  illness
	(Accidental)
		Close case during follow-up
		  investigation

Accidental	CO asphyxiation
	Additional injury (implosive skull
	  fracture)
	(CUPPI)
		CUPPI
		Review crime scene photos and
		  reports
		Prepare report for medical examiner
		  with results of follow-up
		  investigation

Incendiary	CO asphyxiation
	Additional injury (implosive skull
	  fracture)
	(Homicidal)
		Investigate as an arson/homicide
		Fire to conceal prior assault or
		  attempted homicide

Incendiary	CO asphyxiation Additional factors (burns/shock) (Possible suicide)	CUPPI Results of investigative canvass crucial Prepare report for medical examiner Check possible suicide (rare)

Spontaneous Human Combustion

Because of its controversy over the years, I will discuss this ill-conceived concept of self immolation where the human body supposedly self destructs by suddenly bursting into flaming combustion from within and in the absence of an external heat source. Allegedly the internal combustion is caused by an unexplained spontaneous heating from within the victim's body. The "eye-witness" reports of victims' bodies being nearly consumed with only the extremities remaining is only the end product of misconceptions handed down through the years, even centuries, by inexperienced lay persons on the laws of physics and chemistry of fire.

Spontaneous human combustion (SHC) has all the similarities and consistency with those fatal fires involving a number of common factors. The following are but a few of the indicators witnessed and documented by this investigator/author as well as many of my colleagues:

1. The individual was a smoker
2. They were most commonly elderly and sometimes infirm
3. There is evidence of medication and/or alcohol use
4. Frequently the person is overweight
5. The remains of the body are almost always found in the area of the remains of furniture such as a chair, sofa, or bed

These factors combined to allow a fire igniting clothing or bedding to incapacitate the victim through the inhalation of carbon monoxide and subsequent death. The consumption of the body through its own fluids (body fat) fuels the fire, allowing it to continue to burn with intensity, thus accounting for the almost complete destruction of the torso portion of the body and leaving the extremities such as lower legs, hands, and feet partially or unburned.

To date, this author has not seen or read any evidence to confirm or substantiate the phenomenon of spontaneous human combustion.

Follow-up Investigation

The responsibility for conducting the follow-up investigation of fatal fire rests with the police investigator. The purpose of this investigation is to resolve cases referred by the medical examiner's office. The investigative procedure proposed by the medical examiner in phase 4 is normally used as the basis for cataloging cases earmarked for further action.

In many cases, a preliminary follow-up investigation will have started at the time of the fire, based on tentative findings from the examination of the body and the officially listed cause of the fire.

In situations where the death is an obvious homicide (e.g., apparent shooting or stabbing victim, victim's hands and/or feet bound, or ligature tied around the neck), the investigation should be well documented by the time supporting data are received from the medical examiner. Here, the motive for the homicide (e.g., domestic, robbery, narcotics, sex crime) becomes a key issue in identifying a suspect. The fire, if of incendiary origin, was most probably set either to prevent or impede the identification of the victim; to conceal wounds and injuries; or, as in certain sex crimes, to purge or purify the site where, to the psychopathic mind, something evil was committed. (See Chapter 2.)

The investigation of an arson/homicide or felony murder is measurably different from that of a homicide in which the fire was set to conceal the crime. The two investigations are similar only in that, in both cases, numerous sources of information and associates of the victim will have to be identified and interviewed. The greatest distinction between the two is the intent of the actor. In the investigation of an arson/homicide, the key element is the identification of the motive for the fire. The investigator may discover that the fire was indeed set to kill the victim; this would, however, be an exception rather than the rule. In most cases, the arsonist does not intend to kill. There may be no connection whatsoever between the motive for the fire and the death that results; the death is an unintended consequence.

An important point to consider when investigating any incendiary fire, regardless of motive, is the level of sophistication or technical knowledge exhibited by the fire setter. An investigator can, at times, extrapolate enough data in and from the point or area of origin to speculate on such factors as:

- Whether a fire was planned or an impulsive act
- Possible age differentiation (adult vs. child) by target chosen
- Whether the torch was an amateur or professional

To address these questions, the investigator would have to consider:

- The source of ignition (sophisticated, delayed timing devices vs. a common match)
- The first material ignited (were chemicals or other liquid accelerants carried into the premises or were commonplace combustibles simply piled and ignited?)
- Whether any measures were taken to circumvent fire-alarm or -suppression systems
- Other conditions or circumstances peculiar to the case at hand

CUPPI Follow-up

Perhaps the best way to explain the investigation that follows a CUPPI (circumstances undetermined pending police investigation) referral from the medical examiner is to examine a hypothetical example.

Referral from the Medical Examiner: The Case of John Doe

> On Tuesday, July 9, 1982, at 0200 hours, there was a one-alarm fire at 123 Main Street, Garnerville, New York. During the search and rescue operations, the body of a white male, 53 years of age, was recovered in the bedroom of apartment 4B. The fire was brought under control at 0225 hours. There was extensive water and smoke damage on the fourth floor, but limited fire damage.
>
> The fire was declared accidental by Fire Marshal Jones, Shield N. 30764, at 0500 hours of July 9, 1982. The cause of the fire was traced to an overloaded electrical circuit in apartment 3C. All other residents of the building escaped safely.
>
> At autopsy, the victim was positively identified as John Doe. The cause of death was determined to be carbon monoxide asphyxiation. The victim also suffered an implosive fracture on the right side of the head, just above the right ear.
>
> *CUPPI:* How did the victim sustain the fracture to the right side of the skull? Determine if the victim was the victim of an assault.
>
> *Facts:* Cause of the fire — accidental/electrical; cause of death-CO asphyxiation; problem — implosive fracture to the right side of the skull.

Investigative Follow-up on the John Doe Case

Mr. John Doe had lived alone at 123 Main Street, Apartment 4B, for the past 17 years. His sister and her husband, Mr. and Mrs. Thomas Smith of 129 Broadway, Bronxville, New York, had dinner with the victim at his apartment at 8 p.m. on the night of the fire. They stated that the victim was alone when they left him at 11 p.m. The first firefighters at the scene stated that the front door to apartment 4B was locked from the inside, and that they had to force entry.

Review of the crime scene data indicates that the victim was found face up on the bedroom floor, next to a two-drawer night table, approximately 3 feet from his bed. The victim was dressed in nightclothes, and it appears from all available evidence that he was most probably asleep at the time of the fire.

An analysis of all available evidence indicates that the victim awoke in his smoke-filed bedroom. While suffering from carbon monoxide intoxication, he stumbled, fell, and struck the right side of his head on the corner of the night table. The injury took the form of an implosive fracture. After striking his head, the victim fell to the floor, face up.

There is no evidence to indicate the victim was the subject of an assault or any form of foul play. Recommend that the case be closed.

CUPPI: Suicide by Fire

The investigation of a fire death, particularly where suicide by fire is suspected, is a complex exercise. The final determination relating to the circumstances of a suicide by fire can only be made by the medical examiner.

The medical examiner will generally refer such a case to the local police detective unit for additional follow-up. The purpose of this CUPPI referral is to amass as much background information on the victim as possible. This may then be referred to a forensic psychologist or psychiatrist for evaluation, to develop an antemortem psychological profile on the victim. This type of diligent, integrated investigation is absolutely necessary for two reasons:

1. To accurately classify the death as a suicide
2. To verify and document all the available information that may be necessary to defend the classification of death in any future litigation

Suicide by fire is rare in our culture, but fire/arson investigators must know that it does occur and be alert enough to recognize it when it happens. A case in point is that of Mr. Joseph M., an 80-year-old retired fire lieutenant. His body was found tangled in the remains of his bed in the heavily damaged bedroom of his two-family home. The first firemen at the scene thought the body was bound with wire and advised their chief, who contacted both fire and police investigators. A closer examination revealed that the victim had become tangled in the remains of an electric heating blanket and was not bound as was first thought.

The scene investigation uncovered an empty one-gallon gasoline can in the rubble next to the bed, and an undated, yellowed newspaper headline taped to wall in the living room. The headline read, "Fire Chief Dies In Blaze." No suicide note was found.

Interviews with relatives and neighbors, conducted the same day, provided a penetrating portrait of the victim. Mr. M. was a widower and had no children. His wife of 38 years had died 2 years earlier. The victim was pensioned from the fire department on disability, after 24 years of service. He had not worked in the 22 years since. Soon after his wife passed away, he was diagnosed as having cancer. Since that time, he had undergone at least two operations. Relative stated that the victim has suffered terribly and he had been despondent for the past several months.

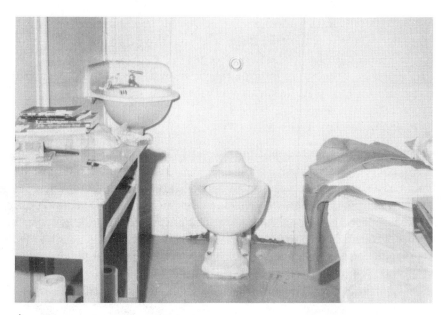

A

B

Figure 7.9 (A) Photograph of an unburned cell in the same cellblock as (B) young male victim who committed suicide by setting fire to his jail cell mattress.

Mr. M.'s death was ultimately classified as a suicide by fire. In this case, the diligence of the investigators both during the scene examination and the follow-up investigation brought the matter to a proper conclusion.

Victim Identified as a Fire Setter

A fire investigator must be alert to the possibility that a body (or one of the bodies) found at the scene may be that of the fire setter. Many inexperienced fire setters, including the home owner or businessman turned torch, seriously injure or kill themselves while setting a fire. This seems either to be due to lack of knowledge of fire behavior and combustibility, or of poor planning. The inordinate reliance upon and excessive use of highly flammable liquid accelerants probably accounts, more than any other reason, for the injury and death of the amateur torch.

The investigator must keep this in mind when conducting the follow-up interviews of the injured. These interviews generally take place at the hospitals to which the injured have been transported. It is important that the investigator pinpoint, through questioning, the actions and locations of the injured up to the time they state they were injured. The investigator can then compare these statements with the information developed during the physical examination.

In one particular case, a building superintendent stated that he was awakened by smoke at about 5:30 a.m. and was injured moments later when he opened a basement door, located in a front hallway in his apartment house. He stated that when he opened this particular door he was "hit in the face with a blast of flame and heat."

An analysis of the already completed physical examination indicated that the fire had started in the rear storage area of the basement and that an accelerant (gasoline) had been used. In addition, it was known that the fire extended into a rear airshaft and that the lateral spread to the front of the basement came much later in the fire. It was, therefore, impossible for the superintendent to have been injured at the time and place he stated. A determination was made that the superintendent was either chronologically confused or lying. Following a well-developed line of questioning, the investigator was able to get him to admit that he had been in the basement when he was injured. He later made statements that led to his arrest: the superintendent "victim" was in fact the torch.

Arrest and Trial

As the case approaches the stage where sufficient probable cause exists to warrant the arrest of one or more suspects, the investigator, working closely with the local district attorney or prosecutor, must carefully consider the options governing the *method of arrest*. This is not a question of tactics, although all arrests do involve some tactical considerations; the method of arrest refers to the authority or agency authorizing or ordering the arrest. A law enforcement officer in the U.S. has only two options:

1. Arrest based on probable cause
2. Arrest with a warrant

Arrest Based on Probable Cause

Probable cause, also referred to as *reasonable cause to believe*, is the minimum level of proof required legally to effect an arrest. The experienced investigator should realize that there are serious weaknesses inherent in choosing to make a summary arrest.

The first shortcoming involves some confusion on the part of the investigator as to his or her obligation to see that the case comes to fruition. The investigator, as previously stated, would be operating at the minimum level of proof necessary to justify an arrest, whereas the district attorney, who is to prosecute the case, must prove every element of the crime beyond a reasonable doubt in order to secure a conviction. It does not serve society to have an arsonist and/or murderer hastily taken off the streets and then freed because of the state's failure to prosecute. Thus, although the initial purpose of the investigation was merely to determine the facts, specific ancillary objectives become important for the investigator as the case builds:

- To identify the suspect(s)
- To gather and present sufficient evidence to carry the case to a successful conclusion

To ensure continuity, the investigator should coordinate with the local prosecutor's office. In this way, weaknesses or problems in the case can be identified and corrected before an arrest is made. The district attorney's office is also the route through which the investigator can gain access to electronic surveillance, eavesdropping, or search warrants, should these become necessary. A second area of concern when a summary arrest is made is the possible problem of civil liability. Many arson cases (because of the nature of the crime) are based largely on circumstantial evidence. The legal principle of "exclusive opportunity" is commonly at issue, and there may not be any hard or direct evidence to positively place the defendant at the fire scene. At arraignment, in such cases, the arresting officer must be eloquent enough to explain the steps that led to the development of probable cause satisfactorily. However, the arresting officer may very well be the subject or respondent of a civil suit charging false arrest. The arresting officer, if an agent of any federal, state or municipal agency, may then be the subject of a federal suit for violation of civil constitutional rights (U.S. Code, Title 18, Sects. 241–242; Title 42, Sect. 1983).

Arrest with a Warrant

A second option available to the investigator, while working closely with the local district attorney, is to effect an arrest under the authority of an arrest warrant issued by a state supreme court or district court judge. An arrest warrant both authorizes and orders the arrest of the person(s) named on the face of the warrant. Such a warrant can be obtained in one of two ways, regional policy or practice notwithstanding.

In one situation, the district attorney presents the case before a sitting grand jury. The members of the jury consider the testimony and physical evidence and vote on the issue. If an indictment results, the district attorney files the indictment (accusatory instrument)* with a local superior court and requests that an arrest warrant be issued.

A second method, which is also a powerful investigatory and prosecutorial tool, is for the district attorney to present the case directly to a superior court judge after filing an accusatory instrument, such as a felony complaint. This method is especially useful in a case where there are a large number of suspects. The investigator and prosecutor can pick one of the defendants, usually the weakest link in the case, and attempt to "turn" him. Using the threat of an indictment and trial on the major count as an inducement, the chosen subject may decide to cooperate with the investigation and testify for the state. This method is often used to build a stronger case against the remaining subjects. In return for cooperation and testimony, the defendant turned informer is listed as an unindicted coconspirator and is given immunity from prosecution.

Trial

The details of the investigator's responsibility during an arson trial are covered in detail in Chapter 13. An arson homicide trial tends to be far more complex, and is, therefore, worthy of special mention. In addition to the points that must be proven in an arson trial:

1. That crime (arson) was committed
2. That the defendant committed the crime

There is an additional burden of proving:

3. That the actions of the defendant led to the death of the victim

---

* In New York State, the right to counsel immediately attaches with the filing of an accusatory instrument.

Additional witnesses, including the medical examiner, serologist, and toxicologist, will be called to testify.

As in the arson trial, the defense attorney's primary attack will focus on the handling and examination of the fire scene. He will challenge the officially listed origin and cause of the fire. If the defense counsel is able to discredit either the qualifications of the fire scene technician or the actual scene examination itself, the people's case against the defendant will come to an abrupt end; if the fire is ruled the result of some accidental cause, then the death that resulted from it was also accidental.

The opening of this chapter described the underlying dilemma faced by every investigator during the investigation of a fatal fire: to separate tragic accidents from criminal matters. The greatest tragedy occurs when, because of investigative laziness or oversight, an arsonist and murderer goes free.

Special Evidence at Fire Scenes

For some time now, bloodstain evidence has been instrumental in determining many different variables at crime scene untouched by fire. In cases where fire has consumed a portion of the scene, either deliberately or by accident, bloodstain evidence can reveal crucial information once thought compromised by the effects of heat and fire. Bloodstain evidence can be observed in two very distinctive categories.

Internal Bloodstains

Internal bloodstains are identified as bloodstains found inside the body. *Livor mortis* or *lividity* is a postmortem discoloration found in the dependent portions of the body. Often referred to as "staining of the skin," this artifact is a product of the collection of blood in the superficial vessels of the skin. Lividity is acted on by gravitational pull and becomes evidence 30 minutes to 2 hours following death. The interpretive value of lividity depends on three elements:

Permanent placement color lividity develops at a progressive rate until it becomes fixed. During the first 10 to 12 hours after death, lividity is transient, that is to say, if the victim has been positioned on the back then rolled over to the stomach, the lividity pattern will migrate to the newly dependent areas of the body. Once the lividity is fixed, and the victim is rolled over, the pattern will remain in its original position and appear inappropriate to the scene. Therefore, the placement of the lividity pattern and the position of the body compliment each other.

The *permanence* of the lividity pattern helps estimate a time frame for the time of death. By pressing on an area where livor mortis is present, before it has become fixed, the stain can be moved or what some investigators call blanched. This is similar to applying pressure to your fingernail and observing the color leave the nail bed. When pressure is released, the color returns.

The *color* of the lividity can help identify specific influences that may have contributed to the death. Normal lividity has been described as a dark red-purple color, often confused with bruising by those not familiar with lividity. When people are alive during the onset of a fire and suffer prolonged exposure to the products of combustion (smoke), the lividity pattern will take on a cherry red color. This color difference is an indicator of the presence of carbon monoxide in the blood.

When a body has been subjected to contact with flames and there is charring of the head, a postmortem *epidural hematoma* (also referred to as an extradural hematoma or heat hematoma) is often found at autopsy. A thick accumulation of blood routinely covers the front and sides of the brain. This forensic artifact often distresses the criminal investigator because hematomas located in the head, in cases other than fatal fires, are often associated with blunt trauma. The antemortem and postmortem epidural hematomas are easily differentiated in color, as the postmortem epidural hematoma is chocolate brown in color, fragile, and has the appearance of a honeycomb structure.

Internal Changes

When blood inside the body is exposed to high temperatures, certain changes occur. Hemolysis is the separation of hemoglobin from the red blood cells. Hemolysis should be considered when interpreting lividity patterns in fire fatalities. This process occurs when the body is exposed to a temperature of 120°F (70°C) and may affect the lividity pattern depending, upon how soon after death the body is exposed to heat. The process of lividity, by itself, does not appear to be significantly affected by the introduction of a heat source, but blood does undergo some change when heat is applied.

External Bloodstains

Blood evidence found outside of the human body is referred to as "external bloodstains." This evidence is acted upon by the laws of physics and maintains specific properties:

Blood has *specific gravity* — blood is affected by gravity and reacts according to gravitational pull.

Blood is a *viscous fluid* — viscosity is a physical property of a substance that depends on the friction of its component molecules as they slide by one another.

Blood has *surface tension* — a single droplet of blood has an outer layer which is referred to as "surface tension." This property has been compared to a water balloon, inasmuch as the water is contained within the skin of the balloon.

In a fire environment where sufficient venting is available, air drafts and turbulence are commonplace. Although gravity is still at work here, these air drafts will alter the path or direction of travel blood will take. For the most part, drops of blood will have already fallen before the ignition of a flame. However, large pools of blood on the floor and wet flow patterns, where victims pressed against a wall depositing blood, can be affected by the heavy air currents inside a structure. Where normally the blood would run straight down a wall until it reaches the floor, air currents will alter the blood flow diagonally or near horizontally, depending on the strength of the shear and volume of blood.

Figure 7.10 Blood stains are commonly preserved on floor surface, particularly carpet.

Heat affects viscosity. When temperatures rise, the viscosity of a fluid begins to break down. The heat emitted from a flame will begin to degrade the bloodstain, and eventually the bloodstain itself will become fuel for the fire. As with other fuel sources at a fire scene, the physical composition of a bloodstain is changed when a heat source is applied over time. The process of physical change in structure at a fire scene is called *pyrolysis*. The human body, blood, and other body fluids are not normally thought of as a fuel source, yet with the onset of heat, their physical composition is changed and they soon may fuel the fire.

Wet vs. Dry Bloodstains

In original experimentation observing dry and wet bloodstains exposed to a heat source, the resulting physical appearances were remarkable. Those stains that were fully dried prior to the introduction of a heat source maintained their original shape and configuration better than the wet stains. Because the dried stains had already undergone a gradual dehydration process, the shapes and configurations of the stains were a permanent marker on the target surface. As heat was introduced to the wet stains, the dehydration process was forced and rapid, which resulted in distortion of the stains, their shape and configuration.

In the presence of heat, the cohesive force of wet blood turns into a membrane-like skin similar to the design of a water balloon. When wet blood is exposed to heat, the outer surface is the first segment of the bloodstain to begin to dehydrate.

That presence of heat, over time, causes the surface tension (outer skin) to become less fluid and eventually better simulate the water balloon with its very resilient outer layer. The internal portion of the bloodstain will eventually reach a point where it also begins to evaporate. This results in the fracturing of the outer membrane in order to release the internal pressures created by the process occurring within. Eventually the entire stain will be dried. When the ambient temperature reaches 160°F (70°C) in a fire scene, blood will rapidly dry, and the process described above will happen systematically. It should be noted that large-volume bloodstains take longer to dry than do smaller volume bloodstains. Therefore, a pool of blood takes longer to dry than a single dripped stain. When high-velocity impact bloodspatter (which is characterized as misted or atomized blood) is released from a gunshot wound, the drying process occurs in a very rapid sequence simply because of the slight volume of the stain.

Interpretation of Evidence

The Human Body

When the body is exposed to heat and flame, it is affected in varying degrees of thickness. The standard measure of these burns are first, second, third, and fourth degree, or superficial, partial, or full thickness, respectively. In first degree (or superficial) burns, the skin appears red and is warm to touch.

Second degree (or partial thickness) burns appear red and, depending on the severity, there may or may not be blisters, and the burned area will heat without scarring. Third degree (or full thickness) burns appear dry and light colored and blisters are not normally seen. If the victim survives, scarring would be certain. Fourth-degree burns involve long exposure to a heat source which results in the partial cremation of the exposed portion of the body and extends into layers below the skin. Tissue burns and eventual charring of the skin is caused by the application of dry heat, such as a flame, radiant heat, or a hot object in contact with the skin. Actual burning of the skin begins when exposed to a temperature of 120°F (30°C) for a period of 1 minute. Long splits in the skin are often seen when examining burned bodies, and may be attributed to the thermal damage rather than antemortem trauma. Bloodstain evidence is often associated with the advent of these splits in the skin and adheres to the properties described earlier. In scenes without fire, hair is often discovered months and even years after death. Cases have been reported where investigators have recovered hair from birds' nests situated near the site where the skeletal remains were found years earlier. In scenes where fire has been introduced, the composition of hair will begin to change. White hair begins to turn yellow at 280°F(140°C) while pigmented hair does not change color. Charring and eventual destruction of hair has been noted to occur at temperatures around 500°F (260°C).

Smoke and Sludge

In a fire environment, smoke is a fuel the fire will eventually consume. Inside, plumes generate a dense layer of smoke that will ultimately fill a closed space from top to bottom. The hotter the upper layer of gas, the greater the degradation of other materials in the room. Smoke represents the material that did not burn completely the first time. This environment is full of char, solid matter in very small particulate form, as well as liquids in an aerosol form. This by-product of the fire is produced by the pyrolysis of the first fuels partially consumed by the fire. When aerosolized liquids that are found in smoke strike a glass surface, the smoke recondenses and a brown sludge is created. Sludge, like smoke, represents fuel for later stages of the fire's development if there is enough thermal momentum to ignite it. Smoke and sludge collect on internal surfaces in structure fires. These deposits cover and sometimes preserve bloodstain evidence on walls and ceilings by establishing a protective layer covering the bloodstain. Conversely, if the thermal momentum of the fire reaches its maximum, the protective layer of soot can become fuel for the later stage of the fire and along with the soot, the bloodstain can be consumed by flames. This phenomenon was observed when blood was deposited on a plate glass window in a controlled structure burn. The blood was coated with soot and sealed to the glass in the initial stages of the fire. As the fire reached its later stages, the soot was wiped clean from the plate glass as were the bloodstains, resulting in a clean sheet of glass.

When the ceiling temperature reaches 932 to 1112°F (500 to 600°C), flashover occurs. At this point, the entire room simultaneously bursts into flames. It is during this phase of the fire that smoke and sludge is used as a fuel and is consumed. When flashover occurs, bloodstains are also pyrolized and change in their physical composition, turning blood into a fuel for the flame. In some cases, windows tinted by smoke and sludge before flashover are wiped clear again when the flame consumes the sooty deposits.

Target Surfaces

Different substrates will conduct heat energy in different ways. Sheetrock surfaces will absorb heat with little conducting ability, while in lath and plaster surfaces the plaster is cooked and the lath superheats until it eventually ignites. When looking at bloodstains on specific surfaces, it is important to keep the exact material in mind. Bloodstains on metal surfaces exposed to high temperatures are literally baked onto the surface. Because of their relative size, bloodstains found on painted, textured surfaces and exposed to heat and flame tend to dry and flake off. Rough and more porous surfaces, like raw lumber and heavy-textured wall paper, allow the bloodstain to penetrate deeper and survive the fire environment longer, if the substrate is not charred.

Paramount to examining bloodstain evidence in fire scenes is determining the extent of damage to the evidence, which is dependent upon the following conditions:

- The applied temperature
- The ability of the target surface medium to conduct away the excessive heat
- The length of time the stain is exposed to the applied temperature

A Case Study

The body of a deceased male was found on the floor of his bedroom. He had been stabbed numerous times and the side of his throat had been cut. The culprit(s) had then set the bedroom on fire by pouring an accelerant on the mattress.

The fire department suppressed the fire, which had been confined to the bedroom. The firefighters removed the body from the house and did not realize that this was a homicide scene until the fire was out.

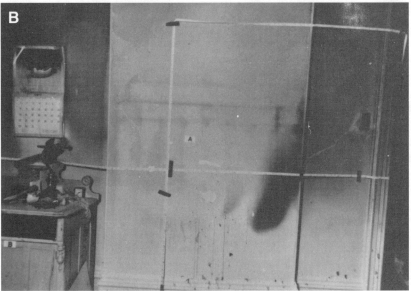

Figure 7.11 (A-B) Scene of a homicide and fire to cover crime.

The fire had altered the general scene conditions and affected the physical appearance of several bloodstains. Projected bloodstains, which were on the wall at the head of the bed, were significantly altered in comparison to the other projected bloodstains found at the scene.

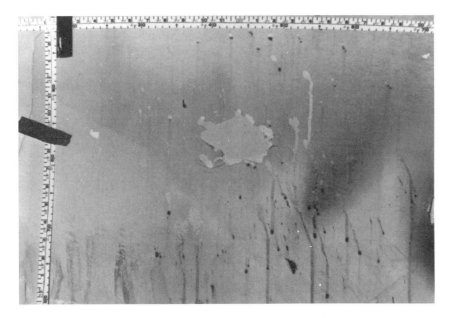

Figure 7.12   Close-up of projected bloodstain on wall behind head of bed. Note change in appearance is similar to bloodstains shown in Figure 7.18.

These projected bloodstains were "faded" and lighter in appearance than the adjacent soot-covered surfaces. In some cases, there was no visual evidence of dried blood in these altered stains. The original shape of each stain was still recognizable, and it was felt that the fire had affected the blood, resulting in the projected stains having a "negative" appearance. The darkening of stain color and the "sooting over" effect commonly observed at fire scenes were not evident on these altered bloodstains.

Subsequent bloodstain pattern analysis answered questions as to the path of travel the victim took once he was bleeding, where he received his bloodletting blows, and the locations of arterial bleeding. Swabs were obtained from the altered bloodstains and were suitable for DNA typing.

Research was conducted to duplicate the "ghosting" or fading image of the bloodstains in question. As the mock crime scenes were being set up, the thought of including a "wet vs. dry effects" experiment was introduced. The objective was to identify any physiological differences between the wet and dry stains, when they were subjected to fire.

This investigation also raised questions which were not fully addressed within any known bloodstain or crime scene publications.

- What factors contributed to the fading of these bloodstains?
- Are these stains recognizable as being altered bloodstains?
- Are these altered stains present in some or all fire scenes?

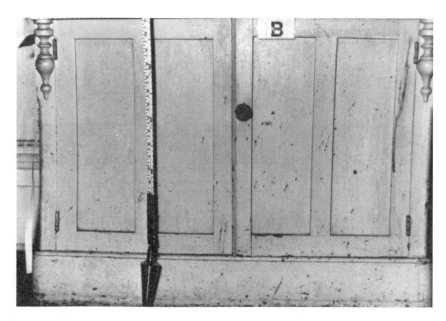

Figure 7.13 Close-up of nightstand front located to left of bed in Figure 7.11. Note bloodstains.

Figure 7.14 High-velocity impact spatter on the ceiling above suicide victim, post fire.

In an endeavor to answer these questions,* a joint project between the Halifax Regional Forensic Support Section of the Royal Canadian Mounted Police and the Level II Arson Course of the Canadian Investigative Fire School was initiated.

Procedure

An old motel was being used by the Fire School to conduct arson investigations. Two units of the motel were chosen as "crime scene" sites and were set-up as bloodletting scenes.

Human blood was deposited in the rooms to simulate realistic crime scenes. Bloodstain patterns (projected, transferred, wipes, swipes, and cast-off stains) were deposited at various locations within these rooms.

The rooms were then set afire and allowed to burn for approximately 10 minutes. The fire suppression teams were advised to fight the fires as normal. When they knew they had entered a crime scene, they were to be aware of any potential physical evidence.

The crime scenes were then examined by the blood stain pattern analyst, to assess the physical evidence that may have been altered by the fire or firefighters.

Scene One

Purpose — To duplicate altered bloodstains from the original crime scene.

Application — A single motel unit, consisting of a bedroom and a bathroom, was the scene of a mock sexual assault, homicide and arson. A mannequin was placed on a mattress and a beer bottle was used to strike blows to the head.

Bloodstains — The following bloodstains were deposited:

1. Soaking stain on mattress at head of victim
2. Medium velocity stain on wall at the head of the bed
3. Swipe mark on the wall beside the bed
4. Cast-off stains on the wall, window, mirror, sink, shower, and ceiling
5. Transfer and dripping stains on window ledge and floor

---

* A chapter in *Interpretation of Bloodstain Evidence at Crime Scenes* by William G. Eckert and Stuart H. James, deals with some aspects of bloodstains at fire scenes. This information was authored by David R. Redsicker, and is titled "Recognition and Identification of Bloodstains at Fire Scenes."

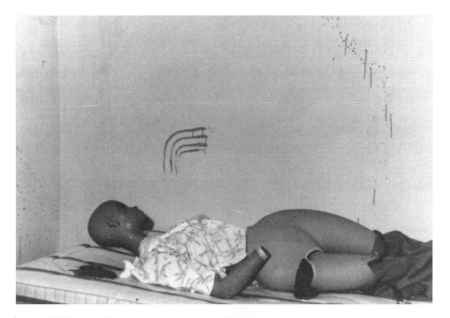

Figure 7.15 Mock crime scene where bloodstains were deposited within scene before setting fire.

The target surfaces included:

1. Painted drywall
2. Painted wood
3. Wafer style ceiling tiles
4. Glass
5. Ceramic
6. Fiberglass
7. Fabric
8. Vinyl flooring and carpet
9. Beer bottle

The bloodstains were applied to all the surfaces and were dry when the fire started. A time span of approximately 20 to 30 minutes elapsed between the bloodletting and the setting of the fire.

Lighter fluid was poured over the mattress and victim and then ignited. The fire was allowed to burn for approximately 8 to 10 minutes and was put out using standard fire suppressing techniques.

Observations:
    Soaking stain (on mattress)
        • Altered due to water
        • Diluted in appearance

Figure 7.16   Bloodswipe on wall next to bed pre-fire.

Figure 7.17   The bed was set on fire using lighter fluid. The fire was allowed to burn itself out.

- Extended beyond original size
- The original outline and shape still visible

Medium velocity stains (on painted drywall)

- Altered significantly by the heat
- Some smaller stains disappeared

- Stains may not be recognizable as a medium velocity pattern
- Some dilution
- Running appearance(due to water)
- Darkening of stain color

Cast-off stains (on wallpaper, walls, glass, fiberglass tub, sink)
- Altered by water
- Running diluted appearance
- Darkening of stain color
- Some running stains (on glass) were lightened

Cast-off stains (on ceiling)
- Stains on ceiling tiles bled into background
- Were diluted by water
- Darkened in color
- Original staining was altered by the appearance of extra stains

Swipe mark (on painted wall next to body)
- Color severely altered
- Density of the stain diminished
- Faded considerably
- Width of stain diminished
- Diluted running stains from swipe

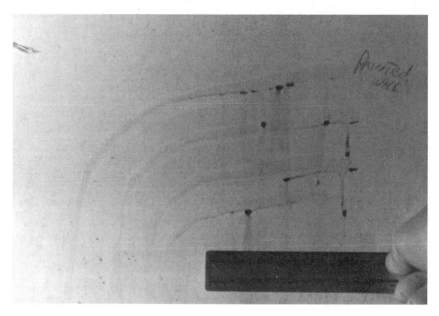

Figure 7.18 Bloodswipe on wall next to bed post-fire. Note they are faded and appear to have a negative appearance.

Transfer and dripping stains (on window ledge, floor, beer bottle)
- Stains on window ledge obliterated by water
- Only recognizable as diluted blood
- Passive dripping on floor was not affected by fire but was altered by the firefighters
- No stains on the floor altered by water damage
- No stains on floor displayed color change from heat or smoke
- Beer bottle on floor was not affected

Scene Two

Purpose: To observe if there were any resulting physiological differences between wet and dry swipe marks, after exposure to fire.

Application:

A hotel unit, consisting of two adjoining rooms and two bathrooms, was the scene of a mock bloodletting and arson.

Bloodstains were deposited on various surfaces within the two rooms. These stains were allowed to dry and prior to setting of the fire, additional bloodstains were applied wet.

The principal purpose of Scene Two was to observe if there were any physiological differences between the general appearance of the dry and wet bloodstain patterns after they were exposed to a fire.

Bloodstains — The following bloodstains were deposited:

1. Cast-off bloodstains on walls, ceiling and glass
2. Soaking bloodstains on carpet, mattress and chair fabric
3. Pooling of blood on floor
4. Swipe marks on walls, chrome and glass
5. Projected bloodstains on painted drywall

The target surfaces included:

1. Fabric covered chair
2. Toaster
3. Paper towel
4. Painted drywall
5. Ceiling tile
6. Glass

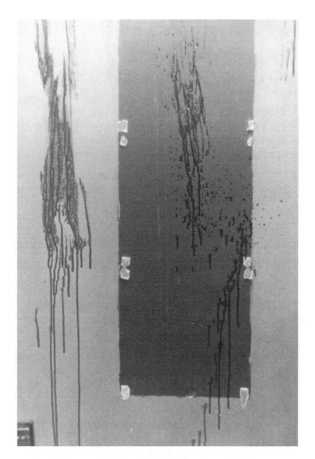

Figure 7.19   Fresh, wet, cast-off and dripping bloodstains just prior to fire.

The fire was set using a toaster and paper toweling, which had been soaked in alcohol. The fire was allowed to burn for approximately 13 to 15 minutes and then extinguished.

General Observations
Cast-off bloodstains (on ceiling, walls, glass)
  • Altered by water damage
  • Diluted and running
  • Darkened in color
  • Stains on ceiling turned black
Soaking bloodstains (on chair)
  • On cloth, still visible
  • Diluted appearance
  • Stains on wood trim not altered

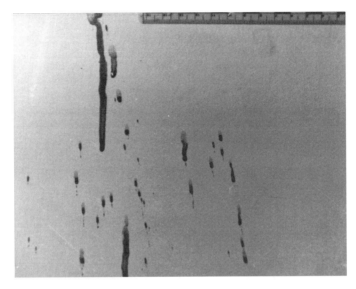

Figure 7.20 Cast-off bloodstains deposited on wall and left to dry prior to setting room on fire.

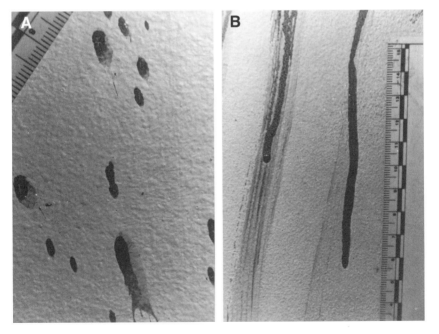

Figure 7.21 Close-up of (A) cast-off and (B) dripping bloodstains. Notice eggshell cracking effect, shiny coagulated finish, and raised appearance-post fire.

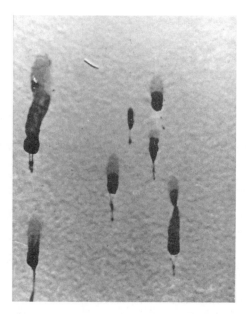

Figure 7.22 Close-up of bloodstains shown in Figure 7.20, post-fire. Note dull appearance; bloodstains are not cracked or shiny as in Figure 7.21.

Soaking bloodstains (on paper towel)
  • Destroyed by fire
Pooling of blood (on floor)
  • Not altered
Swipe marks (on toaster and walls close to fire): the swipe marks were placed on a number of walls at a distance from the fire of 35 cm to 4 m.
  • Stain on the ignition source (toaster) was darkened and had a "baked-on" appearance
  • Stains placed within close proximity to the fire were altered significantly more than stains further away
  • If stain was close to fire, it had a faded appearance; as distance increased, the only change was a darkening of stain color and some dilution (by water)
Projected stains (on wall behind ignition point)
  • Projected stains above the fire source were destroyed by the fire

Specific Observations:
  Wet vs. dry bloodstains: Approximately 8 areas of bloodstains were applied within 1 to 2 min before the ignition of the fire. A significant difference was observed in the individual appearance of these stains when they were subjected to heat and smoke:

Wet bloodstain appearance:
- Surface had a shiny, coagulated finish
- A cracked eggshell appearance
- Some retraction on the edges of the stains
- Raised appearance
- The pooling at the ends of the drip marks as cracked

Dry bloodstain appearance:
- A dull, flat look
- No cracking eggshell appearance
- No retraction of the edges of the stains
- Flat (not raised) appearance
- The ends of the drip marks were not cracked

Results:

The closer the stain to the fire, the more prevalent the physiological changes. The further away the stain, the less prevalent the changes, but these characteristics were still present.

Conclusions:

The initial purpose of this research was to reproduce the ghosting or fading image of the projected bloodstains found in the original homicide investigation. Unfortunately, we were not able to duplicate these stains in these mock crime scene experiments.

It is unknown if the original altered bloodstains (crime scene) were subjected to the same physiological occurrences that the swipe marks (mock crime scene) underwent, or if these changes will occur at every fire scene.

This preliminary study did show that:

- Only swiped bloodstains within close proximity (35 to 50 cm) to the fire faded
- This fading was only seen on one other area of staining, the dripping stain on a piece of window glass
- Stains on painted surfaces were most affected by the fading phenomenon
- Swiping marks situated further than 50 cm from the fire darkened in color
- All projected stains near to and at a distance from the fire were subjected to a darkening effect
- No fading was observed on any projected stains
- The medium velocity bloodstain pattern adjacent to the bed was altered significantly

The effects of water and the actions of the fire fighting personnel accounted for a variety of physiological changes that were recognizable and explainable, except for bloodstains that were totally obliterated.

As to the questions:

> "What factors contributed to the fading of these bloodstains?" It is not known specifically what factors influence the fading of the projected bloodstains.
>
> "Are these stains recognizable as being altered bloodstains?" Yes, the bloodstains are recognizable and if pertinent, should be used as part of the bloodstain pattern analysis. (DNA typing should be conducted on any areas of staining that are being commented on.)
>
> "Are these altered stains present in some or all fire scenes?" This is unknown. Numerous factors may dictate whether bloodstains will be altered (i.e. duration of fire, amount of heat, smoke or water, location of blood in relationship to the fire source, height of the stains compared to height of fire, etc.). What degree and form the altering will take, is also an unknown.

The "wet vs. dry" experiment may prove to be the most valuable piece of information obtained from this study.

The ability to analyze the physiological characteristics observed in the "wet vs. dry" experiment, and the ability to comment on the issue: "Was the blood wet or dry when the fire was set?", may help the bloodstain pattern analyst in reaching conclusions or opinions that were not previously obtainable.

Caution should be taken when evaluating a scene where fire has altered the physical conditions and affected the appearance of bloodstains. The bloodstain pattern analyst should be aware of the probable effects that fire may have on a bloodstain pattern. If these factors are considered in the analysis, then the rendered opinions or conclusions may be more complete.

Please note that this is a preliminary study — additional experimentation is necessary. This is intended as an introduction into recognizing the probable effects that fire, heat, and smoke may have on bloodstains.

References and Selected Readings

Adelson, L., *The pathology of Homicide*, Charles C Thomas, Springfield, IL, 1974.

Ault, R. L., Jr. and Reese, J. T., A psychological assessment of crime: profiling, *FBI Law Enforcement Bull.* 49(3), 1980.

Christman, Daniel, V., Investigator, Snohomish Co. Medical Examiner's Office, Everett, Wash., "Fire and it's Effect on Bloodstain Pattern Evidence," Paper presented at International Assoc. of Bloodstain Pattern Analysts 1995 Convention, Miami, FL.

DeHaan, J., *Kirks Fire Investigation*, 2nd ed., John Wiley & Sons, New York, 1983.

DiMaio, D. J. and Vincent, J. M., *Forensic Pathology*, CRC Press, Boca Raton, FL., 1993.

Geberth, V. J., *Practical Homicide Investigation*, 2nd ed., CRC Press, Boca Raton, Florida, 1996.

Gross, E. M., The role of the medical examiner in homicide investigation, course material, Homicide Investigation Course, New York City Police Dept., undated.

Harris, R. I., *Outline of Death Investigation*, Charles C Thomas, Springfield, IL, 1962.

Hughes, D. J., *Homicide Investigative Techniques*, Charles C Thomas, Springfield, IL, 1974.

Kennedy, J., *Fire and Arson Investigation*, Investigations Institute, Chicago, 1962 (rev. 1977).

Kirk, P. L., *Fire Investigation*, John Wiley & Sons, New York, 1969.

O'Hara, C. E., *Fundamentals of Criminal Investigation*, 5th ed., Charles C Thomas, Springfield, IL, 1980.

Snyder, L., *Homicide Investigation*, 3rd ed., Charles C Thomas, Springfield, IL, 1977.

Spitz, W. U., and Fisher, R. S., *Medicolegal Investigation of Death: Guidelines for the Application of Pathology to Crime Investigation*, Charles C Thomas, Springfield, IL, 1973.

Tomash, M. C. (Craig), Sgt., R.C.M.P., Halifax Regional Forensic Identification Support Section. "How Fire May Effect Crime Scene Bloodstains," Paper presented at International Assoc. of Bloodstain Pattern Analysts 1995 Convention, Miami, FL.

Watanabe, T., *Atlas of Legal Medicine*, J.B. Lippincott, Philadelphia, 1968.

Investigating Vehicular Fires

8

There are tens of millions of motor vehicles on the highways and streets of America. Over the next 12 months, millions of these will be involved in accidents. About one million vehicles will be reported stolen. Thousands more will be abandoned, their derelict frames dotting the landscape. Hundreds of thousands will burn; close to 20,000 of these are classified as vehicular arson each year.

People burn their automobiles, vans, and mobile homes for the same reasons that they burn their homes: the primary motive seems to be money. For the most part, this motive can be described as "selling it to the insurance company." Vehicle values are incentive enough to warrant the investigation of fire losses.

Some enterprising people find an unusual way of getting rid of their cars: by driving them into a ghetto area, well known for its high crime rate, perhaps representing a low socio-economic class. The driver simply parks his or her car and walks away. In a matter of days, the vehicle is usually stripped of its tires, radio, and anything else of value. Soon after that, it may be set on fire, perhaps by a roving band of kids who have nothing better to do. Meanwhile, soon after abandoning the vehicle, the owner contacts the local police and reports the vehicle as stolen.

The investigation of a vehicular fire requires a two-part approach. The first part involves a detailed post-fire *automobile salvage examination* to determine the origin and cause of the fire. The second, which hinges on the determination made during the first, involves the interviewing and/or interrogation of the vehicle's owner (see "Cross Examination" in Chapter 13). If the cause of the fire is determined to be incendiary and the investigator has reason to suspect the owner, then the purpose of the follow-up interview and/or interrogation is to elicit statements that implicate the vehicle owner.

Figure 8.1 Motor vehicle fire incidents continue to increase at a faster rate than any other type of fire incident.

This chapter is concerned with the investigation of vehicular fires and the commensurate responsibility of a fire investigator to investigate and properly classify the cause as either accidental or incendiary.

Many periodicals, references, and manuals refer to intentionally set fire indicators. These include:

1. A sagging roof on the vehicle
2. The color of the chrome on a vehicle (how much heat it has been exposed to)
3. A vehicle whose front fenders are totally burned—devoid of paint
4. Vehicle burn from "bumper-to-bumper"
5. Cars that have been completely burned—with the exception, of course, of the tread that was on the ground, sagging springs or leaves, and an empty engine oil or transmission reservoir
6. The condition of the remaining glass

I mention these because they may have been involved in or near the initiation of the fire and not because someone had ruined an engine or transmission. Small clues such as these are easily dismissed if confronted properly as incendiary indications in court: time of arrival for fire suppression, wind direction, open windows, initial, and secondary fuel loads. When proving a fire cause, I would much rather rely on thorough investigative techniques than look at magic signs. When you eliminate the accidental sources, an incendiary fire can be indisputably determined.

The same is true for showing liability on a product or service by eliminating all other sources of the fire occurrence. Statements from the driver or other witnesses can assist with establishing the origin as accidental. For example:

Bucking or stalling is usually a fuel-related problem
Revving of engine, but no power, may be transmission leak
Loss of power steering may be steering-fluid leak
Loss of brakes may be brake-fluid leak

When it comes to incendiary fires, there are a few things that are not as easily disputable, such as witnesses or gasoline in the back seat, etc. Those are usually definite signs; it all depends on the circumstances. A thorough investigation including statements and pre- and post-fire condition will best back up your final conclusion.

The Four Categories of Fire

Natural

A naturally caused fire is one that has been caused without direct human interventions. A natural cause for a vehicle fire does not seem very plausible. I would think that such possibilities exist in natural disasters. The categories of concern will be accidental, incendiary, and undetermined.

Accidental

These will include, but will not be limited to, misuse of the vehicle (poor maintenance); manufacturing failure or defect; service, repair shop failures or improper procedures; or age, wear, and tear.

Incendiary

There are several different definitions, such as and one "deliberately set on fire under circumstances when the person who is setting the fire realizes that the fire should not be set." This is a vague definition. (For a more detailed definition, see the Glossary.) Arson fire cause is not an acceptable definition. This can only be determined by a judge and jury. An investigator can only state the facts as to whether a fire was accidental, natural, incendiary, or undetermined. Use of the term "arson" is a judicial decision after the fire investigator has completed the investigation.

Undetermined

An "undetermined" fire cause is used when the cause of the fire cannot be proven, whether the fire is still under investigation or awaiting further information. The term *undetermined fire cause* will allow you to keep an investigation open for the event of new pertinent information. The term "suspicious" is an inaccurate definition. Using "undetermined" will allow you to change from what was believed to be "incendiary" to accidental or vice versa, should new information become available.

Requirements Needed for a Fire to Occur

In order to have a fire, four items must be present. This is known as the chemistry of combustion or thefire tetrahedron. According to NFPA 921 Section 3-1.1 (1992 edition), "Fire Tetrahedron", the combustion reaction can be characterized by four components: The fuel, the oxidizing agent, heat, and a self sustained chemical reaction. These four components have been classically symbolized by a four-sided solid geometric form called a tetrahedron (see Chapter 4, Figure 4.1).

Fires can be prevented or suppressed by controlling or removing one or more of the sides of the tetrahedron.

When investigating a vehicle fire, three of the four sides of the fire tetrahedron are present frequently (heat, fuel, and oxidizing agent). The fire investigator must establish the fourth side — what brings them together to cause a fire. The heat can be supplied by anything from the engine to the exhaust system, friction, or a regularly occurring arc or spark within the electrical system. Gasoline is only one of many agents in the vehicle that is a potent and substantial fuel. The oxidizing agent can be considered to be the air that passes over and through the vehicle. The fourth side of the fire tetrahedron would be the self sustained chain reaction (uninhibited chain reaction). This would be the distortion, breakage, deterioration, intentionally caused or other failure in a component or system which would allow the previous three sides of the fire tetrahedron to come into contact with each other.

When a heat source is believed to have been the initiating factor, you must determine if that heat source is of an adequate temperature to have ignited the fuel source. A vehicle that has not been operating for a long time will not have enough heat from the engine or exhaust. In the same scenario, in a vehicle that is also not operating, there are only certain components in the vehicle's electrical system that are still energized.

The investigator must consider the amount of air in comparison to the fuel. This is known as the fuel-to-air ratio where flammable limits must be

Figure 8.2 The origin of the fire was in the passenger compartment, indicated by the classic "V" pattern on the side, and confirmed by positive sample results for presence of gasoline in carpet.

met. (See Chapter 4 "Flammable Limits".) A vehicle traveling at 55 miles per hour with gasoline escaping from the fuel system may not ignite until it begins to slow down or stops, even though fuel, heat, and oxidizer are all present.

Policies

The amount of emphasis that is placed on the investigation of vehicular fires varies widely throughout the country. Certain communities consider vehicles intentionally set afire as a very serious offense requiring a diligent investigation. Other jurisdictions investigate only vehicle fires that involve some other mitigating circumstances: for example death or an organized crime connection. This kind of approach is usually a policy decision mandated by competing interests vying for limited resources. If a specific community is experiencing a major upsurge in crimes such as homicide or rape, how much emphasis in terms of personnel and equipment can be realistically devoted to the investigation of vehicle fires? The local authorities should have a cross-cooperation with other fire investigators, whether from the private sector or the insurance industry. No matter what agency, corporation, or industry that the fire investigator is employed by, our first obligation is safety. For the local municipality, the main interest is to arrest a criminal who is setting fires. The private sector may do the same as the local authorities or investigate more diligently to find that responsibility for the fire occurrence is due to manufacturing defects or service/repair station failure to perform their service. Cooperation between the insurance or private sector with the local authorities is the only way to provide safety for the public or the insurance industry. Many of the items discussed with the local authorities are also relevant to the insurance industry. One of the motivating forces behind the interest in investigations of vehicle fires is not only incendiary vehicle fires, but also to subrogate against responsible parties.

Fraudulent insurance claims involving incendiary vehicle fires have placed a great deal of monetary stress on the insurance industry. This is ultimately paid for by the policyholders in the form of higher premiums.

The basic method of a fire investigation is described in NFPA 921 Section 2-4. Using the scientific method in most fire or explosion incidents should involve the following six major steps from inception through final analysis:

1. Receiving the Assignment
    The investigator should be notified of the incident, what his or her role will be, and what he or she is to accomplish.
2. Preparing for the Investigation
    The investigator should marshal his or her resources and plan the conduct of the investigation.
3. Examination of Scene
    The investigator should examine the scene to collect basic data necessary for the analysis. (This is not always possible, especially for the fire investigator with the insurance industry. This portion of the fire

investigation in vehicle fires can be helpful, but is not an absolute necessity.)

4. Recording the Scene

   The scene should be photographed and diagrammed, and notes on the progress of the investigation should be made. Valuable empirical data should be noted and preserved. (This, again, is not always possible, especially for the fire investigator with the insurance industry. This portion of the fire investigation in vehicle fires can be helpful, but is not an absolute necessity.)

5. Collecting and Preserving Evidence

   Valuable physical evidence should be recognized, properly collected and preserved for further testing and evaluation or courtroom presentation. (See Chapter 9.)

6. Analyzing the Incident

   An incident scenario or failure analysis should be prepared explaining origin, cause, and responsibility for the incident. This analysis should be reported in the proper form. (This is extremely important. It is our primary goal as fire investigators.)

Notification and Response

Once a fire investigator is notified of a vehicle fire, the decision as to whether or not he or she will respond to the scene is usually based upon several factors. All of the factors listed below may not apply to local authorities, and others may not apply to investigators of the private sector.

1. Preliminary determination made by the fire officer who directed the fire suppression operations.
2. Number and type of other fire cases under investigation that require active follow-up.
3. Available personnel.
4. Time of day. Most incendiary vehicle fires occur at night in remote areas where lighting conditions are poor, whereas a detailed examination requires daylight.
5. Mitigating circumstances (a body or contraband [narcotics, weapons, etc.] is involved, the vehicle is connected to a member of organized crime or to the commission of another crime, and classification of the vehicle as abandoned or derelict — in which case a fire investigator would not ordinarily respond to the scene).
6. The location of the fire scene. If the local authorities are concerned, there is usually no problem in examining the scene. For the fire investigator representing the insurance industry or private sector, examination

of the scene is usually not a necessity, since the distance between the fire investigator and scene may be great and the vehicle has most likely been removed from the scene. In many cases, it may have been moved so much further away from the scene that it would make it unwarranted for a scene examination, or such a lapse of time has occurred that a scene investigation is unnecessary or would be unfounded. The information from the scene investigation could be obtained from the local authorities through their field notes.

All telephone or written reports of vehicle fires should be kept in a separate log so not as to confuse them with other calls for service. The log serves as a ready reference and storage of data from monthly and quarterly reports, helps in preparing and updating related crime analysis reports, and ensures equitable distribution of cases among the investigators. Keeping a log of vehicle fires may indicate a trend as to the time of the year or the failure of a specific component in a vehicle.

If a vehicle fire has been declared incendiary or undetermined, or if the fire investigator has been asked to respond, the vehicle should be safeguarded and protected until they arrive. The safeguarding of the vehicle is required by the local authorities, but not as much as by the insurance industry or private sector. The vehicle should not be returned or released to the owner without approval from the assigned investigators and other parties (such as the manufacturer or repair shops) who have an interest in the examination of the subject vehicle fire.

Vehicle Collisions and Relation to Vehicle Fires

Single Vehicle Collisions

The investigation of such accidents is highly specialized, and generally is conducted by special units from local, state, and federal agencies, or the private sector, including the insurance industry. One common exception, however, is the case of a fire of a vehicle supposedly involved in a single-vehicle collision. Certain mitigating circumstances, when carefully considered, may well heighten the investigator's interest in a particular case such as:

1. *The location of the incident.* Is the area populated or is it a desolate area? Did the fire occur in a location where it was highly unlikely for anyone to have witnessed it?
2. *Collision evidence.* Although the vehicle may show signs of collision damage, is there any physical evidence at the scene, independent of the vehicle, that would support the driver's contention? This type of scrutiny is important to avoid the possibility of a prior unreported multiple vehicle

accident now being reported as a single-vehicle accident with a fire to disguise this fact. The reason for this may have been that the person did not carry collision insurance, but did have fire and theft insurance.

3. *Time of incident (daylight vs. nighttime).* Did the reported accident and fire occur at a time when it was highly unlikely for anyone to have witnessed it?

4. *Driver's description of the incident.* Care must be taken to evaluate statements made by the driver to the first fire or police units to arrive. Can incriminating or inconsistent statements be identified?

Multiple-Vehicle Collisions

Collisions involving two or more vehicles, with a fire ensuing later, must be carefully examined. In the vehicle that is fire damaged, an area of origin must be determined. All of the damage sustained from the collision must be taken into account, involving components such as mechanical, fluid transfer lines, electrical systems, or other possible sources for fire occurrence. The compromising of the integrity of any of these systems can easily allow the four sides of the fire tetrahedron to occur and start a fire. Broken fuel lines may also involve other vehicles that were in the collision. The manufacturer may be at fault in some of these fire events. As you probably know, the incidents involving a series of General Motors trucks with side-saddle fuel tanks have been under scrutiny for potential fire hazards when subjected to a side-impact collision. Another example is the recall of the Saab 9000, years 1992 to 1994: even in low-speed frontal collisions, the oil cooler hose assembly could break and leak oil, creating a fire hazard. Making note of this and keeping records of these types of fire events can lead to future recalls and better safety for the public. To find out about recalls and service bulletins. The public is entitled to such information through the Auto Safety Hot Line which keeps a database on vehicle fires and their causes.

Vehicle Identification and Owner Information

Upon arrival, the investigator should first make a complete and accurate description of the vehicle including color, make, year, manufacturer, license plate number, registration, vehicle identification number (VIN), and state inspection code number on inspection sticker, if any. The VIN can be found in various places. If you are unsure where to find the less obvious areas of the VIN number, contact the local dealer and ask the service department.

State Inspection Code Number

By contacting the inspection station, an accurate mileage reading can be obtained from a specific date, along with possible notes on the vehicle's condition. This information should be transmitted to the state department

Figure 8.3 (A) Fatal accidents involving fires require detailed documentation and analysis to determine the sequence of events and responsibility. (B) Impact to the right front of the vehicle engine compartment compromised the fuel lines.

of motor vehicles, local police auto squad, and the National Auto Theft Bureau. These agencies will provide the following identity:

- Name and address of the last registered owner
- Verification of color, make, year, manufacturer and/or code number
- Name of the insurance company and pedigree of the vehicle, including history, dealer information, past accidents if reported, and if the vehicle was subject of a prior insurance settlement (salvage)

Figure 8.4 Was the vehicle reported stolen? Note the vehicle identification number (VIN). Since 1971, the VIN has been located on the upper left side of the dashboard of all U.S.-manufactured and most foreign automobiles.

- A correlation of the engine and vehicle data (9-digit engine serial number is incorporated in the 17 digit VIN)
- Verification of registration and vehicle data (e.g., whether the correct license plates are on the vehicle)
- Possible identification of state-registered inspection

Information on Vehicle Recalls and Service Bulletins

1. Contact a local dealer and speak with a service manager. For recalls, just give him the Vehicle Identification Number. Most dealers have a computer link to the manufacturer. For service bulletins you can give them the VIN but the year, make, and model may also be necessary. This contact with the dealer's service manager is quick and easy, usually taking only 15 minutes.
2. Contact the manufacturer directly. There are 800 numbers for all companies. To obtain your car maker's number, call 800-555-1212. By the phone method you can get an immediate answer whereas it can take a couple of weeks for a written response.
3. National Highway Safety Administration (NHSA) 1-800-424-9393. This is an automated touch-tone service. You can obtain and give information about vehicle fires.
4. Obtain a subscription to *Consumer Reports*. Each monthly issue provides a listing of recalls.
5. Contact your nearest insurance carrier's main office (not agents). Speak with a representative of the salvage department or motor vehicle claims department. Ask who they use for vehicle fire investigations. As an investigator in the field industry, I handle many vehicle fires on a regular basis.

Since 1971, the vehicle identification number (VIN) has been located on the upper left side of the dashboard on all U.S. manufactured and most imported vehicles. These numbers are also incorporated in various other places on the vehicle, especially the newer models of these vehicles in which many of the most valuable pieces, even glass, have the VIN secured to or etched on them. If the vehicle has been reported stolen, the investigator should compare the approximate time and date of the fire with the time and date of the reported theft.

Salvage Examination

Salvage examination is completed in stages. The basic stage is exterior and interior inspections. The fire investigator should thoroughly examine the exterior of the vehicle before starting the interior examination.

Exterior Examination

The investigator should first examine the exterior of the vehicle and the immediately surrounding area. During this stage you should pay particular attention to the following:

1. Tires (extended burning conditions, rims, lug nuts, hub caps, tool marks.)
2. Gas tank (tank flange, cap or filler tube).
3. Suspension system (springs, shock absorbers, sagging, annealed, rubber spacers).
4. Glass (in place, missing, softened, fused, window frames, windows open or closed during fire, amount of soot build-up on the windows, position of roller arm, power windows).
5. Doors (open or closed during the course of the fire. Condition of the locks, any signs of the locks inside the door.)
6. Catalytic converter. (Is there one? Are heat shields in place? This can be determined by a service technician for that particular vehicle. Has recent work been done on the catalytic converter? You may have to remove the catalytic converter and examine the internal components for a breakdown of the material inside).

Figure 8.5 (A-C) During the exterior examination, the investigator should photograph the exterior of the vehicle and the area surrounding the vehicle. Note the general condition of the vehicle, including collision damage. Is the vehicle burned "bumper-to-bumper?" If an accelerant was used, it may be possible to see where the accelerant dripped from the vehicle to the ground.

Figure 8.5

7. Exhaust system (is there fluid coming in contact with the exhaust system and igniting, or are combustible materials possibly stuck or wrapped around the exhaust system?)

8. Brakes (examination of the brake lines on the underside of the vehicle for potential leaks coming in contact with a heat source).

9. Underside fuel lines (possible breakage, tampering or failure allowing fuel to escape and come in contact with an ignition source).

10. Dragging materials creating by friction to ignite combustibles adjacent to and around the underside of the vehicle.

11. Transmission and oil fluid pans under the vehicle. Examine for seal failure, spray patterns, leaks, or fracture of housing. You may even see the fluid coated over the underside. It may be useful to get both oil and transmission fluid samples for laboratory analysis to determine their pre-fire condition. This can determine the condition of the engine or transmission.

12. Drive shaft. Closely examine the entire drive shaft for "fish mouth." This occurs when a severe amount of long-term heat is applied to the sealed hollow drive shaft. The air inside will eventually rise in pressure until the drive shaft literally ruptures and "fish mouths." This can also have enough force to rip a hole in the under side of the vehicle into the passenger compartment. This can indicate a fuel-fed fire, not necessarily an incendiary fire, but it does show that gasoline or other volatile fuel was involved at some point in the fire.

13. Engine and trunk hoods (collision damage, condition of paint, earlier collision damage such as bondo or sheet metal, demarcation of patterns on the hoods, made of fiberglass or metal, forced entry, locks missing. Indications of a CB or mobile phone antenna or signs that they existed at one time, such as scratching or protected areas).

14. Fenders (collision damage, burn pattern on paint, extent of burn pattern on paint, prior collision damage).

15. Grille (collision damage) by looking at the exterior of the radiator which side had received the most heat damage. Since the radiators are made of thin aluminum, impinging flame can create distinct melting patterns indicating direction of fire origin.

16. Bumpers (collision damage) evidence that vehicle was pushed or towed to site; made of plastic or metal, were there bumpers on the vehicle before the fire? Some vehicles such as trucks are not equipped with rear bumpers, except as an option.

17. Doors (collision damage) burn pattern on paint, were they open or closed during the fire, were locks in place, had they been tampered with, possible tool marks in and around the window frame.

18. Lights (collision and/or fire damage).

19. License plates (registration/inspection stickers and service stickers, usually located inside the driver's side door or in the left corner of the windshield).

All information gained in an investigation should be noted in the investigator's notes by photographs and written notes. Any collision damage should be photographed. The total extent of fire damage should be noted. Any vehicle fire which extends from bumper to bumper should be thoroughly scrutinized.

How long did the vehicle burn?
What type of fuel load was contained within the vehicle?
Was it a newer or older model?
Was the engine on or off at the time of the fire occurrence?
Was it being driven, stationary and idling, or just parked?

An extensive burn pattern is highly unlikely if the fire was noticed quickly and was caused by an electrical failure. You must take into account the witnesses' and/or vehicle owner's statements.

An investigator must realistically consider what parts of the vehicle are combustible: whether hoses, wire insulation, tires, rubbers, grease and oil, floor mats, carpeting and seat padding, undercoating, ornamentation, and personal property were involved. A fire that accidentally starts in one of the three interior compartments will usually tend to stay in that compartment unless enough time has passed before fire suppression efforts or a flammable/combustible fuel is involved. Exceptions to this may be a fire originating near the natural openings in the firewall (bulkhead) or the underside involving the transmission or exhaust system.

You also must take into consideration that the release of a fuel line may enter at the rear of the engine compartment close to the fire wall. "Fire wall" is a very poor term, since many new vehicles have fire walls that are built with large openings for the heater vent, wiring, and other components to pass through.

If visible exterior fire damage is pinpointed to the area surrounding one of the interior compartments, the investigator should be able to determine that to be the area of fire origination. If the vehicle fire is small and very localized, and believed to be an electrical fire, the tracing of electrical wiring from the area of origin is possible. It can lead to other smaller failures further down the line.

Tires

A person intending to burn his or her vehicle may remove good tires and replace them with old, worthless ones before starting the fire. What is the condition of the tire tread? How much of the tire was burned? Is the fire and

Figure 8.6 Firefighters risk injury fighting vehicle fires in which the vehicle owner's intention was to "sell the car to the insurance company." In this photograph, gasoline had been poured in the passenger compartment and the vehicle was set ablaze. The vehicle had been intentionally placed in a very secluded area. Note the snow tires mounted on the front wheels of a rear-wheel-drive automobile. The subsequent investigation revealed that the burnt auto had been towed to the scene.

heat damage more severe to the inside of the tire and/or rim, or to the outside, indicating path of fire travel? Even when the whole tire burns, there is usually a section left between the rim and ground due to the lack of oxygen. From this, the investigator can determine the condition of the tires.

The lug nuts and hub caps should also be examined. If the vehicle had hub caps and they are not on the rims, are they nearby? Are any lug nuts missing? Are there any tool marks on the lug nuts indicating that the tires were recently changed? Do the tires match the ones the owner claims were on the vehicle? Verify by questioning the owner about where the tires were purchased and follow-up with the dealer.

Gas Tank

The fire investigator should examine the gas tank, gas tank filler tube and gas cap. You will want to answer questions such as:

Is the gas cap on the car?
If not, is it lying nearby?
Is the gas cap metal or plastic?
If plastic, there will be the remains of a spring and signs of the plastic residue or protected area on the threads.
If the filler neck is still in place, check inside for a siphoning tube.
Does the gas cap show signs of being blown off or failed?
Was the drain plug for the gas tank in place or had it been removed to allow gasoline to pool under the vehicle?

Examine for tool marks. Is the drain plug collar in place? If the collar is in place and the drain plug is missing, it is almost impossible for an explosion to have displaced the drain plug. It is almost impossible for the gas tank to explode in a fire; both the collar and plug would have blown free. If a gas tank explodes, it usually ruptures at its weakest point, the seam. There are chemicals that can be introduced into a gas tank to cause a volatile chemical reaction resulting in an explosion.

Are there any puncture marks or tears? There is a difference: gas leaking from a tear, such as can occur when a vehicle backs over an object that could have punctured the tank, would make significantly different markings from a punctured gas tank and will usually show striations with directionality. Some newer vehicles have gas tanks of fiberglass and special plastics. These will melt with the gasoline to fuel a fire.

Suspension System

The failure or sagging of the vehicle's suspension system as indicated by annealing of the chassis "leaf/coil" springs or by the collapse of the shock absorbers due to the fusing of internal bushings indicate that these components have been subjected to intense heat. You must determine whether gasoline was placed under the vehicle or escaped from the fuel system. With an electronic fuel pump, only a certain amount of gas will be dispensed and will not suffice to cause a severe amount of damage to the underside of the vehicle. If the gas tank releases its fuel, there will be extensive heat damage.

The annealing of suspension springs is in indirect proportion to the following factors:

Temperature. How much heat was the particular component exposed to? Steel will soften at approximately 1000°F and may fail between 1500°F and 1700°F.

Duration. How long was the particular component exposed to the high temperature? If the steel was exposed to a temperature below 1000°F for a long time, this would show the same results as temperatures that reach over 1000°F for shorter periods of time.

Mass. What are the measurements of the component (diameter, weight, and size)? A thicker, more solid object will withstand more intense heat than a thinner one made of the same material.

Examining the Windshield and Other Glass

If the glass is intact, check for tape or tape residue on the windows. This may indicate that a "for sale" sign had been displayed. Safety plates or bottle glass

Figure 8.7   Examine interior of door for presence of window glass and position of lift arm to confirm status of window (open or closed) at time of fire.

for the windshield will craze (crack) at approximately 800°F, soften at approximately 1000°F, and fail at approximately 1400°F. The material will, under certain conditions, release a flammable gas. The kind of safety glass used in most cars bubbles and softens at approximately 250°F. The type and amount of soot on the inside of the windows will also give some insight as to the type and magnitude of the fire. Is the glass checkered, cracked, or fused? These factors can indicate heat ranges and serve as heat indicators as well as direction of fire travel (Chapter 5, "Fire Language"). Examination of windows and doors should also show whether they were open or closed during the fire and whether there were certain power options (power windows, mirrors, locks, etc.). Examination inside the door will reveal whether the roller arm is in the up or down position. Often it remains in that position after the fire. Tracks on the inside of the doors may show protected areas (where the rubber guards line the tracks), showing whether the window was up or down. Inspections inside the vehicle and door can show whether the window was in the up or down position by the amount of glass that had melted either to the inside of the door or into the passenger compartment. If there is a lack of glass or there are indicators that the glass was not in place, even though the roller was in the up position, this may indicate that the window had been broken out before the fire. Since the entire passenger compartment is surrounded by glass, this is a good indicator as to where a fire originates if it is within the passenger compartment. It will tend to have more severe melting of glass in one area of the vehicle and less in another.

Catalytic Converter

In 1975 the *catalytic converter* was introduced with the advent of unleaded gasoline. A catalytic converter is a metal housing that contains a chemical substance — a metallic catalyst (platinum or palladium) in a porous ceramic foam. This unit converts hydrocarbons, carbon monoxide (CO), and nitrous oxides to less toxic compounds. The normal operating catalytic converter ranges in temperature from 800°F to 1800°F. The internal compounds (the ceramic matrix) melt at about 2300°F along with the malfunction of the internal catalytic converter at 2500°F. An improperly running engine or leaded gasoline can cause a converter to overheat, which could easily ignite combustible materials in close proximity, whether on a floor pan, the opposite side of the floor pan, or combustible materials on the ground. If the catalytic system becomes overheated, its internal ceramic matrix can become brittle. An impact to the converter itself can cause the internal ceramic matrix to shatter. These broken pieces can become lodged within the muffler system, still active as a converter material causing overheating and blocking the muffler.

Heat shields have been added to catalytic converters to protect the underside from overheating and igniting combustible materials in that area. Often these heat shields are removed due to an impact or the repair/servicing of the exhaust system. Even a properly operating catalytic converter can serve as an ignition source for flammable/combustible fluids once they come into contact with the exhaust system.

Multiple Points of Origin

The presence of either separate (distinct) or primary and second burn patterns on the exterior suggests intentional damage. Primary and secondary burn patterns may indicate that the original fire burned itself out, possibly due to the lack of oxygen, and neither windows nor doors were open to supply additional oxygen where a secondary fire was started in the same area. These distinctive burn patterns may indicate that two fires were burning at the same time in different compartments. Both the engine hood and trunk lid show signs of fire damage. If there is no fire damage to the vehicle roof (over the passenger compartment), this would indicate that the fire did not spread from one compartment to the other. However, if you had an electrical failure in one compartment, such as the trunk, an electrical failure with the same wiring in the engine compartment or blown fuse or overheated wire with sagging insulation, this would indicate that the ignition source was electrical. Generally the extent of damage would not be severe. Again, if the vehicle was not running, there are only limited origins for an electrical fire.

If possible, the investigator should examine the fire scene for the presence of distinctive patterns indicative of accelerant spatter or splash. If an accelerant

Figure 8.8 Evaluation of fire patterns assists in identifying area of origin and potential fuel and heat sources at the point of origin. (C) Melting of the valve cover indicates point of fire origin below. (D) Arrow indicates transaxle cooling line failure at connector that sprayed atomized fluid on the exhaust header.

was poured on the outside of the vehicle and ignited, the burn pattern will correspond with the path or flow that the liquid followed as it spread over the vehicle's body. If enough accelerant was used, it may be possible to see where the accelerant dripped from the body of the vehicle to the ground. If this is the case, soil samples should be taken from these areas and correctly packaged (see Chapter 9) and forwarded to a laboratory for analysis. The investigator should also examine the underside of the burned exterior, such

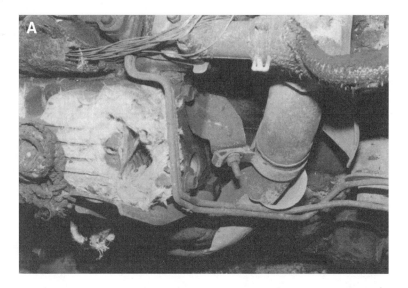

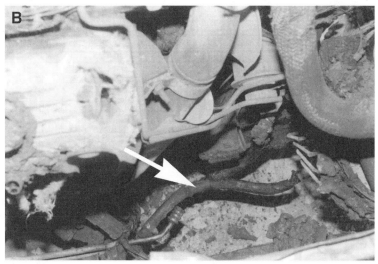

Figure 8.8 (continued)

as the underside of the trunk or hood, for corresponding heat damage and document accordingly. One warning: make sure that multiple points of origin in an incendiary fire are not the result of an overheated wire causing multiple electrical failures.

Flashback

Flashback is an unintentional recession of flame. Examine the ground under and around the vehicle for any signs of this. Such evidence would indicate either that an accelerant poured in the vehicle's interior may have dripped

Figure 8.9 An investigator can no longer rigidly interpret the role of a vehicle's roof panel in the total evaluation of a vehicular fire. Modern engineering considerations have affected the burning characteristics of vehicle models produced since 1969.

to the ground under the car and ignited, or that, while being poured on the vehicle, some accelerant spilled on the ground. If there are signs of flashback, the investigator should take soil samples from the area.

Heat Indicators

This part of fire investigation has been widely theorized about. Discoloration of chrome, melting of copper and aluminum, and patterns on painted panels of the vehicle are all included. Approximate melting temperatures of metals found within the vehicle are as follows:

Tin	449°F
Solder (silver)	190°F
Zinc	786°F to 878°F
Aluminum	1220°F
Brass	1575°F to 1800°F
Silver	1761°F
Bronze	1910°F
Copper	1981°F
Steel	2350 through 2675°F
Stainless steel	2550°F
Plastics	532°F to 898°F

Figure 8.10 This vehicle (A) had a malfunction of the throttle-body fuel system (B), resulting in the vehicle starting, moving forward, striking the building, and burning.

If one of these materials has melted, you know that it has reached at least that temperature. In examining that area, you should be able to document a fuel source capable of reaching those temperatures for a long enough time to melt these metals. It is common to find any one or all of those items melted in an area. However, if you find melted aluminum near to some copper wiring that has not melted, the range of temperatures reached above 1220°F, but below 1981°F for a short amount of time. An electrical failure in the dashboard assembly in most cases will not cause the aluminum of the radiator at the engine compartment to melt.

The Second Vehicle

The information about second vehicles is best obtained from and by local authorities. The investigator should be conscious of additional tire tracks and foot prints in the area surrounding the suspected vehicle. These may suggest that the vehicle was pushed or towed to the scene where it was burned, or may indicate the presence of a second automobile. If the vehicle was pushed or towed to the scene, the investigator may find recent striations on the rear bumper or on the frame below the front bumper. A second automobile, possibly driven by an associate of the suspect, may have been used to drive that person away from the scene.

The Panic Stop

The panic stop may not be evident because the driver of the vehicle may have only noticed smoke or an odor along with the loss of power or interruption of power. Then, only when the vehicle was stopped, is there enough air to fuel the mixture ratio needed for flaming combustion to begin.

This determination is best used by local authorities when they have had an opportunity to examine the scene where the vehicle burned. You can look for skid marks indicating panic stops. However, if the vehicle has an anti-lock brake system, skid marks may not be evident. This evidence is best used when questioning the suspect about the incident. This would be especially true if he or she claims to have been driving when the car suddenly burst into flames. Normally, a person confronted with these circumstances may be expected to hit the brakes, pull off the road, and quickly leave the vehicle. If the suspect makes such a claim, he would be asked to describe and explain his actions. Does it appear that there was an attempt to extinguish the fire? Is the dirt or sand next to the vehicle disturbed to the extent that it appears likely that it may have been used as an extinguishing agent?

Interior Examinations

During interior examination of the three compartments, you will list the accessories or major components, such as four-wheel drive or two-wheel drive, automatic transmission or manual, air conditioning, power seats, personal supplies in the trunk, and a list of components in the engine compartment. (See Appendix for a sample vehicle inspection form.)

The first examination of the engine compartment should verify that the basic valuable components of the vehicle are still present. If you find certain items missing that would make the vehicle inoperable, make note of these. This may indicate an intentionally set fire. A simple test to see whether the engine will turn over is that of applying a ratchet to the center of the main drive pulley; it should turn a full 360°. The full turn is difficult, but if it turns all the way without ceasing, it indicates that the vehicle is operable. Missing screws, bolts, and other items that would not normally be consumed by the fire should also be noted. Is the battery in place and connected? Are the spark plugs/wires in their positions? Doing an overall review of the engine compartment to establish that the components are or were in place at the time of the fire will help you to evaluate which areas have been more severely damaged by the fire and if, in fact, the fire started within the engine compartment. This can be confirmed by whether certain materials had been burned at that area of the engine compartment. The more easily burned materials other than the fuels are the rubber and neoprene hoses, belts, and other plastic components. If those combustible materials are completely missing in one area, you must consider other melting temperatures such as aluminum. Then consider the condition of other metals including brass, copper, and then steel. In a normal vehicle fire, steel will not melt unless an extreme weight distorts it. Melting is quite unusual except for thin materials such as the underside of the hood, which will start to sag. By considering the different melting temperatures, you can determine the area of origin of greatest fuel load as different melting temperatures give you lines of demarcation which will further help identify a location. Once the area of origin has been determined, consider the possible types of ignition and fuel sources. Starting with fuel, the vehicle has a fuel pump, fuel filter, pressure regulator valve, injectors, rails, connecting lines and hoses, and fuel vapor canister.

Air Induction

When vehicles have sensor-related problems, the vehicle can be getting too much fuel. This excessive fuel may build up within the air intake hose. The vapors can come into contact with a regularly occurring spark or arc within the engine compartment. Also, with the air induction system, there may be a problem, especially during the fall, with leaves and other materials being drawn up inside, and beginning to accumulate. They can accumulate to the point where they come into contact with the exhaust manifold or another potential heat source.

Electrical System

As for the electrical system, you should consider the battery (was it in place), primary and secondary wiring (from the battery to the coil [primary] and from the coil to the distributor and the spark plugs [secondary]) wiring harness and related wiring.

A short circuit in the primary wiring often will leave arc signatures and/or fusing of the metal.

Overloaded wiring will cause wire to heat up severely, and this in turn can cause the insulating materials to reach their ignition temperature. Certain surrounding components can further insulate these overheating wires, such as other wires in a harness, seats, or carpeting which will not allow the heat to dissipate adequately. This compounding heat build-up may not trip the fuse or links.

Overloaded electrical wires can be thought of as a garden hose with the water running and the nozzle turned off. The water pressure builds up and the entire length of the hose is affected. It begins to expand, and the connection areas can be where the most activity will occur. The metal or plastic connections will not expand at the same rate as the hose itself, which can cause a failure at these points. Overloaded electrical wiring heats uniformly through its length between its connections or between the point of a short circuit and the energy source. Keep in mind that the heating of the entire length may not pose a threat until it is restricted or occurs where the heat cannot dissipate. Investigate the possibility that wiring or fuses were tampered with or repaired. This is especially true for the amateur who puts radios into older model vehicles where the connections are few. New model vehicles should not be handled by an amateur. Loose connections will spark and arc, creating enough heat to start a fire. Overly tight connections or wires that have been bound together may break down the insulation through the severe pressure and vibration. Severing wires and their insulation also will cause arcs and sparks, which in turn may lead to a fire.

Vehicle batteries contain oxygen and hydrogen. The changing of a battery or a direct short can release enough hydrogen to be ignited by a spark or arc. A lack of ventilation while the hydrogen is being produced can create a serious unrecognized fire risk.

Other engine compartment fluids are in brake lines, power steering lines, transmission fluid, and engine oil. Along with the brake lines, there is the reservoir of the master cylinder and the metal lines that transfer brake fluid to the lines at the brakes in the wheels. Also, newer vehicles with antilock braking systems have distribution lines to another component within the engine compartment.

Other Factors

1. Power steering pump, fluid reservoir, connection and transfer lines.
2. Transmission (whether automatic or manual). With an automatic transmission, there are the transaxle coolant lines that enter the side of the radiator by metal lines and/or neoprene hoses, and the transmission filler neck. An overheating engine or a heavily loaded vehicle can cause the transmission fluid to froth out above a portion of the exhaust

manifold which, of course, is usually sufficient to ignite the transmission fluid. An example of frothing is the boiling (bubbling) of the transmission fluid.

3. The engine oil can spray or atomize from leaks around the valve covers. Other leaks can occur at the oil filter and on some vehicles with engine oil coolant lines which go to the radiator by metal and neoprene lines.

4. Check the condition of the engine block and transmission assembly. A blown engine often causes fractures to the housing releasing the combustible oil. This is also true of the transmission housing.

Once you determine which components are in the area of origin, you need to assess a possible fuel source, whether the vehicle was on or off, if there was a recent problem with one of the systems that would require service work. If the vehicle still has engine oil or transmission fluid in it, a sample can be taken for laboratory analysis. A test will identify the metal count within these fluids to determine the amount of engine wear before the fire. This can also determine whether there was coolant in the engine oil. Coolant and water that is introduced into the engine oil by a seal failure or other failure within the engine compartment will mix with oil while it is going through the regular cycles in the engine compartment. It will not be confused with water that was used to extinguish the fire or the fact the vehicle may have sat exposed to other water sources after the fire occurrence. Windshield wiper fluid and radiator coolant both are alcohol-based fluids but with differing gylcol content. Their vapors can be ignited if sprayed on a hot surface or if they come into contact with a regular spark or arc (open windings). The amount of these fluids that is diluted will have a direct effect on the ease with which they will ignite. Check both reservoirs; they are usually made of plastic and will melt, but it is possible for these fluids to start a fire.

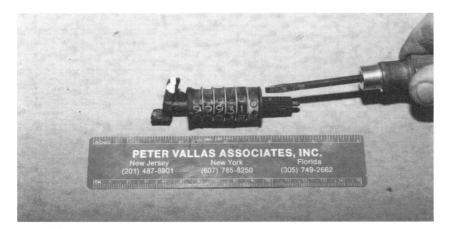

Figure 8.11 If the face of the odometer is melted, remove it and check the number sequence.

Passenger Compartment

The investigator should note the mileage on the odometer and check if the odometer has been tampered with. Tampering is more difficult with newer vehicles. If the face of the odometer is melted, remove it and check the number sequence. The investigator can also check the inside of the door for the vehicle identification number and the date of manufacture. Service records are often kept on the inside of the door and may still be recoverable because of the lack of oxygen to support burning at this part of the door. This information may show that the vehicle was recently serviced, or determine if there was a previous problem with it and whether the work was ever completed. If it has been determined that the fire started in the passenger compartment, the potential sources are few. They include electrical faults and accidental discarding of an ignited object such as a cigarette. The vehicle console acts as a barrier which can help identify on which side of the passenger compartment the fire started.

An attempt should be made to locate the ignition assembly. Almost all new vehicle ignition assemblies are made of a light, easily melted metal. It is usually a white pot metal that has a melting temperature of 562° to 752°F. Many of the springs from the ignition assembly may be difficult to find. The ignition wires are close to the steering column and are of a heavier gauge than the other wires in this area. Many times, a person will leave the keys in the ignition assuming they will melt in the ensuing fire. They are, however, often recovered on the floor beneath the steering column.

The investigator must consider all of the wiring in the passenger compartment including the dashboard, inside the doors, under the seats, and other accessories that might be inside the vehicle, such as a mobile telephone, CD player, or radar detector. By examining inside the doors, you can usually determine if the windows were in place, intact, in the up position or missing at the time of the fire fire. If they were in the down position, all of the melted glass would be inside the door. The roller bar would be in the down position. If they were in the up position, often parts of the track will show protected areas and lines of demarcation different from unprotected areas. The condition of the other windows may verify the amount of glass that has melted back into the vehicle or whether they were in place or not at the time of the fire.

Figure 8.12 Vehicular fire investigation applies to all forms of transportation including commercial trucks, farm, and construction equipment, as well as recreational vehicles. (A) This 35′ cruiser was deliberately burned and sunk, but was recovered from 65′ of water. (B) A coordinated effort by local sheriff department divers and the insurance investigator resulted in recovery, arrest, and conviction of the owner. (C) Inventory of minimum content further documented owner's attempt to defraud the insurance company.

Figure 8.12

Usually the fuse panel box is in the passenger compartment, but many newer vehicles have two, with one in the engine compartment. You must try to determine if fuses have blown or if they are still intact. Sometimes much of the plastic around the fuses melts and the removal or visual examination cannot be done without breakage. You can also inspect the fuses with an ohmmeter first, but they must be removed from the fuse panel.

Comparing the condition of the carpet from the front to the rear and left to right will also help determine where the fire started. This would be important in a case where the entire passenger compartment appears to have been gutted.

Examination of the space underneath the seats should be done to see if foreign combustible material was added to promote ignition or supply additional fuel load.

Some possible accidental-appearing, but yet intentionally set fires may involve candles, flares, and burning of oily food products such as potato chips.

Trunk Compartment/Cargo Area

The trunk/cargo area is probably the least common area of origin. Things to consider when performing an investigation include the electrical wiring or items stored in this area. Some people keep an extra can of gasoline for emergencies. There are, of course, organic compounds that could self-heat and start a fire. Other items to consider are flares or cat litter (for traction). Conduction from a fire below this area may ignite combustible/flammable items within the trunk or cargo areas.

An inventory of materials present in the trunk/cargo area, and a follow-up with the owner or other involved parties should be conducted to evaluate the available fuel load and its relevance to the origin and cause of the fire.

Some of the best experience you can obtain is by seeing the vehicles. A suggestion is to contact a few local salvage yards and ask to see vehicles that are to be sold, not vehicles on hold, as you wouldn't want to disturb an ongoing investigation. By examining vehicles on a regular basis you pick up on consistencies. Check even the small fire losses — these can help you to visualize how and where fire patterns progress.

References and Selected Readings

Kennedy, John, Fire and Arson Investigation, 1962 (revised 19??).

DeHann, John D., Kirk's Fire Investigation, 3rd Edition, Brady: A Prentice Hall Division, 1993.

NFPA 921, *Auto Fire Investigation.*

APPENDIX: Sample Vehicle Inspection Form

VEHICLE INSPECTION FORM

File #   Investigator:

Date:

Location:

DESCRIPTION OF VEHICLE

Date of manufacture: Mileage:

Year: VIN #

Make: Plate #

Model: Body condition:

Color:

Doors:

INSPECTION OBSERVATIONS

Exterior: Tires/Wheels

Underside: Windows

Passenger:
compartment   Trunk

Fuel cap   Accessories

Engine compartment

Oil   Problems observed

Transmission   Engine

Brakes

Electrical

Comments: _____

_____

_____

ENGINE COMPARTMENT

Oil –   Carb/fuel system

Transmission –   Vapor recovery

Brakes –

Electrical (power distribution panel)

PASSENGER COMPARTMENT

Ignition –   Seats –

Radio –   Personal items –

Accessories –   Fuse box –

Carpet –

FIRE PATTERNS

Area of Origin –

Location of samples taken –

Unusual problems –

Comments: _____
_____
_____

Evidence 9

Evidence may be defined as anything that is legally seized and submitted to a court of law for consideration in determining the truth in a matter. Investigators have traditionally viewed evidence as anything that a suspect leaves at or takes from a crime scene, or anything that may be otherwise connected to the crime under investigation. Physical evidence is defined as any finite or tangible material, whether in trace or gross quantity, that may assist with proving elements of a crime. The proper recognition, documentation, collection, analysis, and interpretation of physical evidence can provide valuable information to the investigation.

1. Facts and reconstruction of events to provide that a crime has occurred
2. The method utilized to commit the crime
3. The linking of a suspect with a victim and/or the crime scene
4. Supporting or refuting a suspect's version of events
5. Identification of a suspect
5. Exoneration of the innocent

The value of legally seized evidence is directly related to the role it plays in the solution of a case at hand.

As discussed in previous chapters, the scientific method is the accepted procedure for fire origin and cause analysis. Applied to fire investigation, the two most time-consuming steps are the collection and analysis of the data. For fire investigators, this includes the collection and the laboratory analysis of the evidence. Sometimes during the analysis of the property removed from a scene, further information and additional data needs to be obtained before an opinion can be rendered as to the origin and, specifically, the cause of the fire. Therefore, the collection of evidence is crucial in understanding how and explaining why a particular fire occurred. Oftentimes, investigators have no difficulty finding the origin of the fire; the problem arises in identifying the cause of the fire. The exact cause of a fire may not be positively confirmed during the on-site examination. Many questions can be and are answered once items are collected and tested in greater detail in a controlled environment, such as a laboratory. Consequently, evidence collection is critical in determining an investigator's opinion as to the origin and cause of a fire.

When called to the scene of a suspicious fire, an investigator's first interest is to determine the origin and cause of the fire. If he determines that the fire was intentionally set, his concern shifts to the discovery of evidential material that will support his contention and prove the elements of the crime of arson in a court of law. Throughout the investigative process, the investigator will be seeking evidence to identify and connect a suspect to the crime, as well as any documentation tending to expose a possible motive. Evidence, regardless of its form (business records, photographs, sketches, incendiary devices, etc.), must be identified, collected, and correctly packaged throughout the case-building process.

As mentioned in Chapter 5, the overhaul and general cleanup operations should have been halted or delayed until the officer in charge and the investigator have had an opportunity to examine the scene. Even if these operations take place in an area that seems remote from the point of origin, they may still destroy evidence vital to the investigation.

Regardless of the circumstances involved in a case, not only is the initial collection of evidence imperative, but once an item or items have been secured, the preservation of the collected property becomes paramount. Today, any inclination of potential spoliation of evidence can run the risk of having the evidence declared inadmissible in a court of law. A break in the chain of custody, or damage to the smallest component of an appliance believed to be the cause of a particular fire, could be detrimental in either a criminal or civil case in the eyes of the court.

The fire investigative field has become more organized and professional in the past 15 to 20 years. It has also become more technical and legally scrutinized. Criminal and civil cases alike depend on the manner in which evidence is collected and preserved from the initial inspection date to the day it is presented in court. With the crowded court system of today, the interval between inspection date and trial date could be several years. Everyone in the fire investigative industry, whether in the public or private sector, should understand that the rules and standards established for the collection, preservation, and testing of evidence are becoming more and more stringent.

Figure 9.1 Gasoline had burned on the tongue-and-groove flooring pictured here. Note the puddling effect.

Accelerants and Related Burn Patterns

An *accelerant* is a substance that is used to accelerate (and sometime direct) the spread of a fire. The most commonly used liquid accelerants include gasoline, lighter fluid, kerosene, and turpentine.

A *plant*, sometimes referred to as a *booster*, is either a pool of liquid accelerant or a pile of combustibles (oily rags, newspaper, painting supplies, etc.) that is used by an arsonist to enhance the quality of fire in a selected location. An accelerant-soaked mattress or couch could serve the same purpose. A plant is meant to boost the progress of a fire by producing a large body of fire. A *trailer*, sometimes referred to as a *streamer*, is an arrangement or configuration of flammable or combustible materials that is intended to carry fire from one location to another (or from one plant to another). Commonly used trailers include gasoline-soaked towels tied end-to-end, liquid accelerant splashed across the floor, lengths of safety fuse, or accelerant-soaked newspaper. When used, a liquid accelerant is generally accompanied by distinctive burn patterns, as well as unnatural fire spread and intensity. A typical burn pattern resulting from the use of a liquid accelerant is called *puddling*. This burn pattern is distinctive and should not be confused with other irregular patterns that might result from drapes or clothing burning on a floor. When spilled on a tongue-and-groove (hardwood) floor, liquid accelerant is drawn down between the floorboards. Once ignited, the accelerant burns up through the spaces between the floorboards. In the case of a tiled floor, the accelerant seeps down between the individual tiles and, once ignited, causes the edges of the surrounding tiles to curl. In addition, since only the vapors burn, the pool of liquid accelerant itself serves as an insulating barrier between the burning vapors above and the floor below. As the pool of liquid burns from its upper surface down and inward from its perimeter, it leaves a burn pattern that is deeper at the perimeter of the pool than toward its center.

When the liquid accelerant is spilled on a concrete floor and ignited, *spalling* may result. The heat from the burning accelerant causes trapped moisture within the concrete slab to turn to steam. The resultant steam pressure causes the surface of the slab to pop, leaving behind a very uneven (pitted) skin.

Accelerant splatter may occur in several different ways. It is usually identified by the presence of distinctive, finger-like patterns found under the following circumstances:

1. *Accompanying the puddle effect.* When liquid accelerant seeps down through the floor, it may contact and run down the face of the floor joists.
2. *Below the exterior of a window.* When fire extends through a window, it naturally laps up the face of the structure above the window. The existence of an unusual finger-like pattern *below* a window may suggest that a Molotov cocktail thrown by an arsonist shattered against the window and that its flammable contents ran down the exterior wall before igniting.
3. *Around the holes cut in interior walls for introducing accelerant.* While cutting such holes, the arsonist, may have inadvertently spilled excess accelerant down the face of the wall in the area of the hole. This liquid, in addition to running down the face of the wall, may have seeped in behind the wall molding at floor level.

Legal Aspects of Evidence Collection

As with policing operations, fire investigators, whether they are associated with a governmental agency, or institution or with the private sector retained to perform the investigation, are subject to rules and regulations. It should be known, there are only four possible ways to gain entry into a particular structure in order to conduct an investigation and collect evidence. They are as follows:

"Exigent Circumstances"

The first method is referred to as exigent circumstances. This method is generally recognized when fire department personnel enter a building or structure to suppress and extinguish a fire. Any evidence obtained during the subsequent investigation is considered legal and admissible in court, because the fire department has an obligation and duty to the public to attempt to determine the origin and cause of the fire occurrence.

Consent of the Property Owner

The second method of entry is by *consent of the property owner*, whether a private individual or a management corporation. Often, insurance investigators gain access to a fire scene by consent of the property owner, insurance company, or public adjuster for the property owner. Once the property owner submits a claim to the insurance company, the insurance company may retain the services of an investigative firm to conduct the origin and cause investigation. Insurance companies have this right to have the structure investigated once a claim has been filed by the insured because it is a provision stated in the insurance policy. Nearly all insurance policies (contracts) have an incorporated clause stating that the insured must produce the damaged property as often as the insurance company reasonably requests. This clause can usually be found under information stated in the general policy provisions.

Administrative Search Warrant

An administrative search warrant is normally granted when an agency has the responsibility to investigate the origin and cause of a fire. Situations such as these can occur if permission to investigate the scene has not been attained or has been denied by the property owner. An investigation under an administrative search warrant is limited to the documentation of the origin and cause of the fire occurrence. If, at any time during the investigation possible criminal evidence is discovered, the investigation must stop and a criminal search warrant must be obtained.

Criminal Search Warrant

In order to obtain a criminal search warrant, "probable cause" of a crime must be presented in front of a judge. The judge decides if enough evidence has been presented to suggest a crime at the location has been committed. If the judge does not feel enough evidence has been presented, the warrant will not be granted because the rights of an individual supersede the right of government intervention.

The Supreme Court has had numerous decisions involving evidence collection, primarily associated with evidence collection by police departments or agencies. In 1978, the high court ruled on the first case involving fire investigative agencies. *Michigan v. Tyler* (98 S. Ct 1942, 56L. 2d 486) established the precedents which are followed by government agencies investigating a fire scene.

The circumstances of the case are as follows:

> Shortly before midnight on January 21, 1970, a fire occurred in a furniture store. The fire chief arrived at the scene approximately 2 hours later, just as the fire department was extinguishing the blaze. He entered the building to conduct a preliminary origin and cause investigation. During his examination of the scene, two plastic containers were discovered; these containers stored a flammable liquid. The fire chief called the police department and a detective was sent to the scene. The police detective photographed the scene as well as the containers, but stopped his investigative efforts due to the smoke and steam still present in the building. The fire was completely extinguished around 4 a.m., January 22. At this time, the fire chief and police detective secured the two containers and left.
>
> Both returned to the site about four hours later. During the second investigation, additional evidence was removed and secured. Nearly a month later, a state police arson investigator conducted yet another origin and cause investigation. With subsequent visits, more evidence was removed from the scene. All these investigations were conducted without a search warrant. During the criminal trial, all the evidence was presented and Mr. Tyler was convicted of arson.

The Supreme Court ruled that only the evidence removed during the initial investigation could be presented at Mr. Tyler's trial. The evidence removed from the scene the following morning could also be used because this investigation was conducted during a "reasonable period of time" from the extinguishment of the blaze. The subsequent investigations required a search warrant to enter the premises or remove any items. If a reasonable period of time has expired, no evidence can be removed from a fire scene unless a warrant is obtained. One item rarely mentioned regarding the Tyler decision is that, although all the evidence secured from the subsequent investigation was excluded, it had been obtained with Mr. Tyler's permission. For all who may be associated with government agencies, this is a valuable point to remember. Although one method of entry is by consent of the property owner, a government agency should always obtain a search warrant — administrative or criminal — if the reasonable period of time frame has passed.

Figure 9.2   The investigator should identify, collect, and preserve all evidence pertinent to proving an incendiary fire. (A) The arrow indicates an ignition device missed by local authorities, although it is shown in this original police scene photo. (B) This photo, taken by the author, documents the evidence still at the scene 10 days later.

Evidence Collection

What to Collect

At some point during the investigation process, the question of what property or items should be collected arises. The decision to secure any physical or tangible items lies solely with the investigator. Any possible ignition source at or near the area of origin should be removed and secured, especially if the item cannot be eliminated during the on-site inspection.

In some instances, it may be beneficial to remove property which has been eliminated, to further an investigator's conclusion on the cause of the fire. Such cases include, but are not limited to, cases involving large monetary losses, fires involving many exposures and/or many insurance companies, fires where many agencies investigated or will investigate, cases where a death has occurred, and cases of suspected arson. In all these cases, the items removed from the scene can serve to prove a product or a person is responsible for the loss. It may also disprove any other possible theories as to what caused the fire.

In cases involving a possible product defect or malfunction, it is good practice to obtain any items connected with or related to the suspected component or appliance. For example, during a particular investigation, the fire, heat, and smoke patterns all indicated that the fire originated on a counter top in a corner of the kitchen. After reconstructing the scene, a toaster, microwave, coffeemaker, and blender are found in the corner. All the electrical appliances have been plugged into one outlet box with four receptacles. What items are to be removed?

At this point, too many variables exist to possibly know the correct response. If all items can be eliminated except the coffee maker, then at least the coffee maker and the outlet as well as the circuit breaker or fuse controlling the outlet should be inspected more closely at the scene and removed for further analysis. If none of the appliances can be eliminated at the scene, all of them as well as the outlet and circuit breaker should be removed and examined more closely.

This example assumed the fire originated in an owner-occupied dwelling. However, given the same circumstances, what if the fire occurred in a two family household, with both dwellings rented out to tenants, both having a renter insurance policy? If we assume the investigator is retained by the building owner's insurance company, the investigator can legally remove only the outlet and the circuit breaker and any of the electrical appliances owned by the building owner. If the investigator is retained by the tenant's insurance company, the investigator can only remove those items owned by the tenant. The outlet and the circuit breaker cannot be removed unless authorization is given by the building owner.

If, however, the investigator is retained by the second tenant's insurance company, he or she may not even be allowed to examine the apartment where the fire originated. Even if access into the apartment is permitted, the investigator cannot remove any item from the scene. Regardless of what insurance company the investigator may represent, he or she should be aware that all the appliances may not be present at the scene when the investigation is conducted.

If this fire occurred in a large Victorian house worth $1 million, the investigator may remove all of the appliances, even if they are eliminated during the on-scene investigation, to confirm that the coffeemaker was responsible for the fire loss.

It is easy to understand, in every fire investigation, that the investigator must not only assess the loss, but also consider many additional factors which will ultimately dictate what evidence is removed from the scene. The legality of removing certain items, the size of the investigation, or the liability potential are primary considerations to keep in mind when collecting evidence. A fire investigator must use discretion when removing items from a scene and collecting evidence. Whatever circumstances surround a fire loss, assume that every case investigated will, one day in the future, be presented in a court of law. This manner of thinking asserts how critical the collection of evidence is in determining the origin and cause as well as identifying the party responsible for a fire.

Influences on Evidence Collection

Physical evidence at a fire scene can exist in a variety of forms. Several factors, including the physical state, physical characteristics, fragility, and volatility, influence an investigator on how the evidence is collected. For every investigation, an investigator must be prepared and equipped to collect the evidence which needs to be secured.

In whatever physical state — solid, liquid, or gas — the evidence is found at the fire scene, an investigator must have the capability and equipment to collect and preserve the property. Collection of physical evidence in the solid form can be done by simply removing the item or items from the area of origin. Sometimes an item may be too large and unwieldy for one or two persons to handle. If the evidence cannot be removed from the scene, the investigator will have to return to the scene with the appropriate equipment to secure the property.

Potential evidence remaining at a scene in the liquid state may or may not be absorbed by solid structural materials such as wood, carpet, plastic, or masonry. The liquid material has been diluted, absorbed, or removed by the water used during the suppression and extinguishment of the fire. The only way to ascertain whether an accelerant may have been used in a fire loss is to remove solid samples which might have a trace of the accelerant or liquid material in them. In studies, it has been proven that the more porous a material is, the greater is the possibility an accelerant will be detected during chemical and forensic testing.

Figure 9.3   When evidence is collected at the scene of a suspicious fire, it should be packaged in air-tight containers. Pictured here is a 1-gallon metal evidence can with an evidence label affixed.

In collecting samples for laboratory analysis, two rules should be followed. First, for every solid sample collected, a comparison sample must be taken as well. If comparison samples are not taken, and an accelerant is detected in one of the removed samples, the investigator has no idea whether the accelerant was inherent in the material or not. A prime example is turpentine in pine wood. Turpentine is an inherent component of pine wood and testing results will reflect this fact.

A second rule for the collection of a solid sample is that only one type of material should be isolated and collected per container. For example, if, in the area of origin, a hardwood floor is covered by linoleum and the linoleum is covered by carpet, at least six, possibly eight, samples may need to be taken. One sample each of the carpet, the linoleum, and the hardwood floor at or near the area of origin plus three comparison samples. If the carpet has padding material, a sample of the padding should be taken from the area of origin as well as a comparison sample.

When collecting the samples, if a sample cannot be separated and the padding has melted into the carpet, four comparison samples, each containing a single specimen per container, should still be taken. A qualified forensic chemist will be able to analyze the data and clarify if an accelerant was used for the initiation or spread of a particular fire occurrence.

If several points of origin are found during an investigation, the number of samples removed can easily number a dozen or more. However, if the structure contains all hardwood floors of the same material, only one comparison sample needs to be removed and tested. On rare occasions, a gaseous sample may have to be obtained. The collection of a gaseous sample can be extracted in several different ways. The three most common methods for removing gaseous samples from the scene are through the use of a mechanical sampling device, through air sampling cans, or by pouring distilled water over the area the investigator wishes to take the air sample.

Mechanical sampling devices are designed to remove a sample of the air and store it in a collecting chamber, by using a charcoal filter or a filter of a special polymer substance. The filter then can be tested later. Specially designed evacuated air sampling cans are also available to collect gaseous samples. The atmospheric air is removed from these cans to avoid the possible dilution of the air sample.

These products may be too expensive for an organization to buy, or possibly used too seldom to warrant keeping a supply of them. The least expensive method for collecting a gaseous sample involves a bottle of distilled water in preferably a glass container. A plastic container, however, may also be used if circumstances warrant it. To collect the sample, the distilled water must be poured in the area where the sample is to be collected. As the water leaves the container, it creates a vacuum, collecting the surrounding air in the container. The container is then recapped to preserve the sample. Distilled water is used because it has no impurities, eliminating any future questions regarding the validity of the sample.

A second consideration in evidence collection is the physical size, shape, and/or weight — or the physical characteristics — of the items to be secured. The investigator should be prepared with a variety of equipment to secure the necessary items. Such instruments as a hammer, screwdrivers of various sizes, pliers, wire and bolt cutters, lengths of rope, as well as other common household tools are as essential to the fire investigator as a shovel, broom, and flashlight. In some incidents, however, equipment from outside sources may have to be used, including lifts, cranes, forklifts, bulldozers, backhoes, or excavators. Machinery such as this can either be rented or contracted through an outside company. Whether the machinery is contracted to another company or the equipment is rented, be sure the operators of the equipment are qualified so no evidence is lost or destroyed.

Yet another consideration to be addressed during the evidence collection process is the fragility of the items or samples. An investigator should always use utmost care when transferring secured evidence between any two locations. However, during the initial handling of the evidence an investigator has a greater chance of further damaging the equipment and therefore losing small assemblies or components which might positively prove how the fire originated. Remember, by the time an investigation is completed, the items have been subjected to extreme temperatures, have had other items or materials collapse on them, were possibly thrown away from the area of origin during the overhaul procedures, or damaged during the clearing and sifting of the debris. The property is brittle and can easily break further if great care is not used. Consequently, the investigator should never carelessly place the removed property in a vehicle and then stack a toolbox, flashlight, or other items on the evidence. If the actual assembly or component responsible for the fire is lost or damaged by the investigator, an incorrect conclusion may be drawn, especially if the damage occurs before the laboratory analysis of the property.

The final factor to consider during the collection of evidence is the volatility of the evidence. The volatility of evidence — or how easily it may evaporate — deals primarily with evidence in the liquid state, but is applicable to gaseous samples as well. Alcohol, for example, will be absorbed by water and will also evaporate quickly if exposed to air. Gaseous samples have to be collected quickly or they will dissipate. They are also extremely volatile and a delay in the collection of the sample may change the results.

Recognition and Documentation of Arson Evidence

It is the responsibility of the trained scene investigator to recognize the potential evidentiary value of physical evidence that may be present at a fire scene during the course of the scene reconstruction and the determination of the cause and origin of the fire. The types of physical evidence that may be present at an arson scene should be photographed in place, exactly as found, documented in crime scene notes, and carefully located on the scene sketch. Items such as containers of gasoline or other volatile liquids, ignition devices (e.g., matches or candles), delayed timing devices and trailers present few problems in terms of recognition and documentation. On the other hand, the selection process involved in the recognition of charred or burned fire debris suspected of containing an accelerant residue is one that requires prudence and discretion. Care must be taken to select samples that afford the greatest potential for a positive laboratory result. The thoughtless and indiscriminate selection of random charred areas of a fire scene for sample collection in the vain hope that a forensic laboratory will, through advanced technology, be able to obtain a positive result, is in most cases, a total waste of investigative and laboratory time.

The advantages of glass jars over other storage containers is that the contents can be seen without removing the cap or breaking the seal. As with metal cans, glass jars are readily available and reasonably priced. Glass jars are not as susceptible to the atmospheric or climatic problems as metal cans. Glass jars can be stored for a long period of time without fear of corrosion or corrosive action. Some glass jar manufacturers use metal lids or caps. If such jars are used, the lids must be stored in a dry atmosphere or corrosion could accumulate on the lid and possibly contaminate the sample.

Glass jars also have some disadvantages. They break rather easily and are not as durable as metal cans. Another disadvantage is that the sizes of glass jars are not as varied as metal cans or plastic bags.

Plastic bags are also used for the collection of physical evidence. Plastic bags are handy because they come in a variety of sizes, shapes, and thicknesses. Small items such as beaded wires, a smoke detector, or an outlet, can be securely placed in a sandwich bag. Bulkier items can be placed in large trash bags.

Plastic bags are extremely inexpensive and for that reason, they can be doubled or tripled up to prevent sharp or broken items from puncturing or tearing the plastic and spilling the contents. It is recommended that clear bags be used, regardless of the size, in order to see the contents within the bag without actually opening it up.

Another advantage of plastic bags over metal cans and glass jars is that they can easily conform to the shape of the property. An outlet can easily fit in a sealed and secured sandwich bag. However, the same outlet does not fit conveniently into a metal can or a glass jar, needing more space to store it. Plastic bags, however, can be easily damaged, punctured, or torn, which can result in the contamination or spoliation of the property. Large plastic bags can sometimes trap small components and these can be accidentally discarded if the evidence is transferred to another container carelessly.

Normal bags from the grocery or convenience stores should not be used to collect liquid and solid accelerant samples, because often they can be difficult to seal air tight. Light traces of hydrocarbons can therefore be lost, altering the forensic testing results. Furthermore, common plastic bags contain residual traces of hydrocarbons which can produce invalid test results.

To remedy this problem, special evidence plastic bags are available. Their chemical composition eliminates the possibility of incorrect test results. These bags cannot be found at the local supermarket, but can be obtained easily. They also cost more, but are generally still inexpensive. The special plastic bags come in a variety of sizes and shapes to accommodate the dimensions of the collected samples. Special evidence bags are transparent so the sample can be viewed without opening the bag. Evaporation of a sample does not occur because the bags remain air tight.

Remember, these bags are plastic, and can be easily damaged — punctured by a sharp object, ripped or torn open, or crushed, compromising the air-tight seal — and contaminate the sample. Another problem with the special evidence bags is the seal or plastic material can be attacked in the presence of some specific types of accelerant material, compromising the integrity of the seal of the bag. Therefore, if a sample is collected in the evidence bags, it may benefit the investigator to place a small amount of the sample in a glass jar or metal can upon returning from a fire scene.

One final note on special evidence bags: always double check the seal to confirm that it bonded properly. There is no excuse for an improperly sealed bag. Slipshod work habits can cause the evidence to be excluded or excused in a criminal case. Often, a bag may appear to be sealed properly; however, the seal may not be entirely secured. A poor seal may contaminate the collected sample. If an investigator uses all of the evidence containers, a sturdy cardboard box is sufficient to remove appliances and items. Each item and its related controls should be placed in the same container. The container should also be intact with no holes in the material to prevent losing small components.

Identification of Evidence

Before removing any evidence from a scene, it has to be identified. This does not mean, for example, that the age and the manufacturer of an appliance have to be known. Identification in this instance relates to the location and description of the property or sample removed. If possible, accelerant samples are taken and measurements from secure or definite objects documented. It is preferred that the same objects are used in measuring the distances to avoid any confusion as to the exact location from which each sample was taken. Usually, using two definitive objects is enough to pinpoint the area from which the sample was removed. However, circumstances in possible arson cases will dictate if triangulation of the scene should be performed to pinpoint the location of the removed samples. Triangulation is more common when government agencies conduct their investigation than with insurance industry investigators. These measurements should be written both in the field notes and on the scene diagram. Identifying evidence at the site will also eliminate any confusion once the items are returned to the laboratory or storage facility. When many similar items are removed from one fire scene, such as outlets, smoke detectors, or power cords, identifying them at the scene, photographing them at their pre-fire position, and documenting their location on a diagram will save time and frustration at the laboratory several hours later.

In larger, more complicated cases when many items are removed, identifying the property at the scene is a necessity to prevent mislabeling or confusion in later stages of the investigation. It will give the investigator a quick and simple reference for all items removed; it will also serve for quick and accurate reconstruction of the scene at the laboratory.

On occasion, fire investigators will perform more than one investigation in a given day. On-scene identification is imperative to prevent the possibility

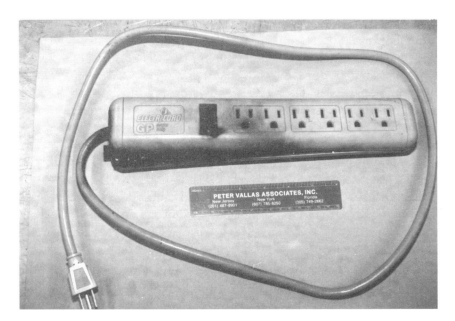

Figure 9.4 A scale of reference should be used when photographing evidence during laboratory analysis.

of combining or confusing the evidence for two or more cases. Be sure to keep all the evidence from one fire scene together to prevent them from being mislabeled or misplaced. In identifying any evidence, some general information needs to be included. The case or file name and number should appear on every evidence tag. Other information which should be placed on an identification tag is the date and time the evidence was taken. Of course, a general description of the items removed could be extremely detailed — i.e., "sample of wood flooring removed from the northwest corner of the first floor living room" — or generally vague — e.g., "oil burner parts and burned debris." A prevailing rule in collecting evidence is to provide a detailed description of samples taken and the location where each sample was extracted. For appliances, electrical cords, and most other items, a brief description of the evidence will suffice. Exceptions are commonplace, and again the investigator's discretion will dictate the information to be written on the identification tag.

When investigating explosions, identification tags may simply include a number or letter to label the item and the measured distance from the explosion's point of origin. Sometimes, a description of the material is included in an attempt to categorize similar materials together for reconstruction purposes.

Before removing any evidence from the scene, a receipt should be signed by the party or parties who granted permission to enter the premises. Persons who entered the premises under exigent circumstances have been excluded from following this procedure in the past, but most government agencies are now obtaining written authorization to remove property, out of the fear that any samples removed may be contested in a court of law.

Insurance investigators are now discovering that all items removed from a particular scene must be authorized by the owner of the property. Samples cannot be removed unless the owner signs a receipt, or the samples may be disallowed during a trial.

In some instances with insurance investigators, permission is granted over the telephone or through the mail. The combination for a lock is given or the key for the an entrance door is mailed. In cases such as these, if any items are removed, a receipt form should still be completed and a copy left behind in the structure or even mailed. This will establish the initial link in the chain of custody.

Because of legal challenges and litigation tactics, a chain of custody must be established at the earliest possible time. From the moment any evidence is taken from the scene to the time authorization for the disposal of the evidence is given, a chain of custody has to be maintained. Chain-of-custody requirements used to pertain only to criminal cases, but with an increase in the insurance industry pursuing subrogation claims, these standards are infiltrating into civil cases as well. A break in the chain of custody can occur at any given time. An alert attorney will use what may appear to be an insignificant lapse in the custody chain, and question how the evidence may have been altered and possibly contaminated. To ensure that there can be no question of contamination or spoliation of the evidence, the items should be identified and labeled at the scene, and a receipt should be signed by the appropriate party to remove any property from the site. If that is not possible, leave a copy of the receipt behind at the scene. Once returned to a laboratory facility, the evidence should be documented in a logbook or saved on a computer disk.

Once the on-site examination is completed, before removing any property from the scene, all items should have an identification tag or label affixed to them or their container, whether an unlined metal can, glass jar, or plastic bag. By completing this task on site, the chain of custody begins. All items should be noted on a receipt form which is to be given to or left behind for the person who granted entry into the structure.

To prevent cross-contamination of evidence, the investigator should wash his tools with alcohol. In order to preserve the chain of custody, an investigator should complete a receipt which should be signed if possible. Both measures demonstrate the investigator's thoroughness and reasonable attempts to prevent the contamination of the samples and establish the chain of custody. We have already mentioned that care should be taken when

Figure 9.5 Molotov cocktails are still popular devices with amateur arsonists. An investigator should be aware that the neck of the bottle used or at least some section of the neck will very often survive both the bottle's shattering and the resulting fire.

placing of evidence in a vehicle to prevent additional damage or property being confused with another case. Great care should always be used in the transportation of evidence from the fire scene to the laboratory facility. Most items are brittle and delicate due to the damage sustained during the fire. Common sense dictates that property should not be thrown in a vehicle or that heavy objects should not be placed on top of the items. Likewise, if a large appliance is removed, secure it tightly to the vehicle to prevent the possibility of its falling or tipping during transportation.

Many common items are useful to carry in a vehicle which will help in identifying evidence at the scene as well as prevent damage occurring while transporting the items to the laboratory. These suggestions are in addition to the required or necessary tools and instruments needed by a fire investigator. Identification tags are, of course, a must. If tags are forgotten or depleted, 3" × 5" index cards will do for temporary tags.

Various kinds of adhesive tape can be stored in the vehicle, because cello or masking tape are not always sufficient. Clear packaging tape may be used to protect brittle beaded wire failures from further damage. The tape's transparency also allows other parties to examine the wire without further damaging it or disturbing it.

Another handy item to have is a roll of numbered electrician's tape. This can help in the identification of numerous wires, power cords, or extension cords found at various scenes.

One or two sections of a mop or broom handle can be placed in a van or similar vehicle; these can be placed on the bed of the van or truck and used as rollers for moving large or heavy appliances from a scene. Less effort is used to position the item in the vehicle, especially if the vehicle is a van or a pickup truck with a cap over the box.

Any property removed should not be left in the vehicle overnight if the vehicle is not in a secured area. Again, the chain of custody question will arise, and possible spoliation of evidence will be addressed by an attorney or authority if the property remained in an unsecured vehicle over an extended period of time.

In cases involving large losses, or when several large or unwieldy items must be secured, an outside towing company may be used to haul the property to the laboratory. Show good judgment is choosing a towing company which will understand the risks of handling such equipment. Oversee the loading and unloading procedures. Follow the towing vehicle to ensure no items have a chance to fall off the truck or fall onto, and possibly damage, other items. If possible, have the investigator or another person ride in the vehicle. Do not forget that all items removed must be accounted for when the trip is completed. Extra protection of delicate components and assemblies should be practiced in order to preserve them.

Once liquid and solid accelerant samples are secured and returned to a laboratory or storage facility, they should be documented in the logbook and stored in an easily accessible area until a decision is made on whether they will be tested. Remember, if the containers are airtight, samples can be kept in storage for quite some time before forensic testing. Often, however, the samples are tested at the earliest possible time. If a question exists as to whether a particular fire was intentionally set, the insurance company needs to know within 90 days. Most policies are written in a way that allows the insurance company 90 days to pay the claim, once submitted; an insurance company cannot deny payment of a claim after 90 days unless extenuating circumstances exist. Consequently, when samples are submitted for forensic and chemical analysis, a quick turn-around time is essential for the insurance industry.

Laboratory Analysis and Testing

Once the property has been taken to its destination, the items should be documented in an evidence logbook, either handwritten or computer generated. This provides the investigator with a quick and easy reference of the evidence on all the claims he or she is involved. The same basic information written on the identification tags should be included in the property logbook. Again, this is necessary to preserve the chain of custody. For example, if an investigator writes his or her description of the evidence on the tag as "oil burner parts and burned debris," the same description should be written in the property logbook. Providing all the relevant information in the logbook decreases the time spent retrieving and reviewing the file to confirm that all the items are present. Some firms have additional information stored in the logbooks such as the date(s) when the property was examined, shipped, returned — and to whom — and/or discarded. Other information which is useful in the logbooks is the location of the property, and name of the person who logged the property in the storage facility. This further preserves the chain of custody. If the property has to be retrieved, it can be done efficiently. When the evidence is to be returned to the facility, it helps to place it in the same location. If this is not possible or if another person returns the property, the logbook will have the name of the last person who handled the property and the date.

Once evidence is returned from the scene, laboratory analysis can be performed in a controlled environment, allowing scrutiny of the items which was not possible at the loss site. During this initial laboratory examination, the investigator has to be careful in his or her proceedings: with the numerous judgments and rulings regarding the spoliation of evidence, during the initial laboratory examination, destructive and invasive testing should not be conducted. Destructive and/or invasive testing refers to permanently altering the shape, integrity, or condition of the evidence in a manner which prohibits the item from physically returning to the state in which it was found by the investigator.

Performing nondestructive and/or noninvasive testing does not limit an investigator or engineer from visually inspecting the item or even dismantling it. Internal examinations on components in small appliances can be done as long as the panels or components can be reassembled once the analysis is completed or at any time in the future. Panels may be removed from large appliances to examine and test the motor assemblies, compressors, or any other electrical component. Thermostats can be tested to see if they operated properly. Microswitch housings may be removed to see if the internal components were severely affected by the fire, which may be a key in proving an investigator's hypothesis on how the fire originated.

If a question exists as to whether an examination may be destructive or invasive in nature, it would be beneficial not to conduct it until all involved parties have been notified. A joint inspection with all the involved parties is a good idea, when an investigator does not precisely know his or her inspection will be completely nondestructive or noninvasive.

When dismantling property at the laboratory, photograph the steps taken, videotape the entire process or preferably do both. Each step in the dismantling process should be documented. Since some cases may take several months or years before other experts or engineers examine the evidence relating to a particular loss, questions will be asked on how the property was handled and treated during the unsupervised inspection. Videotaping and photographing the process will prove no destructive or invasive testing was performed; it can also refresh an investigator's memory regarding relevant information.

If several inspections are performed on the same evidence, one videotape can be used to document the various inspections. The date and times of the subsequent inspections should be noted on the tape. Similar documentation should be used when photographs are taken; the photographs should be separated according to the date of inspection.

Another factor to be considered is the severity of the loss. If the dollar loss for the fire is high, or if several other structures or dwellings were burned or damaged in one fire, the investigator may request an immediate joint inspection with all the involved parties. If, however, only one room in an owner occupied structure was damaged, and in this room are the burned remains of a coffee maker, with all the fire patterns consistent with the fire originating at that point, then a more thorough and detailed laboratory analysis can be performed. The investigator's discretion will dictate if all the involved parties should be notified before or after the initial laboratory examination.

It should be reemphasized that all laboratory analyses should be photographed. Videotaping will encompass the entire process and can include any discussions between the experts. During the introduction between the parties, a formal explanation should be made to notify all the parties that a video of the proceedings will be taken. Each party will be given a copy of the videotape with a written transcript of the proceeding if desired.

If videotaping is not feasible, a dictaphone or tape recorder can be used to document the proceedings. This should not discourage discussion. Providing all the parties with the same opportunity to examine the property should stimulate discussion regarding the possibilities on how the fire started. Many times the parties agree to conduct destructive or invasive testing during this inspection or at a later date to resolve the unanswered questions.

Although initially notifying all parties and arranging a suitable date for the experts and engineers to conduct a joint inspection may delay the investigation, it will eliminate any potential questions regarding the spoliation of the property. Conducting investigations in this conservative manner will limit the litigation revolving around the spoliation issue. Since all involved parties are present at the inspection(s), the responsible party cannot raise the spoliation issue.

Nondestructive Testing

Nondestructive testing should be conducted at every available opportunity. Nondestructive or noninvasive procedures should be exhausted before any destructive or invasive testing is done, unless all involved parties agree to perform destructive analysis.

Radiography is probably the most used nondestructive testing procedure in fire investigation. This nondestructive analysis can examine gas pipe fittings for porosities caused by poor castings or laps in the base metal which weakened its capability to support appropriate loads or allowed gas to permeate from the pipe. Radiography may also be used to ascertain what position a toggle switch or solenoid switch was in at the time the fire occurred. These results usually help the fire investigator in determining the cause. Results may confirm an investigator's preliminary conclusion that an appliance, a faulty switch, or a malfunctioned component was the reason for the fire.

Other forms of nondestructive testing include ultrasonic testing, magnetic particle testing, dye penetrant testing, and eddy current. These forms of analysis are limited in fire investigation and are geared more toward engineering losses involving metal fatigue or the quality assurance of the metal materials.

Preparation of Samples for Testing in the Forensic Laboratory

The term "accelerant" as used frequently during arson investigation refers to any agent, frequently an ignitable or flammable liquid, used to initiate or speed the spread of fire. An accelerant may be a solid, liquid, or gaseous substance. Most accelerants detected through analysis in the forensic laboratory are either a type of petroleum distillate or a nonpetroleum product such as turpentine or alcohols. If not consumed in the fire or otherwise evaporated, these volatile substances are absorbed within the matrix of charred materials such as wood, carpet, and other building materials at a fire scene.

Solid and liquid accelerant samples can be tested by various methods. When these charred materials, unknown liquids and comparison samples.

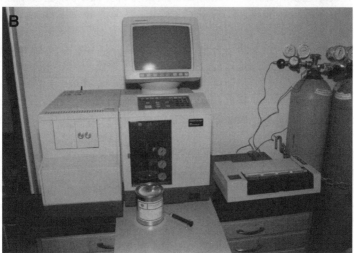

Figure 9.6   (A) Clean, unused metal cans are currently the recommended choice of sample containers for the collection of solid and liquid samples. (B) The technique of gas chromatography is the most commonly utilized for the detection of accelerants in fire debris; (C) samples are heated prior to headspace injection into the gas chromatograph. (D) samples are injected into the injection port of the gas chromatograph and transported via a gas carrier through a column designed to separate the components of the sample.

are received in sample containers and logged at the laboratory, they are subjected to an organized process of isolation or concentration, detection, and identification. Unknown and comparison samples as well as known laboratory positive standards or controls are treated in a similar manner.

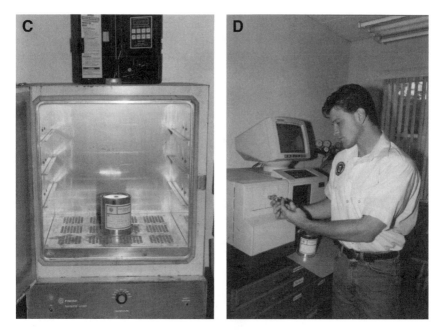

Figure 9.6 (continued)

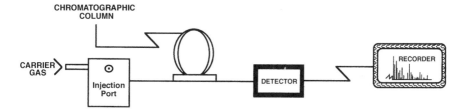

Figure 9.7   Gas chromatograph.

There are four general methods for isolating or concentrating accelerants from fire debris:

1. *Steam distillation* — This involves the heating and distilling with steam of the charred material and trapping the distillate with a cold water condenser. The volatile hydrocarbons are collected in a liquid form before analysis.
2. *Solvent extraction* — The sample of charred material is extracted by mixing and shaking with a known solvent such as carbon disulfide, methylene chloride, or hexane, which dissolves the petroleum distillates and other volatiles into the known solvent. This extract is then evaporated to a small volume which concentrates the sample for analysis.

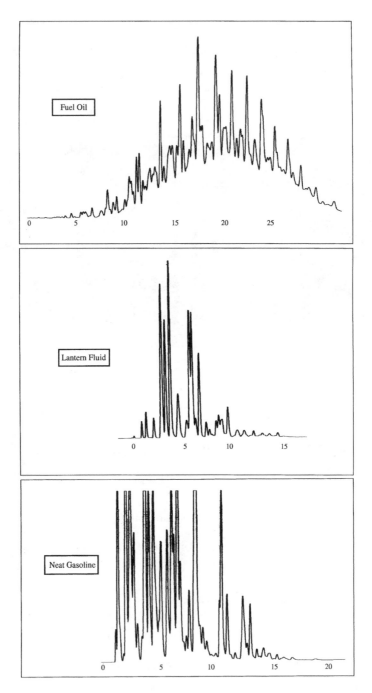

Figure 9.8 These chromatograms are examples of the most common acceler-ants used by the arsonist.

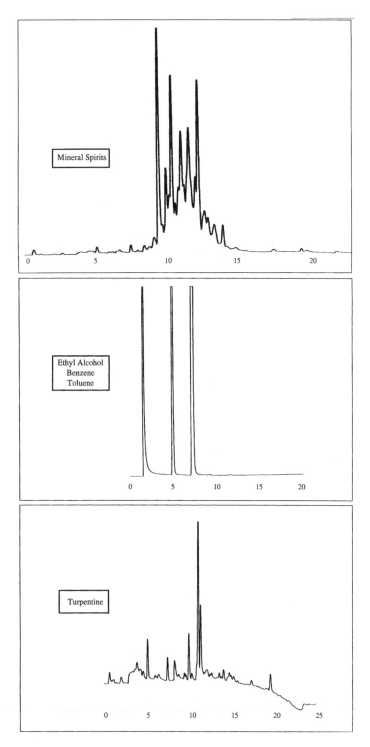

Figure 9.8 (continued)

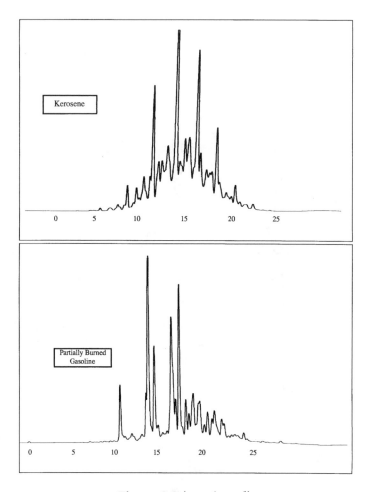

Figure 9.8 (continued)

3. *Cold head space* — the top of the sample container is punctured and a stopper inserted so that a headspace vapor sample can be removed with a syringe for subsequent analysis.

4. *Heated head space* — after the stopper is inserted into the top of the sample container, the vessel is heated to approximately 100°C or slightly lower. This technique concentrates the head space vapors since the heat drives the volatiles from the charred matrix. This method is popular and more sensitive than the cold head space technique.

5. *Vapor concentration on charcoal* — this method uses an inert gas purge with nitrogen or air of the heated samples container which carries volatiles through a small tube containing charcoal where they are concentrated. The charcoal is desorbed by heat or a small volume of a solvent such as carbon disulfide and thus prepared for analysis.

FLAMMABLE AND COMBUSTIBLE LIQUID
CLASSIFICATION SYSTEM

Class Number (Class Name)	Peak Spread Based on N-Alkane Carbon Numbers	Examples
1 Light Petroleum Distillates	C4-C8	Petroleum ethers, Pocket lighter fuels, some rubber cement solvents. Skelly solvents, V M & P Naphtha.
2 Gasoline	C4-C12	All brands of automotive gasoline, including gasohol. Some camping fuels.
3 Medium Petroleum Distillates (MPD)	C8-C12	Paint thinners, mineral spirits, Some charcoal starters, "dry-cleaning" solvents, some torch fuels.
4 Kerosene	C9-C16	No. 1 Fuel oil, Jet-A(Aviation) fuel, insect sprays, some charcoal starters, some torch fuels.
5 Heavy Petroleum Distillates	C10-C23	No. 2 Fuel oil, Diesel fuel.
0	Variable	Single compounds such as Alcohols, Acetone, Toluene, Xylenes, some lamp oils, camping fuels, lacquer thinners, turpentine and others.

Figure 9.9   Flammable and combustible liquid classification system.

Computer Modeling

In a society where technology and computers have made so many advances, the field of fire investigation has also been affected. Many computerized fire modeling programs exist. Computerized fire-modeling can highlight any conceivable aspect of a particular fire: fire behavior under different environmental circumstances, fire propagation, initiation of a fire, etc. Computer modeling can provide a three-dimensional, working progression of a fire which cannot be depicted in photographs or videotape.

Although computer modeling does not test actual evidence removed from a scene, it can help the investigator in testing a hypothesis on how the fire started, propagated, and travelled. In theory, an investigator is testing the evidence he or she has accumulated from the scene.

In years to come, computerized fire modeling will, in all probability, become more universally accepted and more affordable.

Evidence Storage

Once the evidence is removed from a scene and taken to a laboratory for further testing and examinations are performed, what becomes of the items? Can they be discarded if they were not found to be the cause of the fire? Is it acceptable to keep only the items found to be responsible for a particular fire? Once removed samples are tested can they be discarded? Do they have to be held even if no accelerant was detected in the sample? What if the samples were never tested? Obviously, the correct response to all these questions is no. Removal and subsequent securing of physical evidence are the first stages of evidence collection not the last. Physical evidence has to be preserved for months, sometimes years after an incident has occurred. In civil cases, and subrogation claims, files can remain active for 5 or more years depending on the statute of limitations for a particular state. Therefore, any evidence removed from a scene has to be preserved until the case has been finally settled or the statute expires. The most desirable place to preserve evidence is in a specially designed storage facility. A steel-frame constructed unit with a poured concrete slab flooring is ideal. The complex will have to preserve large items such as kitchen appliances, as well as small items such as coffee makers, toasters, and accelerant samples. The storage facility should also maintain a dry climate; excessive moisture or humidity will generate rust and corrosive action on metal components. Although on large appliances, mild amounts of rust and corrosion may not alter the unit, smaller, more brittle items like beaded wires and other small components stand a greater chance of being affected by a humid atmosphere.

In most areas, self-storage facilities can ease the problem of storing evidence. These units offer a safe protective shelter from the natural elements. Usually, self-storage facilities are not placed in low-lying areas susceptible to flooding or other natural disasters. Before renting space in one of these facilities, confirm that the area does not flood. Also check to see if the structure is sturdy enough to withstand severe wind gusts. Check the overall construction to verify the structure has been built competently. It should be equipped with a sprinkler system so in the event a fire occurs, a quick and efficient suppression is provided.

Do not feel comfortable using a noncombustible structure without a fire suppression system. Most units contain combustible items which are literally packed into the rented space. As fire investigators, we know a discarded cigarette can easily ignite a couch, sofa, upholstered furniture, or cardboard boxes. If this occurs during the early morning hours when most facilities are not staffed, a small fire can quickly become a large uncontrolled fire.

All evidence removed from a fire scene has to be secured. It should be preserved so that if and when the evidence is requested to be examined by another party or presented in a court of law, it will be in the same condition as it was when removed from the fire scene. Evidence in criminal cases on the whole is usually held for less time than in civil cases; civil cases tend to continue in litigation and arbitration for years. Throughout this process, the evidence collected will be examined and reexamined by other experts for the other involved parties. If, at any time, a question or concern of spoliation or contamination of the evidence is introduced, the possibility exists for the case to be dismissed or, at least, for the evidence to be excluded. It is recommended that all evidence be kept in a safe and dry environment from the time they are first secured until they are no longer required.

Shipment and Transferral of Evidence

When authorization is received to transfer evidence either to another laboratory for further analysis or to the opposing side for inspection, the evidence should be hand-delivered if at all possible. Delivery by hand ensures the property arrives at the correct destination and intact. (See "Evidence Chart" Appendix 9.2.) Once the item is transferred, a receipt should be signed to preserve the chain of custody. If any destructive or invasive analysis has been conducted, this should be mentioned either on the receipt or in a brief accompanying letter. Also include the names of persons and the companies which agreed to the destructive or invasive testing.

If the property is sent to a laboratory for further analysis, a letter should be included outlining the scope of work to be performed. This is required so the laboratory does not accidentally alter or damage the property or conduct testing which is not requested.

When transferring evidence, a container should hold only the property involved in one particular case. If evidence from more than one case is being shipped or transferred, these items should be packaged separately.

Even before the property is shipped, a sequence of steps should be followed to protect the investigator from accusations regarding the spoliation of the evidence. A photographic survey of the items together as well all the items individually will prove the items were not altered and no invasive testing was performed. On those rare occasions where the evidence *did* have destructive or invasive testing performed, include this in the letter accompanying the items. Also, photograph the unsealed container with all the items placed in it, and finally photograph the sealed container.

Photographing and documenting the items during the packaging process is essential when evidence is to be shipped through a mail or carrier service. When a laboratory or investigator receives evidence, a photographic survey of the property should be done as well to confirm that all items are present and establish the condition they are in upon arrival.

Always request a signed confirmation from the company receiving the package in order to preserve the chain of custody. If the property is being shipped to another firm or company, send a letter explaining that they now have custody of all the property retained by the investigator for that specific case and they are now assuming all responsibility for these items. Notification should be given to the receiving party outlining the inspections that have been performed to date.

Presenting Evidence in Court

Some cases enter the litigation process and are settled, while others go through the entire process and are decided by a jury. In criminal cases, the time between the actual fire investigation and the trial is usually less than in a civil case. Some exceptions may occur when a number of arson cases over several months or years are linked together and the arsonist is finally caught. Most times, however, because the Constitution grants anyone indicted in a criminal action the right to a speedy trial, criminal cases are processed relatively expeditiously compared to civil cases.

Civil cases commonly get bogged down in legalities and arguments which can leave the case active for years. There is also the possibility of hung juries and appeals which delay the ultimate decision. In either case, it is very rare for the actual fire scene to remain preserved for the jury to inspect or examine.

Consequently, photographs taken by an investigator at the scene, during any laboratory examinations, and in preparing the evidence to ship are critical in explaining the origin and cause of the fire, and how these were determined.

Unless a case involves a large monetary loss or the loss of life, the actual evidence may not even be introduced in the court of law. Sometimes the items removed are too large, or too many items were initially removed to adequately place them in the courtroom. Even if the evidence is not bulky, usually photographs which are a true and accurate representation of the component or item are used in court.

Because the use of photographic equipment is necessary in the field of fire investigation, many court decisions over the years have established the parameters and standards for the industry. A brief synopsis of these rulings will show how photographs and videotapes are introduced into court as evidence.

Photographs have been used in the court system since 1875, with the first use of color prints in 1946. Initially only photographs taken by professional photographers could be introduced in a court of law. However, by 1940, with the technological advances over time allowing cameras and photographic equipment to be more accessible and affordable to the ordinary person, a Pennsylvania court ruled in *Adamczuk v. Holloway* that "any competent investigator can take photographs which will be suitable for the introduction as evidence."

The Federal Rules of Evidence has outlined the criterion for photographs in order to be introduced into court. The criterion established in the Federal Rules of Evidence was adapted from various lower court decisions. The photograph must have significance to the case at hand. A photograph of the second floor bedroom may not be introduced if no fire or heat patterns are observed in the room, or if the fire did not travel into the room. However, if the cause of the fire is incendiary and the lock on the bedroom window is in the open position, a possibility exists that the photograph will be admitted into a court of law to prove the structure was not secure at the time the fire originated.

A photograph may be introduced if it refutes the matter being questioned. If the opposition states the first floor window lock was forced before the fire, photographs refuting the claim can be introduced. Photographs of protected areas or items and components are often admitted to determine the position of an item or component during the fire.

The second criterion needed for a photograph to be admitted into court is that the witness identifying the photograph must be familiar with the portrayed scene. If the witness cannot identify the location portrayed in the photograph, he or she will not be able to introduce the photograph.

An additional measure in the Federal Rules of Evidence states the witness must be familiar with the day and time of the scene portrayed on the photograph. In other words, does the photograph accurately depict the scene when the photograph was taken?

In some instances, such as vehicle reconstruction and accident cases, the photograph must depict the scene at a relevant time, day, month, or season. The weather also has to be taken into account. If an accident occurs at 6:00 p.m. on a weekend during a rain shower, a photograph of the scene at 9:00 a.m. on a clear day during the rush hour of a work week is useless and will probably not be introduced in court. Lighting and weather are two extremely important factors in vehicular accident cases. For fire losses, these factors are not as important and the scene does not have to be photographed under the same conditions as when the fire occurred. However, the weather, including wind direction, should be known to help an investigator in understanding seemingly confusing or unusual fire patterns.

Finally, the evidentiary value of a photograph must supersede any effects of undue bias or prejudice created by the photograph. For example, in cases involving fire deaths, a photograph submitted to the jury documenting the protected areas where the bodies of a family were found may be allowed while photographs of the actual bodies may not be admitted. By removing the most graphic items of a photograph, the jury can concentrate on the entire photograph which may demonstrate that the window near the fire escape was nailed closed.

The arguments produced by the lawyers and the idiosyncrasies of a given judge are other considerations to take into account when introducing a photograph into court. If an attorney does not exhibit a strong argument why a photograph should be admitted into the court as evidence, then it may not be allowed by the judge. Furthermore, if a certain judge prefers graphic photographs to be taken with black and white film, an attorney will have to have an extraordinarily good argument to allow a color photograph of decomposed or burned bodies to be introduced.

Disposal of Evidence

Disposal measures for property are becoming increasingly difficult and complex. Long gone are the days when the client calls and informs the investigator the evidence he or she is storing on a particular case can now be disposed. All disposal requests should be written on the client's letterhead or stationery to confirm authenticity of the request. Once the request is received, the investigator must get authorization from the property owner or his attorney. This is usually the most difficult because in some instances after the claim was originally settled by the insurance company to the property owner, contact with the property owner ceases. Also, some cases are litigated for several years and policies could be canceled, which creates additional difficulties in locating the property owner.

On occasion the actual property owner cannot be located because he or she has left the state or country, died, or changed names. In such cases a judge may sign a court order to permit the disposal of the property. This should only be the last resort. If an investigator has sent letters with a return receipt with no response and attempted to contact the employers, relatives, or the public adjusters associated with the owner of the property without ascertaining the location of the property owner, then the investigator can request authorization from the local judge. In requesting permission from the court, an investigator must state that every avenue has been pursued with no correspondence stating an interest for continued storage of the property or turned over to another party from the property owner, attorney, or relatives.

In cases involving several parties, the disposal of the evidence cannot be done until all known involved parties agree to have the evidence destroyed. Although the insurance company which retained an investigator's services may not require the storage of the property, other insurance companies and/or attorneys may need the evidence to pursue litigation against the manufacturer or perhaps a company which recently serviced the appliance or installed an addition to the premises. Consequently, if the client authorizes disposal of the property, a letter to all the involved parties must be sent stating this fact. If another party would like to store the evidence and preserve the items, then they may do so. Notifying all interested parties will eliminate any potential issues regarding the unauthorized destruction and spoliation of the evidence.

Governmental agency employees normally do not remove evidence from a fire scene if the cause of the fire is ruled accidental. In smaller districts and municipalities, however, it is not uncommon for the fire department or police department to remove the items they believe are responsible for the origination of the fire. After the cases are closed, these items are discarded without contacting the property owner or his or her insurance company to ascertain if they would like them returned or if an investigation for insurance purposes is to be conducted. If the municipality you are in operates in a similar fashion, the standard of operations should be changed. Before any evidence is discarded, receive permission from the property owner and his or her insurance company. Although the fire is accidental, the insurance company may want to pursue legal action against the manufacturer of the product believed to be the cause of the fire.

Time-Delayed Ignition Devices

In an incendiary fire, the source of ignition may be direct or time-delayed (indirect). *Direct ignition* involves the direct application of an ignition source (e.g., match) to a combustible fuel. The fuel used may range from a crumpled newspaper to a liquid accelerant. Many novice "torches," who know nothing about the combustibility of different types of fuel, are seriously injured or killed when they become trapped in their own fires. However, the use of a time-delayed ignition device allows the arsonist to leave the scene safely *before* ignition occurs. Some of these devices are crude and unpredictable; others are very sophisticated and give the arsonist enough time to set up and develop seemingly flawless alibis. The following devices are commonly used:

Electronic timers. An electronic timer, which can be bought almost anywhere for well under $10, can delay ignition for anywhere from a few minutes to almost 24 hours. It is used in conjunction with an ignition source (e.g., soldering iron, heating element), which is simply placed in a combustible fuel (e.g., sawdust) or a flammable liquid (e.g., gasoline).

Cigarette matches. A lit cigarette can serve as a 10- to 12-minute fuse when used in combination with a book of matches. The lit cigarette is simply tucked into a closed book of matches, and the device placed close to a combustible material.

Candles. A candle with a 7/8-inch diameter (2 11/16-in. circumference) will burn 1 in. in 57 minutes in a draft-free environment. A 6-in. candle with the same diameter and circumference provides almost 6 hours of burn time before ignition of an adjoining combustible.

Chemicals. Certain terrorist groups have been very successful in the use of chemical igniters. One of these has been the combination of potassium chlorate, powdered sugar, and sulfuric acid.

Countless other devices (including common light bulbs) have also been used, limited only by the imagination of the arsonist.

During the examination of the fire scene, the investigator must be able to recognize the remains of a time-delayed device. He or she must also be aware of the fact that more than one device may have been secreted in various areas of the structure.

Collection of Samples for Accelerant Testing

The investigator's experience and skill dictates the best areas at a fire scene from which to obtain samples for laboratory analysis. The chances of finding an accelerant depend on a variety of factors which should be given consideration.

1. Time lapse between fire and collection of samples
2. Location of sample in reference to the origin(s) and observed pour patterns of the fire
3. The heat intensity of the fire
4. Amount of destruction caused by fire
5. Evaporation rate of the volatile accelerant
6. Type of material or substrate that may contain accelerant

In many cases, a suspected accelerant may have burned away or evaporated, due to the nature of the fire and the environment. Fire-fighting operations may have washed away or diluted traces of accelerant residue. Liquid accelerant may be applied unevenly in different areas and absorb differently within different substrates (wood flooring vs. carpet). It should be recognized that liquids are subject to gravity and will flow, seeking the lowest point depending upon the slope. The number of samples that should be collected from a suspect arson fire scene may vary, depending upon the number of points of origin, pour patterns, etc. However, accelerants applied to different areas of the same pour pattern may be consumed at different rates, so there may be positive and negative areas within the same pattern. Research into sampling at fire scenes performed by Michael Byron of Forensic and Scientific Testing in Atlanta, Georgia, has shown that the percentage of positive samples increases by approximately 10% with each sample as the samples taken per case increased from three to five. When five or more samples were taken, approximately 65% of the cases were positive. There was no appreciable increase beyond five samples, which was considered representative sampling of an area. Further sampling was considered unnecessary except to help determine multiple points of origin or with very extensive destructive fires.

In conjunction with the collection of burned fire debris samples, the investigator should collect comparison samples of the same material or substrate that showed the point(s) of origin or pour patterns that were produced by suspected volatile accelerants. Ideally, these comparison samples should be taken away from the burned areas where the presence of the accelerant would not be expected to be present. The analysis of comparison samples allows the forensic laboratory to evaluate possible contributions of the material or substrate components with respect to volatile hydrocarbons or pyrolysis products that may interfere with the interpretation of the results and possibly produce a false positive result, much as wood, carpet, linoleum or other building materials can all produce volatile hydrocarbons when they are burned. Comparison samples help the analyst understand the chemical composition of substrate materials at a fire scene and help to determine which volatile hydrocarbons are natural to the substrate and which are foreign and considered to be volatile accelerants.

There are substrate materials which produce residues upon burning that are similar to common accelerants which have been recognized by forensic laboratories. Asphalt-containing materials can produce volatile hydrocarbons similar to fuel oil residue. Some printed materials such as newspaper may contain trace quantities of petroleum distillates used as ink solvents or cleaning agents. Synthetic carpet materials, on burning, may produce volatile hydrocarbons that may simulate components of gasoline. Tile and linoleum floor adhesives may contain traces of volatile organic solvents. The burning of plastics and foam rubber products can produce volatile hydrocarbons that may be hard to interpret. The identification of turpentine as an accelerant in charred wood samples is particularly difficult to establish, since pine is a commonly used building material. Pine naturally contains turpentine and is often present in both burned and unburned samples of this type of wood.

In many samples, the common petroleum distillates are easily recognized despite the background material containing volatile materials. In these instances, the lack of a comparison sample will not compromise the results.

However, there should always be good communication between the laboratory analyst and the field investigator at fire scenes when questions arise. It is a good idea to collect comparison samples in conjunction with the unknown charred samples since it may be impossible to revisit the scene at a later time.

Contamination of Samples

Throughout the process of collecting and securing evidence samples, the investigator must be careful not to contaminate the samples. Questions of contamination usually occur during trial proceedings, when a defense attorney questions the investigator who collected the samples. Therefore, the investigator must attempt to show that he or she tried all reasonable measures to prevent cross contaminating samples.

An investigator's tools such as a shovel, broom, wood chisel, and gloves are usually the first focus of a defense attorney to show the possibility that contamination of the scene led to the detection of an accelerant. Be prepared to handle questions concerning the number of investigations preformed using the same tools. Were the same tools used in all of these investigations, and if so, how many investigations were performed where samples had been collected? An attorney will also focus on the number of arson investigations done by the investigator where the same accelerant was used, and how much time had elapsed between the two investigations.

To prevent or at least limit this line of questioning, the investigator does not have to buy new tools for each investigation. This is an unreasonable and ridiculous request. In the eyes of the court, it is today acceptable to reuse tools such as shovels, brooms, and chisels as long as they are washed down with alcohol to prevent cross-contamination of the scene. Alcohol is preferred because it is water soluble and it evaporates quickly; therefore the residue will only remain on the tools for a brief period of time. Brooms should be replaced and new ones used if the circumstances warrant that decision.

Regarding the investigator's gloves, he or she should have a pair of work gloves and also carry a box of latex or surgical gloves when removing samples. Surgical gloves are readily available and relatively inexpensive. When each sample is collected, a photograph should be taken to show the contents of the container as well as the gloves used by the investigator to take the sample. For the next sample, the investigator should use another pair of gloves.

Questions about the contents of a sample will be addressed to the investigator. If a sample testing positive for an accelerant contains burned oak wood flooring and linoleum but the comparison sample only contains the oak wood flooring, the results will be questioned. Was the linoleum a product containing hydrocarbons? What about the adhesive for the linoleum? If a comparison sample of the oak flooring and a comparison sample of the linoleum are tested and the results proved the linoleum contained no traces of hydrocarbons, it would confirm an accelerant was used.

The actual collection of charred samples and comparison samples at a fire scene should be done so as to minimize the possibility of contamination. Contamination of physical evidence can occur from improper methods of collection, storage, or shipment to the laboratory.

1. Cross-contamination between samples can be avoided by the use of plastic or latex gloves when placing samples into evidence containers. There should be a change of gloves between successive sampling. The investigator can alternately use the lid of the evidence container as a means of scooping the fire debris into the evidence container.

2. The evidence containers should be clean before the introduction of the sample. It is advisable to give the laboratory analyst an unused clean evidence container that can be tested and serve as a blank to ensure that components of the container to not contain volatile reacting materials that could interfere with the analysis.

3. Sample containers should be filled with an adequate amount of suspect and comparison material, respectively. Whether the container is a pint, quart, or gallon size, the container should be 50 to 75% full of the solid materials.

4. Liquid volatile samples such as gasoline or kerosene found in containers at a fire scene should be transferred in small quantities (1 ml is more than adequate) to clean evidence containers. Cotton or gauze can be added to the container to absorb the liquid.

5. Gaseous samples require either commercially available gas sampling devices, evacuated air sampling cans, or the use of a glass bottle filled with distilled water. At the scene, the bottle is emptied and replaced by the gaseous sample. The fire investigator should consult with the local forensic laboratory for help with the collection of gaseous samples.

6. Samples should be secured within their respective containers to insure that leakage or evaporation does not occur, especially with the liquid samples. Solid samples should not be placed in plastic or paper bags, but rather sealed in the evidence container at the scene.

Sample Containers

Due to the increased scrutiny of collection methods today by attorneys and the legal system, all items must be accounted for once they leave the scene. Any item, component, assembly, and sample should be placed in a container to ensure no piece or fragment will be misplaced, lost, left behind, or incorrectly filled with evidence from another fire. The three kinds of containers most commonly used by professionals today are metal cans, glass jars, and plastic bags.

Most organizations and professionals prefer new, unused, unlined metal cans when collecting liquid and solid accelerant evidence. When collecting evidence in a metal can, the recommended practice is to fill the can approximately two-thirds full in order to have adequate space remaining so the vapor from the sample can be extracted. A new unlined can will not contaminate the sample or give incorrect results. If a lacquer-lined metal can is used to collect the sample, a contention can be offered the lacquer coating within the can had contaminated the sample and tainted the results.

The cans should of course be unused and clear of any rust accumulation or corrosion. Once a can is used, it should never be used to collect samples again, even if has been cleaned with alcohol.

Metal cans have many advantages as evidence collection containers. They are more durable than glass or plastic containers and are not susceptible to breaking or tearing and spilling the contents; they are also readily available and inexpensive. Many paint stores and hardware stores stock unlined metal cans in a variety of sizes. When buying the cans, however, make sure they are free of any corrosion build-up. Furthermore, unlined metal cans can store materials over an extended period of time without allowing volatile liquids to evaporate.

The greatest disadvantage of unlined metal cans is that they must be stored in a dry atmosphere until they are used; a moist atmosphere may produce condensation which can corrode the metal.

Another disadvantage of metal cans is that they must be opened in order to view the contents. Therefore, in cases involving the transfer of evidence from one party to another, the lid must be removed to verify that the contents within the can are, in fact, the materials stated on the label.

Glass jars are also acceptable for the collection of liquid and solid accelerant evidence. As with metal cans, common glass jars should not be used; this includes mason jars with rubber gaskets. The caps for the glass jars should not have liners adhering to the cap because the glue or adhesive agent usually contains solvents which can contaminate the sample. For some accelerants, the vapors can violate the integrity of the rubber gasket or seal creating the potential for the vapors to leak and escape from the jar.

Methods of Analysis and Identification of Accelerants

Early attempts to identify accelerants from fire debris involved the measurement of physical properties of the volatiles such as color tests, boiling point, flash point, density, and refractive index, and comparing the results to known data. Ultraviolet (UV) and infrared (IR) light have also been used. These techniques have been less than satisfactory, due to lack of sample purity and low sample volume. Fire debris samples rarely contain accelerant material of high purity and often contain burned residues of plastics, wood, carpet, and other building materials.

Gas chromatography is the most common method for detecting accelerants in fire debris in forensic laboratories. It has been used since the 1960s when investigators relied on packed columns and thermal conductivity detectors. Since then, the sensitivity and resolution of volatile components has vastly improved with the use of capillary columns and flame ionization detectors. Gas chromatography is essentially a separation technique capable of separating mixtures of petroleum distillates and volatile organic compounds into individual peaks, which form a pattern for comparison with known standards. Liquid or headspace samples are injected into the injection port of the gas chromatograph and are transported by a carrier gas through a column designed to separate the components of the mixture of organic components. Components having a greater affinity for the moving gas phase will travel through the column at a faster rate compared to those having a greater affinity for the stationary column material. The separated components will eventually emerge from the column. These components are then carried into a detection system such as flame ionization. The ionized components create electrical signals which appear as a series of peaks on a monitor, strip chart recorder, or printing device. The time of emergence assists with the identification of the peak or peak patterns when compared to known standards.

In some cases, the intensity of the fire, its duration and the water used to suppress and extinguish the fire, can dilute the amount of accelerant remaining at the fire origin(s). The gas chromatograph may not detect the presence of an accelerant if too dilute in a given sample. A possible remedy for this problem has recently been introduced to the market. It is a double-sided screened filter used to trap the accelerant vapors emitted during the heating process. These filters concentrate the residual properties and improve the chances of detecting an accelerant in a given sample

The introduction of mass spectroscopy coupled with gas chromatography (GC-MS) as well as infrared spectroscopy coupled with gas chromatography (GC-IR) permits specific identification or fingerprint of the molecules to be made. Some forensic laboratories have the capability for identification and use the gas chromatographic pattern recognition of the more common accelerants. Some accelerants are easily recognized by their GC patterns in the absence of interfering substances that may mask them. Examples of these are turpentine, gasoline, kerosene, and the heavier fuel and diesel oils. Those laboratories without GC-MS or GC-IR certainly have the option of further analysis performed by a laboratory with those capabilities, if deemed necessary.

Five classes of complex liquid product are recognized by the American Society of Testing Materials (ASTM) as usually identifiable by GC-FID patterning alone when recovered from fire debris. The standard is only intended to allow isolated residues to be characterized as one of the five types of petroleum distillate products listed above (See Figure 9.9). Other characterizations of samples are possible as shown in the O classification.

Other tests can be used to analyze the known samples to see if the liquid under certain circumstances will exhibit self-heating properties and the possible flash and fire points of the liquid. A complete listing of these tests can be found in the NFPA 921 Standard."

Regardless of the method used in testing, the quality of the physical evidence submitted to a forensic laboratory for analysis and interpretation is largely governed by the skill and thoroughness of the investigator with respect to initial recognition, documentation, collection, and packaging of evidentiary materials. Continuity of the chain of custody must be maintained throughout the entire process, including the analysis and subsequent storage of the evidence. This is necessary to ensure the admissibility of physical evidence in judicial proceedings and trial of the accused.

Conclusion

Evidence collection has evolved over the past 20 years as an essential element of fire investigation. Every aspect of evidence collection is now scrutinized in much greater detail than in the past by other investigators, lawyers, and the judicial system. From the beginning of an investigation, the investigator has to be aware of measures to eliminate the possibility of cross contaminating evidence removed from a fire scene. Proper and continual documentation of the removed property must also be provided by the investigator in order to establish an acceptable chain of custody. These two issues — cross-contamination and initiating a traceable chain of custody — are the primary concerns the investigator faces today when collecting evidence from a fire scene. Regardless of the cause of the fire — whether it is accidental, incendiary, natural, or undetermined — an investigator must show that every possible attempt has been made to collect and preserve the evidence from the time the property was first removed.

Contaminated or altered evidence will not be admitted in a court of law. Evidence collection can no longer be approached in a nonchalant manner, but rather, must be viewed as critical in determining the origin, cause, and possibly the party or parties responsible for the fire.

References and Selected Readings

1. Deforest, P. R., Gaensslen, R. E., and Lee, H. C. *Forensic Science — An Introduction to Criminalistics*, Series in Criminology and Criminal Justice, McGraw-Hill, Englewood Cliffs, New York, 1983.

2. Saferstein, R., Ed., *Forensic Science Handbook*, 2nd ed., Prentice-Hall, Englewood Cliffs, N.J., 1981.

3. Saferstein, R., *Criminalistics: An Introduction to Forensic Science*, 2nd ed., Prentice-Hall, N.J., 1981.

4. National Fire and Explosion Protection Association, *Fire and Explosion Investigations*, Boston, 1992.

APPENDIX 9.1   Requesting Laboratory Assistance*

This information should be consulted to facilitate the submission of requests to the Laboratory Division.

Requests for Examination(s) of Evidence

All requests should be made in a written communication, in triplicate, addressed to the Director, Federal Bureau of Investigation, with an attention line in accordance with instructions below and contain the following information:

A. Reference to any previous correspondence submitted to the Laboratory in the case.

B. The nature of and the basic facts concerning the violation insofar as they pertain to the laboratory examination.

C. The name(s) and sufficient descriptive data of any subject(s), suspect(s), or victim(s).

D. The list of the evidence being submitted either "herewith" or "under separate cover." (*Note:* Due to evidential "chain of custody" requirements, all evidence sent through the U.S. Postal Service (USPS) system must be sent by registered mail and not by parcel post or regular mail. If United Parcel Service, Federal Express, or air freight is used, utilize their "acknowledgment of delivery," "protective signature," "security signature," or any other such service which provides the same protection as USPS registered mail.)

   1. "Herewith": This method is limited to certain small items of evidence which are not endangered by transmission in an envelope marked clearly as containing sealed evidence, and attached securely to the written communication which should state "Submitted herewith are the following items of evidence..."

   2. "Under separate cover": This method is generally used for shipment of numerous and/or bulky items of evidence. The written communication should state "Submitted under separate cover by (list the method of shipment, be it USPS Registered, United Parcel Service, Federal Express, or air freight) are the following items of evidence." For further information concerning the preparation of packages sent under separate cover see Packaging Chart elsewhere in this section.

---

* Reprinted with permission from the Federal Bureau of Investigation's *Handbook of Forensic Science.*

E. A request. State what types of examinations are desired, to include, if applicable, comparisons with other cases.
   1. Evidence will not be forwarded by the Laboratory Division to the Latent Fingerprint Section, Identification Division, for latent fingerprint examination unless specifically requested to do so in the written communication.
F. Information as to where the original evidence is to be returned as well as where the original Laboratory report is to be sent.
G. A statement, if applicable, as to whether
   1. The evidence has been examined previously by another expert in the same technical field.
   2. Any local controversy is involved in the case.
H. Notification of the need and the reason(s) for an expeditious examination, bearing in mind this treatment should not be routinely requested.

Attention Lines for Communications and Packages

The following guidelines should be adhered to as closely as possible to avoid any unnecessary delay in the routing of mail at FBI Headquarters.

A. Requests for Laboratory examination *only*, should be marked "Attention: FBI Laboratory."
B. Requests for a fingerprint examination *only*, should be marked "Attention: Identification Division, Latent Fingerprint Section."
C. Requests for *both* a fingerprint examination and Laboratory examination of any type should be marked "Attention: FBI Laboratory."

Shipment of Evidence

The following steps should be followed to properly prepare a package for shipment of numerous and/or bulky items of evidence. (*Note:* Comply with steps A through I if a cardboard box is used and step J if a wooden box is used):

A. Take every precaution to preserve the items of evidence as outlined in the applicable sections of the Evidence Chart (Appendix 10.2) as well as afford appropriate physical protection of the latent fingerprints thereon to include identification with the word "latent."
B. Choose a cardboard box suitable in size.
C. Wrap each item of evidence separately to avoid contamination.
D. Do not place evidence from more than one investigative case in the same box.
E. Pack the evidence securely within the box to avoid damage in transit.
F. Seal the box with gummed tape and clearly mark the outer portions of the box with the word(s) "evidence." (*Note:* If any of the evidence in the

box is to be subjected to a latent fingerprint examination, also clearly mark the outer portions of the box with the word "latent.")

G. Place a copy of the original written request for the examination(s) in an envelope marked "invoice" and securely affix this envelope to the outside of the sealed box.
H. Enclose the sealed box in wrapping paper, seal the wrapping paper with gummed tape, and address the package to the Director, Federal Bureau of Investigation, Washington, D.C. 20535, with the proper attention line as outlined above.
I. Ship the package via U.S. Postal Service, Registered Mail, United Parcel Service, Federal Express, or air freight.
J. Choose a durable wooden box suitable in size and
   1. Comply with the above steps A, C, D, and E.
   2. Securely fasten the lid on the box and address it to the Director, Federal Bureau of Investigation, Washington, D.C. 20535, with the proper attention line.
   3. Place a copy of the original written request for the examination(s) in an envelope marked "invoice," place the invoice envelope in a clear plastic cover, and tack it to the box.
   4. Comply with step I above.

Evidence Chart

The following chart (Appendix 9.2) is provided to give assistance in the collection, identification, preservation, packaging, and sending of evidence to the laboratory. This chart should be used in conjunction with similar evidence information contained elsewhere in this section under each type of examination desired. This evidence information and chart are not intended to be all-inclusive.

Hazardous Materials

Over 3,000 items, including flash paper, live ammunition, explosives, radio-active materials, flammable liquids and solids, flammable and nonflammable gases, spontaneously combustible substances, and oxidizing and corrosive materials are currently considered as hazardous materials. All require special packaging, and the amount of each item which can be shipped is regulated. Therefore, the applicable action listed at the top of the opposite page is to be taken:

A. Flash paper: Contact the FBI Document Section for shipping instructions *each and every time* this item is to be submitted to the Laboratory.
B. Live ammunition: For shipping instructions see paragraph regarding Live Ammunition.

C. Other hazardous materials: Contact the FBI Explosives Unit for shipping instructions *each and every time* any hazardous material, except flash paper or live ammunition, is to be submitted to the Laboratory.

Nonhazardous Materials

If evidence of this type is not found in this chart or elsewhere in this section, locate a specimen which is most similar in nature and take the appropriate actions or call the Laboratory at 202-FBI-4410 for general instructions.

APPENDIX 9.2   Evidence Chart

Specimen	Amount Desired		Send by	Identification	Wrapping and Packing	Remarks
	Standard	Evidence				
Abrasives, including carborundum, emery, sand, etc.	Not less than one ounce	All	Registered mail or Federal Express	On outside of container: Type of material. Date obtained. Name or initials	Use containers, such as ice-cream box, pillbox, or plastic vial. Seal to prevent any loss	Avoid use of envelopes.
Acids	250 milliliters (ml.)	All to 250 ml.	Contact FBI Explosives Unit for instructions	Same as above	Plastic or all-glass bottle. Tape stopper. Pack in sawdust, glass, or rock wool. Use bakelite or paraffin-lined bottle for hydrofluoric acid	Label acids, glass, corrosive
Adhesive tape	Recovered roll	All	Registered mail	Same as above	Place on waxed paper or cellophane	Do not cut, wad, or distort
Alkalies — caustic soda, potash, ammonia, etc.	250 ml/100 g	All to 250 ml All to 100 g	Contact FBI Explosives Unit for instructions	Same as above	Plastic or glass bottle with rubber stopper held with adhesive tape	Label alkali, glass, corrosive
Ammunition (cartridges)				Same as above		Unless specific examination of cartridge is essential, do not submit
Anonymous letters, extortion letters, bank robbery notes		All	Registered mail	Initial and date each unless legal aspects or good judgment dictates otherwise	Place in proper enclosure envelope and seal with "evidence" tape or transparent cellophane tape. Flap side of envelope should show 1) wording "Enclosure(s) to FBIHQ from (name of submitting office)," 2) title of case, 3) brief description of contents, and 4) file number, if known. Staple to original letter of transmittal	Do not handle with bare hands. Advise if evidence should be treated for latent fingerprints

Specimen	Amount desired	Amount to furnish	Method of shipment	Identification	Wrapping and packing	Remarks
Blasting caps			(Contact FBI Explosives Unit for instructions)			
Blood						
1. Liquid known samples	Two tubes each (sterile) 5 cc, 1 tube—blood only. 1 tube—EDTA and blood or heparin and blood	All	Registered airmail special delivery	Use adhesive tape on outside of test tube, with name of donor, date taken, doctor's name, name or initials of investigator.	Wrap in cotton, soft paper. Place in mailing tube or suitably strong mailing carton	Submit immediately. Don't hold awaiting additional items for comparison. Keep under refrigeration, *not freezing*, until mailing. *No* refrigerants and/or dry ice should be added to sample during transit. Fragile label
2. Small quantities: a. Liquid questioned samples		All	Registered airmail special delivery	Same as above	Same as above	If unable to expeditiously furnish sample, allow to dry thoroughly on the nonporous surface, and scrap off; or collect by using eyedropper or clean spoon, transfer to nonporous surface and let dry; or absorb in sterile gauze and let dry
b. Dry stains, not on fabrics	As much as possible		Registered mail	On outside of pillbox or plastic vial: type of specimen, date secured, name or initials	Seal to prevent leakage	Keep dry. Avoid use of envelopes

APPENDIX 9.2 Evidence Chart (continued)

| Specimen | Amount Desired | | Send by | Identification | Wrapping and Packing | Remarks |
	Standard	Evidence				
c. For toxicological use		20 cc. (blood and preservative mixture)	Registered airmail	Same as liquid samples	Medical examiner should use a standard blood collection kit	Preservative desired (identify preservation used). Refrigerate. *Can freeze*
3. Stained clothing, fabric, etc.		As found	Registered mail, Federal Express, United Parcel Service (UPS)	Use tag or mark directly on clothes: type of specimens, date secured, name or initials.	Each article wrapped separately and identified on outside of package. Place in strong box placed to prevent shifting of contents	If wet when found, dry by hanging. *Use no heat to dry.* Avoid direct sunlight while drying. Use no preservatives
Bullets (not cartridges)		All found	Registered mail	Initials on base, nose, or mutilated area	Pack tightly in cotton or soft paper in pill, match or powder box. Label outside of box as to contents	Unnecessary handling obliterates marks
Cartridges (live ammunition)		All found		Initials on outside of case near bullet end	Same as above	
Cartridge cases (shells)		All	Registered mail	Initials preferably on inside near open end and/or on outside near open end	Same as above	
Charred or burned documents		All	Registered mail	On outside of container indicate fragile nature of evidence, date obtained, name or initials	Pack in rigid container between layers of cotton	Added moisture, with atomizer or otherwise, not recommended

Type of evidence	Amount desired	Method of transmittal	Identification	Wrapping and packing	Remarks
Checks (fraudulent)	All	Registered mail	See anonymous letters	See anonymous letters	Advise what parts questioned or known. Furnish physical description of subject
Check protector, rubber-stamp, and/or date-stamp known standards. (Note: send actual device when possible.)	Obtain several copies in full word-for-word order of each questioned check-writer impression. If unable to forward rubber stamps, prepare numerous samples with different degrees of pressure	Registered mail	Place name or initials, date, name of make and model, etc., on sample impressions	See anonymous letters and/or above	Do not disturb inking mechanisms on printing devices
Clothing	All	Registered mail, Federal Express, or United Parcel Service (UPS)	Mark directly on garment or use string tag; type of evidence, name or initials, date	Each article individually wrapped with identification written on outside of package. Place in strong container	Leave clothing whole. Do not cut out stains. If wet, hang in room to dry before packing
Codes, ciphers, and foreign language material	All	Registered mail	Same as anonymous letters	Same as anonymous letters	Furnish pertinent background and technical information
Drugs: 1. Liquids	All	Registered mail, UPS, or air express	Affix label to bottle in which found, including name or initials and date	If bottle has no stopper, transfer to glass-stoppered bottle and seal with adhesive tape	Mark "Fragile." Determine alleged normal use of drug and if prescription, check with druggist for supposed ingredients
2. Powders, pills, and solids	All to 30 g	Registered mail, UPS, or air express	On outside of pillbox, name or initials and date	Seal with tape to prevent any loss	

APPENDIX 9.2 Evidence Chart (continued)

| Specimen | Amount Desired | | Send by | Identification | Wrapping and Packing | Remarks |
	Standard	Evidence				
Dynamite and other explosives	(Contact FBI Explosives United for instructions.)					
Fibers	Entire garment or other cloth item	All	Registered mail	On outside of sealed container or on object to which fibers are adhering	Folder paper or pillbox. Seal edges and openings with tape	Do not place loose in envelope
Firearms		All	Registered mail, UPS, or Federal Express	Mark inconspicuously as if it were your own. String tag gun, noting complete description on tag. Investigative notes should reflect how and where gun marked	Wrap in paper and identify contents of packages. Place in cardboard box or wooden box	Unload all weapons before shipping. Keep from rusting. See Ammunition, if applicable
Flash paper	One sheet	All to 5 sheets	Contact FBI Technical Evaluation Unit for instructions	Initials and date	Individual polyethylene envelopes double-wrapped in manila envelopes. Inner wrapper sealed with paper tape	Fireproof, place in vented location away from any other combustible materials, and if feasible, place in watertight container immersed in water. Mark inner wrapper "Flash Paper Flammable"

Evidence			(Contact FBI Explosives Unit for complete instructions.)			
Fuse (safety)						
Gasoline	500 ml	All to 500 ml	Contact FBI Explosives Unit for instructions	On outside of all-metal container, label with type of material, name or initials, and date	Metal container packed in wooden box	Fireproof container
Gems		All	Registered mail, insured	On outside of container	Use jeweler's box or place in cotton in pillbox	
General unknown 1. Solids (nonhazardous)	500 g	All to 500 g	Registered mail	Name or initials, date on outside of sealed container	Same as drugs	If item is suspected of being a hazardous material, treat as such and contact FBI Explosives Unit for shipping instructions
2. Liquids (nonhazardous)	500 ml	All to 500 ml	Registered mail	Same as for liquid drugs	Same as drugs	Same as above
Glass fragments		All	Registered mail, UPS, or air express	Adhesive tape on each piece. Name or initials and date on tape. Separate questioned and known	Wrap each piece separately in cotton. Place in strong box to prevent shifting and breakage. Identify contents	Avoid chipping and mark "Fragile"
Glass particles	All of bottle or headlight. Small piece of each broken pane	All	Registered mail	Name or initials, date on outside of sealed container	Place in pillbox, plastic or glass vial; seal and protect against breakage	Do not use envelopes
Glass wool insulation	1" mass from each suspect area	All	Registered mail	Same as above	Sealed container	

APPENDIX 9.2   Evidence Chart (continued)

Specimen	Amount Desired		Send by	Identification	Wrapping and Packing	Remarks
	Standard	Evidence				
Gunshot residues						
1. Cotton applicator swabs with plastic shafts (*do not use wood shafts*)		All	Registered mail	On outside of container, date and name or initials. Label as to name of person and which hand	Place swabs in plastic containers.	Do not use glass containers
2. On cloth		All	Registered mail	Attach string tag or mark directly: type of material, date, and name or initials	Place fabric flat between layers of paper and then wrap so that no residue will be transferred or lost	Avoid shaking
Hair	Dozen or more full-length hairs from different parts of head and/or body	All	Registered mail	On outside of container: type of material, date, and name or initials	Folded paper or pillbox. Seal edges and openings with tape	Do not place loose in envelope
Insulation (See glass wool insulation)						
Handwriting and hand printing, known standards			Registered mail	Name or initials, date, from whom obtained, and voluntary statement should be included in appropriate place	Same as anonymous letters	

Matches	One to two books of paper. One full box of wood	All	UPS or Federal Express	On outside of container: type of material, date, and name or initials	Metal container and packed in larger package to prevent shifting. Matches in box or metal container packed to prevent friction between matches	Keep away from fire. Use "Keep away from fire" label
Medicines	(See Drugs)					
Metal	One pound	All to one pound	Registered mail, UPS, or air express	Same as above	Use paper boxes or containers. Seal and use strong paper or wooden box	Melt number, heat treatment, and other specifications of foundry if available. Keep from rusting
Oil	250 ml together with specifications	All to 250 ml	UPS	Same as above	Metal container with tight screw top. Pack in strong box using excelsior or similar material	Do not use dirt or sand for packing material. Keep away from fire
Obliterated, eradicated, or indented writing		All	Registered mail	Same as anonymous letters	Same as anonymous letters	Advise whether bleaching or staining methods may be used. Avoid folding
Organs of the body		200 g of each organ	UPS, air express, or registered airmail special delivery	On outside of container: victim's name, date of death, date of autopsy, name of doctor, name or initials	Plastic or glass containers. Metal lids must have liners	"Fragile" label. Keep cool. Send autopsy report. Add no preservatives to the organs. Use dry ice in the package
Paint: 1. Liquid	Original unopened container up to 1 gallon if possible	All to ¼ pint	Registered mail, UPS, or air express	On outside of container: type of material, origin if known, date, name or initials	Friction-top paint can or large-mouth, screw-top jars. If glass, pack to prevent breakage. Use heavy corrugated paper or wooden box	

APPENDIX 9.2 Evidence Chart (continued)

Specimen	Amount Desired		Send by	Identification	Wrapping and Packing	Remarks
	Standard	Evidence				
2. Solid (paint chips or scrapings)	At least ½ sq. in. of solid, with all layers represented	All. If on small object, send object	Registered mail, UPS, or air express	Same as above	If small amount, round pillbox or small glass vial with screw top. Seal to prevent leakage. Envelopes not satisfactory. Do not pack in cotton	Avoid contact with adhesive materials. Wrap so as to protect smear

Documenting the Fire/Crime Scene 10

The proper inspection and accurate documentation of a fire/crime scene is the most important initial step in any investigation. The notes, photos, and sketches generated to document the scene and the discovered evidence serve as an aid and ready reference throughout the investigation. More importantly, they provide the foundation for any criminal prosecution or civil action that follows. Fire scenes have traditionally been one of the most poorly documented and underrated classifications of crime scenes. The chief reason for this lack of documentation has been the investigator's traditional reliance on sketchy notes and personal recollections when preparing official reports or describing the circumstances of the fire to a jury or other judicial body. Other reasons for the lack of the proper documentation include:

- Ignorance of proper crime-scene techniques
- Lack of equipment (e.g., cameras, film)
- Time constraints
- Shortage of qualified personnel, and
- Lack of motivation (e.g., laziness, poor attitude, apathy)

The fact that fire scenes are unique and their analysis time-consuming and sometimes arduous does not relieve the investigator of the responsibility to adhere to proper crime-scene techniques.

The Crime Scene

In a fire investigation, the crime scene should include the area surrounding the location where a crime (arson) may have been committed and where

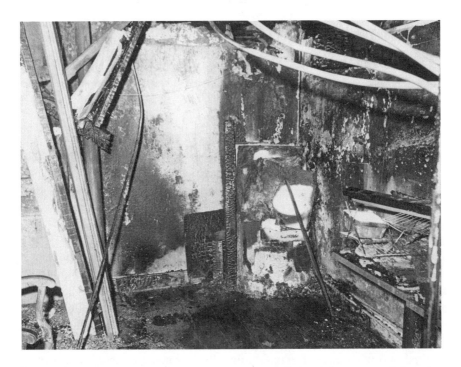

Figure 10.1 Every scene of a serious crime, regardless of the nature of the crime, should be documented by means of photographs, crime scene sketch, detailed notes, and a thorough search for evidence.

evidence pertaining to the investigation of that crime may be found. It should include all entrances and exits or paths to and from the scene.

Under normal circumstances, a criminal investigator is called to the scene of a crime (e.g., homicide) that has occurred. However, a fire investigator is called to the scene of a *fire*, where a crime may or may not have been committed. That determination is to be made (tentatively) upon the completion of the physical examination, but what the fire investigator sees and hears at the scene may be the basis for the entire case. The treatment of all fire scenes as crime scenes is purely a precautionary measure.

"Seat" of the Crime

The "seat" of the crime is the area of the crime scene evincing the greatest impact between the criminal and the commission of the crime. In an arson investigation, this would be the point of origin. In a fatal fire, it is the area of greatest impact among the criminal, the victim, and their surroundings. If the fire was set to conceal a homicide, the seat of the crime is the area around and including the body. If the victim died as a result of the fire (arson/homicide), the seat of the crime is the point of origin of the fire.

Protecting the Crime Scene

An investigator must realize that mistakes made during certain phases of the preliminary investigation may be rectifiable (say, by re-interviewing witnesses), but errors made in the processing of the crime scene can never be corrected. Once the scene has been left unprotected for any length of time or released to the owner, reentry to the scene must be made with a search warrant or with the consent of the owner unless the structure has been abandoned and the owner no longer has a reasonable expectation of privacy. In any case, the admissibility of any evidence found during the later entry is at best questionable, due to the break in the chain of custody (see Chapter 9).

The responsibility for protecting the fire scene varies nationally according to local custom, size, and setting of the municipality (rural or urban), and the availability of personnel (paid or volunteer fire department vs. police department). Regardless of local custom or procedure, however, the ultimate responsibility for the preservation of the fire scene (unit and investigator arrives) lies with the chief or line officer (volunteer or paid) who declared the fire suspicious. This issue is rarely addressed in fire officers' training programs conducted by municipal, regional, or county fire-training academies.

Several investigative and legal questions would be simplified if a firefighter were left at the scene. It would also be beneficial if the fireman who is left to protect the scene was from one of the first fire units to respond. This would maintain the fire department's presence at the scene and prevent the unintentional release of the building back to its owner. It would also afford the responding investigator the opportunity to interview an individual who has first-hand knowledge of conditions in the structure during the actual fire-fighting operations. Should the investigator arrive while fire-fighting operations are still in progress, the questions of the chain of custody and scene protection become moot.

The guarding officer must avoid unnecessary conversations with reporters or people who may congregate at the scene, especially at a fatal fire. Reporters should be told that the matter is under investigation and be referred to the investigator assigned to the case for further information.

Documentation Sequence

There is a specific five-step sequence to be followed in documenting a crime scene:

1. Visual inspection
2. Note taking
3. Photographs

4. Sketches
5. Search for evidence

Step 5 has already been discussed in Chapter 9; steps 1 to 4 are treated in the following sections.

Visual Inspection

The visual inspection of a fire scene uses the investigator's ability to read the observable burn patterns and "push the fire back" to its point(s) of origin. The investigator should try to reconstruct mentally what occurred and be constantly looking for and aware of the unusual such as:

- Unnatural lateral spread of fire
- Evidence of plants, trailers, and accelerants
- Unlikely relationship between the point(s) of origin and the body (a fatal fire)
- Heat indicators
- Evidence of a delayed ignition device

Note Taking

One of the most important operations mandated by proper crime-scene techniques is the preparation of a written record of the investigator's observations and impressions at the crime scene; this is known as *note taking*. An investigator should not rely on memory alone; information left to memory is easily forgotten. If the case goes to trial months or years later, the notes prepared at the fire scene are accessible to a defendant's attorney and will be used by the investigator to refresh his memory while testifying. The notes will also be scrutinized by the district attorney who is preparing and prosecuting the case. With these considerations in mind (and to avoid embarrassment), the crime-scene notes should be arranged and prepared in a deliberate manner. Several principles govern the preparation of these notes:

- Make prompt, accurate
- Give observations in chronologic order
- Avoid discernible codes and cryptic abbreviations
- Be clear
- Make decisions as to what is really important

In addition to being useful when preparing for court, crime-scene notes will be of value in the following ways:

- Providing ready reference for reports to be prepared
- Highlighting points of conflict to be resolved
- Refreshing the memory of witnesses
- Yielding new information to be evaluated
- Aiding in the development of logical and pertinent questions for interviews and interrogations
- Identifying recurring names
- Ensuring that important data are not omitted

Included in an investigator's written record of observations and impressions should be the following:

- Time of the investigator's arrival
- Exact address of the fire
- Weather conditions*
- Identity of persons present
- Statements made (verbatim, if possible)
- Odors detected at the scene
- Extent of damage and room or area of origin
- Anything unusual (e.g., dead pet, lack of furniture in a supposedly occupied apartment)
- Anything else that the investigator may feel is important

The original handwritten notes prepared by the investigator while walking through the fire scene should be *kept* in the case folder. Too many investigators, upon completion of the required follow-up reports, discard or otherwise destroy the handwritten notes. A defense attorney who, during questioning, discovers that the investigator's original notes have been destroyed, may suggest that information beneficial to the defendant was included in those notes (that being the reason the investigator destroyed them). Such an argument may have an effect on the jury.

It is becoming increasingly popular and effective to use cassette recorders for note taking at the scene. These taped notes are transcribed. In lieu of original handwritten notes, the audiocassette(s) should be filed. Removing the two little plastic tabs on the top edge of the cassette will prevent anything from being recorded on the same tape (or over the notes).

However, if it is the standard procedure or policy of your organization to reuse cassette tapes, then the transcribed rough notes should be maintained

---

* The reference to weather conditions is a subtle way of pointing out the investigator's concern in preparation of the notes. The underlying impression suggested is that the level of diligence carries over to the rest of the investigation.

in your files even though a formal report may be prepared from them. I caution the investigator who uses a tape recorder for all note taking. Sometimes it is prudent to use hand written notes in addition to the tape recording, particularly when documenting critical evidence and information from witnesses.

Photography

The fire scene should not be disturbed before the fire/crime scene photographs are taken. Every piece of evidence should be photographed in place (over-all and close-up) before it is removed for processing.

It can be very difficult to photograph a fire scene. Photos of the interior can be especially hard to take because of poor light and extensive carbonization. Regardless of the difficulty, such documentary photographs are an absolute necessity. Juries have come to expect them (prints, slides, and video), and prosecutors rely on them for graphic corroboration of verbal testimony. The technical language of fire science can be disquieting to a jury. Such intricate testimony can be better deciphered if its essence is clarified or illustrated photographically.

An investigator should be prepared to take photographs both in color and in black and white. During a trial for arson/homicide, a judge may admit black and white photos of the victim to evidence after refusing to admit color photos of the same victim, on the grounds that the latter may be prejudicial to the defendant. The first photos taken should be of the exterior of the building. At least one exterior photo should include the address of the building. The sequence of photos that follows should take the viewer into the building, then gradually to the room of origin, and ultimately to the point of origin. This sequence should closely resemble the steps taken by the investigator during the physical examination to determine the cause and origin of the fire.

The suggestions listed in Appendix 10.1 can be applied with certain modifications to virtually any type of fire/crime scene, whether large or small, vehicle or structure. To simplify matters, the term "structure" will be used to denote the item involved. An all-encompassing standard operating procedure must be written from the assumption that you arrived early in the fire, that the fire is in process, and that the structure is still standing. A total burn situation requires a somewhat different approach and will be discussed later. Appendix 10.2 is a general outline for establishing or revising such a procedure.

Certain precautionary measures should be taken by the investigator to ensure that the photographs taken at the scene will be admitted into evidence.

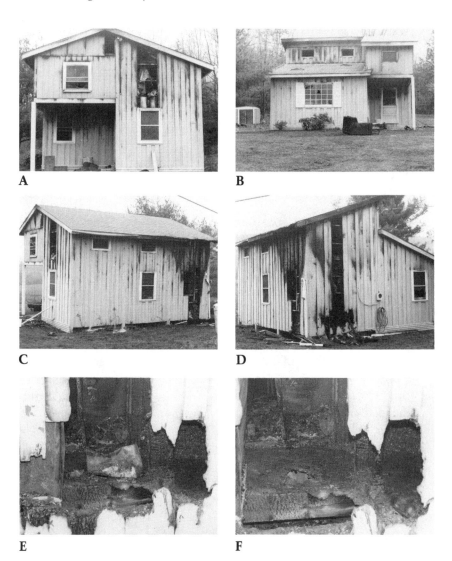

Figure 10.2 (A–D) The exterior of a fire-damaged building should be documented photographically. The photographs illustrate the value and necessity of a detailed external fire scene examination. (A) and (B) show little exterior damage. (C) and (D) isolate the area of greatest damage. The lowest area of burning and a distinctive V pattern are clearly illustrated. (E) Looking into the structure through the exterior damage. The remains of an electric heater are visible on the floor in the center of the photograph. (F) During the interior examination, the area where the electric heater was found was determined to be the point of origin. The area was carefully cleared of debris. A second photo was taken through the exterior wall isolating the point of origin.

The investigator should list in written notes or on the back of the actual photographs the following information:

- Type of camera used and its serial number
- Type of film used, ASA number (film speed)
- Lens setting (f-stop)
- Name and shield/badge number of photographer
- Case number (if assigned) and address, including apartment number of location photographed
- Number of the photo in the chronologic sequence

Nearly every fire scene you photograph, whether by night or day, will require some kind of supplemental lighting. The very nature of the dark, light-absorbing, charred and smoke surroundings requires more illumination.

If the scene must be photographed with supplemental lighting, the following are suggestions for auxiliary light:

1. Electronic flash synchronized with camera with the use of film speed — minimum of 100 ASA up to 400 ASA is acceptable
2. Flood lights (provided electricity or battery packs are available)
3. Bracket each photograph — in other words, shoot one at the recommended or suggested speed (f stop) and then reshoot the photo at one f-stop higher and lower
4. Painting with light; this is best done with at least two people and the following equipment:
   a. Camera with a lens focal length between 28 to 55 mm
   b. Tripod
   c. Locking shutter-release cable
   d. Portable electronic flash with manual firing capability
   e. Film (ASA 400 is preferred, but others are satisfactory)
   f. Lens cap or other suitable light-proof cover

Select a place for the camera in relation to the subject so that no strong lights are shining toward the lens. Streetlights, signs, and vehicles must be eliminated if at all possible. Set the camera at eye level on a tripod. Prior to taking any photos, you must determine the area you wish to photograph and the number of flashes required to cover it. First, determine the left and right extremities of the viewing area of the lens. This can be done by having an assistant holding a small lighted flashlight walk slowly outward perpendicular to the object to be photographed. The photographer watches these proceedings through the camera viewer, and when the assistant steps outside the viewing area, the light can no longer be seen in the viewer. A marker of some

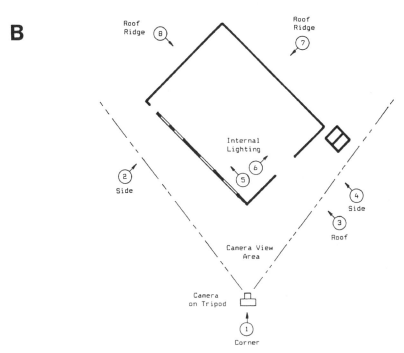

Figure 10.3 (A) Example of multiflash painting-with-light technique. (B) Sequence and flash positions used to produce the image in (A). (From Redsicker, D. R., *Practical Methodology of Forensic Photography*, Elsevier, New York, 1991, 67. With permission.)

sort should be placed an additional 2 to 3 feet beyond this point of disappearance. Perform this procedure for both left and right boundaries of the viewing area. Several boundary markers or the use of barrier tape may be necessary on each side if the area to be photographed is extensive. This will ensure that the flash operator or spectators do not venture into the viewing area and appear silhouetted in the photo.

If you are alone, the viewing area boundaries may still be determined. While observing through the camera viewer, shine a spotlight down either the left or right side of the viewing area. Move the light so that its center spot travels in and out of the viewing area. Note the points of disappearance and mark them as described previously.

Once you have established the area to be photographed, it is necessary to determine the number of flash firings required to illuminate the subject and surroundings. This will vary, depending on whether the subject is light or dark, the texture of its surface, the distance between the subject and camera, and the power capability of the flash. For example, if the area to be photographed is 100 linear feet and your flash properly illuminates a 25-linear-foot area, four separate flash firings will be required.

When you have determined the viewing area and number of flash firings, you are ready to begin painting with light. Proceed with the following:

1. Adjust the lens opening to F3.8 or larger
2. Set the shutter speed indicator to B (bulb)
3. Attach shutter-release cable to the shutter-release button
4. Adjust the release cable to lock the shutter open
5. Focus on an image at the halfway point into the field of view
6. Cover the lens with a lightproof, loose-fitting cover, such as a cloth
7. Advance the film one frame
8. Set the portable flash to full power for maximum distance.

Always remember to point your portable flash away from the camera and toward the scene to be illuminated — never back toward the camera. When done by two people, the person assigned to operate the camera always remains there to operate the equipment and to protect it from being knocked over in the dark. Upon receiving a verbal "ready" signal from the person operating the portable flash, the camera operator will remove the lens cover carefully — so as not to move the camera — and tell the flash operator. The first flash illumination will then be reactivated from above and behind the camera lens, toward the subject. After this happens, the camera operator will re-cover the lens. (If you are working alone, it is necessary for the lens cover to remain off until after the last flash illumination is made.) The flash operator repositions at intervals along the outer edges of both sides of the scene, using caution not to position his or her body between the area being illuminated and the camera lens. Such positioning will cause silhouettes of the flash operator to be photographed, as mentioned previously. At each new position, the sequence of uncovering the lens, firing the flash toward the subject, and re-covering the lens is repeated. Visible roof areas and foreground should also be illuminated as the flash operator advances. A sequence of firings out of sight behind the subject, directed toward the outer edges of the top and sides, will produce a distinctive outline of the subject. Upon completion of the last illumination, replace the lens cap and release the shutter cable lock, thereby closing the shutter.

The painting-with-light procedure is now complete. Proper application of this process can produce exceptional photos; all it takes is practice.

Videography

Why video? The first answer is simply that it exists. Every suspected or known fire/crime scene should be documented in three ways: by making sketches, by taking still photographs, and by video taping. Video should not replace the sketches and still photographs, but rather complement and support them.

There are many other reasons for video recording. Two apply universally: to document and to visually prove an event. The most basic and often overlooked reason is to visually prove that a fire or crime actually took place.

Additional reasons for using reasons for using video are to document:

1. The extent of damages and extent of material not damaged
2. Items of physical evidence present or absent at the scene
3. Injuries sustained and individuals who have no injuries

Such documentation is extremely useful, not only during the investigation and trial, but also in the settlement of insurance claims. Insurance claims for inventories are rarely for less than the actual loss, and mysterious personal ailments and incapacities crop up between the time of the occurrence and court dates. Without proof to the contrary, you may be in for a tough case and lose it in the end.

Usually it is not practical to physically transport the jury, judges, lawyers, witness, and other trial participants to and from the fire/crime scene. Often, by the end of the trial, the scene has been contaminated or altered beyond usefulness. It may, in fact, no longer exist. Because of these possibilities, probably the most important reason to make a video is because, like no other medium, it has the ability to bring a fire or other crime scene into the court room, place it visually in front of all concerned, and to walk the judge and jury through the scene as it was at the time. With video, visual revisitations can be made as many times as required.

Figure 10.4 Documenting a fire scene with videography: like no other medium, it has the ability to revisit the scene as many times as required.

Reviewing video tapes to refresh your memory can be a great aid to interviewing and preparing reports. Once you start using video, other advantages that are applicable to your particular operations will become evident.

Sketches

The drafting of a thorough and accurate fire/crime scene sketch (drawing or diagram) is the next essential step in the documentation of a scene. The purposes of the sketch are several:

1. The primary purpose is orientation, to show the relationship of objects to each other
2. To give an overall view of the scene that cannot be correctly depicted by photographs
3. To eliminate clutter and items not important to the investigation;
4. To clarify issues and refresh the memory of witnesses during interviews
5. To avoid unnecessary and, at times, legally prohibited return trips to the scene

While at the scene, the investigator should prepare a rough sketch. To complete this, the investigator will need paper, pencil, a ruler or straight edge, and a measuring tape. Sketching material should included 1/4-inch graph

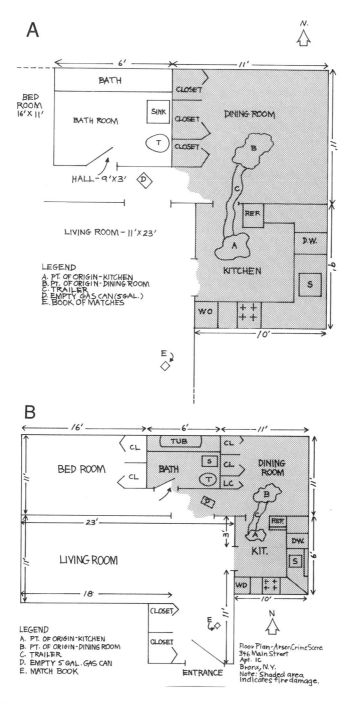

Figure 10.5 (A) Rough sketch — proportional; measurements exact. (B) Rough projection sketch. (Sketch by Det. Joseph Long, measurements by Chief Jones, 3rd Battalion, 9/15/83 — 0600 hr.)

paper. A *rough sketch* is drawn *in proportion* to the shape of the room, not to scale. However, measurements taken of room and to locate evidence in the room must be exact. In those fire origin and cause cases where the conclusions are obvious and simple, approximate measurements will suffice.

In those situations where there may be litigation, the rough sketch will serve as the basis for a finished sketch, which will be drafted later in the investigation and drawn to scale. Items of evidence depicted in the sketch should be lettered and listed separately in a legend. *Every* item should be included in the sketch/diagram; unnecessary items can be deleted later. An arrow labeled *N* should be included to indicated north (as on a map).

To show relationships involving movable objects, the investigator should use either the coordinate method or the triangulate method. The *coordinate method* is often used to located movable objects in a room or other small area. Two measured perpendicular lines are drawn from the object to the nearest walls. The *triangulate method* is most often used to locate movable objects in large buildings such as warehouses or factories and also at outdoor crime scenes. Three measured lines are drawn. The investigator selects two fixed objects (structural pillars, telephone poles, trees, etc.) and measures the distance between each of them and the items to be located, as well as the distance between the two fixed objects themselves.

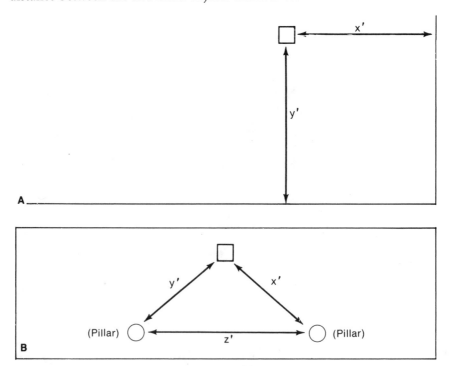

Figure 10.6 (A) Coordinate method. (B) Triangulate method.

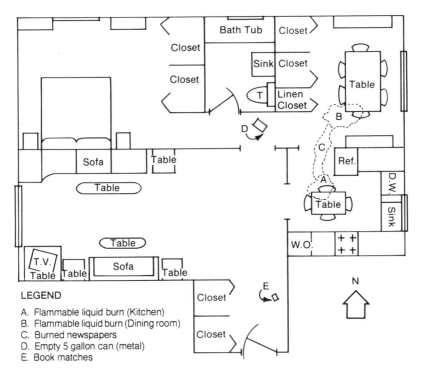

Figure 10.7 Finished sketch. Note there is no indication or phrasing on sketches that tends to draw conclusions for jury. Do not use terms like "trailer," "incendiary device," "accelerants," etc. It is acceptable, however, to refer to these items as "burned newspapers" instead of "trailer," or "flammable liquid burn pattern" rather than "accelerant pour." (Sketch prepared by Det. Joseph Long, 9/15/83 — 1030 hr. Measurements by Det. Vincent Farry.)

The *finished sketch* is drafted to scale (usually 1 inch equals 4 feet) and is generally prepared for court presentation. The investigator may also have to prepare a *projection sketch*, when the investigator wants to focus attention on a particular location of area. A dotted line is normally used to indicate motion. Photographs are located on a sketch by means of numbered triangles.

References and Selected Readings

Geberth, V. J., *Practical Homicide Investigation, 2nd ed.*, CRC Press, Boca Raton, FL, 1983.

Kirk, P. L., *Crime Investigation*, Wiley, New York, 1974.

O'Hara, C. E., *Fundamentals of Criminal Investigation*, 5th ed., Charles C Thomas, Springfield, IL, 1980.

Redsicker, D. R., *Practical Methodology of Forensic Photography*, Elsevier, New York, 1991.

Svenson, A., Wendel, O., and Fisher, B.A.J., *Techniques of Crime Scene Investigation*, 3rd ed., Elsevier, New York, 1981.

Ward, R. H., *Introduction to Criminal Investigation*, Addison-Wesley, Reading, MA, 1975.

APPENDIX 10.1 Existing Structure Fire/Crime Scene Standard Operating Procedure Photo Requirement

Category	Photos to Be Taken
1. Incident identifier	a. Close-up of 3 × 5 card with incident data for film identification
2. Incident location	a. Street name, structure number, rural mailbox number, and name. Include structure and identifier in an overall photo
3. Exterior	a. Straight-on 90-degree shot of all four elevations.
	b. 45-degree off-the-corner shots showing two adjoining elevations at each of four corners
	c. Close-ups of all doors, windows, and any other means of entry or egress
	d. Close-ups of both inside and outside of accesses having forced entry signs
	e. Macros of forced entry signs on both outside and inside of forced access
	f. Documentation of condition of roof taken from elevated position. Four sides and/or corners if possible
	g. V patterns at doors, windows, and other openings
	h. Melt patterns of vinyl siding, window frames, doors, and soffits
	i. Suspicious tracks, containers, or other items unnatural to the scene
	j. Nearby livestock, pets, vehicles, and related housing
	k. Conditions indicating missing livestock, pets, vehicles, and related housing
	l. Scene from witness's viewpoint
4. Exposures	a. Sides exposed to the fire and 45-degree corner shots at each end
	b. Interior of exposures if exteriors damaged
5. Spectators	a. Document onlookers and vehicles, especially recognized suspects and persons who stand out because of their actions and/or inappropriate attire
6. Apparatus	a. Overall shots showing emergency vehicles, equipment, and manpower
7. Suppression	a. General views showing firefighting efforts, including hand lines, snorkels, laddering, rescue, overhaul, ventilation, medical, injuries, and deaths
8. Fire progression	a. Repeat Steps 3a, b, f, g, and h and entire categories 4 through 7 periodically until fire is extinguished
9. Utilities (general)	a. Electrical: on or off, entrance, meters, fuses, circuit breakers, wiring, outlets, switches, evidence of tampering or repair, etc.
	b. Gas (city or propane): on or off, valves, meters, piping, connections, evidence of tampering or repair, etc.
	c. Water (city or well): on or off, valves, meters, pumps, piping, connections, evidence of tampering or repair, etc.
10. Utilities (detailed)	a. All utility services located at or near the area of origin should receive detailed photographic documentation from point of origin to entry into the structure

APPENDIX 10.1 Existing Structure Fire/Crime Scene Standard Operating Procedure Photo Requirement (continued)

Category	Photos to Be Taken
11. Interior	a. All rooms, halls, stairways, closets, cabinets, storage areas, attics, and cellars b. Include walls, ceilings, and floors c. Furnishings and contents including location and arrangement
12. Extinguishment systems (general)	a. All types: on or off, valves, meters, gauges, piping, pumps, pressure systems, connections, and evidence of tampering or repair
13. Extinguishment systems (detailed)	a. All extinguishment systems located at or near the area of origin should receive additional detailed photographic documentation from point of origin to entry into the structure
14. Fire/heat flow indicators	a. Heat, smoke, burn, and char patterns throughout structure, from least affected area to area or point of origin b. Include walls, ceilings, and floors c. Directional pointers to area of origin caused by softening or melting of light bulbs, glass, plastic, candles, toys, etc. d. Rounding of edges of furnishings and structural members e. Tapering of structural members f. Point(s) of lowest burn g. V patterns h. Clocks
15. Heat sources (general)	a. Overall location and close-up of all heat sources throughout structure. Must confirm or eliminate all possible causes of fire
16. Fuel sources	a. All flammable items and materials contributing to growth and extension of fire: gas lines, paint, thinners, furnishings, foam, propane/acetylene/oxygen tanks, etc.
17. Area of origin	a. Before, during, and after excavation and reconstruction of area of origin, such as a particular room or dimensional radii from suspected point of origin b. Detail photos of burn patterns, char depth, damage, and destruction c. Location of heat sources in area d. All exterior sides of heat sources and general views of interiors e. Detail interior and exterior close-up/macro views of isolated damage areas of heat sources f. Nameplates and make, model, and serial number designations g. Installation, operation, and maintenance instruction plates
18. Point of origin	a. Record evacuation and reconstruction of point of origin b. Repeat Steps 17b and c above c. Show proximity of heat source(s) to combustibles/flammables d. Repeat Steps 17d through g above
19. Evidence	a. Each item of evidence taken: one alone *in situ* and one with identifier and scale

APPENDIX 10.1   Existing Structure Fire/Crime Scene Standard Operating Procedure Photo Requirement (continued)

Category	Photos to Be Taken
	b. Each control sample for evidence item taken: one alone *in situ* and one with identifier and scale
	c. General overall of area with identifiers marking locations of evidence taken
	d. Same overall of area in Step 19c but without evidence location identifier
20. Scene irregularities	a. Anything that is out of place or foreign to the area in which found
	b. Any artificial means used to increase the rate of fire spread as opposed to those conditions that would normally be responsible
	c. All indicators of possible arson
21. Controlled substances, hazardous materials, explosives, arms and ammunition	a. Document item and location usually under direction of law enforcement in authority
	b. Container designation and make, model, and serial numbers
22. Fatality	a. Location of body(ies) with respect to one another and surroundings immediately upon discovery
	b. Position and condition of unexcavated body
	c. Excavation of debris from and around body
	d. Position and condition of excavated body
	e. Obvious wounds and injuries
	f. Underside surface of body
	g. Surface body laid upon
	h. Weapons or personal items
	i. Recommendations of coroner
23. Autopsy	a. Condition of body exterior including lividity, soot, skin, hair, and extremities
	b. Wounds and injuries
	c. Condition of respiratory organs affected by heat, smoke, toxic fumes, or flames
	d. Condition of respiratory organ not affected by heat, smoke, toxic fumes, or flames
	e. Condition of organs indicating cause of death
	f. Recommendations of medical examiner
24. Forensic	a. Usually taken by a lab technician under controlled conditions using special equipment rather than the fire/crime scene photographer

From Redsicker, D. R., *Practical Methodology of Forensic Photography,* Elsevier, New York, 1991, 39–42. With permission.

APPENDIX 10.2 Total Burn Fire/Crime Scene Standard Operating Procedure Photo Requirement

Category	Photos to Be Taken
1. Incident identifier	a. Close-up of 3 × 5 card with incident data for film identification
2. Incident location	a. Street name, structure number, rural mailbox number, and name. Include structure and identifier in an overall photo
3. Exterior	a. Straight-on 90-degree shot of all four elevations
	b. 45-degree off-the-corner shots showing two adjoining elevations at each of four corners

Note: In incidents where portions of the structure have been preserved because of outward collapse, the following photos should be taken:

c. Close-ups of all doors, windows, or other means of entry or egress

d. Close-ups of both inside and outside of accesses having forced entry signs

e. Macros of forced entry signs on both outside and inside of forced access

f. Documentation of condition of metal roofing taken from elevated position. Four sides and/or corners if possible

g. V patterns at doors, windows, and other openings

h. Melt patterns of vinyl siding, window frames, doors, and soffits

i. Suspicious tracks, containers, or other items unnatural to the scene

j. Nearby livestock, pets, vehicles, and related housing

k. Conditions indicating missing livestock, pets, vehicles, and related housing

l. Scene from witness's viewpoint

4. Exposures

Note: Burn patterns, heat, and smoke damage on close exposures tend to reflect what was affecting the total burn structure.

a. Sides exposed to the fire and 45-degree corner shots at each end

b. Interior of exposures if exteriors damaged. Document structure and contents

5. Spectators	a. Document onlookers and vehicles, especially recognized suspects and persons who stand out because of their actions and/or inappropriate attire
6. Apparatus	a. Overall shots showing emergency vehicles, equipment, and manpower. May consist of only wet-down or standby operations
7. Suppression	a. General views showing firefighting efforts including hand lines, snorkels, laddering, rescue, over-haul, ventilation, medical, injuries, deaths, etc. May consist of only wet-down or standby operations

APPENDIX 10.2   Total Burn Fire/Crime Scene Standard Operating Procedure Photo Requirement (continued)

Category	Photos to Be Taken

8. Utilities (general)

Note: Present location of some utility equipment may be outside and/or inside the foundation, depending on original location and direction of collapse.

    a. Electrical: on or off, entrance, meters, fuses, circuit breakers, wiring, outlets, switches, evidence of tampering or repair, etc.

    b. Gas (city or propane): on or off, valves, meters, piping, connections, evidence of tampering or repair, etc.

    c. Water (city or well): on or off, valves, meters, pumps, piping, connections, evidence of tampering or repair, etc.

9. Utilities (detailed)

    a. All utility services located at or near the area of origin should receive detailed photographic documentation from point of origin to entry into the structure

10. Interior

    a. All rooms, halls, stairways, closets, cabinets, storage areas, attics, and cellars

    b. Include walls, ceilings, and floors

    c. Furnishings and contents, including location and arrangement

Note: Categories 11 through 21 will generally be located in the debris within the confines of the foundation. Extensive and cautious excavation may be required.

11. Extinguishment systems (general)

    a. All types: on or off, valves, meters, gauges, piping, pumps, pressure systems, connections, and evidence of tampering or repair

12. Extinguishment systems (detailed)

    a. All extinguishment systems located at or near the area of origin should receive additional detailed photographic documentation from point of origin to entry into the structure

13. Fire/heat flow indicators

Note: Indicators in a total burn will usually be limited to noncombustibles. Combustible indicators are sometimes protected and preserved, and they provide valuable clues when found. Therefore, several combustible burn indicators are included below.

    a. Deformation, melting, and heat and rust patterns on metal beams, posts, ceilings, and roofs

    b. Heat, smoke, burn, and char patterns throughout the foundation from least affected area to area or point of origin

    c. Include walls and floors

    d. Directional pointers caused by softening or melting of light bulbs, glass, plaster, candles, toys, etc.

    e. Rounding of edges of furnishings and structural members

    f. Tapering of structural members

    g. Point(s) of lowest burn

    h. V patterns

    i. Clocks

APPENDIX 10.2 Total Burn Fire/Crime Scene Standard Operating Procedure Photo Requirement (continued)

Category	Photos to Be Taken
14. Heat sources (general)	a. Overall location and close-up of all heat sources throughout structure. Must confirm or eliminate all possible causes of fire
15. Fuel sources	a. All flammable items and materials contributing to growth and extension of fire: gas lines, paint, thinners, furnishings, foam, propane/acetylene/ oxygen tanks, etc.
16. Area of origin	a. Before, during, and after excavation and reconstruction of area of origin, such as a particular room or dimensional radii from suspected point of origin
	b. Detail photos of burn patterns, char depth, damage, and destruction
	c. Location of heat sources in area
	d. All exterior sides of heat sources and general views of interiors
	e. Detail interior and exterior close-up/macro views of isolated damage areas of heat sources
	f. Nameplates and make, model, and serial number designations
	g. Installation, operation, and maintenance instruction plates
17. Point of origin	a. Record evacuation and reconstruction of point of origin
	b. Repeat Steps 16b and c.
	c. Show proximity of heat source(s) to combustibles/ flammables
	d. Repeat Steps 16d through g above.
18. Evidence	a. Each item of evidence taken: one alone *in situ* and one with identifier and scale
	b. Each control sample for evidence item taken: one alone *in situ* and one with identifier and scale
	c. General overall of area with identifiers marking locations of evidence taken
	d. Same overall of area in Step 18c above but without evidence location identifier
19. Scene irregularities	a. Anything that is out of place or foreign to the area in which it is found
	b. Any artificial means used to increase the rate of fire spread, as opposed to those conditions that would normally be responsible
	c. All indicators of possible arson
20. Controlled substances, hazardous materials, explosives, arms, and ammunition	a. Document item and location usually under direction of law enforcement in authority
	b. Container designation and make, model, and serial numbers

APPENDIX 10.2   Total Burn Fire/Crime Scene
Standard Operating Procedure
Photo Requirement (continued)

Category	Photos to Be Taken
21. Overhead views	a. Entire foundation area: overall and sectional shots b. Entire area surrounding and adjacent to foundation area c. Close-ups of areas of interest
22. Fatality	a. Location of body(s) with respect to one another and surroundings immediately upon discovery b. Position and condition of unexcavated body c. Excavation of debris from and around body d. Position and condition of excavated body e. Obvious wounds and injuries f. Underside surface of body g. Surface body laid upon h. Weapons or personal items i. Recommendations of coroner
23. Autopsy	a. Condition of body exterior including lividity, soot, skin, hair, and extremities b. Wounds and injuries c. Condition of respiratory organs affected by heat, smoke, toxic fumes, or flames d. Condition of respiratory organ not affected by heat, smoke, toxic fumes, or flames e. Condition of organs indicating cause of death f. Recommendations of medical examiner
24. Forensic	a. Usually taken by a lab technician under controlled conditions using special equipment, rather than the fire/crime scene photographer

From Redsicker, D. R., *Practical Methodology of Forensic Photography*, Elsevier, New York, 1991, 46–49. With permission.

Surveillance

11

Surveillance is the covert observation of people, places, or objects with the intent to obtain information. It may be awkward or impossible to acquire this information in any other manner. At times, to seek such information through other sources might jeopardize the investigation. The time lines of the information may also be an important factor.

Every competent investigator is a trained observer. Surveillance, like all of the other parts of an investigator's repertoire, is an acquired skill. It is learned by doing, and "the street" is the best classroom. Few facets of the investigative function are more amenable to improvement through practice than surveillance. Surveillance is not a haphazard operation, nor should it ever be regarded as one. The planning and familiarization phases must not be viewed as secondary to the actual field exercise; they are crucial to the success of the operation. Once the field exercise has commenced, reorganization is virtually unfeasible.

Possible objectives for surveillance operations are the following:

- To identify a pathological firesetter
- To obtain evidence of a crime
- To protect informants and undercover investigators
- To develop probable cause for a search warrant
- To find suspects or wanted persons
- To identify associates and co-conspirators
- To develop background information for use during subsequent interviews/interrogations
- To corroborate the reliability of an informant
- To prevent an arson
- To corroborate a suspected motive

Planning the Surveillance Operation

All members of the surveillance team should be present during each planning session. They should be directed by one team leader, appointed on the basis of rank, position, or seniority. The team should check all available files and other information sources for data relating to:

- Name(s) used by the subject
- Address(es) used
- Known associates
- Mannerisms, characteristics, and habits
- Probable area of operation (type of neighborhood, character or population, types of occupancy, etc.)
- Vehicles used by subject and associates (year, color, make, and license number)
- Type of equipment (e.g., electronic surveillance) that might be necessary

Reconnaissance

Time permitting, the team members should survey the possible area(s) of operation to determine:

- Supplemental information not available in the files
- Street names, traffic conditions, location of one-way and dead-end streets
- Other modes of transportation available to the subject (e.g., subway or train, buses, taxicabs)
- Best method of surveillance to be used and the number of investigators needed

The reconnaissance phase may also permit each member of the team to gain a personal view of the subject. Photos of the subject may be taken at this time; later these will be carried by each member of the team.

Surveillance Methods

The methods of surveillance that are universally recognized are on foot, by automobile, and by electronic devices. When available, aerial surveillance by helicopter can be an excellent investigative tool. The choice of method is determined by the location and prevailing conditions of the area to be surveilled and by the number of investigators available.

Foot Surveillance

Of the methods available, one-man foot surveillance represents the weakest form and should be avoided. Without backup, the single tailing investigator is, of necessity, required to maintain close contact with the subject in buildings and other off-street locations. The tailing investigator should position himself on the side of the street opposite the subject and stay abreast of him.

Two-man foot surveillance affords the tailing officers much greater latitude, since they can each maintain an "eyeball" on the subject. One investigator positions himself at some distance opposite and abreast of the subject. This right-angle approach is effective in having at least one investigator reach an approaching corner of intersection with the subject, thereby minimizing the possibility of losing the subject if he should suddenly turn the corner. The two tailing investigators may, instead, both choose to follow the subject on the same side of the street, maintaining the "eyeball" position.

Another variation involving three investigators would have two investigators remaining behind the subject, while one positions himself in front of the subject, again all on the same side of the street, maintaining the "eyeball" position.

Another variation involving three investigators has two investigators remaining behind the subject, while one positions himself in front of the subject, again all on the same side of the street.

In the field, be conscious of counter surveillance. If you believe that you are being followed, cross the street in the middle of the block and use a store window as a mirror. If you find that someone is tailing you, double back and challenge him or lose him in a crowd or busy restaurant.

Automobile Surveillance

The number of vehicles used in an auto surveillance is determined by availability, setting (rural/urban), traffic conditions, and availability of other resources. The vehicle to be used should be nondescript, and should not be the standard, official (unmarked) fleet automobile used exclusively by law enforcement agencies and recognizable to a criminal. A wide variety of vehicles should be used, possibly including those seized or impounded in other investigations (narcotic, untaxed cigarettes, etc.).

Auto surveillance in a congested, urban area is very difficult. Heavy traffic flow, traffic lights, and the mix of one-way and two-way streets mandate the use of several tail vehicles. Radio contact is essential. A subject who is either paranoid or aware of the tail will use the traffic conditions to advantage. He may, for example, drive through a red light and watch to see if another vehicle takes the light behind him. He may turn into a dead-end or one-way street the wrong way, again to see if anyone follows. He may turn a corner sharply and immediately park or cut a corner by driving through a gas station or parking lot, observing the reaction of other vehicles.

A moving automobile surveillance operation on a multilane freeway or expressway is called a *convoy*. Multiple tail vehicles are needed. As in foot surveillance, vehicles should periodically rotate their position. The appearance (in the subject's rearview mirror) of the vehicles used in a nighttime moving-surveillance operation can be disguised by alternating parking lights with high and low beams.

Electronic Surveillance

Electronic surveillance involves the use of sophisticated audiovisual equipment to monitor conversations and the physical movement.

Recording and/or listening to verbal communication without the consent of one of the parties involved in the conversation is unlawful and cannot be conducted without a judge's authorization. This authorization takes the form of an *ex parte* warrant. Because there is a great deal of case law regarding electronic surveillance, an investigator should consult legal counsel before conducting it in any form. Electronic eavesdropping is commonly called "wiretapping" or "bugging." However, these terms are not synonymous.

Wiretapping is the cutting in on (tapping of) a telephone line to overhear or record the conversation that passes through the line. A direct tap is completed by connecting an additional earpiece to the telephone's electric circuit anywhere between the transmitter and receiver.

Bugging is the use of concealed microphones (bugs) or other such devices (e.g., transmitters) in a room to overhear conversations. A telephone head piece may also be bugged (fitted with a microphone) as opposed to tapped. A *mini microphone* may be hidden on a person so that direct person-to-person conversation can be overheard (transmitted) and/or recorded.

Electronic surveillance and eavesdropping provide a qualified investigator with a wide range of technical support. Some of the more commonly used equipment in this area allow an investigator to:

- Trace or tap telephone calls
- Record dialed telephone numbers
- Trace the movement of vehicles or packages
- Receive or transmit telephone or person-to-person conversations
- Photograph or videotape movement or meetings occurring in almost complete darkness

Fixed Surveillance

Fixed or stationary surveillance applies to the observation of a fixed point, premises, or object. A van or truck, equipped for surveillance (including a portable toilet), is ideal for this type of an operation. The van is maneuvered

Figure 11.1   The use of rearview mirrors in surveillance photography can produce very effective reflective images of the subject. (From Redisicker, D. R., *The Practical Methodology of Forensic Photography*, CRC Press, Boca Raton, 1994. With permission.)

into a position offering a good vantage point of the target. Once there, the driver locks the vehicle, and walks away. The surveilling investigators, secreted in the rear of the vehicle, have a full view of the target area through one-way mirrored glass. Such a seemingly unoccupied commercial vehicle, legally parked, draws little attention.

If a surveillance van is not available and another vehicle is to be used, certain precautions must be taken. If the vehicle is to be manned by one investigator, it should be driven several doors beyond the target and parked legally. The driver should move to the passenger side after turning off the motor. The passenger-side rearview mirror should be adjusted to give the investigator a good view of the target. The investigator should avoid turning around in the seat and viewing the target through the rear window, which may draw attention. Female investigators are ideally suited to be part of a two-person operation: a man and a woman in a parked car are less likely to draw attention than two men.

Because automobile surveillance may be prolonged and confining, investigators should plan for their own creature comforts by bringing food and drink. Empty containers are also useful, particularly if the vehicle is not equipped with a portable toilet. The lighting of cigarettes at night should be avoided, but when needed, the car's lighter, *not matches*, should be used.

If foot surveillance is to be used to observe a fixed point, the investigator(s) should try to gain a vantage point in another building on the same block. For long-term, fixed surveillance, an empty apartment several stories above the target is ideal. Criminals will routinely and habitually look up and down a street as they enter or exit the target building; rarely, if ever, will they look up to the roofline or windows above them. An investigator trying to watch the target building from adjacent or opposite doorways is very obvious.

Moving Surveillance (Tailing)

If the target is likely to move, then the team surveillance must choose the type of *tailing* (moving surveillance) required; that is, close, loose, or progressive (leap frog).

Close

In *close* surveillance, the investigator maintains a short distance between himself and the subject. Various circumstances require close surveillance, particularly if the tailing is to take place in a highly congested urban area. Under these circumstances, the investigator has to maintain close contact with the subject to avoid losing him in a crowd. In this circumstance the subject is not aware that he is being tailed.

The subject *is* aware of the tail if the close tail is intended to create psychological pressure. The subject may panic and say or do something that benefits the investigation. Close tailing also forces the subject to change plans in an effort to avoid making prearranged contacts with persons whose identities he does not want revealed to the investigators. At other times, the subject and the matter being investigated are of such a sensitive nature that the tailing investigator(s) dare not lose subject contact. For example, the subject may be the target of death threats, or may have made known his intention to leave the country.

Loose

A *loose* tail allows greater distance between the subject and the tailing investigator. If the investigator maintaining a close surveillance believes that he has been "made" (detected) by the subject. Rather than break off the tail completely, the investigator simply follows at a longer distance until a second tailing investigator can take the "eyeball" position. It is imperative that the subject not become aware that he is being tailed.

Progressive

Progressive or *leap-frog* surveillance requires that the operation be broken into several segments. For example, on day 1, the investigators tail the subject from his home to a second point, then break off the tail. On day 2, the tailing investigators go directly to point two, pick up the subject and follow him to point three, where they again break off the tail. This tactic continues until a connection is made between the subject and a particular location or person.

There are drawbacks associated with the progressive approach. In one case, several investigators had been assigned to tail a particular organized crime figure. On day 1, they followed him from his home in Brooklyn to a point just within Manhattan and broke off. On day 2, they waited for the subject at a point where they had broken off the day before. The subject, however, never appeared. The tailing investigators returned day after day to point 2. After 5 days, just as the investigators were about to scrap the operation, the subject finally appeared. Some time later, when the subject was finally arrested, the investigating officers questioned him about the route that he traveled between his home and a particular restaurant. The subject said that he followed a different route each day. One of these routes required that the subject travel through New Jersey, almost 50 miles out of his way. The subject admitted that he believed he was being followed (even when he was not) and that the telephones in his home were tapped (which they never were).

It is important to realize that full-time criminals may exhibit paranoid behavior. They unreasonably believe that their every action is being recorded or photographed, and may routinely take evasive action. Inexperienced tailing officers often misconstrue this odd behavior, believing that they have been "made", even though these criminals behave this way whether they are tailed or not.

Applying Surveillance to Arson Investigation

Identifying a Pyromaniac

When the totality of circumstances (reported fires, arson analysis, and pin maps) leads an investigator to believe that a pyromaniac is operating within a specific area or neighborhood, it is imperative that a detailed surveillance operation be mounted. The size of the area to be covered (streets/city blocks) and the times of such coverage can be determined from a careful analysis of available fire/arson data. A neighborhood that has suffered numerous losses due to a seemingly random fire/arson pattern can be narrowed down (through the use of *pin maps*) to a few streets with the highest concentration of fires. This are a is known as the *saturation area*, and every block within it must be covered by a surveillance team during the hours of highest incidence.

To be most effective, these surveillance teams must be in constant radio communication with each other and should have the following types of equipment available:

- Binoculars
- Nightscope (for night surveillance)
- Camera equipment, including videotape capability

A surveillance van or truck is ideally suited for this type of work. Specially equipped closed-circuit television (CCTV) systems, originally installed to monitor and deter violent street crimes, can also be used for fire/arson surveillance.

Cancellation of Insurance

Certain real estate holders and building owners have a much higher incidence of suspicious fires in their buildings than others. In some of these cases, the building's owner may be suspected of having started some or all of these fires. The real estate holder and his or her various properties may be targeted for special attention and immediate response by an investigative team in the event of any reported fire.

When an investigator is warned that a notice of cancellation has been sent by an insurance company to a targeted building owner for coverage on one of his or her holdings, then a fixed surveillance of that building should be started and maintained on a 24-hour basis until insurance coverage is actually terminated. This is to deter any attempt to cash in on the insurance before it lapses.

Confidential Informants

A registered confidential informant may provide information, either that a particular building has been targeted to burn or that an identified "torch" has been contracted to burn some unknown building.

In the first instance, fixed surveillance at the building should be started immediately to try to catch the torch before the act. If probable cause is developed and it seems likely that the building's owner contracted the arson, then a court-ordered wiretap or other form of electronic surveillance should be used in an attempt to listen to and record conversations that demonstrate a conspiracy to commit the crimes of arson and/or insurance fraud.

When the torch is known, but the target building and the date and time of the planned fire are unknown, then all legal attempts should be made to monitor the torch's telephone, person-to-person conversations, and physical movements.

If the informant has access to the suspected torch and is willing to cooperate with the authorities, he can hide an electronic transmitter or body recorder on his person and try to engage the torch in a conversation about the planned fire. The following information should be elicited from the torch:

Who hired him?
What building is to be burned?
How much is he to be paid?
When and how does he plan to burn the building?

If it is necessary to tail the torch, then a detailed surveillance operation should be planned. This would include:

Fixed surveillance of the torch's residence
Moving surveillance (automobile and foot) of the torch's movements outside his residence
A tracking device wired to the torch's car

Wiring a Co-conspirator

In some cases, investigators have been able to infiltrate organized arson rings. In one case, a torch willingly cooperated with authorities after discovering that his co-conspirator had put out a contract to have him killed. More common is the situation where a torch has been indicted or convicted of a serious crime (e.g., arson, sale of narcotics) and, through his attorney, agrees to cooperate with authorities in the infiltration of ongoing arson conspiracies. This cooperation comes before sentencing in the torch's conviction in order for him to show good faith, influence the trial judge, or reduce his possible jail time.

If the decision is made to use this co-conspirator as an informant against the others involved in the arson conspiracy, an investigator must choose between two operations:

1. Wire the cooperating co-conspirator with a wireless transmitter or body recorder and try to record the incriminating conversations of the other conspirators
2. Have the co-conspirator introduce an undercover investigator to the other conspirator as a trusted friend or relative who needs and is willing to do anything for money

The second option is preferable; it ensures that trained personnel are carrying out the operation, and eliminates the need for a warrant when actions sufficient to establish probable cause for arrest occur in the presence of the undercover investigator.

Appearance and Behavior

The appearance and behavior of surveillance personnel should follow these guidelines:

• Be inconspicuous, of medium height and weight
• Fit the environment, dress, and demeanor of the neighborhood
• Do not wear conspicuous jewelry or other distinctive articles
• Maintain normal gait and manner

- Do not do anything that would attract attention (shout, wave, peek around corners, etc.)
- Have a hat, glasses, and other accessories available in order to change appearance
- Do not make eye contact with the subject
- Have a cover story prepared, if challenged
- Carry loose change, tokens for local modes of transportation, contact telephone number (in case you get separated from the team), credit cards, and cover credentials
- Plan for every eventuality – know what you would do if the subject suddenly enters a taxi, bus, train, or elevator
- Avoid drawing attention of the public and of law enforcement officers who may not be aware of your operation

Recording Observations

The investigator must accurately record his observations, either as written notes and/or still photographs, videotape, or motion pictures. A chronologic log should be maintained, describing actions taken and observations made during the operation. The following types of equipment have traditionally been used during surveillance operations:

Photographic. The best all-around camera format is the 35-mm, except for the rare occasion when a smaller, concealable camera might be needed. The 35-mm format provides the greatest versatility in lenses and films. Since surveillance photography relies on secrecy, the use of auxiliary lighting is out of the question. To make up for the lack of light, the appropriate film (low speed; infrared) and night vision equipment have enhanced the quality of the final photographic images.

Electronic. Portable radios, cellular phones, tape recording equipment, homing devices, additional batteries and cassettes, a watch, binoculars, and/or other night vision equipment are all part of the technology necessary for successful surveillance documentation. New technology is even being applied in the area of computers and "video image capture" or digital imaging. These images can be transferred and stored in computers and later retrieved for court evidence in enlarged still photographic format.

Summary

Good surveillance techniques can be learned, but must be practiced. Teamwork and proper preplanning are the keys to success. Choose the method of surveillance (or combination of methods) that best suits the circumstances. Remember that there is no shame attached to losing a subject. One-on-one surveillance, whether by foot or auto, is generally unproductive and frustrating. Several surveillance officers can bracket the subject and periodically change positions. Inexperienced surveillance officers commonly misinterpret a subject's deceptive tactics; not realizing that the behavior is routine, the officer will mistakenly think that he has been "made." Remember, you are not as conspicuous as you think.

References and Selected Readings

Kirk, P. L., *Crime Investigation*, Wiley, New York, 1974.

O'Hara, C. E., *Fundamentals of Criminal Investigation*, 5th ed., Charles C Thomas, Springfield, IL, 1980.

Redsicker, D. R., *Practical Methodology of Forensic Photography*, Elsevier, New York, 1991.

Scott, J. D., *Investigative Methods*, Reston Publishing, Reston, VA, 1978.

Ward, R. H., *Introduction to Criminal Investigations*, Addison-Wesley, Reading, MA, 1975.

Interviewing and Interrogation

12

Regardless of the investigator's field of expertise (arson, homicide, robbery, etc.), the one predominant skill that cuts across all investigative endeavors is the ability to elicit information through interpersonal communication. The incriminating or contradictory statements made by a suspect, along with information gained from interviews of victims and witnesses, tie the investigation into a narrowly circumscribed, cohesive package. The overwhelming majority of the testimony presented at trial will involve information gathered from other than physical evidence.

The fact that a crime was committed may well be determined after a diligent examination of the scene. However, the development of a valid link between that crime and a suspect will probably result from the skillful application of carefully selected interviewing and interrogation styles.

Interview.   The questioning of a person who is believed to possess knowledge of official interest to the investigator and who is not reluctant to furnish such information. It is interpersonal communication meant to gather information about an event, person, place, or thing; some exchange of information is understood and expected.

Interrogation.   The questioning of a person who is reluctant to make a full disclosure of information; a goal-oriented interview without the free exchange of information.

Investigative Canvass

An investigative canvass is a door-to-door and street-to-street quest for local residents and people on the street who may have information about an

363

Figure 12.1   The primary purpose of an interview is to obtain information that is pertinent to the investigation.

incident under investigation. A thorough canvass is an integral part of any criminal investigation. Canvassing investigators should record the name and address of each person interviewed and whether that person could provide any information. Buildings and residences facing, adjoining, and to the rear of the fire building should be given special attention.

In larger urban areas, an investigator can almost assume that someone will have been looking out a window, regardless of the time of day or night. Bus, taxi, and truck drivers who travel through and frequent the area should also be questioned as to anyone that they might have discharged or picked up around the time and location of the fire.

Not every investigator is a good or even adequate interviewer. Even with extensive training, some otherwise excellent investigators exhibit such serious shortcomings in this area as to be dysfunctional to the case.

Evaluating the Subject

The subject of a forthcoming interview or interrogation must be evaluated (sized up) in relation to the circumstances of the case and with regard to the timing and environment in which the interview or interrogation will take place. Understanding the subject's background and experiences may give insight into how best to pursue or evaluate the interview.

Anxiety

Many people who witness or are the victims of violent, life-threatening circumstances experience varying degrees of *psychological trauma* — emotional shock accompanied by high levels of anxiety. This adversely affects a person's ability not to only to recall the incident, but also to cooperate with the authorities. Many investigators, failing to recognize trauma for what it is, tend to label a traumatized witness an uncooperative witness.

Patience and tact are required to coax the witness to talk about his or her fears. A sympathetic approach will facilitate emotional unblocking and release *(catharsis)*. Your willingness to hear and, to some extent, share in the witness's traumatic experience will lessen the anxiety and promote the flow of information.

Motivation

Is there any hidden agenda motivating the person to come forward or to cooperate with the investigation? A registered informant may be seeking a monetary reward. A criminal may be trying to eliminate his competition. An injured party may be seeking revenge. An investigator must separate the "good-guy" informants from the "bad-guy" informants.

Location

What is the best place to conduct the interview? Would the interviewee be more at ease discussing the case in the comfort of his or her own living room? If the interview were to be conducted in the "official setting" of a police station, would it encourage cooperation? It generally helps to categorize witnesses into "street people", "good citizens", and "professional types." For example, a "street person" would probably want to avoid being seen with a police officer or being interviewed at home. For such a person, an alley or the back of a patrol car might be the best location.

Previous Encounters with Law Enforcement

Another factor that may affect both the style of interview chosen by the investigator and the attitude displayed by the interviewee is the nature of any previous encounters between the interviewee and other law enforcement bodies. A street-wise person will react differently than the average citizen, as will a person who has a criminal record, is on parole, or may have had negative interactions with other official investigating units.

Possible Involvement

Every investigator must be ever mindful of the fact that a supposed witness may have been an active or passive participant, or at least an interested party, in the criminal enterprise. If self-incriminating statements are made, the interview must be stopped and the Miranda warnings given. The totality of the circumstances surrounding the interview will be closely examined and actively contested when and if the case goes to trial.

Timeliness

The longer the time between the incident and the follow-up interview, the greater the opportunity for other factors to cloud the witness's recollection:

1. The witness may "fill the gaps" in his recollection of the incident by adding inferences. The witness may subsequently find it impossible to distinguish between the facts and his fabrications.
2. The witness may not have attached much significance to the incident when it occurred. This failure to attend to the particulars or circumstances of the event may adversely affect later recollection.
3. The witness's recollection of the incident may be colored by his observations and the conversations about the event since its occurrence.

For these reasons, the witness should be interviewed as soon as possible after the incident. However, even under ideal conditions, an investigator must use every verbal skill within his repertoire to determine what the witness actually observed.

Many cases have been "made" by the investigator standing in the street, mingling with the occupants of a still-smoldering apartment house. These possible victims do not need to be reminded of the experience they have just endured or be motivated in any other way. The smell of the fire is still fresh in their clothing; the level of anxiety and confusion is very high and easily perceived. Under these circumstances, the investigator needs only to listen. If any of the occupants has any reason to believe that the fire was not an accident, it will be evident from their conversation. In one case, a woman who had just lost all of her belongings in a two-alarm fire was overheard to say, "That son of a bitch went too far this time!" With one simple question, "What son of a bitch?" the investigator had the name and apartment number of a possible suspect. In another case, a woman still clinging to her two children, stated, "I'm going to kill the motherfucker in 3B. He almost killed me and my kids!" A possible suspect in the case has been identified.

Physiological stress during the course of the interview/interrogation causes people to react in a variety of ways. They know within themselves when they are withholding information or are reluctant to talk to you. This defensive attitude can often be clearly perceived, and the successful interview/interrogation will depend on a number of factors.

1. The physical and emotional make up of *you*, the interviewer
2. The physical and emotional make up of the person being interviewed
3. The subject of the questioning as it relates to the person being interviewed
4. The location where the interview takes place

The relative importance of these factors may vary from situation to situation, but each will play some role in every interview/interrogation. During the course of the interview, a person will react in a variety of ways when under stress. The investigator should recognize the various indicators of stress or its absence. The successful interviewer will be open-minded and confident. You are a fact gatherer. You should not be prejudging the person. In addition, you should be prepared with your questions so that you will be successful in the gathering of the necessary information. You must show interest in the witness and the information being given to you. Be firm but courteous. Do not back down or get sidetracked, and do not appear overbearing.

When it becomes apparent that the person is not responding, be flexible and alter your approach. You may have to be a salesperson and convince the witness that you are there to help him/her so that he/she is willing to give you information. Be very observant. Watch the person as well as listen. How they react is as important as what they say. Look for unusual changes in their behavior. Finally, patience is a virtue. You must be willing to devote as much time as necessary to the interview/interrogation. Do not rush the person or he/she will feel that his/her information is unimportant.

Some basic definitions in the field of interviews and interrogations follow.

Kinesics — the study of body motion (body language) as it relates to speech.
Nonverbal response — a physical reaction to stress.
Verbal response — an audible reaction to stress in the form of an answer to a question, or outburst such as crying, laughter, etc.

The following are some examples of nonverbal and verbal responses:

Nonverbal responses
Reddening of the eyes
Evasive eye contact
Evasive body position
Pretense of boredom (slouching, yawning)
Dryness of mouth (licking of lips)
Repeated swallowing
Hand over mouth
Combing hair

Cleaning fingernails
Lint picking
Excessive use of bathroom
Hand wringing
Foot tapping
Excessive perspiring
Pulsing of arteries in the neck
Red face
Can't sit still

Verbal responses
Excessive swearing
Feigned loss of memory ("I can't recall" or "I don't remember")
Crying spells
Laughing
Complaining
Delayed responses
Pat answers (answers before question is completed)
Always qualifying answer
Voice cracks
Overly polite and/or apologetic
How an individual says no can also indicate stress of lying
   "No" after evasive contact
   A profound emphasis on "No" emphasized by shaking head vigorously
   "No" with eyes closed
   "No" followed by changed in physical (crossing legs or arms)
   "No" that is mumbled
   "No" that appears to be apologetic in tone
   A long drawn out "No."
   A loud and defiant "No."
   A breathless "No."
   A "No" accompanied by a blank stare

Two additional negative responses induced by stress and also found to be very effective indicators of deception are:

Freudian slip. In this response, the subject reveals information inadvertently and then tries to correct the statement by saying "I am sorry. That's not what I meant. What I meant to say was..."

Echo answer. In this response, the person repeats your question or asks you to repeat the question before they answer in an attempt to stall for more time to come up with an answer they hope will satisfy you.

Physiological Response Analysis

During the interview, you must evaluate the physiological response based on the following criteria. How did the individual respond and what type of question was it in response to?

Look for normal behavior in the person, as many will have normal nervous conditions in a stressful situation, such as being interviewed. Also, some people may perspire easily or their red faces may be due to high blood pressure. Further, talking with a hand over the face may be due to embarrassment because of poor teeth or braces. The important thing to notice is, when did the person's behavior change and, in particular, when those changes took place.

A truthful response from a person is usually shown by a relaxed attitude. They are unequivocal in their response and usually friendly and cooperative. In essence, their story has a nice ring to it. It sounds like the truth.

Miscellaneous Considerations

Stress is a key factor behind a person's physiological responses. Stress in any form affects an officer's judgment as well as a witness's reliability.

Two things happen under stress.

1. A person sees more than they hear
2. All that they perceive will be distorted

Personality conflicts between you and a witness may result in a loss of important information. If this happens, the investigator should withdraw and allow another investigator to conduct the interview/interrogation. From time to time you will encounter a reluctant witness: one who refuses to talk to you. An individual has the right to refuse for any number of reasons. Usually they involve inconvenience, fear of involvement, resentment toward authority figures, covering for a friend or relative, and fear of retaliation. If you have any doubts regarding a subject's truthfulness, ask the following questions. The answers to these questions have shown that truthful people tend to respond a certain way and those who are hiding something or lying respond quite differently. You must present these types of questions during a conversation, not in a question and answer manner. Also, remember that one deceptive response does not prove guilt; however, when several negative responses are elicited, then you can rely more on your own conclusions.

Who do you think had a reason to set this fire?

A truthful person will recognize why you are asking this question and that you have a reason for questioning them in this incident. The response would probably be, "Well, it could be one of us." (A good question to ask in the investigation of a commercial business fire.)

A deceptive person will try to mislead the investigation and take the heat off themselves by saying, "Gee, it could have been anybody."

What do you think should happen to the person responsible for this fire?

A truthful person with nothing to fear from the results of the investigation will probably say "Lock him up;" or "He should be punished." A deceptive or involved person would tend to rationalize by saying "Whoever did this must have had some real problems for them to resort to this act." (In other words, "Take it easy on me.")

Is there any physical evidence to connect the person to the fire?

The truthful person will not be concerned and will state very clearly a negative response to this question. However, the deceptive person will be very concerned and quite often fabricate a story as to why they might be inadvertently connected to the physical evidence.

Unique Interview Situations

Every interview situation is unique in some aspect, whether it is the location, specific information or circumstances. However, some situations by their nature alone require additional considerations when confronted — situations such as interviews involving juveniles, females, the elderly, a language barrier, the handicapped, and a dying witness.

Juveniles

Juveniles up to 16 years of age are going to be considered not only by their chronological age, but also by their mental age. Some are more mature at age 5 than others at twice that age. In most states, the age at which a child may testify under oath is 12. However, a child less than 12 years old may testify if the court is satisfied that the child understands the nature of an oath. The investigator's initial contact is important in establishing a comfortable rapport with the child and it enables him or her to assess the level of comprehension.

If a child happens to be in the crowd at a fire scene, he or she may be interviewed as to name, address, parent's name, and what was observed. If the child is a potential witness or suspect, you are required to contact the parent or legal guardian for permission to conduct a further interview, usually in that person's presence.

Depending on local policy, an interview conducted in school may require the parent and/or legal guardian or a designated school official to be present during the interview. If the child is going to be interviewed at the police station, most states require an area designated for this purpose.

A critical area for the successful interview of juveniles is establishing a rapport. Spend time getting acquainted. Do not rush into the interview. Be friendly and patient. If necessary, have the parents introduce you if the situation dictates. Kids are impressionable, so avoid situations with "yes" or "no" answers. Let the child speak at their own level of comprehension. A useful item in establishing a rapport and identifying important facts about a fire is the use of a sketch pad; this lets the child feel that they are an important part of the investigation and that they are helping. Kids are also often interested in hearing their voices on a tape recorder. It may be useful in your documentation of the interview if you have to concentrate on writing down their responses.

Females

Because of the potential for conflicts in the male/female interview situation, it is advisable to set up this type of interview up by appointment when possible.

The interview should be conducted at the investigator's office at a predetermined time. Avoid hotel rooms, bars, restaurants, or the person's home. As for the number of interviewers, whether at the investigator's office or especially in a more compromising situation (such as a vehicle, the witness's home, a place of employment, etc.) it is advisable to have at least two investigators present. The gender situation may involve male and female, two males, or even two females as the investigator partners. Before starting the interview, decide who will be conducting the interview. The second investigator should be responsible for taking notes. The second interviewer's position is slightly behind and to the side of the witness. From this vantage point, they can observe the witness without being distracting. The primary interviewer should be face-to-face with the witness to see physiological reactions.

The Elderly

They are our forgotten group. We tell our kids they should be seen and not heard, and we see the elderly around us every day and we do not listen to them either. Avoid the most common mistake made by investigators of *not asking!* Most elderly people will talk to you if you take the time. You may have to verify their information. These people may be afflicted with disorders common to old age. In other words, check on their physical disabilities such as hearing and eyesight. In addition, when you are asking questions about how young or how tall a person is, remember that in reference to age and size, a person who is described as "young" may be a person in his/her sixties to a person who is eighty. Clarification can be as simple as asking if the person they are describing was younger or older than yourself. Also, when relating questions about physical description, including height, weight, size, etc., have the witness relate it in reference to *your* physical stature.

Language Barrier

From time to time, the investigator will face a witness who does not speak or understand English. This situation is further complicated by the presence of an additional person acting as interpreter.

If you use a friend or relative of the witness, it may help to relax the interviewee. However, be aware of misinterpretation or cover up of information. If the witness makes an incriminating statement, the interpreter may not relay information or may change it.

It is advisable to use a tape recorder so that the interview may be reviewed by another independent interpreter. Sources for interpreters include local churches, ethnic organizations, immigration and naturalization organizations, and schools and universities.

Mentally or Physically Handicapped

Everyone is a potential witness, including the handicapped. However, the individual dysfunction may affect how they perceive what they have observed. Also, it will play a part in the way you approach the interview situation. The mentally handicapped must be represented by a parent and/or legal guardian. It may be necessary to use these family members as interpreters. You must also determine the person's level of comprehension. It may be necessary to have a doctor to help interpret the accuracy of the responses. Most of all, you must be very patient and understanding to establish a trust between yourself and the witness.

Physical handicap. A deaf mute requires someone proficient in sign language. "American Sign Language" is the only recognized sign language in the United States. However, each countries sign language is different. There is no universal sign language. "Signed English" is not a language. It is a code of the oral, spoken English language. Be sure the interpreter you use is A.S.L. (American Sign Language) certified. This can be time consuming, particularly if you have to use written questions and responses for the interview process.

The blind. You must weigh the value of a blind person's information against other witnesses' statements. A blind person's other senses may be very acute and help establish important facts, particularly sounds he/she may have heard or distinct odors they may have noted.

Also, if a person is color blind, you may want to ask this question of the individual, particularly when the information is relative to color identification (flames, smoke, vehicles, clothing, etc.)

Other handicaps. If a person has a speech impediment (stutters, etc.), avoid embarrassment to the witness by being very understanding and patient. A paralyzed witness may be affected by his/her ability to sign a statement which would require a tape-recorded statement witnessed by another investigator and/or family member. Before giving the statement, the witness could be sworn by a notary public or a court officer.

Dying Witness

At some point in your fire investigation career, you may be confronted with a situation where the witness is going to die. It makes no difference if the dying witness is an innocent victim or a responsible party in the fire. There are certain criteria to be considered when taking a "dying declaration."

The individual must be made aware that he or she is dying or going to die. This is usually done by a doctor. The statement must be witnessed by a medical person, either the doctor or nurse, as well as the investigator, district attorney, and an optional family member or friend. Finally, the statement must be recorded or taken by a stenographer so it can be used in court.

Initial Interview Procedure: an Example

A businessman who, either on his way from work or while on his lunch hour, sees someone throw a Molotov cocktail through the window of an occupied building, tells what he has seen to responding emergency units, who, in turn, tactfully hold him until the investigator arrives. A sharp investigator, realizing that the witness will be anxious to get to work should:

- Quickly explain that he needs only 5 minutes of the witness's time
- Request that the witness accompany the investigator to the investigator's office, if nearby
- Guarantee the witness that he will be driven to where he was going as soon as the brief interview is completed

Once in the office:

- Obtain a complete background of the witness
- Get as accurate a description of the suspect as the witness can recall
- If possible, have the witness draw a sketch of the location where the crime occurred

The sketch should be drawn on blank typing paper and include as much information as possible. For example:

- Where was the witness standing in relation to the building and in relation to the other buildings on the block?
- If the suspect fled in a vehicle, where had the vehicle been parked? Was anyone else inside it?
- Through which window was the Molotov cocktail thrown?
- What other information might affect the investigation?

Intentional Loss of Memory

People, in a moment of confusion or at the height of anxiety, will make statements spontaneously. In time, however, their stories may change completely or be lost to lapses of memory. This is one of the reasons why investigators should elicit as much information as possible at the first meeting.

The *intentional* loss of memory, however, is a condition with which investigators must cope frequently. This problem is not apparent until the second time you meet the witness, during the follow-up interview. Although full of information at the first interview, the witness now tells you that he cannot remember anything. This strange loss of memory is usually self-induced after the witness has had an opportunity to discuss the incident with his fellow workers, family, or friends. Now, his boss wants to know whether he is going to lose any time at work. In addition, his wife, family, and friends have convinced him that if he cooperates with the authorities, the suspect will probably retaliate.

An experienced investigator will identify this far-too-frequent scenario immediately. Uncooperative and "forgetful" witnesses regularly frustrate investigations. The witness must be rehabilitated through either rational argument or investigative ploy. The investigator can point out the witness's obligation to the people who suffered as a result of the fire he witnessed, in an effort to touch some "sensitive nerve." Alternatively, the investigator may try to convince the witness that he is already deeply involved in the investigation. This ploy depends to a great extent on the witness's level of sophistication. The documentation needed for this ploy to work include:

- Any number of serialized, official reports prepared after your first brief meeting. These complaint reports, investigative follow-up reports, and so on will list and categorize all of the witness's prior statements in the case.
- The witness's rough sketch of the crime scene, now vouchered as evidence.
- All of the other forms of official crime-scene reports and requests for information that could be found in any case folder.
- The arson case folder itself, the jacket of which is now covered with case and control numbers, telephone numbers for notifications made,

and other pertinent data. These official-looking and -sounding forms, reports, and materials might be enough to convince the witness that he is indeed an active participant in the investigation, causing his memory to return as well.

Be aware that "civilians" locate incidents chronologically in terms of routine events that occur during the course of their daily activities. Try to equate each incident with a specific time on the 24-hour clock:

"I had just opened the store" = (0730 hours)
"I had just put out the garbage" = (1745 hours)
"I was watching television" = (2130 hours)
"I was walking my dog" = (1930 hours)

Try to get the witness as involved as possible in the limited amount of time you have. If the witness explains that he must leave:

Give him a business card and request that he call you if he recalls anything in addition to what he has told you;
Advise him that you will get back to him in a few days; and
Arrange to have him driven home or back to work.

Interviewing and Interrogation Strategies

The underlying assumption in every interview should be that the person being interviewed has information that is pertinent and material to the case. The investigator's task and intent should be to extract that information. Several strategies may be used in interviews. Each is situational, designed to elicit information from a respondent under interrelated and particular circumstances. No one strategy will suffice under all practical conditions; and the investigator, to be successful, will probably use a combination of strategies.

Role Playing

The investigator must be able and willing to play the role that is required depending on the circumstances, in order to promote the most open response of the interviewee. Possible roles to be assumed include:

- Father-confessor
- Concerned listener
- Best friend

- Protector
- Benefactor
- Tough cop
- Many others.

The father-confessor and concerned listener roles are quite similar. In both, the investigator maintains a nonjudgmental attitude and conveys a feeling of sympathetic understanding. The interviewer offers a "sympathetic ear." In the *father-confessor* role, the investigator plays the part of an understanding minister, and the interview takes on the character of a religious confession. The subject of the interview is encouraged to:

- Unload his feelings
- Release the tension by talking about the sources of the tension
- Discuss his feelings of guilt and pangs of conscience

As the *concerned listener,* the interviewer plays the part of an understanding stranger. The line of communication sounds more like a conversation between two frustrated people over drinks in a neighborhood bar than an interview. The investigator tries to have the subject believe that he (the investigator) not only understands and identifies with the subject's predicament, but that he grudgingly accepts the subject's choice of criminal act to solve or deal with a problem. To be successful, the investigator must avoid threatening words such as "jail," "crime," "punishment," "arson," "prison," "arrest," "sentence," and "confession" in favor of words such as "incident" or "problem."

During the early stages of the interviewing process, an investigator may realize that a witness, victim, or criminal has a personal problem — defense mechanism, fear, or other more conscious reaction — that prevents him from cooperating in the investigation. It is imperative that the interviewer identify and address the interviewer's problems before trying to conduct the interview. For example, the investigator may play the role of a *best friend* to a person who has been traumatized by his arrest. By taking the time to explain the arrest process, offering coffee, and so on, the interviewer may put the person at ease and foster further communication.

Some witnesses and victims are reluctant to cooperate with authorities because they fear for their personal safety or because they fear that their involvement will create an undue burden (time, money) on their families. In these instances, the investigator may attempt to calm the person by playing the role of a *protector* or *benefactor.* The police cannot guarantee protection but can often allay the person's fears by explaining the full range of agency resources that are available. Some larger investigative and prosecutorial agencies even provide car and babysitting services when necessary.

When interviewing the streetwise person or habitual criminal, the investigator may find it useful to play the role of *tough cop*. This role requires the investigator to control the pace of the interview and to structure selected questions in such a way as to have the interviewee believe that the questioner knows more than he actually does. The investigator must be prepared to summarize ideas quickly and to constantly redirect the flow of conversation toward the desired objective.

Common Interviewing Errors

Although there are many common interviewing errors, two seem to be the most common:

1. The interviewer does not allow the interviewee to tell his or her story.
2. The interviewer talks too much.

The first is easily understood when you realize the normal career path followed by the average public investigator. A police investigator (detective) most probably served in a uniform assignment for several years before being selected or promoted to the investigator's rank. The bulk of the uniformed officer's time was probably devoted to preparing complex crime reports. In time, report writing became a mechanical skill: just "fill in the boxes." This matter-of-fact, mechanical approach to dealing with crime victims, witnesses, and suspects tends to carry over, unconsciously, into the person's approach to the investigation, and manifests itself in the form of constant interruptions; these interruptions confuse the interviewee and result in a disjointed account of the incident. This is illustrated in the following exchanges during the initial interview of a cooperative witness:

> WITNESS: "I had just put out the garbage, when I heard what I thought was an explosion."
>
> INVESTIGATOR (*interrupting*): "What time was that?"
>
> WITNESS: "I saw these two guys run from the building and get into a car."
>
> INVESTIGATOR (*interrupting*): "Can you describe them and the car?"
>
> WITNESS: "All of the sudden the building burst into flame."
>
> INVESTIGATOR (*interrupting*): "What color was the flame and smoke, and where did you first see the flames?"

In these illustrations, the investigator is actually interrupting the natural thought processes of this cooperative witness by unconsciously shifting into a report-writing mode. He has disregarded several basic principles of interviewing. If this type of approach continues through the course of the investigation, it will certainly have an adverse impact on its outcome. This investigator should have allowed the witness to talk *without interruption*, permitting the witness to "tell his story" in its entirety at least once, and perhaps several times, before asking the first question.

The second common problem is that the interviewer tends to talk too much. As stated earlier, some exchange of information is expected, but not to the extent that the investigator describes the case in detail. An interviewee should not end an interview knowing much more than when he was first approached.

Summary of Guidelines

1. The investigator must control the interview or interrogation.
2. Preparation is essential. Review the facts of the case and all available records and data before starting the interview. Know what you are talking about.
3. Carefully evaluate (size up) the subject of the interview.
4. Play whatever role is required to facilitate the free flow of information.
5. Tactfully select the best combination of verbal strategies to use.
6. Do not automatically discredit information that is favorable to the suspect.
7. Remember that your job is to *gather information*.

Provocation

It is sometimes necessary to motivate or induce a response from a prospective witness. The person may or may not have information; however, the mere fact that he or she does not want to get involved does not warrant exemption from examination. The investigator, after questioning, can determine whether this witness can be of any further value.

In provoking a reaction or response, the investigator is attempting to keep the conversation alive. Statements such as "I don't know anything" or "I don't want to get involved" should not be accepted. The investigator should encourage the person to cooperate by relating the incident to the witness's emotional frame of reference. The following examples illustrate this point:

WITNESS: "I heard about the fire, but I don't want to get involved."

INVESTIGATOR: "Listen, I'm trying to save your neighborhood, but I can't do it without your help."

INVESTIGATOR: "A couple of innocent people died in that fire, and your family could be next if we don't stop the arsonist."

This type of emotional stimulus will generally induce either a verbal or physical reaction.

Paraphrasing

The investigator might *paraphrase* a response, twisting it to his advantage. Paraphrasing, in this context, is the careful rewording of another person's response in order to test or alter its meaning. It is not the mere parroting of what the person has said. The investigator must be prepared to test the witness's commitment when he appears to respond to provocation in a positive way. For example:

WITNESS (*provoked response*): "You have to get that guy before he hurts anyone else."

INVESTIGATOR: "Then you'll talk to me for 5 minutes? I can't stop this guy without your help."

WITNESS: "I'll see what I can find out."

INVESTIGATOR: "Then you'll find out what the 'word' is out on the street and get back to me?"

Empathy

Empathy is the feeling associated with an emotional identification with another person. In some cases, where the victims are children or elderly, the investigator's concern for them may be sincere and easily expressed. In other cases, it is no more than an act. When used correctly, the mutual concern (real or imagined) that results will ensure a free flow of information. In fact, when used properly, the empathetic approach is the most effective interviewing technique. The interviewer must follow these guidelines for its effective use:

Appear sincere
Use a very understanding approach
Have a nonjudgmental attitude
Be careful to disguise negative feelings and lack of compassion for the respondent

The investigator's manner of speech, choice of language, and facial expressions will serve as the focal points for the respondent.

"Let's Make a Deal"

In this strategy, the investigator may induce the cooperation of an otherwise uncooperative subject by offering a concession in exchange for specific information. Conversely, the witness may intimate that he might have information to exchange. In either case, the agreement to act by one party requires a reciprocal agreement by the other:or

> WITNESS: I may know something about the fire, but I don't want to get into trouble."
>
> INVESTIGATOR: "Tell me what you know and I'll tell the prosecutor that you cooperated."

This approach is often used when dealing with a registered informant. It is fairly common to meet an uncooperative informant at his place of work or other area where he is well known, the idea being that the informant does not wish to be seen talking to the authorities. This type of meeting might involve the following conversation:

> INFORMANT: "Are you crazy, man? I told you not to come around here! Are you trying to get me killed?"
>
> INVESTIGATOR: "You've been trying to avoid me. I need information about the fire on 3rd street."
>
> INFORMANT: "O.K. man, I'll meet you tomorrow night at 11:00 p.m. at the usual spot. I'll see what I can find out."

The investigator, in this example, is making a deal with the informant, securing the informant's cooperation in exchange for implied agreement not to be seen in the informant's company in the "wrong" places.

"Choice of Evils"

This approach can be used only when the investigator is dealing from a position of strength. The uncooperative respondent is offered a "choice of evils" — one alternative is more distasteful than the other, and no other options are offered. It may be used when the investigator has a good understanding of the facts in the case and knows that he is interviewing or interrogating a "weak link" in the case. For example, take the case of two partners who jointly own a failing business. One partner opted to "sell the business to the insurance company"; the other tried to disuade his associate but did not notify the authorities. This second partner is a family man whose son worked full-time in the business and knew nothing about the fire.

As the motive for and circumstances of the fire become clear to the investigator, he might well choose to attempt to break this "weak link." After giving the second partner his Miranda warnings, the investigator may offer him a choice between two undesirable alternatives: (1.) he can either discuss the case with the investigator, or (2.) the investigator can discuss the case with his son.

The Lying Witness

Investigators must often deal with respondents who lie during an interview. One might expect the person to lie only when he or she has a vested interest in the outcome of the case. In fact, complainants, witnesses, and even victims lie in their conversations with the authorities.

It is important and necessary for the investigator to identify lies and confront the liar as soon as possible. The method of confrontation should be determined after a careful evaluation of the respondent.

In some cases, a direct attack is warranted. After listening to an obviously untruthful account offered by a streetwise person, the investigator may choose to call that person a liar to his face. The investigator might add that he is determined to find out what happened and that it might be in the respondent's best interest to cooperate.

In other cases, a more subtle approach works best. The investigator tactfully makes it clear to the respondent that it somewhat difficult to accept the story. The investigator might then review the respondent's account of what happened, pointing out the various inconsistencies and illogical statements. Afterwards, the respondent should be asked again to describe the incident to the best of his or her recollection without adding to or omitting information.

An investigator must be cautious to avoid misinterpreting a witness's inconsistent statements by inferring that the witness is lying intentionally. Ten different people can watch the same event and, when interviewed, relate ten different descriptions of the event. As previously mentioned, a traumatized witness might be unable to cooperate if questioned too soon after the incident and might, in fact, invent a story to placate an overzealous investigator. Some witnesses exhibit psychological defense mechanisms, which the investigator, in his haste, may fail to recognize. How many investigators would react favorably when the victim of a fire laughs or giggles? What about the victim who refuses to believe that the event ever took place (denial of reality)? Other witnesses are unable to relate correctly to questions due to chronologic confusion. Thus, the order in which they relate the event may be difficult to comprehend, even though their facts may be accurate.

Constitutional Rights of the Individual

The Fifth and Sixth Amendments of the Constitution of the United States guarantee, among other things, "the right to be represented by legal counsel and that no person shall be compelled in any criminal case to be witness against himself."

> **Amendment V:** No person shall be held to answer for capital or otherwise infamous crime unless on presentment or indictment of a grand jury, except in cases arising in the land or naval forces or in the militia, when in actual service in time of war or public danger, nor shall any person be subject for the same offense to be twice put in jeopardy of life or limb, nor shall be compelled in any criminal case to be witness against himself, nor be deprived of life, liberty, or property without due process or law, nor shall private property be taken for public use without just compensation.

> **Amendment VI:** In a criminal prosecution, the accused shall enjoy the right to a speedy and public trial by an impartial jury of the state and district wherein the crime shall have been committed, which district shall have been previously ascertained by law and to be informed to the nature and cause of the accusation, to be confronted with witnesses against him that have compulsory process for obtaining witnesses in his favor and to have the assistance of counsel for his defense.

Two landmark cases caused the Supreme Court to spell out the information which must be provided to anyone who is accused or suspected of committing a criminal act prior to any question by officers or other people of authority. The first was *Escabito v. Illinois,* 378US478 (1964). This was decided under the Sixth Amendment right to legal counsel applied to states by the Fourteenth Amendment.

Miranda v. Arizona, 394US436 (1965). This was decided under the Fifth Amendment providing protection against compulsory self incrimination.

For a statement (confession) to be ruled voluntary, the suspect must be made aware of his/her rights (only when suspect is in custodial care). The person must understand each and every one of the rights and must knowingly waive these legal rights before questioning can begin. Individual rights under the Miranda decision are as follows:

1. You have the right to remain silent and refuse to answer questions.
2. Anything you say may be used against you in a court of law.
3. You have the right to consult an attorney before speaking to police and to have an attorney present during any questioning or in the future at any stages of the proceedings.

4. If you cannot afford to hire an attorney, one will be provided for you without cost at any time.
5. If you do not have an attorney available, you have the right to remain silent until you have had an opportunity to consult with one.
6. If you are willing to answer questions without an attorney, you have the right at any time to stop and consult an attorney or stop for any reason. Finally, now that I have advised you of your rights, are you willing to answer questions without an attorney present?

After giving the Miranda warnings, the investigator should ask the following questions:

1. Do you understand each of these rights I have explained to you?
2. Do you wish to give up the right to remain silent?
3. Do you wish to give up the right to speak to an attorney and have him present during questioning?

The suspect can invoke these rights before questioning or at any time during questioning; however, once he has invoked his right by requesting an attorney, all questioning must cease.

The Miranda warnings should be given when the person being questioned is "in custody." "In custody" is any time the person is not free to leave the scene or area of questioning. Generally, custodial care is present when the suspect is under the control of the investigator.

Miranda warnings are not required when a person volunteers information or when, not being questioned, the person offers to make a confession or statement, and also when the person is being questioned by a private investigator, such as an insurance company investigator — also, when the person being questioned is not in custody and his/her freedom of movement is not restricted. Miranda warnings are not necessary during routine questioning involving nonincriminating statements, such as, "where do you live?" or "what is your name?"

The best way to avoid conflicts or challenges of the rights is to document them on audio or video tapes. These should be preserved even after they have been transcribed.

References and Selected Readings

"Fire Scene Interviews and Interrogations", New York State Fire Academy Course, 1984 Zulawski, D. E. and Wicklander, D. E., *Practical Aspects of Interview and Interogation*, CRC Press, Boca Raton, FL., 1991.

APPENDIX 12.1   Sample Owner/Tenant Interview Form*

I am _____ of the _____

                                                    (*Department/Agency*)

interviewing Mr./Mrs. _____ concerning the

fire at _____

                                                    (*address*)

that occurred on _____ at approximately _____ AM/PM.

              (*date*)   (*time*)

1.   Your full name is _____
2.   Your age is _____
3.   Your date of birth is _____
4.   Are you aware that this statement is being recorded? _____
a)   Do we have permission to record your statement? _____
5.   Mr./Mrs. _____ do we have your permission
     to enter upon your property at _____
     investigate the fire, and remove any evidence that may point to the cause
     and origin of the fire?
a)   If necessary, do we have your permission to return to your property at
     a later date to collect evidence from the fire? _____
6.   Your present address is _____
7.   Your present phone number is _____
8.   Were you the owner or tenant of property located at _____
     _____ at the time of the fire? _____
9.   Are you the sole owner? _____ If a partnership, who is the other owner?
     _____
10. Are you married? _____
11. Wife's/husband's name _____
12. Is he/she on the deed to the property? _____
13. Is he/she named on the insurance policy? _____
14. Do you have any children? _____

* Courtesy of David Redsicker, New York State Fire Academy.

15. Their names and ages: _____

_____

_____

16. Do you have any pets? _____
a) Were they injured in the fire? _____
17. How long have you owned the property at _____
_____? (Weeks/months/years) _____
18. Did you and your wife/husband live in the house? _____
19. Where were you when the fire occurred? _____
20. How did you find out about the fire? _____

_____

21. Who was the last person in the house? _____
22. Did you personally lock up the house when you left? _____

_____

23. Have you had the locks changed since you have owned the house? _____
24. Who has keys to the locks? _____
25. Have you had any burglaries/prowlers? _____
26. Were there any signs of forcible entry when the fire department arrived?

_____

27. Have you had any electrical problems recently? _____
28. Have you had any heating/furnace problems recently? _____
29. Have you had any TV problems recently? _____
30. Do you or your wife/husband smoke? _____
31. Were you smoking before you left the house? _____
32. Did you have any visitors prior to leaving the house? _____
33. Are you aware of any enemies that would want to start a fire on your
property? _____
34. Do you know for sure how the fire started? _____
35. Do you have any idea how the fire started? _____
36. Do you know who started the fire? _____
37. Were there any flammable liquids stored in the building? _____

_____

38. Have you ever had a fire before on this or any other property? _____

_____

39. Have you ever had an insurance claim before? _____
If yes, what company, when, and where? _____
40. Has the house been for sale recently or were you going to sell it? _____

_____

41. Has the house been appraised recently? _____ If yes, what value
and why the appraisal? _____
42. Have you done any remodeling recently? _____ If yes, exactly
what? _____

43. What was the purchase price of the house? _____

44. From whom did you purchase the house? _____
    _____ On what date? _____

45. Where is the house financed? _____

46. What are the monthly payments? _____ Are they current or in
    arrears? _____

47. Do you have any other loans or debts?

Where	Amount	Monthly Payment	Current or in Arrears

48. Do you have any other insurance besides this policy with _____
    _____? _____

49. Was anything removed from the building prior to the fire? _____

50. Was anything removed from the building after the fire? _____

51. Did you find anything missing after the fire that would indicate a burglary?
    _____

52. Are you planning to rebuild the property? _____

53. Can you think of anything else that would help us with the investigation?
    _____

54. Were there any liens or judgments against you or the property? _____

55. Do you have any health, sanitation, zoning, or building violations
    against the property? _____

56. Are there any county, township, or city violations against the property?
    _____

57. If a business place, what was the approximate amount of daily or weekly
    business (net)? _____

58. Are all of the statements made by you in this recorded statement true
    and complete to the best of your knowledge? _____

59. Please state your name again. You are aware this statement was being
    recorded, and we had your permission to record it? _____

60. This statement was completed at _____ AM/PM on _____

Court Qualification and Testimony 13

An investigator's responsibility is far from over with the arrest of one or more suspects. Pure theorists may argue that once the investigator has introduced the defendant to the judicial system, his job is done. However, this theoretical approach flies in the face of reality. A good investigator attentively follows a case through to its end. Preparing for and undergoing cross-examination by a skilled defense attorney is hardly an experience that can be accurately described by theorists; it is the type of experience that must be endured to be appreciated. The trial is the point in an investigation when many months of rigorous digging, persuading, interviewing, and analysis are put to the test. To think that an investigator has no vested interest in its outcome is ludicrous: the sleepless nights and countless hours on the telephone and in the field, gorged with coffee, seeking leads, and double-checking information hardly represent a fleeting interest.

In most contested arson cases, the fire investigator is the prosecution's principal witness. The criminal prosecution may fail unless the investigator:

- Dresses appropriately and gives a professional appearance
- Has been properly prepared by the prosecutor
- Knows the rules of evidence
- Presents his testimony clearly, understandably, and in a forthright manner.

Pretrial Testimony

In most criminal cases, an investigator will have testified several times about the facts of the case prior to the trial. He may have testified under oath before the grand jury that handed down the indictment in the case, or at various pretrial hearings where a defense attorney contested the legality or constitutionality of seized evidence, a confession, or lineup procedure. This prior sworn testimony may be used to impeach the credibility of that witness who tenders contradictory statements during the trial.

Over the years, an experienced arson investigator may have testified as a court-recognized expert at numerous trials. The court records of those trials, absent unusual circumstances, are a public record. A practical defense attorney, knowing that investigator Jones is the state's principal witness in an upcoming trial, could gain access to Jones's prior testimony, a painstaking analysis of which could yield an interesting and informative portrait of the investigator. The defense attorney is likely to focus on certain material elements, such as: reaction to stress under different questioning techniques; quality of testimony, including weaknesses and strong points; and apparent level of the investigator's expertise and training. This type of pretrial intelligence would be a valuable tool when designing the defense strategy.

Trial Preparation

The fire investigator in a civil case is often the private sector investigator representing an insurance company. Pretrial testimony may be depositions where adversarial attorneys inquire into the content of your file on a fire loss. Their inquiry will also delve into your training, education, experience, and expertise. It is important to document each time you have testified in any type of legal proceeding, whether a deposition, an arbitration, or in court. This is all part of creating and developing a *curriculum vitae*, which is basically your pedigree as an expert in a particular field.

Preparation for trial is much more than simply reviewing one's notes, although the review of all notes, reports, and evidence pertaining to the case is a necessary element. Scrutinize every piece of paper prepared during the investigation. Look for mistakes, omissions, and inconsistencies — a defense attorney certainly will! Discuss any problems or inconsistencies with the prosecutor before the trial commences; do not ignore them or write them off as inconsequential. Are there any photos, reports, statements, and so on in the case file that might be construed as beneficial to the defendant and therefore "Brady" material?* If so, discuss them with the prosecutor. To knowingly disregard this type of material constitutes malfeasance and may be grounds for mistrial.

---

* According to *Brady v. Maryland* (373 U.S. 83, 83 S.Ct. 1194), suppression by the prosecution of evidence favorable to an accused (exculpatory evidence) who has requested it (discovery) violates due process where the evidence is material either to guilt or to punishment, irrespective of the good or bad faith of the prosecution.

Ensure that the witnesses, assisting investigators, laboratory personnel, and the coroner or medical examiner (if necessary) will be available at the time of the trial.

If the jury has already been selected (as in a Federal case, where the judge selects the jury), ask the prosecutor if any common thread or line of questioning was obvious during the defense attorney's *voir dire* (preliminary examination regarding competency) of the potential jurors. The prosecutor may be able to identify the defense attorney's trial strategy, e.g., prosecution witnesses are all liars; the defendant was away or abroad at the time of the fire (or other alibi); or the Prosecution expert witness is not an expert, and defense expert will present the "true" facts.

Remember: "Forewarned is forearmed."

Witness Stand Behavioral Guidelines

Expect the defense attorney to stand away from the jury, on the opposite side of the courtroom. This is intentional. We have a tendency to look and talk to the individual who is questioning or talking to us. This defense tactic, although subtle, is intended to prevent the witness from making any eye contact with the jury while answering questions. Remember, the judge is the trier of the law, but the jury is the trier of the facts. Look at the jury when answering questions.

The following guidelines should be followed when testifying in court:

- Identify yourself to the court stenographer, by name, rank, and assignment or unit, in a clear and audible manner.
- Stand erect and respond with an audible "I do" when the oath is administered.
- Sit erect with both feet on the floor and hands in a natural position.
- Tell the truth, remembering that it is *how* you tell the truth that makes the difference.
- Assume that the defense attorney has visited the fire scene and reviewed every shred of evidence, piece of paper, and photograph concerning the case.
- Consider the defense attorney to be a master of the English language.
- Do not become aggressive or "cute" in your responses to defense questions.
- Listen carefully to questions and delay at least 3 seconds before answering, allowing the prosecutor sufficient time to object.
- Allow the judge to rule an objection before answering.

- Do not exaggerate answers.
- If you do not understand a question, wait until it is explained or rephrased before answering — chances are the jury did not understand it either.
- Do not volunteer information — where appropriate, answer with a simple "yes" or "no."
- Request the judge's permission before referring to your notes or a memo book to refresh your memory.
- If a question requires a technical answer, explain the technical language to the jury in simple, understandable terms.
- Remember that, many times, the prosecutor can rehabilitate damaging testimony during the redirect.
- If you cannot remember a specific fact or piece of information, simply answer, "I don't remember," *not* "I don't know."

When the prosecutor asks your opinion of the cause of the fire, the proper answer is "I could find no natural or accidental cause," not "Arson." In testifying about patterns from accelerants, refer to them as "pour patterns" to show deliberateness, as opposed to "spill," which may imply accident.

Cross Examination

Be prepared for and expect an aggressive defensive counterattack during your *voir dire* as an expert witness. Keep available an updated résumé listing formal and specialized education and training, total number of cases investigated (separating physical examinations and automobile salvages), and all the courts where you have been previously recognized as an expert. Remember, when you qualify as an expert in an arson trial, you are qualifying as an expert in the entire field of fire investigation; as such, you are subject to a wide and diversified range of questions, some (or all) or which may have little or nothing to do with the circumstances of the case on trial.

Cross examination could proceed as follows. The defense attorney approaches the witness stand carrying a number of textbooks. The subject or topic covered in all of the books is fire and/or arson investigation. Handing the witness one book after the other, the defense attorney asks whether the witness recognizes the author as an expert in the field of arson investigation. The witness is then asked if he has read the book and whether or not he views it as the product of the author's expertise.

The prosecutor's witness is in a very difficult position, regardless of his answers at this point. If he answers that the authors are in fact recognized experts in the field of arson investigation, but he either does not recognize the book as the product of that expertise or has never read it, the defense attorney will claim that a "supposed" expert witness does not take the time to stay current in his field. If the witness states that the authors are recognized experts and that the book is indeed, the product of their expertise, then the witness will be asked at random, whether or not he agrees with any particular author's opinion on any given issue. Unless the witness is very well read and has a superhuman memory, he is about to made to look foolish before the judge and jury. It is almost a no-win situation. Regardless of how the judge rules on the prosecutor's contention that his witness is an expert, the defense counsel has scored a major point. Even if the judge rules that the witness may testify as an expert, the defense attorney has succeeded in damaging that witness's credibility with the jury.

Answer what might be considered "trick" questions with special care. For example:

- "Did you discuss this case with anyone?" The answer is "Yes." You discussed the case with your partners and the prosecutor.
- For questions using the words "ever" or "never" — "Mr. Jones, do you ever make mistakes?" — an appropriate answer might be, "Yes, but not in this case."

The defense attorney, after soliciting a long litany of "I do not remembers" and "I do not knows" from a witness may add, for effect, "Well, what *do* you know?," just before stating that he has no further questions. This is intended to damage your credibility by having the jury believe that you really do not know anything. An inexperienced investigator might sink into the witness chair, feel intimidated, or sit silently waiting to be dismissed. Think! The defense attorney has asked a wide-open question. Answer by telling the jury what you *do know* about the case: "Well counselor, I do know that your client told me he started the fire, but did not intend for anyone to get killed." To stop you from answering, the defense attorney will have somehow to object to his own question.

Defense Expert

The defense in an arson trial has the right to introduce and court-qualify its own professional fire investigator as an expert witness. This witness will have examined the same fire scene, evaluated the same evidence, and yet reached a totally different conclusion as to cause and origin. Although you have stated that the fire was not an accident, he will testify that the cause could not be determined, or that it was, in fact, accidental in origin. The language and terminology used to describe the fire scene and the various phases of its examination are very technical and, no matter how simply expressed, can confuse a lay jury. Unless there is other overriding evidence to the contrary, a jury deliberating guilt or innocence may well find for the defendant. After all, if two equally qualified experts cannot agree on the cause of the fire, how can the jury be expected to do so?

Standard for Professional Qualifications of Fire Investigator

In 1993, the National Fire Protection Association established NFPA 1033, Standard for Professional Qualifications for Fire Investigator. "This standard identifies the professional level of performance required for fire investigators. It specifically identifies the job performance requirements necessary to perform as a fire investigator."

The purpose of this standard is to specify in terms of minimum job performance requirements the minimum standards for service as a fire investigator in both the private and public sectors. It is not the intent of this standard to restrict any jurisdiction from exceeding these minimum requirements. Job performance requirements describe the performance required for a specific job. A complete list of requirements for each duty describes the task an individual must be able to perform in order to successfully carry out that duty; however, they are not intended to measure a level of knowledge. Together the duties and job performance requirements define the parameters of the job of fire investigator.

The standard addresses the general requirements for job performance, definitions, description of duty in scene examination, documenting the scene, evidence collection/preservation, interviews and interrogation, post-incident investigation, and presentation, which includes preparation of a written investigation report (see complete standard).

Legal Aspects 14

Introduction

In the first edition of this book, this chapter was titled "New York State Law Governing Arson." It was, and still is, an excellent reference for the various legal considerations which have an impact on the origin and cause of fire investigation. However, in the rewriting of this chapter, I have decided to broaden the scope of the legal aspects and bring them more into line with the National Fire Protection Association Standards under NFPA 921, Chapter 5, "Legal Considerations."

In today's profession of fire investigation, it is even more important that the investigator be aware of the latest legal considerations that may affect every phase of an investigation. The laws vary from one jurisdiction to another and from time to time these laws change either by amendment or repeal.

The common law definition of arson is "the malicious burning of the house of another." However, depending on the jurisdiction, the definition may take on additional elements such as felony degrees depending on the intent, recklessness, or involvement of other people either as participants or victims.

An example of a model penal code states:

A person is guilty of arson, a felony, if he starts a fire or causes a explosion for the purpose of a) destroying a building or occupied structure of another; or b) destroying or damaging any property whether his own or another's to collect insurance for such a loss.

Problems of Proof in Arson Prosecutions

Search and Seizure in Premises Where Fire Occurred

Evidence acquired without a search warrant while firefighters are lawfully on the premises putting out the fire or within a reasonable time thereafter is admissible under the "plain view" doctrine [see People v. Calhoun, 90 Misc.2d 88, 393 N.Y.S. 2d 529 (Sup. Ct. Kings Co. 1977), aff'd without opinion, 67 A.D. 2d 1110, 413 N.Y.S.2d 535 (2d Dept. 1979), aff'd 49 N.Y.2d 398, 426 N.Y.S. 2d 243, 402 N.E.2d 1145 (1980)]. But once the fire has been extinguished, is a warrant required before a fire marshal may search the burned premises and make observations or seize evidence for use in an arson investigation?

The trial court in Calhoun rejected defendant's contention that such a search violated the Fourth Amendment. Defendant, a tenant, was charged, inter alia, with second-degree arson in his New York City apartment, which he was occupying at the time of the fire, although an unexecuted dispossess order had been issued by the Civil Court. Two fire marshals arrived at the defendant's apartment approximately 4 hours after the fire had been extinguished and the firefighters had left the premises to investigator the origin of the fire pursuant to New York City Administrative Code §488(2)-1.0, which authorizes fire marshals to investigate "[t]he origin, detail, and management of fires in the city, particularly of supposed cases of arson, incendiarism, or fires due to criminal carelessness." [Other subdivisions of Administrative Code §488(2)-1.0 authorize fire marshals to inspect for violations or Administrative code safety provisions.] The defendant's apartment was open when they entered, since the door had been destroyed in the fire. At defendant's trial for arson, he objected to the proposed introduction of testimony by one of the marshals and photographs of the apartment, citing People v. Tyler, 399 Mich. 564, 250 N.E.2d 467 (Sup. Ct. Mich. 1977), in which the Supreme Court of Michigan had held that such evidence seized without a warrant violates the Fourth Amendment. An appeal in Tyler was decided by the U.S. Supreme Court in Michigan v. Tyler, 436 U.S. 499, 98 S.Ct. 1942, 56 L.Ed.2d 486 (1978), and will be discussed infra.

The trial court in Calhoun first distinguished the case from Tyler, finding that since defendant's apartment was destroyed by the fire and was no longer habitable, the premises were in effect abandoned and defendant had no reasonable expectation of privacy in the premises, a prerequisite to a Fourth Amendment right, citing Katz v. United States, 389 U.S. 347, 88 S.Ct. 507, 19 L.Ed.2d 576 (1967). The court further found that since a fire is an emergency and the prompt warrantless investigation of a fire is authorized by the Administrative Code, it is an administrative search in an emergency situation and, therefore, is permissible under Camara v. Municipal Court, 387 U.S. 523, 87

S.Ct. 1727, 18 L.E.2d 930 (1967). The trial court analogized the case to *People v. Neulist*, 43 A.D.2d 150, 350 N.Y.S.2d 178 (2d Dept. 1973), which held that a police warrantless search of premises where a death occurred, subsequent to a finding by the medical examiner that the death was a homicide, was valid since the police entered originally to answer an emergency call, and a specific local law (Nassau County Government Law 2101) gave the medical examiner power to investigate the circumstances of a death.

The New York Court of Appeals affirmed Calhoun's conviction and upheld the reasonableness of the search, although on a different ground than that upon which the trial court based its decision. The Court specifically rejected the trial court's finding that the occurrence of a fire renders a premises abandoned:

> The classic statement that even a "ruined tenement" may be secure against the sovereign (see *Miller* v. *United States*, 357 U.S. 301, 307, 78 L.Ed.2d 1332) is literally applicable — for people often continue to live and work in buildings that have sustained fire damage and, even when the ensuing destruction has made that impossible, remaining personal effects may invoke continued and respected expectations of privacy. To reinforce this protection, a warrantless intrusion by a government official is presumptively unreasonable, the burden of justifying it devolving upon the *People (Vale* v. *Louisiana*, 399 U.S. 30, 34, 90 S.Ct. 1969, 1971, 26 L.Ed.2d, 409; *People* v. *Hodge, supra*, 44 N.Y.2d, p. 557, 406 N.Y.S.2d, p. 737, 378 N.E.2d, p. 101). (*Calhoun*, 426 N.Y.S.2d at 245)

Citing *Michigan* v. *Tyler*, the court then affirmed the trial court's holding that the occurrence of a fire, whatever its cause, falls within the scope of the so-called emergency exception to the search warrant requirement. This doctrine sanctions warrantless searches and seizures in circumstances presenting immediate danger to life or property, or, on the same general principle, threat of destruction or removal of contraband or other evidence of criminality. The Court then reviewed the role of the fire marshal in New York City. It noted that, although the marshals do not respond to every fire as a matter or routine, there was proof that their task was to investigate all fires of undetermined origin, rather than to conduct a search for evidence of arson. In this case, the fire marshals had no actual knowledge until hours after their arrival that arson was a possibility, for it was only then that they learned that the defendant had made arson threats to his landlord. While arson was a possible cause of the fire, other causes, natural and accidental, were theories to be tested by the marshals at the time of their arrival. The Court stressed that if there had been a finding by the trial court that the fire marshal's visit to the premises was motivated primarily by intent to gather evidence for an arson prosecution, the warrantless intrusion might well have exceeded the bounds of the emergency exception and trespassed on the constitutional guarantee of the Fourth Amendment.

The New York Court of Appeals in *Calhoun* relied in part in its decision on the recent opinion of the U.S. of Supreme Court in *Michigan* v. *Tyler*, 436 U.S. 499, 94 S.Ct. 1942, 56 L.Ed.2d 486 (1978), decided after the decision of the trial court in *Calhoun*. In *Michigan* v. *Tyler*, the U.S. Supreme Court reviewed the decision of the Michigan Supreme Court in *People* v. *Tyler, supra*, to consider the applicability of the Fourth Amendment to official entries onto fire-damaged premises. Defendants in *Tyler* were lessees of a furniture store that had burned down on January 21, 1970. Firefighters called in the police after they had just about quenched the fire, because of the discovery of two containers of flammable liquid. The police came and took several pictures, but had to leave because of the smoke and steam. Four hours after the blaze was extinguished, a fire inspector came, left, and returned an hour later with a detective. They discovered suspicious burn marks in the carpet and a piece of tape with burn marks on the stairs. On February 16, the police returned, investigated, took pictures, and seized a piece of fuse.

At defendant's trial, a police officer testified that his investigation had determined that the fire was not accidental. Defendants did not challenge the admission of photographs taken while the fire was smoldering, but challenged the admission of the evidence seized 5 hours later and the evidence seized during, and testimony relating to, the search on February 16, on the ground that a search warrant was required by the Fourth and Fourteenth Amendments. The Michigan Supreme Court had held that "[once] the blaze [has been] extinguished and the firefighters have left the premises, a warrant is required to reenter and search the premises, unless there is consent or the premises have been abandoned" (*People* v. *Tyler*, Mich. at 583, 250 N.W.2d at 477).

The Michigan court accordingly reversed defendant's convictions and ordered a new trial, having found neither consent nor abandonment.

The U.S. Supreme Court, in reviewing the holding of the Michigan Supreme Court, first reiterated the principle that the protection of the Fourth and Fourteenth Amendments applies to any search by a government official, even if it is an inspecting "administrative search" (a search to enforce a nonpenal statute or regulation), unless the premises search involved a heavily regulated industry, such as alcohol or firearms, citing its recent decision in *Marshall* v. *Barlow's Inc.* 436 U.S. 307, 98 S.Ct. 1816, 56 L.Ed.2d 305 (1978).*

---

* After both *Marshall* v. *Barlow* and *Michigan* v. *Tyler* were decided, the U.S. Supreme Court in *Donovan* v. *Dewey*, 452 U.S. 594, 101 S.Ct. 2534, 69 L.Ed.2d 262 (1981) ruled that in a regulated industry such as mining, where work place safety is crucial, a warrantless inspection in compliance with specific authorized statutory procedures or regulations (the Mine Safety Act) does not violate the Fourth Amendment.

The U.S. Supreme Court rejected the prosecution's argument that burned-out premises are "abandoned"; that is, that the occupants and/or owners have no reasonable expectation of privacy because (a) if they set the blaze, they have abandoned the premises, and (b) even if they did not set it, their privacy interest is rendered negligible by the damage. The Court stated:

> [E]ven if the petitioner's contention that arson established abandonments be accepted, it second proposition — that innocent fire victims inevitably have no protectable expectations or privacy in whatever remains of their property — is contrary to common experience. People may go on living in their homes or working in their offices after a fire. Even when that is impossible, private effects often remain on the fire-damaged premises. The petitioner may be correct in the view that most innocent fire victims are treated courteously and welcome inspections of their property to ascertain the origin of the blaze, but "even if true, [this contention] is irrelevant to the question whether the…inspection is reasonable within the meaning of the Fourth Amendment. [Citation omitted.]

Once it is recognized that the innocent fire victims retain the protection of the Fourth Amendment, the rest of the petitioner's argument unravels. For it is of course impossible to justify a warrantless search on the ground of abandonment by arson when that arson has not yet been proved, and a conviction cannot be used *ex post facto* to validate the introduction of evidence used to secure that same conviction.

Thus, there is no diminution in a person's reasonable expectation of privacy nor in the protection of the Fourth Amendment simply because the official conducting the search wears the uniform of a firefighter rather than a policeman, or because his purpose is to ascertain the cause of a fire rather than look for evidence of a crime, or because the fire might have been started deliberately. Searches for administrative purposes, like searches for evidence of crime, are encompassed by the Fourth Amendment. And under that Amendment,

> one governing principle, justified by history and by current experience, has consistently been followed: except in certain carefully defined classes of cases, a search of private property without proper consent is "unreasonable" unless it has been authorized by a valid search warrant. [Citation omitted.]

The showing of probable cause necessary to secure a warrant may vary with the object and intrusiveness of the search, but the necessity for the warrant persists. (*Michigan* v. *Tyler*, 436 U.S. at 505-7, 98 S.Ct. at 1947-8)

The Court added:

> To secure a warrant to investigate the cause of a fire, an official must show more than the bare fact that a fire has occurred. The magistrate's duty is to assure that the proposed search will be reasonable, a determination that requires inquiry into the need for the intrusion on the one hand, and the threat of disruption to the occupant on the other. For routine building inspections, a reasonable balance between these competing concerns is usually achieved by broad legislative and administrative guidelines specifying the purpose, frequency, scope, and manner of conducting the inspections. In the context of investigatory fire searches, which are not programmatic but are responsive to individual events, a more particularized inquiry may be necessary. The number of prior entries, the scope of the search, the time of day when it is proposed to be made, the lapse of time since the fire, the continued use of the building, and the owner's efforts to secure it against intruders might all be relevant factors. Even though a fire victim's privacy must normally yield to the vital social objective of ascertaining the cause of the fire, the magistrate can perform the important function of prevent harassment by keeping that invasion to a minimum. See See v. *City of Seattle*, *supra*, at 544-545, 87 S.Ct., at 1739–1740; *United States* v. *Chadwick*, 433 U.S. 1, 9, 97 S.Ct. 2476, 2482, 53 L.Ed.2d 538; *Marshall* v. *Barlow's Inc.*, 436 U.S., 323 98 S.Ct., at 1826. (*Michigan* v. *Tyler*, 436 U.S. at 507-8, 98 S.Ct. at 1949)

The Court noted that another purpose of the warrant is to provide the property owner with information to reassure him of the legality of the entry. The Court further held that where the investigators find evidence of wrongdoing in a search under an administrative warrant, it would be admissible in an arson prosecution and could be used to establish probable cause for a search warrant to gather additional evidence. The Court also ruled that where the officers are seeking evidence of arson, the court in which they apply for the search warrant must determine the existence of probable cause to believe a crime was committed before it issues the search warrant. The standard is more stringent than the standard of reasonable cause sufficient to justify the issuance of an administrative search warrant. Reasonable cause for an administrative search warrant exists when conditions are present that reasonable justify a search under the statute or regulations sought to be enforced. The reasonableness of the administrative criteria for the search is determined in light of the specific purpose of the particular statute or regulation.

However, the Court further ruled that there is an exception to the warrant requirement where a fire has occurred. The existence of "exigent circumstances" creates a recognized exception and [a] burning building clearly presents an exigency of sufficient proportions to render a warrantless entry "reasonable." Indeed, it would defy reason to suppose that firemen must secure a warrant or consent before entering a burning structure to put out the blaze. And once in a building for this purpose, firefighters may seize evidence of arson that is in plain view. *Coolidge* v. *New Hampshire*, 403 U.S. 433, 465–466, 91S.Ct. 2022, 2037–38, 29 L.ed.2d 564. Thus, the Fourth and Fourteenth Amendments were not violated by the entry of the firemen to extinguish the fire at the Tyler's Auction, nor by Chief See's removal of two plastic containers of flammable liquid from the floor of one of the showrooms. (*Michigan* v. *Tyler*, 436 U.S. at 509, 98 S.Ct. at 1950)

The Court added that the Michigan Supreme Court had recognized a right to make a warrantless entry in an emergency such as fire, but then had held that the need for a warrant arises when the last flame is extinguished. The U.S. Supreme Court ruled that the Michigan Court's holding was too narrow, declaring that officials may remain on the premises for a reasonable time thereafter where the condition of the building, as in *Tyler*, prevents them from making an effective inspection. The Court found that a warrant was not necessary for the early-morning reentries on January 22, since these entries were an actual continuation of the first valid entry. However, the Court agreed with the Michigan Supreme Court that the subsequent warrantless entries on February 16 were unconstitutional and, accordingly, affirmed that court's decision ordering defendant's new trial, stating:

> In summation, we hold that an entry to fight a fire requires no warrant, and that once in the building, officials may remain there for a reasonable time to investigate the cause of the blaze. Thereafter, additional entries to investigate the cause of the fire must be made pursuant to the warrant procedures governing administrative searches. See *Camra*, 387 U.S., at 534–539, 87 S.Ct. at 1733–1736; *See* v. *City of Seattle*, 387 U.S., at 544–545, 87 S.Ct. at 1739–1740; *Marshall* v. *Barlow's Inc.*, 436 U.S. at 320–321, 98 S.Ct., at 1824–1825. Evidence of arson discovered in the course of such investigations is admissible at trial, but if the investigating officials find probable cause to believe that arson has occurred and require further access to gather evidence for a possible prosecution, they may obtain a warrant only upon a traditional showing of probable cause applicable to searches for evidence of crime. *United States* v. *Ventresca*, 380 U.S. 102. (*Michigan* v. *Tyler*, 436, U.S. at 511–12, 98 S.Ct. at 1951)

In a recent case, the U.S. Supreme Court dealt again with administrative warrants. In *Michigan* v. *Clifford*, 104 S.Ct. 641 (1984), the Supreme Court held that a warrantless search at the residence of a couple who were out of town, five hours after firefighters extinguished a fire of suspicious origin and left the premises, violated the Fourth Amendment. The 5-4 decision refused to exempt from the warrant requirement all administrative investigation into the cause and origin of a fire.

The majority concluded that where reasonable expectations of privacy remain in fire-damaged premises, either consent or exigent circumstances must be present to justify a warrantless search. Here, the occupants of the private home were not told of the search and took steps to secure their remaining privacy interests in the damaged home against further intrusion. Moreover, several hours separated the initial exigent intrusion to extinguish the fire from the search in question. When a warrant is required, an administrative warrant is sufficient if the primary purpose of the search is to determine the origin and cause of the fire, but a criminal search warrant based upon probable cause is required when authorities seek evidence of criminal activity.

In this instance, a basement search revealed the cause of the fire, so that the search of the rest of the house would have required a criminal search warrant even if the search of the basement was valid.

Other Legal Considerations

In today's litigious climate, every consideration must be given to ascertaining the authority to conduct an investigation. The authority is generally granted to local authorities through the laws and codes of their jurisdiction. As for the private sector investigator, he may be acting under the contractual agreements of the insurance company (insurance policy) or other private authorization by individuals or their representatives. In any event, proper documentation is advised when embarking on such an investigation where entry onto private property for the purpose of origin and cause analysis is intended. Such documentation may require written authorization from a local authority, insurance representative, property owner, or representative (attorney, public adjuster, etc.).

Exigent Circumstances

The fire is often not determined to be incendiary in nature until a thorough origin and cause investigation has been conducted at the fire scene. What sets fire investigation apart from all other types is the fact that one must maintain an open mind to the property owner's innocence while conducting a search for facts as to the cause for the fire. Once the fire department is called, they generally have the legal authority as well as an obligation to enter the property for the purpose of extinguishing the fire, and saving lives and property, as well as conducting an investigation of the origin and cause of the fire. The fire officer may call for assistance of the fire investigator in the performance of his duties as to origin and cause determination. One must still maintain strict adherence to the laws of search and seizure in the event the fire is determined to be incendiary. This respect for people's right in regard to post fire investigation activity is clearly outlined by the U.S. Supreme Court in the decision of *Michigan v. Tyler.*

Here the court held that the prosecution's contention that all rights of privacy by the owner were given up by committing a crime was not substantiable. On the other hand, an investigation begun and continued "for a reasonable amount of time" is entirely flexible, depending on the type of building involved, the time and nature of suppression efforts, the complexity of the scene, and the extent of emergency situations. The court reinforced the statement that it is the duty of fire officials to determine the cause of fires. The circumstances defining "reasonable length of time" for an investigator to conduct a warrantless search must be considered by the investigator at the time of the incident.

Further, in the U.S. Supreme Court *Michigan* v. *Clifford*, 82–357, January 11, 1984, the post fire scene investigation is further restricted regarding a private residence. The court held that on Fourth Amendment grounds, evidence found in a fire-damaged residence by arson investigators who entered and conducted an extensive search without obtaining a warrant, consent, or under exigent circumstances some 6 hours after firefighters had extinguished the blaze and left the scene, was seized illegally and therefore must be suppressed. There are especially strong expectations for privacy in a private residence and respondents here retained significant privacy interest in their fire-damaged home. Because the warrantless search of the basement and upper areas of respondent's home was authorized neither by consent nor exigent circumstances, the evidence seized in that search was retained in violation of respondent's rights under the Fourth and Fourteenth Amendments.

Once the "reasonable length of time" has been exceeded or is questionable, the right to privacy of the owners of fire-damaged premises must be acknowledged. To continue a lawful search into the cause of the fire, the investigator may obtain permission from the owner to obtain a search warrant.

Permission To Search

A "consent to search" form may be obtained from the legal owner or person responsible for the property in question and should be obtained in writing.

Administrative Search Warrant

Administrative searches are necessary for reentry onto the fire-damaged premises, when the reentry is not a continuation of an initial valid search and when the purpose of the search is to determine the cause of the fire. Evidence gained from such searches would be admissible to convict a person of arson under the Plain View doctrine.

Criminal Search Warrant

The necessity for a criminal search warrant applies when the reentry onto the fire damaged premises is not a continuation of a valid search and when the reentry is for the purpose of gaining evidence to be used in a criminal prosecution of arson. Of course, assuming a proper criminal search warrant is obtained, the evidence gained from such a search would be lawful, and therefore, admissible in court. (Fourth Amendment to the Constitution of the United States...Protection against unreasonable search and seizure.) Most arson trials involve substantial amounts of circumstantial evidence. Direct evidence may clearly document that the fire was incendiary, but the evidence connecting the defendant to the commission of the crime will be largely circumstantial.

An investigator should expect a diligent attack by a defense attorney against any form of evidence offered at trial that tends to establish the guilt of his client. Case law on evidence and the rules of evidence are strictly adhered to by courts throughout the nation. Any evidence that it suppressed during any of the several pretrial motions, no matter how damaging to the defense case, cannot be brought into evidence during a trial. The primary purpose of the rules of evidence is to insure that the proof offered is reliable.

Federal Rules of Evidence

Evidentiary requirements, standards, and rules vary greatly from jurisdiction to jurisdiction. For this reason, those rules of evidence that are in effect in individual states, territories, provinces, and international jurisdictions should be consulted.

The Federal Rules of Evidence became effective on July 1, 1975. They apply in all civil and criminal cases in all United States Courts of Appeal, District Courts, Courts of Claims, and before United States Magistrates. The Federal rules are recognized as having essentially codified the well-established rules of evidence, and many states have adopted, in whole or in part, the Federal rules. (See NFPA 921, Chapter 5, Section 5-3.1, Federal Rules of Evidence.)

Prosecution for Insurance Fraud

Losses by arsonists are commonly inflated. This is grounds for a prosecution for larceny by false pretense under Penal Law Statutes of the states. Generally defined, *insurance fraud* is a fraudulent insurance act committed by any person who knowingly and with intent to defraud presents, causes to be presented, or prepares with knowledge or belief that it will be presented to or by an insurer or propertied insurer, or any agent thereof, any written statement as part of, or in support of, an application for the issuance of, or the rating of an insurance policy for commercial insurance, or a claim for payment or other benefit pursuant to an insurance policy for commercial or personal insurance which he knows to:

> Contain materially false information concerning any fact material thereto, or to conceal for the purpose of misleading, information concerning any fact material thereto.

Summary

Although it is imperative that the rules of evidence be followed in all fire investigations, one is not expected to be able to quote them verse and chapter. However, a competent fire investigator should be able to go to his or her resources and follow proper procedures in the preparation of a case. Further, if the investigation follows the general guidelines for proper procedures within the NFPA 921 Standards Guide for Fire and Explosion Investigations, there should be no problems with the admissibility of the case.

Index

405